RED HAND: THE ULSTER COLONY

Red Hand: The Ulster Colony

CONSTANTINE FITZGIBBON

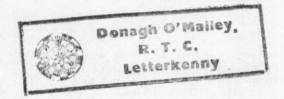

LONDON : MICHAEL JOSEPH

First published in Great Britain by
MICHAEL JOSEPH LTD
52 Bedford Square
London, WC1
1971

7181 0881 7

Set and printed in Great Britain by Northum-
land Press Limited, Gateshead in Georgian
eleven on twelve point and bound by the
Dorstel Press, Harlow

A/941.6

To all Irishmen and Irishwomen of goodwill,
and to their true friends in
other lands across the seas

IRISH REPUBLIC

SCOTLAND
NORTH CHANNEL
Irish Sea
ATLANTIC OCEAN
ST. GEORGE'S CHANNEL

NORTHERN IRELAND
REPUBLIC OF EIRE
ULSTER
CONNAUGHT
LEINSTER
MUNSTER

GIANT'S CAUSEWAY
Larne
Belfast
Londonderry
Buncrana
Ardara
Donegal
TWEED · CARPETS
Sligo
L. NEAGH
Portadown
Dundalk
Kells
Drogheda
Balbriggan
Baile Átha Cliath
Dublin
Dún Laoghaire
18 NEW FACTORIES
Mullingar
TEXTILE
Ballina
Westport
Athlone
Ferbane
Mountmellick
Port Laoighise
Kildare
Poulaphouca Res.
Arklow
Wicklow
Galway
Loughrea
Killaloe
Ennis
Limerick
SHANNON
14 NEW FACTORIES
Kilkenny
Carlow
New Ross
Waterford
SHIPBUILDING
Wexford
Rosslare
Thurles
TIPPERARY
Nenagh
Tralee
Listowel
Dingle
Kenmare
Killarney
Bantry
Mallow
Cork
Cobh
STEELMILL
LEATHER · GLASS
Kinsale
Youghal
Blackwater
Mouth of the Shannon

Airports
Seaports
Power stations active
" " under construction
Shipbuilding
New factories (50 more u. construction)
Development area
Oil refinery

IRISH REPUBLIC
Population 2,884,002
94% Catholic
Church of Ireland 4·3%
0·8% Presbyterian
0·4% Methodist
0·5% all others

IRISH REPUBLIC
TOTAL EXPORTS 1967
£ 273·3 Million
79% to UK £ 223·7 m
21% to rest of world

MANUFACTURED GOODS 40%
AGRICULTURAL PRODUCTS 60%

TOTAL IMPORTS 1967
£ 380 Million
51% from UK £ 186·4 m
49% from rest of world

GROWTH OF TRADE EIRE/UK
£ 223·7 m   £ 186·4 m
£ 112 m   £ 109 m
1958–67 EXPORTS to UK
1958–67 IMPORTS from UK

NEW INDUSTRIAL ENTERPRISES
1959–1967
£ 98 MILLION (100%)
(273 Firms)
EXTERNAL INVESTMENT (80%)
£ 78 Millions

UK 40%
USA
West Germany 20%
Netherl. 5%
various European countries 19%
Canada & S. Africa 16%

© GOODWIN

IRISH REPUBLIC

NORTHERN IRELAND 1970

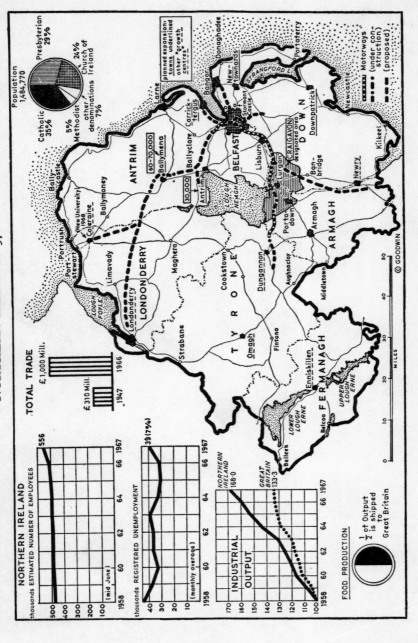

Population 1,484,770

- Catholic 35%
- Presbyterian 29%
- Church of Ireland 24%
- Methodist 5%
- other denominations 7%

planned expansion towns underlined
other "growth centres"
New towns
Motorways (under construction)
(proposed)

STRANGFORD L.

Donaghadee
Portaferry
Bangor
Stormont
BELFAST
Carrick-fergus
Larne
Ballyclare
Antrim
LOUGH NEAGH
Lisburn
CRAIGAVON designated area
Lurgan
Portadown
Banbridge
Newry
Kilkeel
Newcastle
Downpatrick
DOWN
ARMAGH
Armagh
Middletown
Aughnacloy
Dungannon
Cookstown
Maghera
Magherafelt
TYRONE
Omagh
Fintona
Strabane
Londonderry
LONDONDERRY
Limavady
Coleraine (New University 1968)
Port-stewart
Port-rush
Bally-castle
Ballymoney
Ballymena
ANTRIM
LOUGH FOYLE
FERMANAGH
Enniskillen
Belcoo
Belleek
LOWER LOUGH ERNE
UPPER LOUGH ERNE

60-70,000
30,000

© GOODWIN

MILES
0 10 20 30 40 50

TOTAL TRADE

£ 1,000 Mill.
£ 310 Mill.
1947   1966

NORTHERN IRELAND

thousands ESTIMATED NUMBER OF EMPLOYEES

556
500
400
300
200
100
(mid June)
1958   60   62   64   66   1967

thousands REGISTERED UNEMPLOYMENT

39 (7%)
40
30
20
10
(monthly average)
1958   60   62   64   66   1967

INDUSTRIAL OUTPUT

NORTHERN IRELAND 168·0
GREAT BRITAIN 133·3
170
160
150
140
130
120
110
100
1958   60   62   64   66   1967

FOOD PRODUCTION

½ of Output is shipped to Great Britain

ACKNOWLEDGMENTS

Many friends, acquaintances and even strangers have helped me with this book, though for all the opinions expressed and the, generally tentative, conclusions drawn I am, of course, totally responsible. This must similarly apply to any errors of fact that may have escaped their and my own vigilance.

First of all I should like to express my deep debt of gratitude to Professor Kevin Nowlan, professor of history in University College Dublin, who gave a great deal of his most valuable time to assisting me with the historical background which forms the bulk of the book: the 'modern' chapters he did not in fact read and so of course cannot be blamed for any views there expressed. Mr. George Morrison, who has also compiled the illustrative material, is in addition a distinguished student of Irish history, and his comments on my text were also most useful. Those with whom I discussed the subject, at a length that must have at times seemed tedious to my friends, included Mr. Tim Pat Coogan, editor of *The Irish Press*, as well as various soldiers, civil servants and politicians in Belfast, Dublin and London, who would probably prefer to accept my thanks anonymously. The list of acknowledgments to those authors whom I have quoted, and to their publishers, follows, but I should like to express here my quite especial thanks to Mr. Andrew Boyd who gave me his personal permission to quote, at a length that many writers would regard as inordinate, from his *Holy War in Belfast* (Anvil Books, 1969).

My wellnigh illegible manuscript was typed, more than once, with meticulous accuracy and great speed by my friend, Mrs. Robina Quigley. Finally, it is customary for a writer to thank his wife. In this case, however, such gratitude is more than a mere courtesy. Over the past two years Marjorie must have heard far more than any woman from California could possibly wish to hear about Irish affairs, and has borne this travail with a truly astonishing tolerance.

My thanks are due to the following publishers for permission to use material from books in which they own the copyright:

Hamish Hamilton Ltd., for quotations from *The Great Hunger* by Cecil Woodham-Smith.

Faber and Faber Ltd., for quotations from *The Making of Modern Ireland* by J. C. Beckett.

Anvil Books Limited, for quotations from *Holy War in Belfast* by Andrew Boyd.

George Allen & Unwin Ltd., for quotations from *The Irish Question 1840-1921* by Nicholas Mansergh.

Routledge & Kegan Paul Ltd., for quotations from *Orangeism in Ireland and Britain 1795-1836* by Hereward Senior.

Hamlyn Publishing Group Ltd., for quotations from *The World Crisis* by Winston S. Churchill.

ILLUSTRATIONS

Assimilation of Norman and Irish nobility	*facing* 96
Cattle raiding among the 'native Irish'	97
The siege of Enniskillen Castle	97
'Union is Strength'	128
'The Fort', Hillsborough	129
Henry Cooke	129
Hugh Hanna	224
Lord Randolph Churchill	224
Leading Unionists in 1912	225
Sir Edward Carson	225
F. E. Smith	256
Ulster Volunteers in training	256
Carson signing the Ulster Covenant	257

CHAPTER ONE

Throughout most of the middle ages, and particularly during the sixteenth century, Ulster was the heartland of Irish resistance to Anglo-Saxon dominance; perhaps the heartland of the whole 'Celtic' world which stretched along the Atlantic seaboard from southern Brittany to the northernmost isles of Scotland. Until the Irish Elizabethan Wars spread to that province (1596-1603) Ulster had never been really conquered, though it had been raided by Vikings, Normans and Scots and there was, indeed, already a Scots-Irish 'colony' along its eastern seaboard, in what are now the counties Antrim and Down. The Anglo-Normans had overrun almost all of southern and western Ireland, and though they had rapidly been assimilated—had become 'more Irish than the Irish'—they had brought with them a measure of continental modes, of that feudal attitude which, deriving indirectly from Rome, was to lead ultimately to the world of the Renaissance and thus to modern society: primogeniture, that is to say the family rather than the tribe as basic unit of the human community: from this, a firm concept of property and particularly of land as property: a vague heritage of Roman law: and the concept of a centralized government. In Leinster, particularly in the Pale, these ideas took root. In Munster and Connaught they faded among Irish mists, but the memory lingered on among Gaelic-speaking Fitzgeralds and de Burgoes and the other great families of Norman descent. In Ulster, until the Plantation, they were for all intents and purposes unknown. There the ancient laws and customs of the Irish still prevailed over almost all of what later became the Nine Counties, except for the Scots communities, and when it came to fighting the foreigners formidable reinforcements, in the form of mercenaries called 'gallowglasses', could be recruited from the Scottish Highlands and islands. It was there that the greatest and last act of Gaelic rebellion against alien rule and alien ways took place, led by Hugh O'Neill, Ulster's principal chieftain and, briefly, the real

King of Ireland. Descended from Niall of the Nine Hostages, High King of Ireland from 380 to 405, his tribal emblem was the Red Hand which in due course became and has remained the emblem of all Ulster. His attempt to defend, by force of arms, his people's ancient customs and lands, rebellion in English eyes, failed, at last, utterly. O'Neill was forced to flee overseas and died in Rome. His province was in ruins, and most of his people dead. The government in London then moved in, to ensure that such a dangerous rebellion should never happen again. Ulster was planted.

The political and military aspects of the Anglo-Irish wars of the late sixteenth and early seventeenth centuries had quite rapidly polarized about religion. When these wars began the Reformation, in England, was far from complete and still subject to reversion: for purposes of policy Queen Elizabeth I was quite capable of following a more subtle policy than her late sister's and restoring, as their father Henry VIII had wished to do, something like an eotype of the later French 'Gallican' Church. By the time these wars were over events in the Low Countries, the almost perpetual threat of a Spanish invasion with consequent, similar anti-Protestant atrocities in England, and finally the Gunpowder Plot of 1605 had hardened the English into an anti-papist ideology that was to endure for two centuries and more. In Ireland, on the other hand, the process had been precisely reversed. When the Elizabethan wars started religion in Ireland had reached a low point perhaps without precedent before, and certainly since. The old mediaeval Church had declined, at least as much as it had done in England before the Reformation, into a useless, expensive and largely irreligious social organization. Apart from the work of the Franciscan friars it provided little, if any, spiritual leadership for the people: divorce and concubinage were commonplace and brigandage almost an accepted way of life, at least outside the Viking-founded and now partly anglicized coastal cities. When, under the early Tudor monarchs, Church lands and Church property were seized and sold few who were not clerics either objected or were even surprised. However, in Ireland there were virtually no Protestant pastors to replace the Roman Catholic priests. Anglican divines might accept one benefice, or more frequently several, but seldom bothered to visit all their parishes. Ireland was reverting, rapidly, to paganism. The wars both accelerated this relapse into savagery but simultaneously changed, and drastically, the religious attitude of the people.

Ireland and Holland were at this period the two major battle-fields of the massive counter-offensive launched by the Counter-Reformation, soon to be extended into the German Thirty Years' War. Master-minded from Rome and using the might of Spain as its first and principal weapon, this counter-offensive employed as its agents very clever and very brave missionary priests, of whom the most famous were Loyola's new Order of Jesus, and its major emotional-political lever the devotion of those who preferred the Old Faith to the New. In Ireland the priests were extremely effective and regained the respect that had been lost in past generations, while the English enemy became increasingly the Protestant enemy. And when the wars were lost, and the Irish leaders had fled abroad, been killed or reduced to impotence in their own divided territories, after acceptance of English law and an oath of allegiance to the English monarch, it was inevitably to these brave, competent, outlawed priests that the Irish looked for leadership. They were to do so for several centuries, and the tradition lingers on even today, for even today the Thirty Years' War is still being fought in the streets of Belfast.

Thus by the time of the Plantation of Ulster an Anglo-Irish War, now over, had become a Catholic-Protestant confrontation. Therefore when the English government decided to plant Ulster, this could only be a Protestant plantation, to keep down and if possible expel the Roman Catholic 'natives', those dangerous, savage people who had so nearly opened Ireland, and through Ireland England, to the ultimate horrors of Spanish conquest: the English governing class was only too well aware of what Alva had done in the Low Countries.

The whole apparatus of English administration was then imposed upon Ulster, an apparatus infinitely more sophisticated than the old Irish system, complete as it was with counties, shires, sheriffs, the English legal system, the Protestant religion and so on. This in itself, though bewildering to many of the Irish and distasteful to many if not most of the people's temporal and spiritual leaders, was not unacceptable to all. The famished survivors of the terrible war were, as always and everywhere, anxious to see a revival of order, and in such circumstances even an alien order is better than none: nor can the mass of the people have particularly relished the traditional feuding and raiding and raping by the petty chieftains who had ruled their lives for centuries. In such circumstances the peace even of the grave is better than no peace at all. In our own times it was so in Germany in 1945, it will be so in Vietnam tomorrow, and it was so in Ulster in 1604. But then the English began to steal the land, using English legal methods in the province.

CHAPTER TWO

After the soldiers always come the carpet-baggers. Nowhere was this more true than in Ulster after 1603. The English general, Mountjoy, had a very wise respect and, it would seem, even a measure of personal affection for The O'Neill and for his principal lieutenant or ally, the head of the O'Donnells whose land lay to his west. The terms of the surrender were generous. The Irish chieftains were regranted most of their lands, after swearing allegiance to the Crown. This however turned them into feudal lords rather than Irish chieftains, and the change caused immense confusion among their people. As The O'Neill, Hugh had been the local king or *ri*, but had not personally owned any land, for the land belonged to all his people when it did not belong to the peoples of his allies and client kinglets. There were, indeed, no real borders. Since virtually the entire economy of inland Ulster had hitherto been based upon the cow and since the population was almost semi-nomadic in its search for pasturage among the great forests that then covered most of the land, this had led to brigandage, cattle-rustling and petty local wars—a situation not dissimilar to that of the American West as it was opened up in the nineteenth century, where many of the toughest, earliest settlers were, as it happened, the descendants of Ulster Scots-Irishmen.

Once The O'Neill had finally accepted the royal jurisdiction that he was now the Earl of Tyrone, all this changed. The land now belonged to him and should pass to his oldest son or nearest male relative on his death, rather than to the most suitable O'Neill within a reasonably close degree of co-sanguinuity. This meant in effect that what the Ulster chieftains were surrendering to the English was not their own to give away. True, feudal land tenure had long taken root in other parts of the island, particularly in Leinster and in large parts of Munster, but even in those provinces the great Anglo-Norman families, while preserving the principal of primogeniture, had in greater or lesser measure reverted to the sort of primitive communism of co-ownership that had prevailed over all Europe before the Roman conquest and its feudal successor states, and that even then was only moribund in the *mir* system of Great Russia.

Thus O'Neill's surrender was in essence a betrayal of his people and of Gaelic civilization in that civilization's heartland. Red Hugh O'Donnell must have realized this at once, for he fled abroad where he soon died, probably from poison given to him by an English secret agent. O'Neill tried to retain his position, but with the departure of his old enemy-friend, Mountjoy, in 1606 and the increasing pressure of the carpet-baggers, who had London's full support, he realized that without the support of his people he had no longer any role to play in his native land. In 1607 he, with Rory O'Donnell and close on a hundred of the most important persons in Ulster, quietly boarded a ship in Lough Swilly and sailed to the continent, never to return.

It is generally agreed that 'the flight of the earls' marks the real end of Gaelic civilization as a political entity, though as a cultural and even as a social phenomenon the tradition lingered on and flickers still, while Irish patriotism was of course constantly to be revived in a variety of forms and behind a multitude of slogans.

For centuries it was English policy to make Ireland 'pay for itself', that is to say to pay for supporting the English standing army which was there to prevent rebellion and—when rebellion occurred as it had always done and was to do with remarkable regularity almost once per generation—to pay for the cost of subduing the rebellion. In the Ireland of the sixteenth, seventeenth and eighteenth centuries there was virtually no industry or commerce that could be successfully milked, as was to happen in the nineteenth and twentieth, and the only wealth that the English could draw on in Ireland was land. Since land is obviously not transportable, the only way the English could transfer it into cash was to seize it and sell it. This was the primary, economic basis of British colonialism, and remained so until the end of the British empire. From a socio-political point of view this policy of land seizure hid a secondary motive. The purchasers and new landlords were intended to be English or Scots so far as possible. They would bring with them English ways, the English language, English law and the English or Scots versions of the Protestant religion. Since for centuries the English, like their cousins in Germany and their descendants in America, have generally regarded their own methods as being divinely inspired, such a substitution of cultural and spiritual values to replace the benighted ideas and ideals of the ignorant natives could only be, in English eyes, of positive benefit to all, from Drogheda to Delhi. Such was the ideological justification of conquest and plunder. It was later to assume slightly more sophisticated forms of reference, such as the imposition of an incorruptible civil service on the Malayans or Ghanaians, but in Ulster, in the first half of the seventeenth century, the motives behind the Plantation were crude: to make money, to keep the Irish down, and if possible to turn them into second-class Englishmen or Scots or at least to prevent them from speaking, thinking and thus even being Irish.

The Plantation, that first deliberate plantation, of Ulster was very far from being homogeneous. The most easterly counties, Antrim and the northern part of the County Down, already had a largely Scots population. Indeed the sea is there so narrow that the distinction between Scots and Irish was and is almost irrelevant. By the mid-sixteenth century there had been a large Scottish 'colony' in Antrim, the MacDonnells. (The present head of this clan, Lord Antrim, still has his seat at Glenarm and is chairman of the independent television service called Ulster Television.) These areas were therefore not ripe for expropriation and colonization. An attempt to plant northeastern Ulster in the 1570s had failed: the colonists had either sold up and gone home or had married Irishwomen and produced Irish, and Irish-speaking, children as had happened over the centuries in Munster and Connaught. Only in Leinster, and only in parts of that province, had the English *geist* taken firm root. It was therefore to the hinterland that the colonists and the carpet-baggers had to look. They came, they saw, they stole what the soldiers had conquered. Their method was really quite simple.

The province of Ulster consisted in 1607, as it does today, of nine counties. (That part of the United Kingdom usually referred to as 'Northern Ireland', though it does not include the extreme north of the island, contains six of these counties.) Of the nine, two were not meet for plantation: Antrim and Down already contained large Scottish and smaller English settlements, and since after 1603 England was to be ruled by a Scots dynasty for almost all of eighty-seven years, these people were in theory loyal subjects of the London government—which indeed they usually were—and their land was therefore not expropriated. The large estate called Clandeboye in North Down, the property of Con O'Neill, a member of that great family, and consisting of some 60,000 acres that include what was then the village of Belfast, was divided into three. One share went to a keen and efficient Scottish colonist from Ayrshire called Hugh Montgomery, one third, apparently as a reward, to another Scot named James Hamilton who had usefully served the Crown for many years as a secret agent in Dublin; the final portion Con O'Neill was allowed to keep, but within a very few years his new Scots neighbours had, by legal and commercial methods, acquired almost all of his land too. With such people active in Down, and the MacDonnells across Belfast Lough with the utterly loyal settlement at Carrickfergus, there was no need to plant the two eastern counties.

In the southeastern part of the province the small county of Monaghan had already been expropriated in Elizabethan times. This was MacMahon country and when Hugh MacMahon was attainted and executed for collecting his rents by a customary Irish method—that is to say the seizure of cattle—the county was broken up and feudalized in the 1590s. Seven MacMahons and a MacKenna were allotted between two and five thousand acres apiece: they were entitled to demand £10 per 960 acres from each of their tenants: and from this they had to pay a quit rent to the Crown, represented by a Seneschal. This was a comparatively successful implementation of the policy of 'surrender and re-grant' that Queen Elizabeth had inherited from her father, Henry VIII, who had first formulated it in 1541. Its intention was the destruction of the ancient Irish social structure. By 1608 in Monaghan there was no longer 'a MacMahon' but seven great landowners with that name and often at loggerheads one with another. Therefore Monaghan, like Antrim and Down, was not planted. To do so would only have disrupted those long range plans for the substitution of English for Irish methods in social arrangements which it was the English colonialists' intention to enforce. Monaghan, in fact, reverted quite quickly to Irish ways. Together with Donegal and Cavan it is one of the three counties of Ulster that are now part of the Republic of Ireland.

The other six counties of Ulster (Donegal, Coleraine, soon to be renamed Londonderry, Tyrone, Fermanagh, Cavan, Armagh) were to be planted. The first was Cavan in 1605, even before the flight of the earls: the other five in 1608, immediately after that event. And here it is necessary to explain the whole method and motive of 'plantation', in Ireland as in Virginia and elsewhere, which was the main method of early English colonialism.

The basic motive of the plantations—for even in Ulster we must speak of many, carried out over many years—was not, or at least not consciously on the part of the newcomers, the destruction of Gaelic culture nor even in the first instance of the Roman Catholic religion. True, since the Statute of Kilkenny in 1366, the English had made periodic attempts to stamp out the Irish language in the areas they controlled, principally in the Pale of Dublin, and to compel the subject people to dress as Englishmen. These measures were, however, directed more against the Anglo-Norman settlers of the original conquest and their successors, known as the Old English, who were likewise becoming assimilated amidst the native population, rather than against the Irish themselves. In Ulster in the early seventeenth century the Anglo-Normans, small in numbers in any event, were almost completely Gaelicized, and the Old English were also rare. Though the operation was not directed against Irish culture as such at this time—this was to come later—it was directed against the old Irish legal system (the Brehon Laws, which had almost nothing in common with Roman Law), against the Irish economy, which was to be expropriated, and against the Irish people, who were to be in as large a measure as possible expelled to make way for the planters or reduced to the level of second-class citizens.

As early as the reign of Queen Mary, in the 1550s, an attempt to extend the Pale westwards by planting Leix and Offaly with loyal Old English had soon failed, as usual owing to assimilation. (Curiously, the counties, renamed Queen's and King's counties, were allowed to retain their new names throughout centuries of Protestant domination and re-conquest: it was left to the Irish Free State to abolish this memorial to his Most Catholic Majesty, King Philip of Spain, and to his wife, the last Roman Catholic queen to reign over England and Ireland.) An attempt at a plantation in northern Ulster in the 1570s had similarly failed. The plantation of Munster was carried out in far more systematic fashion between the two Desmond revolts and after the final suppression of the second in 1583. This is hardly surprising since the men in charge in London were the two most powerful men in the English government, Burleigh and Walsingham, while the men on the spot included Sir Walter Raleigh and his half-brother Sir Humphrey Gilbert. Sir Humphrey had not only been governor of Munster twenty years before but was to plant the first British colony on the American continent. Sir Walter Raleigh's career as one of the first and perhaps among the greatest English colonists in the New World is common knowledge. It is important to realize that these tough Elizabethan politicians and soldiers regarded the colonization of Munster in exactly the same light, and from the same point of view, as they regarded the colonization of the eastern seaboard of America: it was wealth that they were after, the wealth of the natives. In this they were merely copying—at that time unsuccessfully—their Spanish enemies, with the general backing of Queen Elizabeth and her ministers.

The planting of Queen's and King's counties was not a success. 'Undertakers' were appointed, who became tenants-in-chief to the Crown on the understanding that they import English subtenants. The businessmen found it easier and more profitable to let the land to Irishmen, so nothing was changed save that land-tenure was made to approximate to the English pattern, while the authority of the Crown, in theory at least, was strengthened. Even these English gains were in large measure swept away in the wars. At about the same time a more successful, at least temporarily successful, attempt was made to bring the province of Connaught into the English system, this time without conquest. The so-called Composition of Connaught introduced money rents and English land-titles instead of the prevailing confusion of Gaelic and feudal tenures. This too was to be swept away, though again only temporarily, in the next Anglo-Irish war. The precedents were being slowly and steadily established, but at no profit to the Crown and, indeed, at great expense as army after English army had to be despatched across the Irish Sea only to melt away, more usually of disease or hunger than in battle, in the fearsome, trackless forests or in isolated outposts. Colonies were supposed to pay their way, at least, and were intended to bring in a profit. Ireland was doing neither, and Ulster least of all. Therefore when the Great O'Neill's rebellion was finally crushed, and the earls had flown, and Sir Cahir

O'Doherty's rebellion of 1608—in the course of which he burned Derry—had been crushed and the Irish chieftain killed on Tory Island, it was decided in London that more Draconian, more up-to-date, more efficient and above all more lucrative methods must be employed in the plantations of the devastated, starving counties of Ulster.

One of the most intractable problems of Elizabeth's and James I's Irish operations had been the payment and victualling of the soldiers. The English army at that time was remarkably corrupt at almost all levels. The contractors and sub-contractors stole and sold supplies of food, and even of weapons, intended for the men in the remote fastnesses of Ireland, all the way from Bristol or even from London as the carts creaked along the roads and tracks to Coleraine or Kerry. The officers stole the money with which the troops were supposed to be paid. In vast numbers the penniless, starving soldiers deserted when there was nothing left to loot from the natives, and often there had been nothing for a long, long time. The entire army's pay was almost always in arrears. And neither Queen Elizabeth's nor James I's ministers were anxious to have these 'sturdy beggars' back in England, not so much for fear of those anti-social methods of self-help which they had inevitably learned in the Irish wars but rather because an unemployed military rabble was in itself a highly undesirable component in a fragile, insecure society that was becoming increasingly divided as bitterness steadily increased over religious and parliamentary matters. Therefore, instead of pay, it was decided to plant approximately one-third of the sequestrated land of Ulster with discharged soldiers. No doubt among the clever and educated renaissance men in London and Dublin there were also memories from Oxford and Cambridge—and the brand new Trinity College, Dublin—of Roman methods of colonization, of discharged legionaries keeping Colchester or Trier quiet by their mere presence. It seemed a good financial and political solution. It failed, at first, because the majority of the planted soldiery either became Irishmen, in at least one generation, or sold up to the undertakers or even to the Irish and went home.

The second class of persons who received land-grants were the so-called 'servitors'. They were Irishmen who had in some measure or other proved their loyalty to the Crown in the recent wars. In view of the constant changing of sides for so many years, it must have been even more difficult in Ireland in 1608 to decide who had been a 'servitor' than it was in Germany in 1945 to decide who had been anti-Nazi. In view of the countryman's entirely comprehensible passion for land, his own people's land, in a country that offered no other form of wealth and survival for himself and his people, one does not need to be a psychologist in order to be quite sure that many of these 'servitors' hated the English expropriators, and we know that many of their sort took part in Owen Roe O'Neill's rebellion of 1642.

The third portion of confiscated Irish land—and precise percentages of course varied from district to district and from time to time—was sold to the 'undertakers' to help recoup the Crown for the cost of the wars and to pay for the government of this part of the Irish colony. They were more carefully supervised than they had been in Munster, but though a great deal of this land passed into English or more often Lowland Scots hands, much of it passed only to be resold into Irish hands as the province quite rapidly recovered from the wars. Undoubtedly a great many of the remaining Scots and English settlers were murdered in the rebellion of 1642. Figures, even rough percentages, are of course unobtainable. It would seem probable that the population of Ulster was in the nature of 100,000 in 1642: that perhaps some 10,000 of these were English or Scots living west of the old Scots settlements: and that few of these can have survived the atrocities of the 1640s. Thus the first plantation of Ulster was also, very largely, a failure so far as population was concerned but a success, in the long run, so far as English law and English methods were being gradually accepted as the normal way of conducting legal, economic and to a lesser extent agricultural affairs.

As for the nature, origin and quality of the original colonizers of Ulster in the age of James I and Charles I, there is very little statistical evidence on which to rely. The planted soldiers must have been, in the majority, English or Welsh, though they will have included a proportion of Scotsmen: these last must have been mercenaries as opposed to pressed men, since the union of England and Scotland under James I only came into effect with the death of Queen Elizabeth, an event that occurred only a few days before Hugh O'Neill surrendered and which would probably have postponed and perhaps prevented that surrender had he known of the change of dynasty at the time.

These soldiers were, in general, the scum of the English and Welsh countryside. Shakespeare knew them well and portrayed them in *Henry the Fifth*: Pistol, Nym, Bardolph, Fluellen, Macmorris and Boy were good military material but scarcely the types to colonize Ireland or indeed any other portion of the globe though, of course, there were exceptions. In West Cork, many years ago, I met a family with an English name. He was the blacksmith and was proud that an ancestor had been one of the blacksmiths with Mountjoy's army: he still had his forebear's Elizabethan anvil.

As for the servitors, they were Irishmen, either Ulstermen or men from the other three provinces, perhaps younger sons, perhaps themselves uprooted by earlier plantations. Some may have been of Anglo-Norman stock, and thus have inherited a vague knowledge of feudalism, but in language and manners such people had become almost completely Gaelicized by this time. Some may have been of Old English stock: in which case they were Roman Catholics, almost surely, and on their way to becoming as Gaelicized as the Irish descendants of the Anglo-Normans. And some must have been Scots-Irish, from the comparatively prosperous and comparatively peaceful settlements in the eastern and unsequestrated areas of the province. They would be, almost certainly, Presbyterians or even adherents of the more extreme nonconformist faiths such as Anabaptists.

As for the settlers provided by the undertakers, it is equally difficult to define their origins or qualities. From Massachusetts to Botany Bay, the British empire was colonized, at this level, by citizens who were usually regarded as undesirable, as misfits, in their own, increasingly homogeneous, society. Of course there were great English noblemen with Irish estates, from the time of Raleigh to the present day, but since they usually had and have English estates as well they tended and tend to be mere visitors to their Irish lands, the prototype 'absentee landlord'. The men whom the early undertakers found ready to settle the land were of a different type. In the early seventeenth century the undesirable misfit in England was not so much the criminal or prostitute who was later sent to Australia as the man who worshipped God in a manner unacceptable to the authorities. Get them out! Make life uncomfortable for them, so that they go somewhere else! To this must be added the fact that with

so many Scots nonconformists already settled in Antrim and
Down, with the narrowness there of the channel and the consequent comparative ease of communication between the settlers
and the Lowland Scots, the easiest place for the undertakers to
recruit settlers, and thus make money, was undoubtedly Scotland. It is therefore not illogical to assume that the attempt to
extend 'loyal' Ulster westwards—as it had been attempted
earlier to extend the Pale westwards into King's and Queen's
counties—was carried out in large measure by the importation
of Scots farmers and their families.

The exception was the County Coleraine. This was, in essence,
sold to a consortium of guilds with offices and halls in the City
of London, which is why the city and county were renamed
Londonderry. Modern comparisons are invariably misleading
but, if this is borne in mind, may also be in some measure en-
lightening. Coleraine was sold to the City much as Katanga in
the Congo was 'sold' by the Belgian government to the *Union
Minière*. They could exploit the territory, but must protect it
against its own natives, and a share of the profits must revert,
positively or negatively by savings in defence, to the metropolitan government. Coleraine was allotted to the City companies on the understanding that this, the heart of the O'Neill
country, would be planted and that forts would be built, in
particular that Derry—so recently destroyed by Cahir O'Doherty
—be turned into an impregnable fortress to safeguard the western part of Ulster. In exchange for great financial privileges,
such as Church patronage, the local fisheries and the collection
of customs at a nominal cost, the London consortium agreed to
police their county and to fortify its towns. As early as 1610 a
large body of workmen arrived to rebuild the walls of Derry and
to found other fortified centres, significantly named after City
companies, such as Draperstown and Salterstown. It may fairly
be assumed that the planters they brought in were largely Englishmen. But, to the disappointment of the London government,
the businessmen proved as inefficient in the role of military
engineers as did the soldiers on the farms. Ten years later the
City companies were fined heavily for failing to keep their
promises. Londonderry's walls were still unfinished, and no doubt
many of their English workmen and farmers were fast sliding
into the Irish emotional bog that has embraced so many generations of Englishmen, soldiers and civilians alike.

The problem of what to do with the native Irish in Ulster whose land was escheated was less acute than a similar problem was to prove in parts of that province in the eighteenth century (when great landowners such as Lord Downshire were to 'clear' vast estates of uneconomic peasant-farmers in order to put their farms down for grazing) or in the nineteenth when, again for economic reasons, the eviction of unwanted tenants was almost commonplace all over Ireland and particularly in the west. In seventeenth century Ulster the native population, as already stated, consisted largely of cattle-drovers. Almost all the towns and castles had been burned and very few houses survived the combination of Irish 'scorched earth' policy and the English policy of reprisals. Since the armies of both sides lived off the land, it was the English policy to destroy the crops, the Irish to do likewise when they retreated. Cattle it was possible to hide in the forests, but there can have been few of the beasts left in Ulster in 1608. Sheer starvation drove a part of the population elsewhere in search of food. Some never settled again and it is said to be from these 'broken men' of the sixteenth and seventeenth centuries that many of the tinkers, who still roam the Irish roads and whom foreigners sometimes confuse with Gypsies, are descended. Ulster, after 'the flight of the earls', was in large parts a wilderness, as open to colonization as the lands seized from the Indian tribes in America. Indeed in 1605 Lord Deputy Chichester was thinking principally of Ulster when he remarked that it was foolish for Englishmen to run after empty lands in Virginia, Guiana and elsewhere with Ireland on their doorstep. Sir Arthur, later Baron, Chichester, was the proto-type of the efficient, honest British colonial governor-general. His family struck root in Ulster during the ten years that he was Lord Deputy. Had Ulster been planted as he wished, that is to say with the minimum of damage to the native Irish popula-tion, that first plantation might have endured. But without a civil service to support him and with only a raggle-taggle army that was being rapidly disbanded he had no means to deal with the avarice and incompetence of the undertakers.

One section of the native population with whom it was more difficult to deal were those freebooters known as swordsmen. These were precisely what their name implies. In pre-English days the value of an Irish chieftain was measured by the num-ber of armed men in his entourage. It was they who raided across the undefined borders and stole their neighbours' cattle or who, when their land was raided, fought the other man's swordsmen. It was they, more or less united for once, who had provided O'Neill with almost all his military strength. And now they still clustered around their old chieftains, impoverished though these were, *bouches inutiles* if the province were to be permanently pacified and a constant menace to settlers and peaceable Irish alike if it were not. They had no role whatsoever to play in Chichester's vision of the new Ulster. Some, it is true, had gone abroad with the earls: others had followed, and it was now that the tradition of the Wild Geese, of Irishmen going to Europe to enlist in foreign armies, began, a tradition which was to drain Ireland of as many, perhaps, as 2,000,000 young men throughout the next two centuries. And this was, from the beginning, actively encouraged by the English authorities. Indeed an attempt was made to export some 6,000 Ulster swordsmen to fight in the Protestant armies of Gustavus Adolphus, but at the last moment the Swedish King shrewdly declined the offer of these reinforcements. It was to the Catholic countries that the Wild Geese usually went, to France above all but also to Spain and Austria, though a few were to be found as far afield as in the Russian service. But meanwhile most of the swordsmen chafed around their petty, impoverished and embittered chieftains in an Ulster that was becoming increasingly an extension of the Scottish lowlands as the settlers moved in.

It was a province rapidly recovering from the ravages of war. The more advanced agronomy of the new colonists enabled more land to be sewn with crops than before: towns were built or rebuilt, the currency was reformed; the exportation of timber began, which was to lead in due course to the destruction of the great forests and thus to yet more land being made available for agriculture; the army, greatly reduced in size, no longer roamed the countryside but was stationed in a series of forts, more properly called blockhouses, which ringed the province, where the soldiers were properly provisioned and even paid, and the religious animosities seemed to be quiescent. It was what is nowadays called a lull. In Ireland such lulls have usually lasted for approximately the life-span of one generation, for the conquered do not forget and though the fathers who fought may be dead or exhausted, the sons also remember: they are taught by their mothers, as they grow up with the ruins of the Castle of

Dromore and a score of thousand other ruins before their eyes, that when they are men there will be, for them too, 'work to do'. This lull lasted from 1608 to 1642, the time for a new-born babe to grow to be a man of thirty-four.

Religious animosity during this period of lull was less, probably, than it has been in Ulster at any time since those distant days. The religious division in the Irish wars had first been effectively raised in the South, during the Desmond wars in Munster in the late sixteenth century. But even then the old English of the Pale, though they had generally remained faithful to the Old Faith, had found a more natural affinity for a while with the New English who professed the New Faith. Among the native Irish it was only gradually that the propagandists of the counter-reformation, particularly the English Jesuits, could identify the English enemy with the Protestant enemy. It is said that there is a time-lag in mode of thought between England and Ireland which is dependent on the means of communication but which can nowadays be estimated at quite a short period of time, owing not only to a common language but also of course to technological changes. In the sixteenth and seventeenth centuries it took a long time for 'ideas' to reach so remote a province as Ulster, and even longer for the ideologies of the reformation and counter-reformation to be translated into, and understood in, the Irish language. Besides, as pointed out earlier, the Irish at this time were not politically dominated by sectarianism. The country churches were in ruins : the clergy of the Established Church seldom in evidence and unlikely to speak Irish : the Roman Catholic priests, when they were not political agents, generally simple and semi-educated men.

In these circumstances—apart from expelling the Jesuits for purely political reasons—Chichester and his immediate successors saw little point in enforcing the ever harsher religious discriminations that were becoming state policy in England and, to a lesser degree, in Scotland. Presbyterian Ministers were allowed to occupy many of the vacant Establishment Churches, nor did the local bishops, themselves usually Scotsmen and therefore compatriots, often object. The Roman Catholics, the so-called recusants, were also largely left alone, to celebrate the Mass in their own fashion. This tolerance undoubtedly contributed to the duration, and the success, of the lull.

But in England and Scotland tempers were rising on the reli-

gious issue, a major contributory factor to the Civil War about
to break out in the larger island. In the opinion of this writer while
the liberal and Marxist historians' interpretation of the causes
behind the English Civil War—the emergence and desire for
domination of the *bourgeoisie*—has an element of validity, in
Ireland, and indeed in Irish history generally, the economic
interpretation has had, and has, far less. For the attempts by
Chichester's immediate successors, and particularly by Strafford,
to enforce the rules of the Anglican establishment through his
fiscal policies, both upon the Roman Catholics and upon the
non-conformists, not only caused the Catholics to harden in
their religion and to identify it with their patriotism but also
failed to unite the two subdued religious groups who between
them constituted an overwhelming majority in the Province of
Ulster.

Indeed in the late 1630s politico-religious issues in England,
and above all in Scotland, affected the Scottish settlers to their
detriment far more than they did the native Irish. In order to
enforce the Church of England ritual upon the Scots, Charles
I prepared to invade his second kingdom. In Ireland, his third,
this meant a measure of persecution of the Presbyterian and
other nonconformist sects which they accepted with great
bitterness as they observed the comparative tolerance still extended to the Roman Catholic recusants. By 1641 King Charles
had been compelled by *force majeure* (he had no army on which
he could rely and could call no parliament which would vote
him the money he needed) to give in to the Scots in Scotland.
The Scots in Ulster benefited indirectly from King Charles's
failure and in one of the many paradoxes of history—the history
of Ireland contains more than the histories of most countries—
it was the failure of King Charles and his Irish deputies to ram
the Church of Ireland down the throats of the Presbyterians and
other Ulster noncomformists which led these eventually to turn
all their venom against their Roman Catholic neighbours and
to become the super-patriots of a Scotland-England, which they
have almost always remained. This 'country' to which they
swore and swear allegiance, and for which they were and are
prepared to die and even more readily to kill, has never existed.
It is the mythical component of an ideology, the reality of
which was and is a fear and therefore hatred of the conquered
Irish. This has remained an almost constant factor in the

Ulster equation. By 1641 it has been estimated that of the three and a half million acres of Ulster, three million belonged, by English law, to Englishmen and Scots. However the proportion of the Ulster population was probably in almost exact reverse. The men who worked the land were dispossessed, Irish-speaking Irishmen. And on their diminished acres the Irish chieftains, with their swordsmen around them, watched the English defeated by the Scots, watched England sliding towards civil war, counted the small numbers of ill-trained soldiers who ringed the province from their blockhouses : communicated with France and Spain : listened to fanatical Counter-reformation priests : and decided that the time had come.

In 1642 Ulster rebelled, under the leadership of Owen Roe O'Neill, the nephew of the greater rebel of that name. Soon enough all Ireland was in flames, and in chaos. And after O'Neill came Cromwell.

CHAPTER THREE

The second O'Neill rebellion, and the Cromwellian re-conquest, were the great traumatic experience in Ulster's, indeed perhaps in all Ireland's, history. This may seem a remote and almost irrelevant chapter of history to English, and even more so to American, readers. But unless the events of 1641 to 1652 are understood, at least at the emotional level, it is impossible to comprehend what lies behind the present and future struggles in what are now the Six Counties of Northern Ireland.

Seldom can there have been a more complex situation, even in Irish history. In Ulster there were at least four politico-religious groups involved: the dispossessed Roman Catholic majority, embittered and since 'the flight of the earls' almost leaderless: the Scots-Irish settlers in the East: the new Scots and English settlers and the 'servitors' in the other counties: and a weak English army, dotted about in its forts and itself rent by the strife in the larger island between Cavaliers and Round-heads.

In Ireland as a whole the situation was equally unamenable to clear-cut division. There, too, at least six forces were involved: the native Irish, partly feudalized long ago but still resentful of English rule: the Anglo-Normans, largely Gaelicized and in large measure indistinguishable from the native Irish: the Old English, particularly of the Pale, almost entirely Roman Catholics and therefore anti-Roundhead though not necessarily pro-Cavalier: the new English of recent plantation, who were not necessarily pro-Cromwellians: a very small English army, also split: and finally the Wild Geese who returned, under Owen Roe O'Neill and others to fight for an Ireland that had, during the lull, almost ceased to exist. A statesman and soldier of genius might have united all these forces. None appeared upon the scene.

Behind all this, but highly relevant, was the Civil War in England, in essence a triangular war between Roundheads, Cavaliers and Scots, fought over issues that did not directly affect the Irish, but which obviously affected them indirectly were they to fail to throw off English rule in the smaller island.

In fact here we have, not for the first time and certainly not for the last, an Irish political situation which was alternately to bewilder, in times of crisis, or to bore, in quieter moments, the English, government and people alike. The English had become a very homogeneous people under the Tudor monarchs, the Spanish threat, and the Protestant religion. They had now split on internal, though not on external, issues. From the blood and misery of the Civil War there was, quite quickly, to arise the two-party parliamentary system, which has endured until our time and has been copied in a modified form in England's greatest ex-colony, the United States. Behind this political system there lie certain assumptions, of which two are here relevant. The primary purpose of the two political parties is to decide, by debate and ballot, their relative powers to govern, the principal issues being social and economic—that is to say the redistribution of power or of its easiest symbol, wealth. But when faced by a foreign enemy, whether Spanish, French, German or Russian, the parties tacitly postpone their internal differences until the immediate peril is past.

Therefore, from the English point of view which inevitably they have applied to all their colonies and particularly to Ireland, the art of politics consists in realizing that there are two sides to every question. They are saying so today.

But in colonies, and particularly in Ireland, this assumption is totally untrue. On the one hand there has always been only one side to the question—how to get rid of the conquerors. On the other, in a society fragmented by conquest and colonization, there are numerous sides, almost always in bitter disagreement, as to how this aim should or should not be achieved. It was so in 1641, it is so in Ulster and the Republic of Ireland today.

It is not my intention here to describe the spasmodic, confused and confusing ten-year-war that engulfed almost all Ireland, nor even, in detail, the events in Ulster. Briefly what happened is that in the autumn of 1641 the Roman Catholic population of Ulster rose against the settlers and the military. In the following year, August 1642, Owen Roe O'Neill returned from exile to take command of the Ulster rebel horde, which he transformed into an army of sorts, the only moderately effective army that the Irish possessed. By then much had happened. In that same August civil war had broken out in England, the rebellion in Ireland had spread across the whole island, and a more competent general than Preston, another homing Wild Goose who 'commanded' the Irish army in the south, could quite easily have captured Dublin: a Roman Catholic parliament, the so-called Confederation of Kilkenny, had been assembled in opposition to the Protestant parliament in Dublin: Richelieu's France and other Catholic powers were supplying the Irish with arms and money: and the war in Ireland was becoming ever more a straight religious war, between Catholics and Protestants, almost an extension of the German Thirty Years' War then approaching its climax. Yet to describe events in Ireland during this decade as a war is largely inaccurate, for though there were armies, and even occasional battles and sieges, the Rebellion of 1641 was, like the Rebellion of 1798 and even that of 1919, far closer to a Peasants' Revolt, a *jacquerie*, than to the wars between European sovereign powers in the three centuries to come, with their conventions, even their rules, and their usually clear-cut decision ending in an armistice and ultimately a peace treaty. Indeed it is, perhaps, easier for us to understand the atmosphere of the struggle than it was for our grandfathers: Vietnam is a closer parallel than nineteenth century colonial wars.

It was fought with extreme brutality. Those Protestants who could not flee into Protestant enclaves, such as Dublin, Cork, Bandon and one or two more in the south, to the forts of Enniskillen or Derry in the north, or to the Protestant settled areas of Antrim and North Down, were usually massacred. This seems to have been particularly so in Ulster, where the Catholics and the Protestants were face to face, where there were few Old English Catholics or Gaelicized Anglo-Normans to act as intermediaries, and where plantation was so recent. It was a war, if war it can be called, fought without gallantry or dignity. And it is hardly surprising that when Cromwell arrived in 1649 he regarded the Irish whom he conquered as little better than dangerous wild beasts, to be exterminated.

It has frequently been said that the most repulsive—emotionally repulsive, that is—aspect of the Nazi genocide of the Jews, Poles and other ethnic groups was its scientific, businesslike efficiency. This is a comprehensible anthropomorphic response. We identify a régime with a human being, and since we tend to regard a man who murders in an outburst of passion or insanity as 'superior' to one who carefully and systematically plans his crime, so we tend to be more horrified by the crimes of the Cromwellians than by those of the Ulster peasantry and swordsmen. This is, of course, totally illogical. The Ulster Old Irish population was as determined upon some form of genocide for the English and Scots in 1641 as were the Ironsides vice-versa ten years later. Indeed the crimes of Cromwell in Ireland have almost certainly been exaggerated in popular mythology: modern historians even deny that he killed the entire population of Drogheda. But Cromwellian atrocities have entered into the people's mind, from which they can now never be erased, while the earlier crimes and massacres by his enemies—which incidentally he invoked specifically as justification for his own—have largely been forgotten, save among the Protestant population of Ulster. And the reason for this brings one back again to the parallel with Nazi Germany.

Cromwell's Ironsides were probably the first army in Europe to be inspired by ideology since the armies of the early Crusades. In Germany, during the Thirty Years' War, appalling atrocities were committed on a far greater scale than in Ireland, but these were savageries of another sort. The principle of *cujus regio, ejus religio* (that it was the religion of the local prince or potentate which counted) did not mean that all his subjects were automatically damned, though they might well be mere objects of loot, rape and murder. It would seem that many, perhaps most, of Cromwell's officers and men regarded the Roman Catholic Irish as damned, as inhuman, as fiends incarnate, an impression strengthened by their knowledge of massacres by these people before their arrival in the strange country. It was therefore their duty to exterminate these monsters in human form, and their utterly wicked religion, just as it was the duty of SS men to exterminate Jews and international Jewry. Like most political slogans, 'Hell or Connaught' meant precisely what it says. If the Roman Catholic population, and particularly the population of Ulster, refused to move out and go to the wilderness of Connaught, then they would be murdered: in which case, in the eyes of the Cromwellian fanatics, they must automatically go to hell, a hell in which those soldiers believed implicitly. Why should they not believe in hell, since they were creating it on the Irish soil? If they preferred to go to Connaught, well then, they could quietly starve to death on their own, out of sight and out of mind. In this writer's opinion, if Cromwell and his people had possessed the technical ability to build gas chambers and drop Zyklon B upon the Irish Roman Catholic subhumans, once they had them at their mercy, they would undoubtedly have used such methods. As it was, they did their best. And this has left a far deeper—as always with the conquerors less than with the conquered, though very deep on both sides—political trauma than had the mere colonization and attempts at rebellion of an earlier and later age. Cromwell and his plantation of Ulster planted more than farmers. It set a time bomb which, re-fused in the nineteenth century, ticks away in that province even today and may, with ill luck or through ill management, have finally blown up before these words are printed.

Only towards the very end of the atrocious war was there any real alliance between the native Irish, particularly the Ulster Irish led by O'Neill, and the Roman Catholic and royalist majority in the south. This alliance, if such it can be called, came too late to affect the political or even the military outcome. It did not come too late to affect the post-war settlement. In the eyes of Cromwell and his successors—he did not linger in Ireland after his initial, successful campaign—they had won a Holy War against the papists, and they set about the creation of a Holy Peace, in an Ireland intended to be without papists. Though they disliked the Church of Ireland and even regarded the Scottish Presbyterians as dangerously High Church, for the Roman Catholics they had little save hatred and contempt. The complete extirpation of the Old Faith in Ireland now became official policy. And since the men who set about enforcing it were neither the miserable military nor the venal businessmen of an earlier age, it seems possible that had they had time they might have succeeded and the Irish might have ceased to exist.

The new policy was threefold. First of all the physical transportation of the Irish to the counties west of the Shannon ('Hell or Connaught') and in particular the expulsion of Roman Catholics from all towns and cities. Secondly a massive and far more effective plantation of the escheated lands east of the Shannon, of which ten counties were allotted to the military, the remainder to the adventurers, while only a handful of 'loyal' Irish were allowed to retain ownership of land, though the dispossessed were in theory to be allotted land in Connaught. This proved to

be an administrative impossibility, partly owing to the absence
of an effective civil service and even of maps, partly because
areas of Connaught were also needed to settle the military
colonists. The purpose of this massive transfer of population,
similar though of course smaller in scale to that inflicted upon
the Germans in Soviet-occupied Eastern Europe after 1945,
was to ensure that there were almost no land-owning Roman
Catholics east of the Shannon. Total expulsion there proved an
impossibility, since with the agricultural technology of the age
the new settlers required labour on their farms. But every effort
was made to ensure that such Irish as remained would be pau-
perized, penalized, landless labourers.

Finally a determined attempt was made to stamp out the
Roman Catholic religion as such. The few remaining churches
were destroyed physically. All priests were now outlawed. Indeed a price of £5 per head of a priest was offered, the same
reward as that given for the head of a wolf, for wolves had multiplied in the ruined countryside. Fines for non-attendance at
Protestant churches and chapels were enforced. Here again
given time the Cromwellians might have been successful,
though it seems probable that they came on the scene too late.
By 1651 Irish nationalism had become firmly and inextricably
intertwined with Roman Catholicism, and the now almost total
destruction of the old Gaelic aristocracy and of Gaelic civilization as such meant that the people inevitably looked to their
spiritual leaders, the priests, and to the Roman Catholic Church
to replace the whole external apparatus of Irish life which was
then finally swept away. In no province was this overthrow of
old values more violently carried out than in Ulster, where the
Protestants were already so deeply entrenched in the east and
the Irish so 'wild' in the west: in none did it leave such deep and
enduring scars and hatreds.

The Restoration of Charles II in 1660 was greeted by the
Roman Catholic majority with joy and the expectation that
their wrongs were to be righted, and presumably with a measure
of fear on the part of the new Cromwellian settlers. However
it was not the policy of the new government, either in England
or by extension in Ireland, to put back the clock and restore the
ancien régime. What restitution of property was made was small
and almost exclusively to active royalists in the south, that is to
some of the Old English. The Irish received virtually nothing.

Although the more virulent attempts to extirpate the Irish ceased, the situation, particularly in Ulster, was more or less frozen so far as the recent plantations were concerned. The new settlers and their Irish serfs lived, uneasily, side by side. And another lull, again to last for some thirty years, ensued.

Religious persecution was relaxed, so far as the Roman Catholics were concerned, but with the passing by the Cavalier Parliament of the so-called Clarendon Code stronger measures were taken to put down the nonconformists. In England it was policy to strengthen the established Church. In Ireland this meant full governmental support for the Church of Ireland. Though this met with a measure of success in the southern provinces, in Ulster the attachment of the two main religious groups to their respective faiths was very great. Thus a triangular situation arose: Church of Rome, Church of Ireland, Nonconformists. That situation has endured to this day. In terms of political logic, the oppressed nonconformists and the oppressed Roman Catholics should have united against their oppressors of the Establishment, just as nowadays in terms of economic logic the oppressed proletariat of both faiths should be united against the boss class. But in the 1670s as in the 1970s such a union of interests by the downtrodden did not take place, for emotional division based on religion and on history was and remains too great. Only very briefly, in the late eighteenth century, inspired by the a-religious ideals of the French Revolution and with at least one leader of genius in the person of Wolfe Tone, was it possible for the Irish of all the oppressed faiths to attempt a United Ireland, and even that attempt at national unity was in large measure a failure. But by then much had happened, and much had been repeated. For any student of Irish history the psychological phenomenon called *déja vu* becomes almost a permanent state of mind, and can verge on the obsessive. This can be misleading, for Ulster, though caught in the vice of religious animosity from which it has not yet escaped, was slowly changing, more slowly perhaps than the rest of Ireland and in another direction, far more slowly than England and Western Europe, but changing nonetheless.

During this Caroline lull there was, once again, a rapid and remarkable economic revival in Ulster, more rapid than in the rest of Ireland. When the rating of a country's or a province's economy is zero, as in Ulster in 1651 or in Germany in 1945, a mere return to normality appears to be an economic miracle. This is, however, not the whole story. The Scots settlers and the planted Cromwellians were in general sober, god-fearing, hard-working men. They were good farmers too, and shrewd merchants. It was now that flax became a fruitful crop, and linen a profitable industry. Even today, when one crosses the border, it is striking to see how much better kept the farms in the north are than those to the immediate south. Such is the basic justification of the dour and bigoted Scots-Irish: they are efficient. Cromwellians usually were.

True, the Cromwellian plantation in most of the country and especially in the rural areas soon went the way of the earlier plantations, as the Cromwellian soldiers began immediately to intermarry with Irishwomen. Since in farming communities it is the mother primarily who brings up the children, such marriages bred a new racial mixture, or reinforced the old mixture with new blood, while failing to exterminate old modes of thought and even of behaviour. Now began the emergence of that special type of Irishmen called Ulstermen. Their most distinctive quality was and is a siege mentality that has frequently reached paranoiac proportions. Outside of the forts, such as Derry, which were growing into towns, and the almost homogeneous Scots colonies of the east coast, the Ulstermen might be reverting to Irish ways even when retaining the Protestant religion. But the colonists and their descendants were well aware that in Ireland as a whole they were vastly outnumbered and, without British support, were at the mercy of the conquered majority. Since 1641 they also knew how much mercy they might expect. Meanwhile in Ulster, though not in the rest of Ireland, the disfranchised and spoliated Catholics who had not been driven into Connaught were reminded daily that they too were at the mercy of their enemy, and they too knew the nature of that mercy. In this situation qualities and responses came into being which, curiously, united Ulstermen psychologically, if in no other way, and set them apart from most other Irishmen. If a very rough parallel can be drawn, the conquered Irish of Munster, Leinster and Connaught were closer to the Jews of Eastern Europe—diaspora and all—than to the Israelis: the population of Ulster was closer to the present day inhabitants of Palestine, Israeli and Arab alike. Of course, no two situations are ever the same, but the role of America in Israeli affairs is curiously parallel to that of Britain in those of Ulster. It is also to be remarked that in both places this 'siege mentality' produced and produces soldiers and military commanders of the very highest quality.

Thus Ulster began to develop a 'personality' that set it apart not only from Britain, on which its ruling class relied, but also from the rest of Ireland, to which its countryfolk bore an increasingly closer resemblance. Even Ulster never became a mere extension of England or a Scotland *outre-mer*, while the rest of Ireland quite quickly, and as usual, absorbed most of its foreign conquerors. Nevertheless Cromwell's overthrow of the old order had profound effects which cannot be overestimated in Ireland's history. The determined attempt to expel the Roman Catholics from the towns and cities was only marginally successful: they kept drifting back, and were in any case needed for a mass of menial or semi-menial tasks. On the other hand in the municipalities political power, that is to say the power of the corporations, passed from the hands of the Old English, of the recusants, into those of the new settlers, and was to remain in these hands, in the hands of their descendants, for over two centuries. This has remained the condition in the Six Counties until such time as it shall have been righted by the promised reforms, enforced upon the government of Northern Ireland by the government of the United Kingdom in 1969 and, at the time of writing, being enacted very slowly and amidst growing resentment on the part of Protestant extremists. It is against this rigging of the vote in Derry, Newry, Strabane, Dungannon and of course Belfast itself that the basic campaign of the Civil Rights movement, created in 1968, was first directed. And all this dates from way, way back, from the seventeenth-century concept that in Ireland, and latterly in any part of Ireland controlled by the Crown, it was in the interest of the Crown and, perhaps more important, of basic local political realities that the Roman Catholics be subjected to the Protestants. And it follows from this that trade, and therefore wealth, must be in competent, Protestant hands. The Irish were to be, in their own country, second-class citizens. That they were such inferior persons was already and obviously evident to the English after the Cromwellian plantations, the chance of their remaining so, once 'there was work to do', was a minor consideration, for no pragmatic generation of Teutonic origin thinks beyond its own or its children's lifetime. This Caroline lull lasted for again a generation, and then Ireland blew up once more.

The Stuarts, that most attractive but most inept of British dynasties, had done much harm to Ireland. James I had planted it: Charles I had imposed the tyrannical Strafford upon it: Charles II had failed to redress the wrongs inflicted upon the Irish by his grandfather, his father and the usurper Cromwell: James II, in furtherance of his own aims in the larger island, not only destroyed the new born and very fragile equilibrium that his brother's ministers had helped to create, but also exacerbated religious hatred by his policies, and finally plunged the country into civil war, soon to be followed by international war. He then simply ran away, leaving the Irish to their fate, a nation conquered once again. This deplorable monarch had once been a brave and competent admiral: in Ireland he proved himself a most incompetent and even cowardly soldier. All Ireland had rallied to him save only the key forts of Derry and Enniskillen in Ulster and the Protestant eastern seaboard in that province. (Derry was about to surrender to the Roman Catholic forces in 1689 when the Apprentice Boys seized power within the town, closed the gates, and withstood the siege, an event that is annually commemorated on August 12th of each year.) Any competent general could quite easily have occupied the whole of Ireland, particularly once the efficient and experienced French regiments had arrived to act as a steel backbone for the newly recruited Irish. It was not done. The Ulster coast remained an open beachhead through which King William could pour his English, Scottish, Dutch and other foreign troops, and from which he proceeded to advance southwards and then westwards. He had landed at Carrickfergus with some 36,000 troops on June 14th, 1690. He himself cannot have collected many Ulster volunteers, though some had rallied to his general, Schomberg, who had been in Ulster since the previous winter, for it was only a mere two weeks later that King William's forces met and defeated those of King James at the Battle of Boyne. This was on the 1st of July, new style, but is still celebrated as the great Orangemen's festival on July 12th, the old dating before the Gregorian Calendar reform. It is from this battle, won largely by Danes, Germans and French Huguenots, that the Protestant north derived in large measure its political entity. And it is from the Dutch king, Willem of Orange-Nassau, that the most patriotic and bigoted of Irish Protestants derived their chosen name of Orangemen, their tribal colour and, in due course, their semi-secret society known as the Orange Lodges. Though they had not actually fought the battle in any quantities, they had also not surrendered to a Roman Catholic army which however had scarcely bothered to attack them. It is yet another example of the truism that wars are lost, not won. Meanwhile the events, even the dates of these events, have assumed ever since a sacred, indeed an idolatrous, quality in the minds of the Ulster Low Churchman's mythology. This mythology has been used and abused by extremists in Northern Ireland to this day.*

* In the view of many military historians the decisive Williamite victory was not so much the Battle of the Boyne as the Battle of Aughrim, fought just over a year later, in July 1691. The French regular troops were decimated, their general killed, and the Irish forced to withdraw with all speed behind the walls of Limerick, with Schomberg close on their heels. Aughrim, however, is in Galway, that is to say in the province of Connaught, which is perhaps one reason why it does not figure among the Ulstermen's annual celebrations. Maybe more important from the psychological point of view is the fact that the Boyne was essentially a defensive victory—had King William lost, it is possible that all Ulster would have been overrun—whereas Aughrim was an offensive operation. The former was therefore more suitable to assume traumatic status in its appeal to the Protestant Ulsterman's siege mentality. From that day to this the Ulstermen have, in all-Irish terms, almost always been on the defensive, within their own territorial boundaries: only within those boundaries have they repeatedly taken the offensive, against the Catholic minority. Since Partition, though the illegal Ulster Volunteer Force has committed acts of terrorism in the Free State/Republic—blowing up monuments, occasional acts of arson and a murder or two perhaps—such deeds are insignificant when compared to the attempts of the equally illegal Irish Republican Army to disrupt by violence, in several ill-organized campaigns, the social arrangements prevalent in the North.

CHAPTER FOUR

On October 3rd, 1691, Patrick Sarsfield signed the Treaty of Limerick. For a century, and perhaps for more than two, no other Irishman was to command what could be described as an Irish army in Ireland. The terms of the Treaty were honourable: essentially a return to the *status quo ante*, to the Caroline period. But the English still wished to be rid of the Irish swordsmen. And the Irish soldiers had nowhere to go, save abroad, to King James and to foreign armies. This the English accepted and encouraged. Sarsfield and some eleven thousand Irish soldiers sailed away, some with the French fleet that had arrived just too late to raise the siege of Limerick, but more than half of them in ships supplied by the English government, only too glad to see these dangerous fighting men elsewhere. These joined the five Irish regiments which had sailed to France in the previous year, in exchange for the 7,000 French troops sent to support James II, the remnants of which now also departed.

The flight of the Wild Geese was the flight of the earls all over again, save on an infinitely more massive scale, appropriate to an age that was taking the first steps towards democracy and the importance of quantity of men above quality of lineage in political matters. With the Wild Geese went a high proportion of the Irish, Anglo-Norman and Old English aristocracy. And with the swordsmen and their chieftains gone, the Irish who remained had now no defenders at all. As in Ulster in 1608, so now the other provinces of Ireland were open for the most drastic colonization.

It has been estimated that at the beginning of the Williamite war approximately one eighth of the land of Ireland remained in Catholic hands. Of this eighth, about one million acres were now confiscated and sold on the open market. The old Gaelic aristocracy was, for all intents, wiped out and reduced to the status of a peasantry, soon enough to be almost indistinguishable from the old peasantry save perhaps in a certain retention of manners and courtesies which, indeed, still linger on in many

country cottages. However the whole cultural apparatus of the
Gaelic and Gaelicized Anglo-Norman civilization was now systematically destroyed, and the Irish language rapidly decayed.
It was still spoken by the majority, perhaps by as many as 80%,
of the population, but it was gradually becoming the simple
language of the peasant. Throughout the brilliant, glittering,
endlessly enriching eighteenth century, when every other nation
in Europe was inventing new words to express new concepts and
new discoveries in every field, only in Ireland was the language
of the people contracting within the borders of poverty, disorder
and loss. Oh, there were a few poets, who wrote a few poems
that have survived and doubtless recited many more from an
earlier, happier, richer period.... Gaelic civilization in its external forms was finally killed in the elegant eighteenth century.
No attempt to revive it has ever succeeded, nor now ever will.
But the Irish character, though inevitably modified, was not
destroyed, and if the Irish remain conscious of themselves—as
they still most certainly do—perhaps it will only continue to
change but never die.

King William intended and wished to honour the Treaty of
Limerick to which his name had been appended by proxy. And
this not merely because he was an honourable man but also
because he wished that there be a pacified Ireland behind him
when he turned back to the main objective of his entire career,
the safe-guarding of his beloved Holland and the defeat of
Louis XIV. It was principally in order to achieve this end, and
to prevent Holland being outflanked by a Roman Catholic,
Jacobite England in alliance with France, that he had usurped
his father-in-law's crown, invaded England and re-conquered
Ireland. However in the matter of the Treaty of Limerick, as
in other matters too, he was reckoning without his hosts.

The men who had invited him to England, had organized the
Glorious Revolution, and who had placed the crown upon his
head were the spiritual and temporal magnates of England both
Whig and, to a lesser extent, Tory and their mouthpiece was
Parliament. They were High Church Anglicans and just as they
were determined that this Dutch king whom they had appointed and his successors should never be in a position to govern
without Parliament, so too were they convinced that the Anglican faith was an essential cornerstone of the England they
wished to see. In their view the Established Church could and

should brook no rivals. The atmosphere had been one of mounting hysteria since the days of Titus Oates and his imaginary
Popish Plot in Charles II's time. (This unpleasant incident, 1678-
1680, is curiously reminiscent of the Joe McCarthy period in
the United States, with prominent Roman Catholics being
accused, punished and—unlike in America—not infrequently
killed for taking part in a fictional conspiracy which had little
if any connection with the very real plans of France to impose
the counter-reformation upon England and the other Protestant
powers of Northern Europe.) When Charles II became publicly
converted to Roman Catholicism on his deathbed, it seemed to
many that maybe Oates had been right after all. When James II
deliberately set about overthrowing both Church and State and
persecuting Anglican bishops, in order to restore the Church of
Rome, they became more than ever convinced that Popery was
the prime enemy. They were not going to allow the new crowned
head of their oligarchy to spare the Papists in Ireland, even
though this meant compelling him to go back on solemn and
freely given promises. The Treaty of Limerick was never rati-
fied by the English parliament, nor by the Irish parliament (an
entirely subsidiary and almost irrelevant Protestant organization, powerless to legislate in any important field without Westminster's approval, and used principally for fiscal purposes of
English devising, it was even more a sham parliament, being
entirely of one party and one faith only, than is the present
Parliament of Northern Ireland at Stormont.) Therefore instead
of the comparatively fair and decent Treaty of Limerick, a
series of Penal Laws were passed through the English and Irish
parliaments. These were directed primarily against Roman
Catholics in the two kingdoms, but also against the Dissenters,
which meant against a large proportion of the Protestants in
Ulster, and particularly against the Presbyterians whose large
following and competent organization both there and in Scotland offered an alternative to the Church of England. It has
been estimated that at this time approximately half the population of Ulster was Protestant, and most of these will have been
Dissenters.

The effects of the Penal Laws were far harsher upon the
Roman Catholics, of course. They were forbidden to carry arms
or even to own a horse: to buy land, or if already in possession
of an estate to pass it on intact to a chosen heir, unless that heir

turned Protestant: to obtain any higher education in Ireland or
to attend a university abroad, thus closing all the professions to
the Roman Catholics: and soon enough, in 1728, they were
deprived of the parliamentary franchise. Profession of the
Roman Catholic faith was not, in itself, a criminal offence and
though the few remaining churches were confiscated or destroyed, the country was dotted with 'mass-houses' where it was
permitted that members of the secular clergy might celebrate
the Mass. However the Roman Catholic bishops and regular
clergy were banished overseas. The intention here was obvious,
once the living generation of secular clergy had died out, none
could be ordained. This compendium of cruel, spiteful and often
petty legislation continued to be pushed through successive
dummy parliaments for almost half a century. One wonders
whether the Nazi lawyers who drew up their own even harsher
Penal Laws against the Jews had not studied these earlier, in-
famous legal acts of tyranny. The two sets of laws are remarkably similar; the Irish were comparatively fortunate in that
their persecutors lacked modern administrative techniques.
For instance whenever an Irish industry, such as the woollen industry became a competitive threat to its English
equivalent a heavy duty was placed upon the export of
the Irish goods. Thus were many Irish craft industries
smothered in infancy. But the repeated attempts by legislation
and by fiscal methods to reduce Ireland to utter economic sub-
servience were not entirely successful. One Irish reply was to
create a fairly competent illegal transportation system. Smuggling to and from France and Spain was soon on an enormous
scale. It was not only goods that the ships carried as they slipped
into or out of the innumerable bays and inlets of southern and
western Ireland. Young men left, to join the Wild Geese in the
armies of France and Spain. Others to study for the priesthood.
Few of the soldiers ever came back, but the priests did. Nor was
smuggling the only large-scale form that illegal activity now
took. Many swordsmen in the Irish forces that Cromwell and
Ireton had broken took to brigandage. These tories—the name
was later applied, as an insult, by its enemies to one of the emergent English political parties—remained a scourge throughout
the seventeenth century. Though motivated perhaps by a primitive patriotism and certainly by a hatred of the settlers, these Irish
Robin Hoods might be heroes to their oppressed fellow-country-

men but they certainly impoverished the country as a whole by interfering with communications and hindering trade. However throughout the first two thirds of the eighteenth century there was very little trade outside of the seaports, the Pale and parts of Ulster.

Agriculture in most of the country was in an equally deplorable state. The English confiscations had left most of the Irish landless, while the Penal Laws saw to it that even those who did own land had to subdivide it among their children, in ever decreasing plots. The Irish tenant farmer was completely at the mercy of his English or Anglo-Irish landlord. He had no security of tenure, save that occasionally provided by a form of collusion. If he improved his land, and there were no collusion, his landlord could and not infrequently did raise his rent. Nor was he allowed to sell his tenancy, save only in Ulster, of which more later. If he could not pay his rent in cash or goods and his labour were not needed—and there was very little cash in circulation in Ireland in that century—he could be evicted immediately. To appeal to any legal body would be an appeal to his enemy, in a language he probably did not understand. Agricultural misery was acute. We read of families living in turf hovels with no furniture but only ferns and straw to lie upon, and no clothes save those they wore upon their backs. On the turf that they cut and burned water would be boiled, and into it the potatoes, increasingly the principal and often only food they ever saw, would go. It used to be said of the little black Kerry cows that they 'remember Sunday', because on Sundays they would be bled, and their blood used to enrich the monotonous diet of potatoes.

In such conditions of agricultural misery, most prevalent in the bad lands of the west and south, it is hardly surprising that agricultural crime flourished. The Irish had an age-old tradition of cattle-rustling. From the tories the men of the secret societies of the eighteenth and early nineteenth centuries also inherited the new tradition of armed brigandage directed against the alien landlords. Cattle were houghed, houses burned and looted by the Whiteboys, the Ribbonmen and the other organizations of armed and desperate countrymen that made large parts of the Irish countryside an extremely dangerous place in which to live and an almost impossible territory to farm efficiently. Where such a state of anarchy prevailed, the only restraining force was the priesthood, and even a devoutly Christian priest, though he might preach against murder and theft, could hardly be expected to be enamoured of his persecutors. Only in parts of Ulster, in the Dublin area, and in some though not all of the seaports, was this slide into anarchy halted and even reversed. Thus was the difference between Ulster and most of the rest of Ireland further accentuated.

In 1726 Dean Swift, the herald of a new form of Irish patriotism, wrote: 'The whole country, except the Scottish plantation in the north, is a scene of misery and desolation, hardly to be matched on this side Lapland.' The reason for this difference was two-fold at that time. The Scottish or English landlords and tenants in the predominantly Protestant areas of eastern Ulster and in and around its fortress-cities elsewhere were united in their fear of the Irish, while in the purely Scottish enclaves they were generally united by the Presbyterian religion as well. Though the Penal Laws split the Protestant community, and this perhaps forever, the English believed then that in the last resort they could always rely on the impossibility of united action against their rule by Dissenters and Roman Catholics joining together to rebel.

More important, economically, to the comparative well-being of Ulster was the so-called 'Ulster custom' which was never a law in the sense of being on the statute book, but which was generally observed throughout the province. This gave the tenant one essential right, the right of occupancy. If he wished to sell his tenancy he could do so to the highest bidder, provided that the landlord could not show reason for disapproving of the new tenant, a condition primarily intended to keep out Roman Catholics. If the landlord wished to evict his tenant, then that tenant could either sell his tenancy or the landlord himself could buy him out at the market price. This meant that in Ulster, unlike in the rest of Ireland, it was in the direct interest of the tenant to improve his land and of course this was ultimately in the interest of the landlord. Thus a further community of interest existed here that did not prevail in the other provinces. The agronomy improved slowly, and rents were more regularly paid. Furthermore, while the rest of agricultural Ireland was almost totally devoid of any industry of any sort, so that the rapidly growing population either lived off the land or starved, the linen industry in Ulster, particularly in the growing city of Belfast, both bought up the flax as a cash crop and also provided some jobs in the home and in the mills. There was in fact a certain amount of cash in circulation, very little by English but very considerable by Irish standards.

This does not mean that the Scots-Irish were a happy people, contented with their lot. They most certainly were not, and they proved this in the most effective way next to revolution, which the circumstances rendered impossible: in Lenin's phrase 'they voted with their feet', since there was no other way in which the nonconformists could have a real say in the running of their community.

The emigration from Ulster started in the second decade of the eighteenth century, principally to the American colonies. It continued throughout the rest of the century. By 1770 it was reckoned that some 12,000 Ulstermen were reaching America each year. They brought with them not only their grievances against English overlords—they and their memories played an important part in the American Revolution—but also the savagery instilled into them by generations of bitter strife with the conquered Irish. And as they moved westwards, for they were very prominent along the moving Frontier, they treated the Red Indians as they had been taught to treat the natives in the old country. The expulsion of the Indians from their territories, and the treatment of those who stayed and fought or, when conquered, still remained, was 'Hell or Connaught', set in the Appalachians, the Great Plains, the Rockies and westwards. Others, at least until the American Civil War, did well out of cotton and slavery particularly in the more western of the Southern States. It would therefore seem more likely that Scarlett O'Hara, the fictional Southern-belle heroine of *Gone with the Wind*, bore a name closer to Cameron or MacPherson than to one borne by the old Gaelic aristocracy. It was not until well into the next century that the really massive Irish Roman Catholic immigrations into Canada and the United States took place, and these were in general to the Northern cities.

It was the comparative prosperity in eighteenth-century Ulster that brought about the first great Irish emigration to the New World. Because of the 'Ulster custom' a dissatisfied farmer could sell his tenant's right and buy a passage for himself and his family across the Atlantic. He might even arrive on the far shore with a little cash. A regular passenger trade was soon in existence between Ulster and America. And so the colonists moved on. Meanwhile the destitute younger son or evicted peasant in Munster or Connaught would have no cash whatsoever. When he went to France or Spain he went alone, as a recruit. The fragment of Ireland and Irish ways that he brought with him died when he did, as often as not on some foreign field that never had been, and never would be, Ireland. The most he could pass on was his name, usually corrupted, to the descendants of the son some foreign wife had borne him. But the Ulstermen established communities in America, and intermarried among themselves, and wrote to their friends and relations back home to leave the old misery and join them in this new territory where there was land enough for all, just waiting to be seized from the nomadic Indians. Finally the religious climate in eighteenth-century America was immensely attractive to Presbyterians and, in many parts, even to extreme Dissenters, far less so to Roman Catholics.

Both parts of the island were acquiring a middle class—for lack of a better word—during the first half of this century, but with a difference. In Ulster this new class of professional and business men was almost exclusively Protestant. For the professions, the refusal of higher education to the Roman Catholics is explanation enough: the Presbyterians and other Dissenters were free to enter Glasgow and Edinburgh universities (as did many Welshmen at this time and later) and returned as qualified doctors, lawyers or ministers: the members of the Church of Ireland could of course go to Trinity, Oxford or Cambridge, then the jealously guarded and ecclesiastically controlled preserves of the Established Churches.

Trade and commerce in the North were from the very beginning almost entirely in Protestant hands, and it is there that these have remained. Belfast, rapidly becoming the province's commercial centre, contained only seven Roman Catholics in 1708, and fifty years later what was then by Irish standards a large town was 94% Protestant. Although probably about half the population of the nine counties of Ulster was Roman Catholic throughout the eighteenth century (a figure that has not varied greatly in the two centuries that have since passed, though this proportion does not of course apply to the Six Counties of Northern Ireland today) the Roman Catholic, that is to say the Old Irish, half consisted, almost without exception, of landless tenants and farm labourers. Banned by law from the towns, the Ulster Catholics found that in Ulster, and particularly in Belfast and Londonderry, this ban was enthusiastically and at times brutally supported by the Protestant citizens, entrepreneurs and workers alike. The pattern was set at a very early date....

This new Protestant middle class could not be permanently deprived of all political influence or even of political office at a low level. The Penal Laws against the Dissenters were relaxed or ignored and gradually they gained control of the municipalities, though membership of Parliament was still barred to them, for social as much as for religious reasons. However they were gaining in political experience, and some were indulging in political thought which was to be turned into action before the century was out. Meanwhile throughout the Age of Enlightenment their Roman Catholic fellow-Ulstermen in their wretched cabins among the bogs brooded and remembered, but seldom were able to study. If any of the educated handful wondered whether the new spirit abroad in Europe might not alleviate their lot, the anti-Papist, populist Gordon Riots in London in 1780, in which some 450 people were killed, must have told them that that spirit had not yet reached the English masses. The Gordon Riots, directed against the very moderate, even timid, Catholic Relief Act of 1778, bear a curious resemblance to the similar riots by Protestant extremists nowadays usually called Paisleyites, also directed against measures to increase the civil rights of the Roman Catholics, in Belfast and Derry in 1969.

The situation in the rest of the island was rather different. In the cities, Galway, Wexford, Limerick, Waterford and others, and in particular in Cork and above all in Dublin, a middle class was also rapidly emerging. The majority of the professional men and businessmen belonged to the Church of Ireland; some of the former however were in reality Roman Catholics, and a proportion of the latter openly so, for the attempt to exclude the Catholics from the life of the cities had proved a failure and been abandoned. Furthermore, English upper-class snobbery had in a measure benefited the old Irish upper class. It was then regarded as degrading for an English aristocrat to be 'in trade': the honourable professions were those of land-owner, soldier or Establishment clergyman. Since these three were barred to Roman Catholic Irishmen, and since English prejudices appear weird and distorted across the Irish Sea, quite a number of now landless Irishmen and Anglo-Normans of ancient lineage were quite prepared 'to go into trade'. Many of them, particularly in Cork and Dublin, did well and amassed money. Though they could not enter politics they could, and increasingly did, mingle with their Protestant equivalents, thus gradually destroying the moribund myth that to be a Roman Catholic was the equivalent of being a Redskin or a Hottentot. During the second half of the eighteenth century Dublin flourished, a beautiful city was built, the arts were patronized, and despite the obstructions set up by British capitalists through the Westminster Parliament to protect English and Scottish industries, trade increased and so did wealth. The monuments remain, in the fine Georgian squares of Dublin and in the Georgian mansions that still dot the countryside.

There was of course atrocious poverty in the capital, as in the countryside and the other cities, but in Ireland—and I speak here of the Protestant, more tolerant, middle-class Ireland that was producing such men as Grattan and Flood, Goldsmith and Burke, Sheridan and Thomas Moore—a new Irish nation was arising. And it was a nation that was not deprived by law of political power, for it was in the majority adherent to the Church of Ireland. It was linked to the thoughts of London and Paris, of Vienna and of Boston. This new generation of Protestant Anglo-Irishmen, almost all descended from Cromwellian or Williamite settlers, very rapidly became a new sort of Irishmen. Once again the spirit of the place, the *genius loci,* was conquering the bigotry of past conquerors. Once again events not of Irish origin were to destroy this lull and plunge Ireland, as in the times of the Williamite War, into utter misery. Meanwhile Ireland, Protestant Ireland, enjoyed a brief and beautiful summer.

None of this did much, if anything, to ameliorate the lot of the rack-rented, down-trodden Irish countrymen. There were some 'improving' landlords who, in the spirit of the age in England and elsewhere, attempted to better the living conditions of their tenant farmers and their serfs. Particularly in Leinster there were great noblemen who built beautiful houses and attempted to turn their vast estates into well-kept parks, with fine cattle and crops, cared for, on the English model, by a happy, rosy-cheeked peasantry that knew its place. Unfortunately for the sons and grandsons of conquerors, the memory of the conquered is usually longer than their own. And in the remoter parts of the country the estates that had been given to the soldiers, or sold by them or by the Adventurers, were seldom places where any gentleman would wish to live, let alone to improve. Irish eighteenth-century literature and memoirs, and the reports of travellers from England and elsewhere, give us a most depressing picture of the men, and of their agents when they were absentees, who owned most of Ireland's land and in whose ultimate interest the conquests had occurred: drunken, gambling, illiterate spendthrifts whose only interest in their stolen land was what they could derive from it, totally out of touch with the men who worked it, trying and failing to ape their betters, 'squireens', 'half-mounted gentlemen', they must have been a dreary, uncouth, gloomy and ferocious lot. If those parts of Georgian Dublin that still remain are the finest monument to all that was most elegant among the Anglo-Irish during their brief flowering, then the small, dirty, poor provincial towns and villages of Ireland are an equally eloquent memorial to all that was ugliest.

CHAPTER FIVE

Revolutions, or at least European revolutions in modern times, seem to follow a rough pattern. They seldom occur in epochs of absolute misery, whether economic or political. Neither starving men nor slaves nor illiterates have the wherewithal of physical strength or organizational experience or intellectual capacity to overthrow the governing class, regardless of how incompetent and cruel that class may be. Thus an Irish revolution in 1737 was as unthinkable as a Russian revolution in 1937. (The Irish remained absolutely quiet during the Jacobite invasions of England and Scotland in 1715 and 1745.) It is only when conditions that have been atrocious are beginning to ameliorate that the people, or some of the people, begin to believe that political and economic progress could be vastly speeded up by the overthrow of the old order. Only then does a revolutionary cadre come into existence which when the opportunity comes—maybe defeat in war, a famine, an economic collapse—can mobilize sufficient popular strength to challenge authority. It was so in America in the 1760s, in France in the 1780s, in Russia in the years just before the First World War. It was roughly so in Ireland in the years preceding the establishment of Grattan's Parliament and the first attempt at what later came to be called Home Rule in 1782.

A second phenomenon, common to most but not all revolutions, is that they come in two phases. The first might be described as the constitutional phase. By force, or the mere threat of force, a group of 'new men' compels the power élite to abdicate part or all of its power and then takes over, leaving the basic structure of society largely unaltered, though modified. The 'new men' wish to rule the old society according to their new lights and new ideals. But in order to do this, to overthrow the entrenched men and all their power apparatus, they require a wide measure of support from others outside their own particular group. On the one hand those 'others' will invariably be drawn from the less privileged orders of society and, since

it is not the intention of the 'new men', the new élite, basically
to re-shape that society, the masses will derive little immediate
economic or even political benefit from the new régime:
meanwhile they, or at least their revolutionary leaders, will be
now well aware of the potential power at their disposal, since
without their support, or at least their passive acquiescence, the
recent change of régime could never have taken place. And they
will feel cheated and embittered. In these circumstances a second,
social revolution will almost invariably follow the first—at a
greater or shorter interval—and will invariably be far more
bloody and brutal unless immediately, and brutally, suppressed
by the new masters. In Germany the Peasants' Revolt rapidly
followed the Lutheran reforms, and went down in blood and
fire: Cromwell's republicans, when threatened by proto-com-
munist Levellers, suppressed them brutally: in France the Jacobins guillotined Mirabeau's men and the more liberal Giron-
dins, only to be killed in their turn and rapidly by Napoleonic
Caesarism: in Russia Social Revolutionaries and Mensheviks
alike were butchered by the Bolsheviks, themselves soon to be
exterminated by Stalinist totalitarianism. In fact the second, the
idealistic and ideological, social revolution, has always failed,
has always devoured its children as well as its parents. Only perhaps in the new United States of 1776 was there to be no second
revolution, but that was not a purely European revolution even
though the constitutional revolutionaries were, in thought and
style, entirely European. This may have been due to the surprisingly high intellectual calibre of the founders of the new Constitution: it may have been to the presence of internal enemies, the
Indians, the French and far away the Spaniards: but it was probably due to the fact that there was virtually no urban proletariat,
fewer class distinctions than in Europe, and an unlimited opportunity for the discontented to acquire land. At least, of all the
constitutions devised by the clever, well-meaning and patriotic
thinkers and politicians of the eighteenth and early nineteenth
centuries it was the only one that was to survive, more or less
intact, not only for a few years but even to our own day.

Ireland, in the last quarter of the eighteenth century, passed
through this revolutionary cycle, with a constitutional revolution in 1782 and its pendant, the failed social revolution, in
1798: but, as usual, with its own idiosyncratic difference. This
was two-fold or perhaps three-fold. In the first place the distinc-

tion between those who organized a new Constitution at the earlier date and those who, sixteen years later, carried out a bloody rebellion was, in most of Ireland, not merely one of class or property—though this was important—but one of religion. It was the Catholics who rebelled most actively against a more-or-less free Protestant Ireland in 1798. On the other hand it was a more-or-less free Protestant Ulster that led the movement which sparked off the '98. And religious animosity between the two Christian faiths never disappeared, but was only to be exacerbated by the bloodshed of the attempted social revolution. Thirdly, the course of Irish affairs was affected by influences entirely foreign to Ireland, to an extent that the earlier events in Germany, England, America and France had never been. It is this cross-section both of historical time and of physical geography which, added to the internal complexities of Ireland's own religious and ethnological demography, makes it so difficult for foreigners to understand the developments of the late eighteenth century inside Ireland. In order to grasp the background to the new Ulster which was to emerge from these chaotic years it is therefore necessary to give a brief, and inevitably superficial, outline of the whole country's recent history, for Ulster was still an integral Irish province.

By the 1750s the latest wave of settlers, the Williamites, had been in Ireland for fifty years, and if not in their third they were certainly in their second generation. Their immediate predecessors, the Cromwellians, had been in Ireland for a century, most of the Ulster Presbyterians even longer. Inevitably these people of the Ascendancy* identified themselves more and more with the land in which they lived, the only home that most of them had ever known, though not of course with the alien, Irish-speaking rural proletariat from whose lands these homes had been carved. As the kingdom of Ireland, *their* kingdom as they increasingly felt, began slowly to recover from utter chaos and misery—the last of the really great famines in this century, caused by potato blight, ended in 1741—as trade and commerce began to increase, despite jealous English restrictions, in the coastal towns, as Dublin slowly became a small metropolis, the emergent middle class and the landed gentry inevitably and rightly claimed the credit for themselves. It was, after all, their

---

* According to Lecky this word first appeared in print in the early 1790s, but was presumably in use verbally at an earlier date.

country. They owned it. Yet when they turned to examine how that country of theirs was being run, those who understood anything at all about politics or economics began to see that their country was not being run for their benefit or by their own people. It was being run from England, and for the financial gain of England, and they were a permanent, rooted, unpaid and under-privileged garrison in their own land, their duties being to keep down the native Irish and watch the maximum amount of Irish wealth being exported to England—without even much say in how these tasks were to be carried out.

Their basic complaints were those of all colonial peoples. Their economy was run in the interests of the British economy. Thus so long as the English grew enough corn to export a portion of their crop, they had no wish to see the domestic market undercut by the import of Irish corn. Therefore duties were imposed on Irish corn. Therefore tillage became less profitable than pasturage. Therefore not only were many farm labourers evicted from their livelihoods, and eventually from their cottages—a matter of only passing interest to many of their landlords—but the landlords themselves sometimes lost money. The merchants had seen the Irish woollen industry deliberately destroyed at the beginning of the century and Dean Swift, Dean of St. Patrick's Cathedral in Dublin, had observed the misery of the starving weavers. Perhaps the greatest English prose writer ever to have been ordained into the Church of England, he had, in the 1720s, thundered forth his total disapproval of these commercial-colonial methods. He advocated a complete boycott of all English goods, that the Irish burn everything English save English coal, and his *A Short View of the State of Ireland* is not only the most masterly description of Irish miseries during the penal years but also a fantastically accurate prophecy of the protests that the Patriots were to raise a generation later. Even Ulster's linen trade, the only really successful manufacture in all Ireland, was discriminated against: the export of coloured linens to Britain was forbidden, and other restrictions imposed. This took political effect later, but between 1771 and 1774 some 10,000 Ulster weavers, unable to support themselves at home, emigrated to America each year. The importation of hops was heavily taxed, thus making the Irish brewing industry uncompetitive at home and encouraging the sale of beer brewed in England. It is no exaggeration to say that the authorities in London were determined to crush all commercial or agricultural enterprise in Ireland that could in any conceivable circumstances compete in any way with the equivalent English interests. This affected the whole of Ireland and almost all Irishmen of all classes, races and religious persuasions.

Another source of mounting grievance was the systematic milking of the Irish economy, both officially and by private individuals. Pensions were allotted on the Irish list to persons who had never had any connection with Ireland whatsoever, King George I's mistress, the Duchess of Kendal, being perhaps the most glaring example of this. Sinecures were created, or more often kept in being, and these were awarded to Englishmen, and sometimes to Irishmen who had served the English government well or whom it was considered desirable to bribe. When these pointless offices had any vestigial functions to perform, the officer could employ a clerk to act as his deputy in Dublin while he himself enjoyed his income among the comforts of London or Bath. It has been estimated that by the 1770s absentee pensioners and the holders of sinecures were costing the country something in the nature of £100,000 per annum, or approximately 10% of the whole kingdom's total annual revenue.

In the private sector the principal drain was the export of cash to fill the pockets and meet the gambling debts of the absentee landlords, both English and Irish. It was estimated by Arthur Young in 1779 that this amounted to some three quarters of a million pounds in that year: when this is contrasted with the figure given above for Ireland's annual revenue, approximately one million pounds, it is surely an astonishing figure. It is hardly surprising that there was a chronic shortage of coinage in Ireland. The Irish private banks—the Bank of Ireland was not established until 1783—were usually rickety affairs, prone to going bankrupt, but entitled to issue paper money. The banks folded almost as easily as the banknotes. These were therefore seldom accepted at their face value. Commerce and what industry there was were thus further hampered by a most inefficient financial structure for which absentee-ism must bear a considerable degree of responsibility.

Nor of course was this the end or even the beginning of the evils caused by absentee-ism. Though there were exceptions, most of the absentee landlords were solely interested in deriving a steady income from their Irish properties, which they seldom if ever bothered to visit. Rents would be collected by their agent, or more frequently by one or more principal tenants with the right to sublet. Sometimes there was a whole inverted pyramid of leases, decreasing in size, before one reached the farmer or peasant who actually worked the land and had to support the whole edifice upon his back. Furthermore, since these middlemen did not themselves own the land they seldom had much interest in improving it, being like their landlords essentially exploiters. As the population rapidly increased, from some two million in 1700 to some four million in 1780, holdings for tillage grew smaller and smaller, rents more and more difficult to collect. Simultaneously until 1784 the English corn laws made it virtually impossible to export Irish corn and therefore more profitable to put down the land for grazing than to till it with a peasantry that could not, and would not, pay rent for its subsistence holdings. Only in Ulster did the 'Ulster custom' give some security of tenure, with the result that there was a slow internal emigration from the other provinces towards the northeast and particularly into the border counties. But in Ulster too great estates were being 'cleared' of an unwanted peasantry. When these landless men did not emigrate to America, and of course most of them did not, they found themselves in direct competition for an inadequate supply of land with the newly arrived Roman Catholics from the south. This competition infused new bitterness into the religious animosities and the historical hatreds that were already dangerous enough. It was in the most 'mixed' of the border counties, particularly Armagh, the southern parts of Down and Londonderry, that the tension mounted most rapidly and struck the deepest roots. It is there, and in the poorer areas of the city of Belfast, that it has remained most venomous till today.

Yet another by-product of agricultural depression, and particularly of the decline of tillage in favour of pasture and large scale enclosures, was the increase of agricultural crime throughout the century. This was most marked during the height of this process, during the 1760s, for in 1759 ancient restrictions prohibiting the export of cattle to England were raised and enclosure thus became immediately profitable. In Munster an infuriated peasantry produced the Whiteboys (who wore white smocks over their clothes). Operating principally by night they waged what might be described as a permanent guerilla war against the Protestant landlords and their agents—the rooted garrison—and against the tithe farmers who collected the tithes from the overwhelmingly Roman Catholic populace for the benefit of the Church of Ireland clergy. Their principal methods were the destruction of fences, the killing of cattle, the burning of houses and farm buildings, and on occasion the brutal torture of the most hated among their enemies: murder, however, was rare, no doubt owing to the influence of the priests. The central government was hesitant as this movement spread from the County Tipperary across almost all Munster and into parts of Leinster and Connaught. The local magistrates and landowners —the two terms were almost synonymous at this time—reacted as best they could by arming their few Protestant or otherwise reliable tenants and what had started as a purely agricultural dispute soon became also a religious one. This development, common in all Irish disputes, is being repeated *mutatis mutandis* in Northern Ireland now.

Eventually the government acted, sending in troops and passing repressive legislation—agrarian crime became a capital offence—but it was probably more a general acceptance of the new agronomy combined with a total absence of leadership that led to the decline of the Whiteboys. However they lingered on well into the next century, and left behind them a renewed memory of that violence which never lies far below the surface in Ireland. Bucolic heirs, in some ways, of those broken men of past Anglo-Irish wars, the tories and rapparees, they in turn fathered the Croppies of '98 and, through them, every popular anti-Ascendancy movement throughout the nineteenth century and down to the I.R.A. of 1920 and the Republican Party (call it Sinn Fein or I.R.A. as you wish) in all Ireland today.

Meanwhile a similar Presbyterian movement had come into being for precisely the same reasons in Ulster. The Oakboys— they wore a sprig of oak in their hats—appeared briefly in 1763 in Armagh, Tyrone and Londonderry. They were protesting principally against the methods used by the landlords in pressing men for road-building. They were seldom violent, and when their grievances were met melted away. But in 1770 Lord Donegall, head of the Chichester family, 'cleared' his estates in Antrim by demanding a large bonus payment from any of his tenants who cared to remain. The Steelboys was the people's reply. For some three years they slaughtered cattle and destroyed the property of such new tenants as had moved in. Here the safety valve of American immigration took the steam out of the movement, however. Still, the tradition of direct action remained, and was to be revived in the far more dangerous and sinister Peep o' Day Boys, to be passed on to strong elements of the Orange Order and to the Paisleyites of today.

Thus in the 1770s the condition of Ireland was very disquieting indeed to the new middle class, whether Roman Catholic or Protestant, as well as to those landowners who chose to make it the country of their residence. Both economic and political considerations had combined to produce a crisis, and from the crisis there had arisen the Patriot Party.

The political nature of the crisis was twofold. The Irish parliament was a sham parliament. In theory it could initiate legislation : in practice, since London had complete powers of veto, it could only pass such legislation as was entirely acceptable to London, where Irish bills were usually amended in the English interest. Only after a long struggle did the Irish parliament gain some measure of control over Irish money bills. It was this struggle, incidentally, which brought the Patriot Party into existence. In theory the Lord Lieutenant was the king's representative and since England was more or less a constitutional monarchy, he should have filled the role of constitutional monarch in Ireland : in practice he was a member of the British Cabinet, and his principal function was to see to it that British policy was enforced in Ireland, using when possible the Irish parliament for that purpose. In theory that parliament represented the Protestant population : in practice it represented primarily, through pocket boroughs, the land-owning, not infrequently absentee class in the Commons and the same interest in the Lords, which was also packed with English bishops and archbishops appointed to Irish sees. Furthermore an elaborate system of bribes, in the form of sinecures, pensions for relatives and so on, was used to grease the machinery, that is to say to ensure that the Irish parliament toed the English line whenever a conflict of interests between the two parliaments arose. Finally, in the background, there was always the British army. It can thus easily be seen that the situation was not dissimilar to the one that has prevailed in the Six Counties of Northern Ireland, so far as methods of government and relationship with London go, throughout the last half-century, the great difference being of course that in the Six Counties the Protestants outnumber the Roman Catholics in the ratio of 2:1 and that therefore the more blatant forms of public corruption, apart from religious discrimination in official appointments and gerrymandering the constituency and ward boundaries in mixed areas and cities such as Fermanagh or Derry, have been unnecessary. While it is frequently alleged by Irish Republicans that the huge Welfare State handouts in the North are, in our age of mass democracy, the equivalent of bribes to noblemen in the age of aristocracy, this writer fails to see the parallel or to believe that these doles are part of an English scheme to 'kill Republicanism by kindness' in the North. But of this, more later.

To return briefly to the Irish scene as a whole in the 1760s and even more in the 1770s, what the Protestant Irish patriots saw was the need for constitutional change, without which Ireland's economic wrongs could never be righted. What the government in Dublin Castle saw was a steady erosion of its powers inside parliament as self-interest led more and more of its members to favour the Patriots, soon enough to be led by such competent men as Flood, Grattan and Lord Charlemont. Even that government's most committed placemen were now quarrelling among themselves. In these circumstances, the Castle set about taking away from an increasingly unreliable parliament what few powers it possessed and assuming greater, direct authority for itself. The result of this was soon enough seen. The Castle found itself in direct confrontation with the Patriots, who were on their way to becoming the party of the whole nation, the Protestant nation that is. The vast majority of the Irish nation did not care one way or the other about the Constitution: how their Protestant masters arranged their affairs was no concern of landless peasants in Kerry or Sligo. Indeed in the struggle for power between the Castle and the landlord class the Roman Catholic masses, when not neutral, tended if anything to side with the Castle, of which they knew little, against their old oppressors, the landlords, of whom they knew only too much. Traditionally, it was the Irish parliament which, from the very beginning, had imposed the most savage Penal Laws, while the Crown acting through the Castle had allowed the more vicious of those laws to fall into desuetude. Now, in the 1770s, the Castle and the Patriots began to compete, not for the Catholic vote for the Catholics were still disfranchised, but for Catholic sympathy. In 1771, 1774 and 1778 acts were permitted to go through parliament which gave the Catholics rights in leasehold almost equal to those enjoyed by Protestant tenants, and the first steps were taken towards giving them the franchise by modifying the oath of supremacy so that a Roman Catholic could take the oath without abjuring his faith. Grattan asserted that 'the Irish Protestant could never be free till the Irish Catholic had ceased to be a slave'. The spirit of tolerance, in fact, was in the air, and it must have seemed that the Age of Enlightenment was reaching the Irish shores at last. For the rest of the century it may be generalized that the urban Catholics, particularly those of the merchant class, were perhaps more sympathetic to the ideals and aims of Grattan's Patriots, while the conservative Roman Catholic hierarchy tended to be more timid of change and looked towards the Castle. The countrymen with their country priests, though more likely to be influenced by the hierarchy than the merchants, took little interest in the struggle between the Protestant Ascendancy and the Castle.

In the North the Presbyterians were also only marginally involved. Again the middle class tended to side, and eventually whole-heartedly, with the Patriot cause. However, and even though the Penal Laws had almost completely ceased to apply to Dissenters, the Northern Protestants still regarded themselves essentially as outsiders—that is to say outside the Church of Ireland Ascendancy—but were simultaneously pre-occupied in the majority with preventing the reoccupation of Ulster farms by Roman Catholic farmers. The 'revolution' of 1782 was a middle-class revolution: neither in Ulster nor in the other provinces was the rural proletariat deeply involved, concerned or active. And in Ulster a rapid decline in the linen industry in the 1770s led to a massive emigration of weavers to America. By 1775 one third of the looms were idle. In that same year fighting broke out on the American continent, and American markets, Ireland's best, were closed to Irish commerce. The Ulstermen were forced to rely solely on the land once again. In such circumstances of mounting economic tension any form of Catholic emancipation, whether emanating from the Castle or from the Dublin parliament, which might strengthen Catholic competition for the land, was bound to be unacceptable to the Presbyterian farmers. But for the moment all was quiet, both in the North and in the South, as the constitutional and economic reforms were debated in Dublin and in London. Everybody was now in agreement that reforms of the post-Williamite War settlement were needed: what was under discussion was the nature that these should take.

It was now, apparently for the first time, that an Act of Union was suggested in London, and referred to Dublin, in 1779. This suggestion met with such opposition in Dublin that it was dropped for a decade and more. The only constitutional alternative, now that Britain was fully stretched in America and also losing a war with France and Spain, was to give the Patriots what they wanted, parliamentary control of Ireland. And with 40,000 Volunteers in existence, and most of Protestant and parts of Catholic Ireland united behind them, the English had really no choice. Lord North fell, the Rockingham Whigs took office in London, and the free, Protestant Ireland came about in 1782.

The Volunteers were the lever. They were not the only military force thrown up in Ireland at this time by international events nor, in connection with Ulster's history, the most important. It is therefore necessary here to examine the irregular, volunteer armed forces, some secret and some not, which sprang up in Ireland during this period of crisis that saw the loss of almost all the first British Empire in the New World and that nearly saw the liberation of Ireland as part of the same process. It is these volunteer bodies of armed men that set a pattern which still endures.

By 1760 Ireland had been quiet for sixty years. Although, at the Battle of Fontenoy in 1745, the Irish Brigade in the French service is said to have charged the British column to the war-cry, in Irish: 'Remember Limerick and Saxon perfidy!' this Franco-Irish victory had found no echoes in the Old Country. During the Seven Years' War with France and Spain (1756-1763) no group of Irishmen attempted to turn England's misfortunes into Ireland's opportunity. Indeed in 1759 representatives of the Roman Catholic population sent addresses to the Lord Lieutenant expressing their loyalty to the Crown, while, when war was declared on Spain, the bishops instructed their flocks to pray for a British victory. This greatly strengthened the hand of the Protestant Patriot leaders who, despite the increase in agrarian crime, began to feel that they need no longer fear the Roman Catholic majority as a political force, and therefore felt free to devote all their energies to the constitutional struggle with the Castle and with London.

The Ulster Presbyterians gave even more striking proof of their loyalty to the Crown. In 1760 a small French expeditionary force under Admiral Thurot, in command of three frigates, was landed on the Antrim coast and captured Carrickfergus. At once the countryside rose, but not, as the French had doubtless hoped, against the English. Thousands of armed Ulstermen flocked to the defence of Belfast and thence marched on Carrickfergus. Within a week the French were forced to re-embark. What is significant about this incident is not merely the British patriotism of the Presbyterians—despite their poor economic and political status, this was only to be expected against the traditional, Catholic enemy—but the speed with which a large body of armed men could be put into the field.

This was an important fact to be taken into account when the American war began in 1775. The Lord Lieutenant, Lord Harcourt, wrote to London: 'The Presbyterians in the North are in their hearts Americans.' In the south, too, the Patriots felt great sympathy for the American cause which was, after all, very close to their own: the economic and fiscal policy of a ruling colonist class, which believed itself quite capable of running its own affairs and managing its own natives, controlled in the interest of a Britain that had little to give in return. Only the Papists, grateful for the measure of relief already granted and hopeful of more, listened to the traditional anti-republicanism of the Church of Rome as passed down to them through the bishops who were by now freed from the restrictions of the Penal Laws. A Cork man wrote: 'We are all Americans here, except such as are attached securely to the Castle, or papists.' This somewhat contemptuous reference to the majority of the population is indicative of how little the Ascendancy had come to fear their real enemy in the Age of Enlightenment.

However the Ascendancy had no wish to be left disarmed. When the British realized that George Washington's armies were not quite the rabble they had expected to meet, and that reinforcements were urgently needed, they proposed to move one third of the army in Ireland, then some 12,000 strong, across the Atlantic. The Irish parliament immediately objected, but was overruled. Nor was the request for an Irish militia granted from London. Instead economic concessions were made, intended to keep the Patriots quiet. But this was interpreted by the Ascendancy as a mere proof that London was rattled, and they became even more determined to exploit English difficulties in America in their own interest. Almost fortuitously they soon had a powerful weapon to hand in the form of the Volunteers.

The landlords and Protestant tenants of the South had already a certain experience of this type of voluntary para-military organization, ever since the height of the Whiteboys' agitation, when bands of armed Protestant horsemen had on occasion patrolled the countryside. As early as 1776 these organizations began to be revived, first of all, it would seem, in Wexford. But it was not until 1778 that the movement assumed national dimensions and a national importance, and for this the initiative came from Ulster.

In February of that year, because of the despatch to aid the Americans of Lafayette and his 'volunteers', Britain had declared war on France. Two months later the most famous of all American sea-captains, John Paul Jones, a Scots immigrant, sailed the *U.S.S. Ranger*, a sloop-of-war, into Belfast Lough where he fought and defeated a superior British warship, *H.M.S. Drake*, which he then took as prize to Brest. This happened within sight of land, and caused the most intense excitement in Ulster, and indeed in Ireland generally, which was only increased by the news of the commodore's other successful actions against British warships off the very coasts of Britain.

The result of this was a sort of political schizophrenia in Ulster which has recurred periodically until today. Though pro-American (and John Paul Jones might as easily, perhaps more easily, have gone to America from Ulster as from Scotland) they were violently anti-French, largely for religious reasons but partly because of the memory of Thurot. The American sailor seemed to them to have proved that the Royal Navy was now incapable of protecting the coasts of Ireland, indeed even Belfast Lough, against a French invasion. In something not far from panic they applied to Dublin for troops to protect their cities and their farms. The Lord Lieutenant, stripped of troops for the American war, could only offer them half a troop of dismounted horse and half a company of invalids. Against such resistance even Thurot could have captured Ulster's principal city. And so almost the entire male Protestant population, encouraged and often led by their Presbyterian ministers, enlisted in the Volunteers. We read of clergymen in uniform, only laying aside their weapons when about to mount the pulpit, such as the Rev. William Bruce, an officer in one of the Volunteer regiments, the Lisburn True Blues, preaching to his congregation dressed up, quite literally fit to kill, in 'a short blue coat with white facings, brass buttons, and white breeches'.

Rapidly the Volunteer movement spread across all Ireland, not discouraged by the fondness of Irishmen for dressing up and playing at soldiers. Within a year almost the entire male Protestant population was drilling in the most fanciful uniforms, on foot or better still on horse, to the accompaniment of military bands. In some companies in the South even a few Catholics were admitted, though this was strictly against the law, for Roman Catholics were still forbidden to carry arms. What would have happened had this remarkably caparisoned army met real soldiers, it is hard to say. Indeed they never did. But the spectacle of the whole Protestant manhood armed and parading, theoretically against French invasion but actually against direct British rule, was highly alarming both to the Castle and to London. And Britain was losing the American War.

More important, perhaps, though infinitely less spectacular, was the partial and voluntary embargo of British manufactures in Ireland. Every British administration has, in its dealings with Ireland and its other colonies, always attached the greatest possible importance to its own financial gain. They now found that the entire Irish governing class was determined to use economic resistance unless and until it were granted independence. The last thing the English now wanted was another American situation just across St. George's Channel. The British government fell and in 1782 the Irish Protestant Ascendancy was given the constitution it demanded.

The immediate result was a sharp decline in inter-denominational hatred, and particularly in Belfast, where by 1784 Roman Catholics were being admitted into the Volunteers in some numbers. Lecky quotes from *Thoughts on the Volunteers* of that date: 'The Papist with an Orange cockade fires in honour of King William's birthday. He goes to a Protestant church and hears a charity sermon.... The Catholic who wishes to carry arms proposes himself to a Protestant corps. His character is tried by his neighbours. He is admitted to an honour and a privilege; he receives a reward for his good conduct.... Thus are the best of the Catholic body happily selected, the whole of the Catholic body satisfied, and the two religions marvellously united.' The almost insufferable tone of patronage is, to this day, being repeated. As late as 1969 the British Secretary of State for Home Affairs, Mr. James Callaghan, could say, in Belfast, while Roman Catholic homes were still smouldering ruins after being burned by Protestant fanatics, that more Catholics ought to join the Royal Ulster Constabulary and, later, that they should enrol in the Special Constabulary, the B-Specials, just as soon as this militia should have been given a new name. This English politician then further insulted his audience, in the Bogside, Derry, by telling them that they might call him Seamus. Thus did they and do they speak to Paddy-and-his-Pig who must be 'tried' by his Protestant 'neighbours'. The form of the trial is usually one that, even in the 1780s, was out of date, *peine forte et dure*. And then, under the benevolent and progressive new form of government introduced by Grattan's Parliament, it was to produce almost the same phenomena as have been and are being produced in the Six Counties by the benevolent and progressive Welfare State governments, whether labelled Conservative or Labour, that have long been ultimately, and are now directly, *de facto*, if not yet *de jure*, responsible for law and order, for chaos and disorder, in that province of the United Kingdom.

In the 1780s the Roman Catholic minority banded together to create the Defenders against the physical attacks of the Protestant assailants called, originally, the Peep o' Day Boys. Today they have other names: I.R.A., Sinn Fein, People's Democracy, Civil Rights, Republicans on the one hand, Paisleyites, Ulster Volunteer Force, B-Specials or Ulster Defence Regiment, Orange Lodges on the other. The situation however is scarcely altered, nor the animosity, nor the inability of the authorities to bring peace.

The powder train that was to lead to the second and disastrous Irish revolution of the eighteenth century was laid, more in Ulster than in any other part of Ireland, by the apparently happy outcome of the first. Enlightened legislation and some measure of increased prosperity, desirable in themselves, totally failed to cure the sickness beneath. Georgian elegance and eighteenth-century reason were rouge upon cheeks that were sallow, emaciated and lined with bitterness. Belladonna may cause the eyes to shine, it cannot affect the cruel thoughts that lie behind them. Grattan's short-lived Ireland was a sham, as in any country that is half-free half-slave, as are the Six Counties of Ulster today. But this the English and the Irish Ascendancy largely failed to realize then, as they fail to realize now. Economic and financial palliatives, when applied to such a situation as existed then in all Ireland and as exists in Northern Ireland today, are but a plaster applied to cure a cancer. The English have always regarded money as the beginning and end of their colonialism. The Irish, whether Roman Catholics or Protestants, do not agree.

CHAPTER SIX

As with a child stricken with sickness in early youth and doomed to die before it shall have reached maturity, what we remember of Ireland between the Constitution of 1782 and the final, ignominious surrender of that constitution by the Irish Parliament eighteen years later is, in a word, promise—a promise and an original youthful charm never to be fulfilled. The midwife that brought it into the world was the American revolution. If this fanciful metaphor may be taken a little further, its parents were politically sick, England less so than Ireland, and it was with the Irish people that the new-born Patriot parliament had to live. Furthermore, from the age of seven Protestant Ireland had also to survive beneath the ever-growing, ever darkening, ever more attractive or more repulsive according to taste, ever more powerful shadow of the French Revolution and of its offspring, international Jacobinism. Before it was ten years old the Irish child was obviously sick, by the time it was sixteen it was dying: two years later it was dead. The malady, though inherited constitutionally from its parents, was rendered mortal by infections from abroad. The basic ills, however, were internal, and nowhere was this more apparent than in the province of Ulster.

The newly constituted Kingdom of Ireland was faced with three formidable tasks to solve, the first being its economic status *vis-à-vis* Britain, the second its constitutional relations with King George's other kingdom, and the third its own internal political arrangements and particularly the rights of the Roman Catholic majority. (The more obnoxious of the Penal Laws had already been repealed by 1778 and virtually all of them by 1793.) All three were closely intertwined, so closely as to make one strand within the knot insoluble while the others remained entangled. However the reconciliation of commercial ambitions with religious animosities, of constitutional claims with class interests, of Irish patriotism with loyalty to the Crown, of the age of reason with the history of rebellion, proved too complicated. The injection of French egalitarian ideology into this situation—an ideology scarcely understood, indeed more often misunderstood, by an almost illiterate peasantry—only served further to confuse an already confused situation. The result was the explosion, or series of explosions, of the 1790s. And the short-lived Ireland of the Protestant Patriots went down, first in torture and massacre, finally in a welter of bribery and squalid deals. Yet that brief period of Irish history preserved, both for its friends and its enemies, a curious and exaggerated glamour. Whatever was elegant in eighteenth-century Ireland has come to be, erroneously, identfied with 'Grattan's parliament'. Indeed, its fall as much as its creation made it, for a century and more, a symbol of Irish freedom. It has become one of history's might-have-beens, and nothing is more suited than this to the process of mythopoesis.

As stated earlier, it was English domination of the Irish economy and of Irish commerce—oppression would hardly be too strong a word—that had led the Protestant Ascendancy to unite with the new Catholic middle-class in a mutual desire for some measure of constitutional freedom. Therefore once that measure had been obtained the Irish parliament immediately turned its attention to reform in these fields. And it very rapidly became apparent that, depending on whether the scene was surveyed from London or from Dublin, the new constitution had either gone too far or not far enough.

During the first year and a half of the new system in Ireland, government in Britain was both lacking in stability and pre-occupied with the liquidation of the lost American War. In September of 1783, however, the Peace of Versailles was signed. For nearly nine years Britain was to be at peace. And in December of that same year William Pitt the Younger became Prime Minister of England. His ministry was to survive, indeed to bring about, the death of the newly born Irish Constitution. In these early years, however, Pitt was anxious, both at home and in Ireland, to create a stable atmosphere through reform. In Ireland he was prepared, in 1784, to be a liberal.

What he proposed was, in essence, almost complete free trade between the two kingdoms, with identical import duties should either country decide that a domestic market needed protection, and with the equivalent of what was later to be called a Most Favoured Nation clause so far as trade with countries outside the British Isles was concerned. He perceived, and rightly, that such a common market could only be of advantage to Irish industry and agriculture and was most unlikely to harm the English. Since the foreseen Irish prosperity was likely to increase the Irish revenue, he also demanded an Irish contribution to the expense of maintaining the Royal Navy arguing, again correctly, that that navy was the first line of defence against Protestant Ireland's potential Continental foes and invaders. This demand for what was, in effect, a levy was resisted by the Irish parliament but eventually Grattan proposed a compromise whereby unless the revenue were in excess of expenditure in time of peace, such a contribution to naval expenses should not be imposed. This was acceptable and Pitt's 'propositions' were passed by the Irish parliament in 1785.

They were then presented to the British parliament, where they met a much more difficult reception. The English landed and mercantile class which dominated that assembly was deeply distrustful of Irish competition—lower wages, lower costs—and anxious to preserve the conqueror's ascendancy. By the time the proposed treaty was approved it had been both weakened and so watered down to be almost meaningless as a measure of reform. One new condition was that the Irish parliament was to enact, immediately and without alteration, any meaures concerning navigation, the colonial trade and certain aspects of foreign trade, that had passed through the parliament at Westminster. This was a direct denial of the principal motives of the Volunteers and of the 'spirit of '82', and when this revised bill was presented to the Irish House of Commons, it was thrown out. A great opportunity had been lost: to observant politicians it became apparent that commercial legislation through two Houses of Commons was an exceedingly difficult, if not indeed an impossible, task, and voices began to be raised in favour of a Union, of one Parliament, inevitably in Westminster, responsible for legislation in both the islands. Such a concept was, however, completely unacceptable to the Irish Protestant nation, still intoxicated by its own apparent liberation. Nevertheless, since Great Britain was at peace and was now an importer of foodstuffs owing to its own industrial revolution, and since the Pitt administration was at this time well-disposed to help Ireland, the Irish economy prospered. In Ulster particularly the linen trade revived during the 1780s and a cotton manufacture was begun in the Belfast and Derry areas. In the south as well as in the north the woollen industry was no longer smothered and, at least for the internal market, began to revive: raw wool was no longer exported. And in this almost totally unindustrialized society the only other major industry—namely the brewing of beer—was encouraged by the repeal of duties upon the importation of hops. The brewers' lobby in London might and did protest, but the name of Guinness was to become, in the next century, as well known in its own field as that of the Rothschild family in theirs.

In the South, too, the provisions trade, principally the provisioning of ships for the Atlantic crossing, was of benefit to agriculture generally, while more favourable arrangements for the importation and re-export of colonial goods were a fairly valuable addition to commerce as a whole. Cork, with its deep sea port of Cove (renamed Queenstown when Queen Victoria first set foot on Irish soil there, but now once again called Cobh) together with Limerick, Galway and other southern and western ports assumed considerable importance in the growing transatlantic shipping industry. This was to last as long as the age of sail.

An incidental benefit, and particularly for the Protestant Ascendancy, derived from the increased difficulty the Castle now had in controlling the technically independent Irish Parliament. Since the Administration was not, as in England, ultimately answerable to its legislature, since there was in fact no Irish cabinet in any meaningful sense of the word but only a number of appointments culminating in, and deriving their authority from, the Lord Lieutenant, himself an English politician who received his instructions from London, the quasi-independent Irish Lords and Commons had to be cajoled into following the wishes of the Castle. This meant that the noblemen and gentlemen of the Ascendancy, jealous to guard their measure of freedom both against London and against the disfranchised Roman Catholic majority, had to be far more skilfully, and far more expensively, induced to vote the right way. An attempt was made to approximate to the English model by ennobling many of the principal officials of state, thus giving them seats in the Irish House of Lords, but more often titles were bestowed as rewards for past favours to the government or for favours yet to come, in a word as bribes, and the rest of the century saw a vast inflation of the Irish peerage. More important economically was the fact that the sinecures, pensions and so on which had sucked so much money out of Irish pockets into those of Englishmen were now needed, for political purposes, in Ireland itself. This drain on the Irish exchequer did not cease—it was if anything increased—but at least the money tended to circulate more inside Ireland.

An attempt to legislate against absentee landlords failed, as it was almost bound to fail in a parliament constituted and elected as was that of Ireland. Indeed the amount of money leaving Ireland in this fashion actually increased during this period, though with the growth of prosperity the portion of the national income that moved abroad decreased. And once Pitt's attempts at parliamentary reform had failed in England in 1784, the chances of any such reform in Ireland, always remote in view of the religious division, disappeared. It is very rare indeed that a governing class will vote its power or its wealth out of existence, and that only in a country so homogeneous that a ruling élite can accept a new and diminished future with at least a measure of confidence in the basic goodwill of its fellow-citizens. But no such confidence could possibly exist in any part of Ireland in the late eighteenth century. Throughout the first half of the Kingdom of Ireland's brief life it became increasingly apparent, as the heady and attractive lights of '82's Patriots burned lower in a constitutional imbroglio, that there were only three ways by which Ireland might be governed. One was the present system, unsatisfactory to almost all, of an Irish Ascendancy oligarchy with diminished responsibility beneath an English overlordship: one was something much closer to democracy, which sooner rather than later must imply the emancipation and enfranchisement of the Roman Catholic majority: the third was union with Great Britain on the Scottish model. All three were tried, in turn, to the mounting displeasure of the Protestant Ascendancy. All three failed to solve Irish discontents, and especially so in the Ulster of the Dissenters. Meanwhile, and most particularly in the 1790s, a fourth solution, of neither Irish nor English origin, became particularly attractive to the Northern Protestants. Once again a foreign ideology was imported into Ireland. This time it came from France: it was in its extremer forms an atheistic, egalitarian Jacobinism: its leader and martyr was Wolfe Tone: it took the name of United Ireland: and its bible was not the gospels but *The Rights of Man*, by the

American Jacobin, Thomas Paine. It found its first home and final resting place in Protestant Ulster. Born abroad, it nevertheless had deep emotional roots in and about Belfast among Dissenters, doubters, scoffers, men of violence and men of deep certainties. Time in Ireland is ever a dubious commodity, and history less a steadily flowing river than a lake in a quaking bog, liable to overflow quickly or to dry up completely. Some of the men whom Tone thought to lead were two hundred years out of date, dreaming of a return to a pre-Plantation Ireland freed of the English. As for the Protestants, was Dublin worth a mass? Others were men two hundred years before their time, nurturing ecumenical instincts in remote presbyteries and 'masshouses'. The actual leaders, however, were very much men of their own age. Deists, agnostics, even atheists, they usually equated religion with superstition and privilege with rank. Rank and religion must vanish in a world where Reason was to rule for the material and moral welfare of all. For a while it seemed a most attractive dream, and the ideas, principally French ideas, that it generated were impressive, often useful, and are still with us.

But the eighteenth-century intellectuals, like their successors, played with ideas. The world of Montesquieu, of d'Alembert, even of Rousseau, was a France in which human emotions were but one or more quantities in a complex mathematical equation, which it was their job to solve by Euclidean, Pythagorean, Locke-ian or Condorcet-type methods. Even in France such generous intellectual strivings for noble ends led to massacre and the execution, ultimately, of the intellectuals themselves. In Ireland such an enterprise as the union of all the people beneath banners inscribed Liberty, Equality, Fraternity was doomed from the start. The forces that fractured the United Irishmen were built-in: and nowhere more so than in Ulster. The very background of that organization, which claimed the Volunteers as parent, is enough to see—in retrospect at least—its ghastly doom.

Events to come were foreshadowed as early as July of 1784 and indeed it was then, when the Protestant Nation was not yet two years old, that the gunpowder trail was laid that led to explosion with the second revolution of 1798. Two incidents of opposed significance took place in 1784.

Lord Charlemont was not only titular head of the Volunteers, but also the virtual governor of Armagh, the most southeasterly of Ulster's planted counties and the one in which sectarian strife has perhaps been most bitter from the time of the Cromwellian plantation until the present, for the population is mixed and its people are border people. Even today, when passing from Roman Catholic to Protestant village or hamlet one notices a visible change in the general tidiness and neatness of cottages, streets and fields, while among the farms dotted among the hills it is said that there is no need to enquire of the farmer's religion: the Presbyterians all live on the sunny slopes, or so the Catholics say. If that is true today—and as the events of the past three years have shown, the bitterness lives on both in such towns as Newry and in the countryside—it was far more pronounced in Lord Charlemont's time when the two strands of the population were divided not only by religion and law but also in large measure by language.

James Caulfeild, fourth viscount and first earl of Charlemont, is the epitome of all that was best in the Protestant Nation which he helped to create. A forebear had been granted large estates in the County Armagh by James I and command of a fort (Charlemont, from which the title derived) upon the River Blackwater in that county. These estates had been fought for in the many wars, had prospered, and had been enlarged. The Lord Charlemont with whom we are here concerned was, in fact, an Irish grandee. He was also a highly cultivated man, interested both in literature and the arts, and it is suitable that his Dublin town house should now be that city's second museum of painting and sculpture. He is said to have been a nobleman of great charm, whose personality was much appreciated both in the Irish and in the English capitals. In his forties—he was born in 1728—he became involved in the politics of Flood and of Grattan and he became one of the 'founding fathers' of the Irish Protestant Nation: he would undoubtedly have felt thoroughly at home in the company of Jefferson and Franklin and his other contemporaries and equivalents in America. He died in 1799, a determined opponent of the union with Great Britain that was then being pushed through the Irish parliament he had helped to create. He was also an opponent of Catholic emancipation and it may be assumed, politically at least, that he would have got on well with George Washington, another contemporary and child of the Enlightenment who had no objection to slavery or to the appropriation of Indian lands. In Charlemont's Ireland however, and particularly in his own Armagh, religious division was a far greater threat to the country than was racial discrimination in Washington's United States.

As early as 1784 a number of Irishmen, particularly in Dublin and above all in Belfast, were beginning to feel otherwise. The ideals of the Age of Reason and the economic interests of the urban middle class were, briefly, united, and the ferment caused by the success of the Volunteers lived on, at least in more radical circles, whether Presbyterian or Roman Catholic, though for different reasons. The majority of the Volunteers, of whom Charlemont was not only the head but also the very best prototype, might be happy to stop marching about after 1782, once their immediate aims had been achieved, and their social and political Ascendancy as members of the established Irish Church endorsed by London. Those who were not of that church were less satisfied. The radicals attempted to gain control of the whole Volunteer movement in 1783 but were foiled by Charlemont himself and by the Attorney General, John FitzGibbon later earl of Clare, when they attempted to use the Volunteer Convention of 1783 in Dublin as an alternative parliament and there to override the new Irish parliament with a threat of force. Extra-parliamentary pressure was, according to the views of the gentlemen who sat in that new, real parliament, supererogatory. Legal reforms were one thing, reforms of course to be carried through by themselves: revolution, even the pressure of revolutionary threat, was quite another. Charlemont would have got on well with some of his French contemporaries too, with Turgot and Necker and perhaps even with Mirabeau.

On July 12th of 1784 the anniversary of the Battle of the Boyne was celebrated by the Orangemen of Belfast in a way that would have been inconceivable in any other period of Belfast's history either before or since. They paraded to what was then the only Roman Catholic church in the city, St. Mary's Chapel Lane, and from it they sent a petition to Lord Charlemont which demanded, in essence, Catholic emancipation and freedom for Catholics to join the Volunteers, that is to say to carry arms. (The sacramental test act, as applying to Dissenters, had been repealed in 1780, so that Presbyterians now enjoyed the same civil rights as members of the Church of Ireland.) This demand for Catholic civil rights, and coming from such a source, must have astonished many. Charlemont's reply was characteristic. He disclaimed any religious prejudice, but maintained that this demand for equality was premature: it could only divide the reform party of which he was so prominent an ornament. As for arming the Catholics, he was opposed to this, not on religious grounds, but because in his belief men without property were 'strangers to moderation' and since most Roman Catholics were poor this ruled them out: Q.E.D. Have we not heard precisely these sentiments uttered, in various languages, in our own time? 'Some of my best friends are Jews, but ...' 'Every encouragement should be given to educated negroes, but ...' The first volleys in Ireland's coming, second revolution had been fired when the first was barely two years old.

Even before this interchange between the urban and better educated Presbyterians of Belfast and Lord Charlemont, the inevitable backlash had set in. A few Roman Catholics had already, and illegally, been admitted to the Volunteers. Their numbers had been grossly exaggerated by rumour. The word travelled through Ulster that the Catholics were arming: that the government either could not or would not prevent this owing to repeal of some of the Penal Laws and the reluctance of the authorities to enforce those that remained on the statute book: and that it was once again up to the Protestant Ulstermen themselves to protect their 'freedom, religion and laws' against an imminent Papist revolt. Former Oakboys and Steelboys began to raid the houses of Roman Catholics, ostensibly in search of arms, but actually in pursuance of the age-old policy of frightening them away. Since these raids usually took place at dawn, these new extremists became known as the Peep o' Day Boys. Violence of this sort was frequently triggered off by remarks and threats exchanged between Catholics and Protestants in taverns or at cockfights, the meeting places of the poor. Drink always was, and has remained to this day, a highly inflammable ingredient in the whole Ulster situation. And nowhere were these Peep o' Day Boy raids more prevalent than in Lord Charlemont's own border county of Armagh.

The situation rapidly deteriorated. Two Presbyterians came to blows in the village of Markethill, County Armagh. A Catholic intervened, and the Presbyterian who lost the fight blamed his defeat not on his enemy but upon this intervention. He swore vengeance, raised a gang of ex-Steelboys who were given the curious name of the Nappach Fleet after the village of Nappach, and these toughs carried out raids more violent than those of the Peep o' Day Boys, smashing furniture and destroying the looms of Roman Catholic weavers. Indeed it became apparent soon enough that the motives of the Nappach Fleet were economic persecution rather than disarmament. There was, for instance, a series of attacks on unarmed Catholics in the Loughgall area.

Were they not to be forced to flee their homes, the Roman Catholic peasantry of the County Armagh had no choice but to band themselves together in armed self-protection. Strangely enough it was a Dissenting clergyman who formed the first band of Defenders. Yet is it so strange? The Catholic peasants who had bought farms in Armagh were leaderless: then, as now, there was many a true and often muscular Christian among the Dissenting ministers: and when the Defenders had defeated the Nappach Fleet in a battle or more accurately a brawl, this one persuaded the Protestant extremists to accept a Roman Catholic leader. It was a good idea and other men of goodwill, both cleric and lay, have attempted similar palliations of sectarian strife in Ulster from that day to this.

It did not work. Larger and larger bodies of armed men, soon almost all Catholics or almost all Protestants, were marching about the county, brawling and looting. To this there was added mutual economic boycott. The courts were powerless, since witnesses on both sides were intimidated into silence. In 1787 the Lord Lieutenant sent two troops of horse into Armagh to restore order. They failed. In 1788 it was seriously considered whether the county should not be declared to be in a state of riot. In these circumstances Lord Charlemont decided to enrol a new body of Volunteers from whom both Roman Catholics and Presbyterians were to be, in theory, excluded, that is to say a 'respectable' Church of Ireland force containing neither Peep o' Day Boys nor Defenders, to keep the peace between these brawling religious fanatics and the opportunists, of whatever religion or of none, who were busy exploiting their fanaticism. Already, in 1788, we thus see the Ulster turmoil foreshadowing the turmoil of today, extremist Catholics, extremist Protestants, and law-abiding Protestants, with Dublin called upon to play the role that London is playing today and with embryonic atheistical Jacobins and their sympathizers, very much in the minority but often very conspicuous nonetheless, where embryonic atheistical Communists and their fellow-travellers are to be discerned today.

On the earlier occasion this mobilization of the 'respectable' elements was in part, but only in part, successful. In the first place, there were not enough respectable Protestants to deal with the two factions, and undoubtedly large numbers of Presbyterians were enrolled in the new force, including many Peep o' Day Boys. The new corps of Volunteers rapidly became itself a violently Orange force of armed Protestants, parading with Orange flags and insignia and singing Orange songs, such as the provocative *Boyne Water* as they marched, deliberately, through Roman Catholic areas where the Defenders were strong. Soon enough the attacks began, both by the Volunteers upon the Defenders and by the Catholic militants against their new enemy, or rather the old enemy newly re-named. In July 1789, the month that the Bastille fell, a Church of Ireland clergyman wrote to Lord Charlemont: 'Every opportunity of revenge is eagerly seized upon, and to what length it may at last be carried I tremble to think.' Volunteers were now attacking Roman Catholic processions and committing acts of sacrilege in their enemies' churches. Roman Catholics responded: a Protestant schoolmaster was murdered and Protestant tenants driven from their farms near Forkhill. Further south and west, where the Roman Catholics were in the majority, the Defenders began adopting Peep o' Day Boy tactics, raiding Protestant homes, still allegedly in search of arms but actually to drive out their enemies. By 1790 the Defenders were active as far south as County Dublin. Two years later their activities had forced down rents in the Counties Meath (in Leinster) and Cavan. Peasants bashing one another in unknown villages was just tolerable to the gentlemen in Dublin: decreased land value was not. And as the movement spread southwards, it ceased increasingly to be even nominally defensive but became a recrudescence of the Whiteboy movement with as principal motive the terrorization of landlords, their agents, Protestant clergymen and their tithe collectors. And a year later Great Britain was at war with revolutionary France.

In dealing with the 'Irish question' the English—or perhaps one should always say the British—have repeatedly made the same mistakes, and for much the same reasons. They have long believed that their method of handling their own political and social evolution is superior to that of any other European nation, and in this belief they are probably correct. In essence that method is an alternative of reform and retrenchment, expressed in the two-party system of parliamentary representation. Whig and Tory, Conservative and Liberal, Labour and Conservative governments have replaced one another over two centuries and more. When the electorate felt that change was needed, it would vote in a reforming parliament: when it felt that enough had been achieved it would vote them out again, with the tacit understanding that the new government would not be a reactionary administration, would not repeal the basic reforms of its predecessors, but would consolidate the *status quo*. This meant, in effect, the status of a new power élite that had pushed through the reforms and itself been pushed up by them, whether landowners in the eighteenth century, industrialists in the nineteenth, or the representatives of the working class in the twentieth. Since Britain has been a remarkably homogeneous society, with few if any drastic internal divisions that could not be solved by this method, it has proved on the whole a very successful, if rough and ready, way for a nation to run its own affairs. It even took root in the colonies and later the dominions with a population of primarily British stock and affected the political development of the United States—though not to the extent that many Britons have claimed. But in Ireland it did not work, and this the British refused to recognize for a very long time: indeed it is doubtful if they have even recognized it in Northern Ireland today.

For in dealing with a conquered people, or even with an oppressed minority, the cycle of reform and retrenchment assumes a very different hue and becomes an apparently arbitrary alternation of appeasement and persecution. 'Apparently arbitrary' because the alternation is determined far less by the needs or wishes of the conquered—whose primary wish is to get the conquerors off their necks—than by the moods, needs and political expediencies of their masters. It is these that determine the swing of the pendulum, and the swing between appeasement and persecution is infinitely more violent than that between reform and retrenchment. This is one interpretation of the old saying that when England sneezes, Ireland catches pneumonia. The 1790s was one of the periods of such a sneeze in England.

The age of reform, or appeasement, which had begun at the time of the American War of Independence continued until almost the middle of the century's last decade and then, for both internal and external reasons, rebellion in Ireland and the French Revolutionary War abroad, was violently thrown into reverse.

There were two very important, though small, groups of men in Ireland who, for very different reasons, viewed England's alternating policies towards Ireland with disquiet if not disgust. One was those educated Irishmen, often of English descent though usually thoroughly Hibernicized by this time, who bore the responsibility of governing Ireland, who were well aware of the complexity of Irish emotions and of their fundamentally illogical motivation, and knew that appeasement, no matter how honourable the English intentions might be, would be interpreted by the majority in Ireland as weakness. The chief representative of this group, in Ireland in the 1790s, was the Lord Chancellor, Lord Clare, of whom this writer is a direct descendant. His family was of ancient Anglo-Norman lineage, spoliated in the seventeenth century wars, and I have some reason to believe—but cannot prove—that he was himself all his life a secret Catholic. More important he was, like the hierarchy of the Roman Church, profoundly anti-Jacobin. Being himself an Irishman, he foresaw how his simpler compatriots must misunderstand appeasement, and living as he did all his life in Ireland, he was well aware of how potentially explosive the situation was becoming, and not only in Ulster. In an attempt to steer his fellow-Irishmen of the Old Faith away from Jacobinism he created, in 1795, St. Patrick's College, Maynooth, the first legal seminary for the priesthood on Irish soil for over two hundred years. And moving, as he had done all his life, among the Protestant Ascendancy—he had been a fairly prominent member of the original Volunteers and a friend of Grattan's—he began to be increasingly dubious about the ability of the members of the Irish Lords and Commons to deal with the storms to come. Throughout the 1790s he was the effective ruler of Ireland, a truly thankless task that killed him at an early age.

At the other end of the political spectrum were those Jacobins, of whom Wolfe Tone is the most prominent, who created the revolutionary movement called the United Irishmen. Though most of its leaders were of Protestant origin, and its original centre was Belfast, religion played little if any part in their ideology. Tone's appeal was to 'the man of no property' as he put it. It was in fact an appeal to social revolution, to the expropriation of the expropriators. Their new, revolutionary ideas were originally more acceptable to the better-educated middle, lower middle and working class Protestants in Ulster and Dublin than to the almost illiterate and Irish-speaking peasantry in the other, predominantly agricultural provinces. However Tone and the other leaders quickly realized that middle-class Presbyterian Ulster was too small a base from which to mount a national revolution against the Protestant Ascendancy backed by Great Britain, even with the promised assistance of international Jacobinism in the form of a French expeditionary force. They therefore set about securing the support of the Roman Catholic rural proletariat. It was a task that would have taxed the revolutionary ingenuity of a Lenin, particularly in view of what was going on in County Armagh and elsewhere in the border counties, but initially at least they were remarkably successful.

Thus once again the struggle and the ultimate violence in Irish affairs was on as many levels, often incompatible levels, as a Neapolitan ice. Far out of sight, but never out of the minds of the men at the centre, was the fact that Great Britain was at war with France: as with the Spanish wars of the sixteenth century, a French occupation or liberation of Ireland could and probably would have spelled the defeat of Britain and the destruction of its social system. In Ireland itself the real battle was between the forces represented by Clare in Dublin Castle and the Jacobin leaders of the United Irishmen, and the subject: property. Here both antagonists regarded themselves as patriots, but both had to rely on external support, the Castle on the British, the United Irishmen on the French, neither of whom were really interested in the welfare or happiness of the Irish, both of whom wished to exploit internal Irish antagonisms for their own ends. And yet a third layer was the sectarian strife, the inherited sectarian strife, between Protestant and Catholic, itself fragmented by mutual distrust between Dissent and Church of Ireland, between the anti-Jacobin Roman Catholic clerics and an increasingly revolutionary peasantry, between the English-speaking cities and the Irish-speaking countryside. Yet in an age when revolutionaries could only rely upon the pike or at best the musket, it was necessary to mobilize large bodies of men. This the United Irishmen proceeded to do, while their opponents relied on their authority, their wealth, their armed horsemen who had controlled the Whiteboys, but ultimately upon the British armed forces.

At the lowest level a crisis was reached in September of 1795 when a pitched battle took place at the Diamond, County Armagh, between Peep o' Day Boys who had been attacked by Defenders. The Defenders were utterly defeated. In the following months thousands of Roman Catholics were driven from their homes in Southern Ulster and forced to flee into Connaught. And on the evening of the Battle of the Diamond the victorious Protestants, most of whom must have belonged to the new Volunteers, formed an offensive-defensive society known as the Orange Society, later renamed the Orange Order. It is this semi-secret society which, through its Orange Lodges (its organization is modelled in some measure upon the Free Masons to which society many of its members also belong) has controlled, and still controls, the political activities of what are now called Unionists in Ulster.

It was in these confused circumstances that Ireland became involved in its second, disastrous revolution. The battle, on all its levels, could not be long delayed, but loyalties were unpredictable. And the following year the French were on the seas.

CHAPTER SEVEN

The last decade of the eighteenth century saw, in Paris and in something approaching geopolitical macrocosm, the destruction of what was then the head and heart of European society: and events of that decade's first, five terrible years in France may even be seen by our survivors as early symptoms of that cancer, insensate nationalism, which, combined with senseless materialism, was to destroy Europe's ancient civilization too, for it was there and then that egalitarianism was born as a political force. Ulster on the other hand presents a microcosm. Few beautiful objects, little that was gracious, only coarse and usually violent forms of religious faith were to be found in that northwestern outpost of the Europe that then had Paris as its suicidal capital city. Yet even these were to be transmuted and debased. In Paris Bourbon gold became Napoleonic iron, in Belfast Cromwellian bronze was turned into Orange Lodge pewter by the revolutionaries' alchemy.

Our own century's early scientists or alchemists taught us, through their popularizers, that space and time are but part of the same continuum. So it was then, when the news from Paris took days or even weeks to reach Ireland, when ideas that were commonplace in the boulevard St. Germain of Voltaire's day were to remain incomprehensible in Londonderry for a very long time; perhaps for ever. But to some Irishmen, and indeed to some Englishmen sent over as governors, they were not incomprehensible, though inevitably distorted by distance and circumstance. The ideas and ideals of French thinkers and actors, the glorious and sensible, the ignoble and the wicked, the foolish with the wise, were imperfectly translated into English, even more clumsily into Irish, and were to become totally enmeshed into traditions, modes of thought and feeling, and into a history of which these French thinkers had had little if any concept. It is from this insemination of French thought that modern Ulster, like all modern Europe, was curiously engendered. It was a tragic birth in Ireland that cannot even be rated a tragicomedy. But it is an impossibility to see the events in Northern Ireland at that time in any sort of geographical abstraction, just as it is impossible to view the story of any part of European society, no matter how small and how obscure, without some comprehension of its history. Ulster was and is a part of Ireland. Ireland was and is one of the British Isles. They are very close to Europe. The microcosm, in this case, becomes a part of the macrocosm. It would be impossible to understand the events in Ireland in the 1790s without repeated reference to what was happening elsewhere.

The French Revolution was not, as we are sometimes taught at school, an incident that occurred when the Bastille was 'stormed' on July 14th, 1789. It was rather a lengthy process which had begun in men's minds many years before and which fell into the pattern of a dual revolution outlined in the previous chapter, the first being a revolution of reform, the second a social revolution, the first and successful revolution being in essence bourgeois, the second and failed revolution being more nearly proletarian. The first or constitutional one lasted for some three years and bequeathed to France that social and political structure which, often overthrown by dictators of greater or lesser benevolence and constantly modified by circumstance, has yet remained the French norm, the French phoenix, until today. The second revolution, which we associate above all with the September Massacres of 1792 and the Terror that soon followed, bequeathed a heritage of another sort: the class hatred and mass violence which have also recurred, notably in 1871 and 1945 after lost wars. (It was the spectre of imminent defeat that produced the hysteria which enabled Marat to instigate mass murder in 1792.) This second revolution lasted for a mere two years, yet such was its violence that whereas its positive influence was far less than that of the first, the reactions it created were far greater. And nowhere was that influence, and that reaction, more strongly felt than in Ireland.

The first, reformist French revolution, deriving as it did from the general climate of opinion of the previous half-century and fortified by the success of the American Revolution, was of great and immediate encouragement to liberals throughout all Europe. In Ireland this took on, at first, the character of reform, that great slogan and strength of the English Whigs. Reform in Ireland at that time, as in Northern Ireland at the time of writing, was basically concerned with the granting of political and economic rights to the all-Irish Roman Catholic majority. The two principal organizations, in 1790, that put forward the proposals for reform were the new Whig Club in Dublin (with the affiliated Northern Whig Club in Belfast) and the older Catholic Committee in Ireland. The Whig Club was a Protestant, more precisely a Church of Ireland, association. Founded by Lord Charlemont and Grattan, among other distinguished parliamentarians, its objectives, according to Grattan, were 'to obtain an internal reform of Parliament, and to prevent the Union'. In his *Memoirs* he also described its members as 'steady supporters of settled government—attached to the principles of the revolution of 1688 in England—and proud of that of 1782 in Ireland'. It was not particularly pro-Catholic, for it was merely the more 'liberal' wing of the Protestant Ascendancy, and indeed it might be said that Lord Charlemont, from his vast and troubled estates in the County Armagh, was positively anti-Catholic. However 'internal', that is to say parliamentary and administrative, reforms could in the long run only benefit the Catholics, since any move towards democracy, even the cautious semi-democracy of property-owning Englishmen in the eighteenth century, must ultimately lead to an amelioration in the political condition at least of similarly situated Catholic farmers and merchants. Edmund Burke, that great Irishman and passionate advocate of American independence in the '70s, the intellectual ancestor of the then unborn English Conservative Party, gave his blessing to the Whig Club while almost simultaneously damning Tom Paine and the principles of the French Revolution. The young Wolfe Tone was an early, and brief, member of the Whig Club. The Castle, meanwhile, was violently opposed to it. The reforms it advocated would have undermined the powers of the Castle to co-erce, by bribery and financial intimidation, the legislature, at least until it had found new means so to do. The Whig Club was well-intentioned, within the limits of preserving Protestant Ascendancy (as already stated a phrase first and significantly used at this time), but ineffectual. Had it achieved power, as it hoped to do when the liberal Lord Fitzwilliam came to Ireland as Lord Lieutenant in January 1795, it would perhaps have been, *mutatis mutandis*, the equivalent of the Necker and Mirabeau governments of a still monarchist France that lasted from 1789 to 1792. A similar, and in this case domestic, parallel can be drawn with the O'Neill administration in Northern Ireland that attempted reform, while preserving the *status quo*, in 1968 and early 1969. Such methods were not to the taste of Wolfe Tone, who rapidly became disgusted with the Whigs, and soon left their club.

The Catholic Committee was, at the beginning of the decade, an even more conservative body. Originally formed in the 1750s, it achieved nothing and faded away within a very few years. It was formed anew by Lord Kenmare, one of the few great Catholic landlords, in 1773, and for the next seventeen years was run, rather inefficiently, by himself and others of his type. Their aim was not the enfranchisement of the Catholic masses, but rather the participation of the Catholic aristocracy and gentry in the then exclusively Protestant Ascendancy. This meant that they were the political enemies, though not infrequently the personal friends, of their Protestant peers, particularly the Whigs. Furthermore the reduction of the Roman Catholics to the status of second class citizens in their own country had been, from the very beginning of the Penal Laws period, the work of the Irish and not the English Parliament, and in the last quarter of the eighteenth century the British government was far better disposed towards the Catholics of property, indeed towards the Catholic population generally, than were the Protestant gentlemen who sat in the Irish parliament on College Green. This was reflected in the administration imposed upon Ireland by successive English governments, and the attitude of the Catholic Committee towards the Castle was one of loyalty that at times approached the obsequious. When England went to war, the Catholic Committee issued proclamations of utter fidelity to the Crown. When each successive Viceroy arrived to rule John Bull's other island they submitted addresses of loyalty and did little more than hint at their wish that they too might be permitted a small share in the government of their country, for it was to London and the Castle that they looked for an amelioration of their condition, not to the Protestant magnates no matter how Whiggish these might be. In this law-abiding attitude they had the full backing of the Roman Catholic hierarchy, a support that was of immense value in controlling the peasantry and one which was increased manifold once the French Revolution had begun and the new French government set about confiscating Church lands and Church property. Since the expropriation of the

French aristocracy was already underway this caused the spiritual and the temporal leaders to coalesce in an anti-Republican attitude of mind. There thus came about a superficial and undeclared alliance between the Whigs and the hitherto dominant personalities of the Catholic Committee, observed with approval from London by William Pitt and also by Edmund Burke. (If some historians were ever to justify my suspicion that FitzGibbon was a secret Catholic, he would have been of Lord Kenmare's party, certainly. I first propounded this theory in a book called *Miss Finnigan's Fault*, semi-fictional and historical Irish sketches, published in 1953. My evidence was almost, but not quite, entirely negative: Clare's reluctance to go to a Protestant church on Sundays: the fact that I could find no record of the baptism of his two sons in the churches of Limerick and Dublin that his wife, certainly a Protestant, attended: the statement of a contemporary that his father, ostensibly a Protestant as was necessary for a barrister in Penal days, was 'a notorious Papist': and finally his policy, which at all stages was in full accord with the anti-Jacobinism of the Hierarchy. This theory was not accepted by historians, though no evidence has been produced to deny my hypothesis. Family evidence may here be relevant. His granddaughter and co-heiress to the property, Lady Louisa FitzGibbon, married a son of Lord Dillon, who took her name, in 1847. The Dillons were at that time Protestants, yet their children, one of whom was my grandfather, were baptised Roman Catholics. She herself, twice widowed, died a nun. Her mother, on the other hand, was an English Protestant who married her father after a divorce action, further negative evidence that Lady Louisa's Catholicism came from her father. Finally, her granddaughter and my aunt, Lady Antrobus, has recently told me that her father had told her in her childhood, very many years ago, 'we FitzGibbons have always been Catholics'.) This theory, if provable, would necessitate a certain amount of re-assessment concerning such matters as the Foundation of Maynooth (which Clare desired to see as a University, not a seminary) and the whole problem of Catholic Emancipation and the Act of Union. Research in the archives of the Vatican might well be relevant. Almost all Clare's papers were destroyed at his own request shortly before or immediately after his death. His appreciation of those Protestant Ascendancy men who sat in the Irish House of Commons, whose value he knew since he bought many of them with titles and places, was very low indeed. He was to describe them, to their faces, as 'a puny and rapacious oligarchy, who consider the Irish nation as their political inheritance, and are prepared to sacrifice the public peace and happiness to their insatiate love of patronage and power'. No orator of our time has spoken so strongly about a situation, so similar, in the Six Counties of Ulster. FitzGibbon's greatest enemy, Wolfe Tone, refers to these same parliamentarians in his *Autobiography* as a 'gentry, as they affected to call themselves'. This was unconsciously echoed by FitzGibbon, who had described them as 'the gentlemen who call themselves the Irish nation', and by Grattan, who had once described them as fit only to carry claret to a chamberpot. From three such varied angles, not to mention the voluminous 'amusing' literature of the time we surely get a most depressing picture of the colonizer class, the permanent armed garrison, which was so jealous of its liberties and as determined to control its natives in the 1790s, as are their equally vulgar equivalents of English descent in Rhodesia today.

The spirit of the age was against the Catholic Committee. I quote from William Lecky's *History of Ireland in the Eighteenth Century*: 'another type of Catholic leader, springing out of the rich trading class, was now appearing, and it found a leader of some ability in John Keogh, a Dublin tradesman, who for many years exercised much influence over Irish politics.

'Several circumstances were conspiring to make this party ascendant in the Catholic Committee. Towards the close of 1790 the Catholic Committee waited upon Major Hobart, requesting him to support a petition to Parliament which asked for nothing specific, but simply prayed that the case of the Catholics should be taken into consideration; but their request was refused, and they could not find a single member to present their petition to Parliament. In the course of the same year an address of loyalty, intended to be presented to Lord Westmoreland by the Catholics, on the occasion of a visit of the Lord Lieutenant to Cork, was returned to them, because it concluded with a hope that their loyalty would lead to a further relaxation of the penal code. In the beginning of 1791 a deputation from the Catholic Committee went to the Castle with a list of the penal laws which they were anxious to have modified or repealed, but they were dismissed without even the courtesy of an answer.'

The sequel to this was that Lord Kenmare and some sixty of

the Catholic gentry seceded from the Committee, which passed into the control of John Keogh and the democrats. The agent, or what we would call secretary, of the old Committee had been Richard Burke, appointed principally because he was a Protestant and Edmund Burke's son, therefore acceptable both to the Castle and to the hierarchy. He had not, however, inherited either his father's talents or his tact. Keogh's new Committee chose as his successor in 1792 another Protestant, a young barrister named Wolfe Tone. He later wrote: 'In reviewing the conduct of my predecessor, Richard Burke, I saw that the rock on which he split was an overweening opinion of his own talents and judgment, and a desire, which he had not art enough to conceal, of guiding at his pleasure the measures of the committee. I therefore determined to model my conduct with the greatest caution in that respect. I seldom or never offered my opinion unless it was called for in the sub-committee, but contented myself with giving my sentiments, without reserve, in private, to the two men I most esteemed, and who had, in their respective capacities, the greatest influence on that body—I mean John Keogh and Richard McCormack, secretary to the General Committee. My discretion in this respect was not unobserved, and I very soon acquired, and I may say without vanity, I deserved the entire confidence and good opinion of the Catholics. The fact is, I was devoted most sincerely to their cause, and being now retained in their service, I would have sacrificed everything to ensure their success, and they knew it.'

Thus, in Dublin alone in 1792, there were already five factors at least involved in the equation: the Catholic aristocrats and the Catholic bourgeosie or democrats, the Protestant aristocracy divided into hard-liners and Whigs, and the Castle. In the background was the power of England on the one hand, and on the other, in FitzGibbon's phrase 'the old inhabitants of the island, brooding over their discontents in sullen indignation'. And in Paris the Terror was about to begin with the massacre, principally of Catholic priests or the members of religious organizations, in September of 1792. And in Ulster, more particularly in Belfast, the Presbyterians were coming more and more to accept Jacobin belief, while in the border districts of that province murderous mob fights between Catholics and Dissenters were becoming more and more frequent. There were considerably more than two sides to that particular Irish situation.

In Ulster, too, extreme political complexity existed and one that grew more complex as the decade advanced. Here there were, in appearance, three basic groups, the Protestant Ascendancy, the Protestant Dissenters of whom the majority were Presbyterians, and the Roman Catholics. (That triangulation has continued in the Six Counties of Northern Ireland up to, and will almost certainly continue beyond, the time of writing: at the beginning of the decade of the 1970s it might be personified by the names of O'Neill, Paisley and Bernadette Devlin.) In the 1790s the Ascendancy landlords were identifiable with their cousins in the other Irish provinces, but with this difference: in most of Ulster the small tenant farmers and the peasants from whom the ruling class exacted their wealth were not Catholics and, owing to the Ulster Custom, had more protection than had the poor people in Ireland as a whole. However they were not a yeomanry in the English manner with the ultimate cohesion of patriotism and a shared religion between master and man. The religious difference between Scottish Presbyterians and the English-inspired Church of Ireland was not as great as that between either of those faiths and the faith of Rome: it was still great enough to be divisive, for the Anglo-Scottish War of 1745 was only ten years more remote in the 1790s than is the recent Civil War in Spain, to Spaniards, in the 1970s. The Presbyterians in Ulster, or at least those of them who were not busy bashing the Catholics in Armagh and the other border counties, looked to the American solution when they did not actually emigrate across the seas. A division was here arising between town and country, between the politically educated middle classes of Belfast and the men on the farms who remembered past conquests, which was to produce the strange twin birth of Orange Lodges and United Ireland. Again, and with apologies, of this more in a moment or two.

Of the Catholics in Ulster at that time we know comparatively little. They were almost entirely rural, not urban, small farmers and farm-labourers, an uneducated, land-hungry, often Gaelic-speaking peasantry. Where they collided with their equivalents of settler stock, and particularly in the border counties, there was ill-feeling, sectarian hatred, brawls and murder. The Defenders have left few records of their battles with the Peep o' Day Boys. We have fitful glimpses of mobs, armed with clubs and scythes and knives, and rarely a gun, many half-drunk on poteen, collecting on hillsides, perhaps to attack an isolated inn where the customers were all and always Scots-Irish Presbyterians: of a Protestant mob, slightly better armed, collecting in some muddy village street, inflamed with liquor and religion, marching to attack in reprisal the Catholic village up the valley: of the Gaelic speaking peasant farmer somehow finding the money, and the way, to buy the gun forbidden him by law with which to protect his family in his lonely, mountain cabin, or to shoot his hated Protestant neighbour on the other side of the hill: of the Protestant boys arriving at first light, to seize the gun and cuff the countless children, while the mother sobbed or screamed and even more iron entered into the father's soul, and sometimes to burn the wretched cottage. Such, frequently, was life in large areas of Armagh and South Down and the other border counties in the early 1790s, and this has remained a very important part of the Ulster heritage until today: it is visible on many faces, Protestant and Catholic, north and south of the present border, in that part: it is audible in the accent, harsh and sour to Southern Irish ears: it is almost tangible in Newry, Dungannon, Strabane, other ugly, dreary towns, and above all in Derry and in central Belfast, where the corners of the mouth curve downwards in bitterness and the hands seem formed for fists, not for handshakes, let alone for caresses.

The Church of Ireland ascendancy and the Roman Catholic peasantry were only local, Ulster variants of their equivalents in all Ireland. The Dissenters, on the other hand, were unique. Though they bore considerable resemblance, both in faith and in way of life, to their now remote cousins in the Scottish Lowlands and in the United States, a resemblance that was stronger in the more homogeneous Scots-Irish northeast of the province, history and geography were nonetheless producing a new breed of man, a sort of Irishman who, with the generations, has become almost as alien to his Irish compatriots as he is to the other descendants of his Scots and English forebears or to those now distant cousins whose ancestors, from all parts of Ireland, emigrated to America in the eighteenth and nineteenth century and produced yet another distinctive Irish race, the Irish-Americans. This fissiparous social process, which had been going on for some five generations in 1790, was only marginally biological, for intermarriage was very rare as surnames show (though miscegenation may well have been more common): nor was it therefore a question of the old story of the invader's descendants becoming 'more Irish than the Irish', for this they never did: rather was it, if I may apologize for the invention of a truly atrocious word, a sort of psychoparthenogenesis. A new view of the world was created on Irish soil, in Scots-Irish minds. It is unique. It is sometimes dismissed by those who say that the population of the Six Counties of Northern Ireland are merely old-fashioned, that they are still fighting the religious wars of the Counter-reformation. This is true, in a way, but it is no explanation. The Treaty of Westphalia was signed in 1648. What is unique about the Ulsterman is that, over three centuries later, he has not accepted that the Thirty Years' War is over and is still fighting it out with brickbats, petrol bombs and far more lethal weapons in the streets of Belfast and Derry. The political, as opposed to the emotional, genesis of Ulster can be found in the 1790s. And since the men involved, the Dissenters above all, were Irishmen, though of a specialized sort, the political Ulsterman began as a political schizophrenic. From the same egg came the bigoted, black Protestant Orangeman with his lodges, and the red Jacobin with his dreams of Rousseau's Utopia and guillotines.

One important aspect of the story of the United Irishmen is really encompassed within the short lifetime of Theobald Wolfe Tone. His personal charisma, and the sheer coincidence of the various political posts that he filled, were largely instrumental in the creation of the Society (or conspiracy, according to taste): his absence in America and France during the critical years between January 1795 and July 1798, combined with the arrest of almost all the other United Irish leaders, deprived it of a head during the brief period when it attempted a revolution that might have triumphed if properly led: with Tone's death in a Dublin gaol in 1798, perhaps a murder but more probably a suicide, the Society of United Irishmen really died, though the corpse twitched again with Robert Emmet in 1803, and of course a very important heritage in the whole history of Irish republican nationalism was passed on, to be modified by subsequent generations until today and, no doubt, by future generations too. For the ideals and aims of the United Irishmen were part of the great European ideology that was finding its first positive political expression in Paris when that society was being formed in Belfast and spreading across Ireland. And its finest chronicler is undoubtedly Wolfe Tone himself, whose so-called *Auto-*

biography (in fact a posthumous rag-bag of diaries, memoirs and memoranda) is perhaps the most honest, revealing and self-revealing of books ever to have been compiled from the writings of a great Irishman. Even the fact that his political career was as disastrous for his country as it was for himself and his family is not concealed, let alone excused. Tone was the almost perfect revolutionary, a cool-headed, steely-eyed fanatic, for whom ideas of liberty and social justice were far more real than the realities of terror and injustice then being played out, in their name and almost before his eyes, in revolutionary France.

Tone, like so many revolutionaries of his generation, was of upper middle class stock and had trained as a lawyer. He was a Dubliner and a Protestant, the son of a coachmaker who had squandered what moneys he possessed in litigation concerning an inheritance. It was this family misfortune, combined with the long tedium of his own legal studies, that gave Tone a rooted aversion, indeed a positive loathing, of the law, of English law that is: the French revolutionary laws that sent the king, queen and so many others to their deaths he accepted, if glumly, as historically necessary. Although he seems to have quite enjoyed his student years at the Inner Temple, drinking too much in the pubs and generally behaving as normal young men so often do, he developed an aversion for the English which, for political reasons, became an active hatred. Many a young Irishman has found the snobbishness and materialism of the English repellent, and if the 'beasts' are in his eyes not even 'just beasts' they can have little appeal to one brought up in the easier atmosphere of Dublin. When he returned to that city in 1788, at the age of twenty-five, he was already married, with a small daughter. Early in the following year he was called to the Bar and went on circuit. Almost immediately, and quite deliberately, he became involved in politics. Though, as he says, he was 'far from approving the system of the Whig Club, and much less their principles and motives', he wrote a pamphlet which gave the Whigs, and particularly the Northern Whigs in Belfast, so much satisfaction that they courted him with rather vague offers of briefs, which he badly needed, and perhaps even a seat in the House of Commons. These promises were not kept, or at least not kept with sufficient speed to satisfy Wolfe Tone. It was perhaps for this reason, as well as for other, purely political ones, that he now developed yet a third and dominant hatred, for the land-owning Protestant aristocracy whether Whig or Tory. This was not modified by the fact that many such grandees treated him as an equal (even at the height of their power the Anglo-Irish Ascendancy were never snobbish in the English fashion) and that he counted many personal friends among his political enemies. In fact during the first three years of the French Revolution, even after he had broken with the Whigs in 1791, he was in much the position of some clever *Salonkommunist* in London, Paris or New York in the 1930s. He was such a likeable fellow, so intelligent, so amusing. Aristocrats have always and everywhere listened, with interest, to those who can debate skilfully in favour of the destruction of aristocratic rule, usually without realizing that this means the social, financial and often physical destruction of themselves and their families. (Indeed it would seem a constant that save in times of actual massacre the greater the revolutionary fervour the higher the level of popularity. No eighteenth-century writer was ever so lionized by the *grandes dames* of his age as Jean-Jacques Rousseau: none so esteemed in the highest social circles of tsarist Russia as Leo Tolstoi: outspoken Communist intellectuals are probably, on the whole, more acceptable to sophisticated American millionaires than are anti-Communists. Their talk is seen as original, and their theories produce a pleasurable *frisson* in many of their intended victims.)

Furthermore at this time, that is to say 1790 and 1791, the French Revolution was still intellectually respectable. Although the emigration of aristocrats had begun, the royal family were virtual prisoners, and the expropriation of Church property was being carried out on a massive scale, none of this appeared to affect the Irish aristocracy as a direct peril to themselves. Charles James Fox, an aristocrat if ever there was one, could and did speak in favour of developments across the English Channel: Pitt's government approved of a situation that weakened the French 'natural enemy' and probably numbered an obscure deputy by the name of Danton, among its many Parisian spies: almost alone, Edmund Burke felt the true quality of the rising wind. Perhaps so, too, did Wolfe Tone. Perhaps the imbalance of Irish society had equipped those two great Irishmen with more sensitive political antennae than were to be met with in the more stolid and comfortable atmosphere of Westminster and Mayfair.

The Northern Whigs were of a different breed from their

Assimilation of Norman and Irish nobility. A Clanricarde Burke displaying
a blazon of which one quarter bears the arms of Felim son of Cathal Crob-
dearg (Redhand), King of Connaught, whose daughter Una married Richard
de Burgh, Lord Lieutenant of Ireland.

Cattle raiding among the 'native Irish'.

The siege of Enniskillen Castle.

Dublin colleagues. They were men of Tone's own urban middle class: they were Dissenters though usually, it would seem, religious sceptics like Tone himself and, when they still believed in God, not infrequently Free Masons: they were thus far more inclined to radical, and what we would now call ecumenical, thought than were the land-owning, Church of Ireland grandees of the Dublin Whig Club. Inevitably there was a division between Dublin and Belfast and with equal inevitability Tone was a prime agent in the split. His second pamphlet which he wrote and published in September 1791 over the nom-de-plume 'A Northern Whig' was the catalyst. It is said to have sold over 10,000 copies. It expressed contempt for the Whig principles of Grattan and the other liberals: it demanded a complete severance of all political ties with Britain: and it further demanded an alliance between the urban, Protestant proletariat and the rural, Catholic proletariat to bring this about. This was clearly a straight revolutionary document. The immediate outcome was the creation, in Belfast, of the Society of United Irishmen, of which Tone was the dominant member. Branches were soon established in Dublin and elsewhere. For the first and last time in Irish history an interdenominational, or more precisely an irreligious, political party which could rely on mass support existed on Irish soil.

Five years later, when he was in France and actively engaged in promoting a French invasion of Ireland, Tone described his own attitude at the time when he was creating the United Irish movement. He wrote:

'The dominion of England in Ireland had been begun and continued in the disunion of the great sects which divided the latter country. In effectuating this disunion, the Protestant party were the willing instruments, as they saw clearly that if ever the Dissenters and Catholics were to discover their true interests, and, forgetting their former ruinous dissensions, were to unite cordially, and make common cause, the downfall of English supremacy, and, of course their own unjust monopoly, would be the necessary and immediate consequence. They therefore laboured continually, and for a long time successfully, to keep the other two sects asunder, and the English Government had even the address to persuade the Catholics that the non-execution of the penal laws, which were, in fact, too atrocious to be enforced in their full rigour, was owing to their clemency; that the

Protestants and Dissenters, but especially the latter, were the enemies, and themselves, in effect, the protectors of the Catholic people. Under this arrangement the machine of government moved forward on carpet ground, but the time was, at length, come when this system of iniquity was to tumble in the dust, and the day of truth and reason to commence.'

Having secured one leg of his revolutionary Ireland, Tone now set about the other. He was in luck. The Catholic Committee had split, basically on the issue of loyalty to the Crown. Lord Kenmare and the other Roman Catholics who had run it for so long had, foolishly, resigned. It had immediately been taken over by John Keogh, a great organizer, and other bourgeois, though not revolutionary, leaders. In order to play down their sectarian differences with the Ascendancy, it was their tradition to employ a Protestant secretary. Wolfe Tone was a friend, and soon a very close friend, of Keogh's. It was decided to bring over, as secretary to the General Committee, Richard Burke from England. As Edmund Burke's son it was believed, wrongly, that he could manipulate the levers of power in London in the interests of the Irish Catholics. He accepted the job with alacrity.

The Catholics, who thought that they had hooked a big fish, gave him large sums of money. He scarcely earned them, for he seems to have had little comprehension of the Irish situation— the Roman Catholic hierarchy was becoming increasingly reactionary, as the French revolutionaries increased their spoliation of the Gallican church—and he preferred to spend his time, and the Catholics' money, in England. His arrogant folly made him unpopular with almost everyone in Ireland, and early in 1792 he was given £2,000 by the Committee to go away. Wolfe Tone took over his post with the Catholics and rapidly turned what had been a sort of P.R.O. job into that of secretary to a mass organization with very considerable revolutionary potential. Thus did he find himself not only the founding father of the United Irishmen, but also a key figure, second only to Keogh, in the Roman Catholic political movement, and this at a most critical moment of history. He immediately set about forging what have always been two fundamentally discordant elements, the urban Dissenters in the North and the Roman Catholics in the South, into a single movement for political liberty and social reform in all Ireland. It was a tremendous, perhaps an impossible, task though no greater than the one Lenin attempted and achieved when he forged an alliance between peasants, industrial workers and mutinous soldiers in Russia in 1917 and 1918. But then time and history were on Lenin's side. In the spring of 1792 they appeared to be on Tone's, for this was an age of reform and Tone was well qualified to transform it into an age of revolution. After April France was at war with the Germanic powers from Holland to Austria. Foreign armies, with French emigré recruits, were slowly advancing on French soil. And the country was bankrupt. Although in Paris, in early 1792, the revolutionary clubs were tightening their grip on the people, most of the rest of the country was visibly disaffected and large areas were in open revolt against the central government. Even if the French armies, whose officers' loyalty was to their king living the life of a semi-prisoner in the Tuileries and not to a rabble of deputies in the Assembly, would and could repel the invader, it seemed to many that the French revolution was dying. Indeed some emigrés were beginning to return, under the misapprehension that the worst was over: it had not, of course, begun.

In England the policy of the government was to avoid the French disasters by means of reforms. If Pitt had had his way something not unlike the Reform Bill of 1832 would have passed through both the English and Irish parliaments forty years earlier, rotten boroughs abolished, the franchise extended to a much wider range of property-holders, and religious disqualifications also abolished. However the opposition of the land-owning class to any diminution of their control in parliamentary elections was too great, both in England and Ireland, and before they could be educated to accept the inevitable, events on the continent had drastically changed the climate of opinion in the British Isles and, indeed, altered the whole purpose of the Pitt administration. In religious matters, that is to say the final dismantling of what remained of the penal laws against Roman Catholics and nonconformists, Pitt came into direct conflict with his stubborn monarch, George III, then alternating between stupidity and insanity. In his saner moments he believed that his Coronation Oath forbad concessions to his Roman Catholic subjects, and in this he received a considerable measure of support from the aristocracy which had, and has still retained, a bias against the Catholics. During his periods of insanity, of which the first acute spasm occurred in 1789, it would have been something like political suicide for Pitt to make the Prince of Wales Regent, for that almost equally unstable man would probably have dismissed the government and invited Charles James Fox to head a more liberal administration. Thus in his tentative search for English reform before the outbreak of hostilities with France early in 1793, Pitt found himself in a situation where he could achieve little. Once the great war had started—and like almost all of England's wars it started disastrously—he neither could nor did attempt any reform in his own country.

But so far as Ireland went, in 1792 reforms to the electoral and fiscal system were, as we say nowadays, in the pipeline. Fiscal reforms removed certain punitive taxes hitherto levied on the Catholics alone, and other relics of the Penal Laws, most of which had fallen into desuetude, were finally annulled in that same year. However the Irish parliament threw out a bill that would have given Catholic property-holders the vote. The Catholic reaction was immediate, and surprisingly effective— at least in appearance, to the Irish.

Keogh and Tone had greatly broadened the base of their General Committee. No longer an aristocratic clique scarcely functioning outside Dublin and Catholic country-house drawing-rooms, it now had its representatives, usually solid merchants or farmers, across the length and breadth of Ireland. Through them it preserved contact, of a sort, with the Gaelic-speaking peasantry. This organizational structure had been set up with great speed, a proof of Tone's efficiency. He now proceeded to use it in order to summon an all-Ireland Catholic Convention, which met in Dublin on December 1st, 1792, and there drew up a petition of rights which it proposed to present directly to the king in his capacity as king of Ireland. The men of the Catholic Convention were moderates, and their petition was carefully phrased to avoid frightening the Protestants.

Indeed their attitude was, in appearance at least, traditional: for a century the Catholics had looked to London rather than to the Irish parliament and Dublin Castle. In view of the English administration's known desires for reform, it was only logical that they appeal to the king—that is to say in reality to Pitt—over the heads of the Protestant oligarchy, the rooted garrison, determined to preserve its hegemony of power in Ireland. Furthermore the Protestant Nation had come into existence itself by just such Conventions of its own, only a decade before. The Protestants could hardly take legal exception to methods that they had themselves so recently employed without bringing the legality of 1782, and perhaps even of the Irish constitution itself, into dispute. Tone was, in fact, playing a very clever game, using the enemy's methods and even the enemy's administrative arrangements in order to bring about his enemy's downfall. (It is a classic revolutionary strategy, usually though not always coupled with violence or the threat of violence, and was later employed with great success by the Nazis in Germany between 1924 and 1933.)

That it was revolutionary was, of course, apparent to Fitz-Gibbon, to the Catholics' Belfast allies and undoubtedly to Tone himself. The Catholic Convention met in the Dublin Tailors' Hall in a street called Back Lane. It was immediately dubbed the Back Lane Parliament. The respectable collection of provincial burghers there gathered together to draft their modest petition for a modicum of civil rights did not look like revolutionaries, nor were they. But they did represent, if only indirectly, the majority of the population. They had no Camille Desmoulins, nor even the quasi-legality of the Third Estates meeting, three and a half years before, in the Jeu de Paume, but nevertheless their mere assembly was a revolution in embryo, for no state can tolerate two, opposed parliamentary assemblies without moving towards revolution, or counter-revolution, or civil war.

Of this FitzGibbon had long been well aware. In 1784 the High Sheriff of Dublin had proposed the summoning of a National Convention (Protestant of course) in order to bring pressure on the Irish parliament which had just thrown out Flood's reform bill. Although the High Sheriff had the backing of the armed Volunteers, FitzGibbon, who had just been appointed Attorney-General, did not hesitate to write to him: 'I shall hold myself bound ... to prosecute you in the court of King's Bench for your conduct, which I consider so highly criminal that I cannot overlook it.' When the High Sheriff ignored this warning, and summoned a public meeting, FitzGibbon did precisely as he had said. He was well aware, as a lawyer, of what was constitutional and what was not. So was Tone. The Catholic Convention was therefore most careful not to *appear* as a parliament in rivalry with the House of Commons, though of course in reality that is what it was. Nor did it have any body of armed men at its disposal. It was, in fact, not illegal. It met for only a few days. And it is highly significant that when its delegation set off with its petition to London, it travelled via Ulster. It is even more significant that the delegates were cheered by the Protestant crowds as they passed through the streets in Belfast. Tone must then have thought that his dream of a United Ireland was fast becoming a revolutionary reality: so must have FitzGibbon. And they were certainly in agreement as to the political direction that this revolutionary movement must take. Since the summer of 1792 there had been public subscriptions collected, in the North particularly, to help the French repel their invaders, and in November the Belfast Volunteers had welcomed the deposition of Louis XVI and the proclamation of the first French republic. Those same men must also have welcomed the proclamation by the French National Convention, issued on November 19th, that France would assist all peoples attempting to overthrow their governments. (This news would have reached Dublin and Belfast just about the time that the Catholic Convention was meeting in Back Lane.)

How much the respectable delegates of the Catholic Convention influenced the busy gentlemen in London it is hard to say, but apparently very little. They were treated with scant courtesy, though they did at last manage to present their petition. The dates, however, indicate with certainty that the Pitt administration had already brought sufficient pressure on Dublin Castle to ensure the passage of a Catholic Relief Bill through the Irish Parliament in the 1793 session. No doubt Pitt and Dundas felt reassured by the eminent respectability of the Catholic delegates. What they did not apparently realize was that the Catholic Convention, by its mere existence and the despatch of its delegates to London, was contributing and in some measure creating a Protestant back-lash in almost all strata—outside Belfast—of the Irish Protestant Nation, from the sophisticated gentlemen in Dublin Castle to the Presbyterian peasants in the border counties. Primarily from the former came the disastrous Act of Union of 1800, from the latter the Orange Lodges, of 1795.

I trust that the reader has not been too confused by the confusing events and climates of opinion which were then so soon to lead, first, to the jacquerie of 1798 and, therefrom but slowly to the emergence of an Ulster that is still with us, with an ideology that is still prepared to kill and die for principles and prejudices that have been forgotten or transmuted in the rest of the world. Paradox, all paradox. The crowds who cheered the Catholic delegates as they passed through Belfast are the ancestors of the crowds who attack the Catholic areas of that city nearly two centuries later. An even more atrocious paradox: Wolfe Tone is the political ancestor of Ian Paisley.

CHAPTER EIGHT

The reforms of 1793 produced an atmosphere of mounting excitement, fear and anticipation in Ireland and also a very considerable degree of confusion in simpler Irish minds. To the United Irishmen, or at least to their Protestant leaders in Dublin and Belfast, these reforms were the first step towards democracy on the French model or, for the extremists, to Jacobinism. One more push, preferably with French assistance, and the walls of the Castle must come tumbling down.

> Bliss was it in that dawn to be alive,
> But to be young was very heaven!

The men in the Castle were prepared, with a certain reluctance, to accept these reforms imposed upon them by London. But they too feared that this might be the first step down a slope that could only lead to carnage and disaster for Ireland. They pushed the Bill through the Irish Parliament with surprising ease: their placemen there voted, as usual, as they were told to vote, while the amorphous 'liberal' opposition voted for it on principle. But both the Castle and, soon, the Protestant gentry were to be united in their determination that this first step was enough, that there must not be a second. With England, and therefore Ireland, now at war with France the advocacy of Jacobin opinions became tantamount to treason. The French are not the only nation who can cry, as Danton had just done: 'La patrie en danger!' Just as English Fascists were allowed to air their views in Britain during the early months of the Second World War, but were locked up the moment that war became serious, so the Irish government began locking up the United Irish leaders in 1794, or with surprising and perhaps even misplaced gentleness permitting them to go into exile, usually to America, whence many made their way to France. Wolfe Tone took his family to Philadelphia early in 1795, and himself to France a year later there to plan several invasions of Ireland by

French troops. Only those *salon* Jacobins with the very highest social connections were temporarily left at liberty in Ireland. Lord Edward Fitzgerald was brother to Ireland's largest landowner and only duke. Married to the beautiful Pamela (daughter of the blue-stockinged madame de Genlis and probably of the duc d'Orléans, that Philippe-Egalité who voted for the death sentence pronounced in early 1793 on his cousin Louis XVI) was permitted for some time to dash about Dublin in his curricle, a French tricolour in his hat, his hair cropped in the Jacobin style and his brown suit cut, no doubt by Dublin's best tailor, in the current Parisian fashion. He seems to have been an attractive if savage and not too intelligent a man, but as a revolutionary he was a failure. In his book about '98, *The Year of Liberty*, Thomas Pakenham makes a strong case to show that Lord Edward was scarcely entitled to the place he has always held in the pantheon of Ireland's patriot heroes.

Below, and also as it were above, these two small groups of educated men, other forces were involved and other motives at work. Nations that have a real, historically proved identity are, it would seem, almost indestructible. (Despite all the horrors of the past fifteen hundred years, what European nation has vanished without trace, since Asiatics overran Pannonia and, after the Roman Empire, Illyria? And even there faint echoes of a remote and foreign past linger on among Hungarians and Serbo-Croats.) On the other hand fictitious and rootless nation-states have seldom survived in Europe—or are surviving now in Africa—for more than a generation or two. Many were created, particularly by the first French republic and the first French empire, in this period. None lived long, and few were ever resurrected. Protestant Ireland, as a state, had anticipated the Cisalpine Republic, the Confederation of the Rhine and all those other, bogus political inventions still to come. The Irish Protestant Nation pre-deceased all of them, crushed in this case between the millstones of which the upper was the government in London, the nether its own native population, of varying religious faiths.

The nether millstone was the proletariat, particularly the rural proletariat or peasantry, both Catholic and Protestant. These uneducated and often illiterate masses had only the vaguest idea as to what reform meant. Stories passed rapidly from mouth to mouth, exaggerated in a fashion which has not died out, on

Irish tongues, with the near death of illiteracy and of the Irish language. Soothsayers could chant that the French were on the sea 'says the Shan Van Voght', and wise women would foresee, for 1798, 'a wet winter, a dry spring, a bloody summer, and no king'. The news moved fast across the southern counties and was interpreted in the only way that the dispossessed, spoliated, oppressed, hungry and land-hungry agricultural majority could possibly interpret such weird, exotic information: the English, the landlords and their Church were pulling out. Ireland would soon belong to them, to the Irish, once again. One can almost smell the turf of their fires, can almost taste the violent, sour home-brewed poteen, as the Whiteboys and the members of the other spontaneous, leaderless resistance groups met, and one can certainly sense the mounting excitement beneath the apparent tranquillity. For at last it seemed, pathetic though it now appears, that they had leaders again: Wolfe Tone, Napper Tandy, Lord Edward, the Emmet brothers and many more brave idealists. Soon all rural, Catholic Ireland was behind the United Irishmen. But by 1795 almost every United Irish leader was behind bars or across the seas. And when at last, three years later, a couple of French revolutionary generals arrived they discovered that the Irish masses, their cannon-fodder, believed that those foreign, usually atheist officers were in Ireland in order to restore the supremacy of the Church of Rome. The French were bewildered and surrendered. The Irish remained bewildered, were massacred, but seldom surrendered. How could they? To their conquerors they were traitors.

By 1795 the Irish masses were prepared emotionally for rebellion but were almost without their strategic, that is to say their Protestant, leaders, for their few Catholic leaders had realized, with the hierarchy, the folly or wickedness of importing Jacobinism into Ireland. (Here, a mention of the time element in the continuum, when communications were both slow and inaccurate. When Tone arrived in France, early in 1796, his journals show how keen he was to express his Jacobin enthusiasms. He realized rapidly that he was then tacking on what was very much an ebb-tide, and perhaps never understood why his only powerful patrons, Carnot and Hoche, were repeatedly asking him if FitzGibbon was not their best bet once the French had landed in Ireland.)

Strategically lost by lack of leadership, the Catholic masses were quite rapidly doomed tactically as well. The methods that the Protestant landlords had used, defensively, against the Whiteboys and other agrarian secret societies were now applied, offensively, against the population as a whole. Since the principal weapon available to possible rebels against authority was the pike, and since blacksmiths are the people who make pike-heads and carpenters make the shafts, a pogrom with torture and atrocities was carried out against the members of those two trades. In Leinster and Munster this was a moderately successful way of carrying out total war by a powerful minority against a poorly armed majority in a simple community, though the brutality probably contributed in a large measure to the ferocity, indeed the very arising, of the 1798 rebellion. In Ulster these methods were almost entirely successful. There conditions were very different.

In Ulster the reforms of 1793 were interpreted almost exactly as they were in the other three provinces: Catholic domination was on the way, and the farms would return to the native, Gaelic-speaking Irish. The reaction there was inevitable. The Dissenters had little, if any, love either for the Church of Ireland Ascendancy or for the English, or, come to that, for the parliaments that sat in Dublin or London. But they wanted their farms, and were prepared to fight for them. They did not wish to see their 'Popish' neighbours armed, and when the Irish government set about disarming their enemies they gave that government their full support, moral and physical. When, however, they felt that their government was being dilatory in protecting their interests they took the matter into their own hands. The Peep o' Day Boys was a peasant organization and, as such, disreputable in a society which accepted aristocratic values. When aristocratic rule was itself threatened by French democracy, squeamishness about methods and class became less important. Hannah Arendt has shown, in her great book *The Burden of Our Times* how the Boers of the Dutch Reformed Church rapidly became just another African tribe, despite their religion. This, by 1795, had happened to the Ulstermen, who had become just another type of Irishmen. Complete with secret societies, tenant versus landlord problems, imported English snobbery and class distinctions, second class citizenship, and the rest of the Irish rigmarole of that age. But like the Boers in South Africa, strong religious adherence made the Ulstermen, if

merely another tribe, yet a unique tribe. This tribalism must be
added to economic, that is to say land, interests that then divided them from the other inhabitants of the island. For the
Ulster farmer his farm belonged to him not only by right of
conquest—always suspect in Ireland—but by absolute, moral,
theological right. He was, in his eyes, a better man than his
Catholic neighbour, and, if he were unlucky enough to have
such a one, he would rather that that neighbour went away
before he were forced to question his own moral superiority.
If that neighbour refused to go away, and kept looking over the
fence, then in the ultimate crisis the only solution was first to
scribble 'Hell or Connaught' on his front door and then to burn
him out.

Tribalism is the curse of Ulster, from then till now. Just as the
Boers adopted slavery from the other African tribes, so did the
descendants of the Ulster settlers adopt the conspiratorial, secret
society, murder-in-the-night methods of the conquered Irish.
And both sides in what was a smothered civil war wherever they
collided were as remote as their cousins in the Alleganies
from the aristocracy, the intellectuals and the English. In
Armagh then, as in Armagh, parts of Belfast, or Derry today,
sectarian hatred was the prime political emotion. Then, as now,
the intervention of well-meaning, reasonable gentlemen from
London, Dublin or even from Ulster itself was, and is, regarded
by the rival factions as irrelevant. When their mutual fears and
loathing reach boiling point, only physical force can prevent
them from being at one another's throats.

In England, meanwhile, the Irish situation was as usual only
partly understood. Furthermore after 1793 it was viewed in terms
of a far greater English problem, which was neither more nor
less than the survival of English society and English institutions
as they then existed. One by one England's continental allies
were being defeated by French armies. Republics, more or less
Jacobin in tone, were being set up in Holland, Switzerland,
western Germany, northern Italy. Britain was becoming isolated
behind its navy's wooden walls and, according to the economic
theories of the age, was acquiring such a stupendous national
debt as to be almost bankrupt. Pitt and his colleagues realized
soon enough that this was an international crisis of a gravity
such as England had not seen since the defeat of the Spanish
Armada two centuries before. It was in this context that they

judged the situation in Ireland.

For them Ireland had a dual importance that far transcended natural Protestant affinities or liberal instincts to ameliorate the lot of the Catholics. The population of Ireland then constituted approximately one quarter of the population of the British Isles. The high birthrate, and the economic conditions in Ireland, meant that there was always a very large number of young men who could not find a living in their own country. Most of these, perhaps 80%, were Roman Catholics. With the gradual abolition of the penal laws, more and more of these surplus males had made their way into the British army and navy. Ireland in fact had become the great recruiting ground for the British forces. The Wild Geese were now flying east and not south. Regimental rolls of nominally English regiments, such as the Gloucesters, during that great war reveal a surprising number of Irish names, while the fleet, officered by Englishmen, was in large measure manned by Irish sailors. (These were not all volunteers, even in the sense of being forced by economic pressure into the navy. In Connaught in 1795, the commander-in-chief, Lord Carhampton, quite arbitrarily handed over suspected Defenders to the press gangs, thus almost bringing an end to Defenderism in that province, which remained quiet in the great rebellion three years later.) However, the British government did not wish their principal source of military and naval recruits, whether pressed or otherwise, to be politically and nationally disaffected. Therefore, with impeccable English logic, they decided that more appeasement of the Catholics, by means of further reforms, was desirable.

On the other hand they needed the English and Scottish regiments which, in increasing numbers, had been moved into Armagh and the other border counties as these were declared to be in a state of disorder and the equivalent of martial law therefore proclaimed. So a yeomanry and a militia were raised to free the regulars for service of more immediate importance to England. In Ulster this meant arming the Protestants, in the south the Catholics. The northern yeomanry was almost uniformly drawn from the members of the new Orange Order, and life for the few Catholics who had joined was made so difficult that they did not remain in the service long. In the south the militia was officered by Church of England Protestants, but even so it proved impossible to quarter battalions of different religious persuasions near one another in Ulster. The Ulster yeomanry rapidly became the armed branch of the Orange Order, entirely comparable to the B-Specials of recent years and perhaps to the Ulster Defence Regiment of tomorrow. Their job was, as they understood it, not primarily to preserve the peace but to ensure the continuation of Protestant domination by keeping down the Catholics. Dragooning the Ulster Catholics might be described as a peace-keeping operation: so might the activities of the SS in German-occupied territories during the Second World War or of the Russian tank crews and their local auxiliaries in Czecho-Slovakia today. In all three cases it worked. The British General Lake saw to it that the disaffected, that is to say Catholic or Jacobin elements, in Ulster were disarmed, with very considerable brutality. The violent and dangerous Dissenters who might have followed the United Irish leaders were given more congenial tasks, to their simple minds, than social revolution. Ulster remained quiet when the rebellion exploded in Leinster and Munster, and the minor rebellion that followed in the north was quickly and easily suppressed.

The other major motive in London's policy towards Ireland during this decade, and indeed throughout the long Revolutionary and Napoleonic wars, was to prevent a French encirclement of the British Isles by an occupation of the smaller island. This had been, and was to remain, a constant in all Britain's major wars, whether fought against Spaniards in the sixteenth century or Germans in the twentieth. There were two means of positive defence, the Royal Navy and, less important, the neutralization or annihilation of anti-English forces within Ireland itself, while attempting to preserve the loyalty of the population as a whole.

In the long history of Anglo-Irish relations the pendulum of British policy has always swung between benevolence and persecution, between appeasement and coercion. In times of placidity the swing is slow: in times of crisis it is usually rapid: in times of extreme crisis, such as 1795 or 1917 or 1969, attempts have been made to produce both carrot and stick simultaneously. Then the British government prefers to hand the stick to its subordinates, its Irish administrators, while itself offering the carrot. The ill-advised concept behind this method of colonial administration seems to be that the Irish can well be allowed to hate their Irish masters while being at the same time persuaded that their more remote English ones are well disposed. In effect this policy has always provoked, and is provoking today in the Six Counties of Ulster, a far higher degree of political schizophrenia among those Irishmen whom London chooses to govern than among the governed themselves. Never was this form of schizophrenia more apparent than in 1795. In the very month that Wolfe Tone felt forced to emigrate, at a time when extreme repressive measures were being taken against the pro-French United Irishmen, London sent over, as Lord Lieutenant, a garrulous Whig named Lord Fitzwilliam, who knew nothing of Irish affairs and who talked, too much and too quickly, about more reforms in the Catholic interest. The reaction among the Catholic and the Protestant countrymen was precisely what the Castle had expected, a worsening of the tension. FitzGibbon, who was now Lord Clare, saw to it that Fitzwilliam was recalled within three months. By then Ireland, and particularly the north, was very close to open, not smothered, civil war. From all this alien and unrealistic liberalism there emerged, first, the sectarian battles associated with the Diamond and then the assumption of total, authorized power by the Protestants which continues in Northern Ireland until today.

There was at this time no police force in Ireland in any meaningful sense of the word. The Castle had what we would call a secret police, which was highly efficient, particularly in Dublin. Conspiracy breeds informers and the numerous Irish secret societies did not keep their secrets hidden from the authorities for long. The law, as it affected the masses, was administered by magistrates, who were simply the landlords acting in their capacity as justices of the peace. More serious cases were tried by the Grand Juries, the jurors being selected by the county Sheriff, himself a political appointee chosen by Dublin Castle. Since there was no police force until 1822, the responsibility for dealing with riots, unlawful assembly, and other such affairs, whether political in motive or not, devolved on the military, which meant, increasingly, on the local militia. Thus the whole system of the law, from top to bottom, could be easily, and usually was, rigged in the interests of the Ascendancy. Although the Roman Catholics were no longer virtual outlaws, the emergence of Orangeism in Ulster and, more important, its faint acceptance as an ally against revolution by the Ascendancy, made it very unlikely that a Roman Catholic could expect justice, at any level, in that province. From the yeoman who arrested him to the judge upon the bench who sentenced him, he would find himself in the hands of Protestants, and embattled Protestants at that, fighting to preserve what they regarded as their rights of supremacy and, in Ulster particularly, armed with the certainty of moral and religious superiority.

The corollary was, and has remained, true. It is even harder to convict a Protestant extremist of a crime that is even remotely connected with sectarian, i.e. anti-Catholic, politics than it is to ensure pardon for a Catholic involved in such activities. The secret society ethic, which has always prevailed in large areas of rural Irish life, leads directly to the intimidation of witnesses. In the last century in Southern Ireland it was not only 'unpatriotic' but also extremely unwise to give evidence against Fenians or the killers of landlords: to this day the Civic Guards in the Republic find it extremely difficult to make a case against members of the I.R.A. and indeed, unless murder is involved, frequently do not seem to try. To this, in Ulster, was added the fact that almost all the Protestant male population was soon involved in the Orange Order, a secret society with signs and passwords, and dedicated not only to the preservation of Protestant domination *at all costs* but also to mutual self-protection. An Orange jury was, and is, hardly likely to find a fellow Orangeman guilty for promoting ends in which both he and they believe implicitly. One might just as well expect a white jury in the American Deep South to find against a neighbour who has used violence against a negro in what he and they regard as the defence of white racial supremacy. Members of the Mafia, similarly, do not often get sentenced in Sicilian courts.

The reader will, I trust, excuse this long digression from the affairs of Ulster to those of Ireland and indeed of Europe. The microcosm is incomprehensible without the macrocosm, the story of the past becomes meaningless unless it is told in relationship to the whole. With the establishment of the Orange Order and the Orange Lodges in 1795, a formula was stated, a frame of mind created, that with modifications has endured until today. These will be presented in the later part of this book, for it was in the 1790s that modern Ulster came into existence.

The history of Ireland as a whole, during this period of parturition which became after a hundred and more years partition, can be briefly summarized. In 1796 the French sent an invasion fleet to Ireland. It was commanded by General Hoche, but his ship was blown off course. His second-in-command, General Grouchy, sat in Bantry Bay with some 10,000 excellent soldiers for a few days over Christmas, but did not land his expeditionary force, which would almost certainly have overrun all Ireland. (A dinner party of loyal Protestants was held in Dublin at this time. A toast was proposed, and drunk, to 'the wooden walls of England'. A second toast was proposed, and drunk, to 'the wooden walls of Ireland'. When somebody then asked the proposer to what on earth or water he was referring, he replied that they had drunk to the colonels of the militia.) During the period when the French were on the sea there were no risings by the now almost leaderless United Irishmen.

French strategy was not radically altered in the Anglo-French war by this mishap, but the emphasis was changed. International Jacobinism, that is to say the exportation of revolutionary doctrine and methods, was no longer the main strand of French policy. The principal purpose of the campaigns of the Directory was less to bring freedom than to bring back loot. And Napoleon Bonaparte brought back millions from Italy. The next country on the list to be plundered was England and Bonaparte's *Armée d'Angleterre* was assembled along the Channel with this aim in view. Ireland had little to offer, being too poor. On the other hand it remained strategically of high value in the larger context. Therefore in 1797 and 1798 the invasion of Ireland was handed over to the Dutch navy, which was to transport French troops together with Wolfe Tone and such Irishmen as he had been able to muster, a mere handful as it turned out. Holland, then a French satellite state called the Batavian Republic, had a great maritime tradition and its entire navy was committed to the operation. With immense slowness, warships, transports and men were collected in the Texel. The British fleets based on Spithead and the Nore mutinied, flew the red flag and declared, briefly, a Floating Republic. Tone hoped that their Irish and republican crews would sail the British warships to Irish ports and help the Irish peasants who had risen in Leinster and Munster. The rebellion of 1798, ill co-ordinated for it was almost leaderless, was rapidly put down by British and Irish troops. The mutiny in the British fleet was also quite quickly suppressed, and when at last the Dutch warships put to sea that same British fleet blew the Dutchmen into matchwood at the

Battle of Camperdown. Any large invasion of Ireland was now off. So for the next few years was a direct attack on England. Bonaparte marched his *Armée d'Angleterre* down to the Mediterranean, and set off to plunder Egypt, perhaps Turkey, and with luck India as well. That army never returned.

Small French forces, little more than the equivalent of commando raids, were sent to an Ireland which was now being 'pacified', the gallows being the principal means of pacification. They achieved nothing. In one raid Wolfe Tone was captured, and soon dead. In another Nappy Tander became so drunk that he was put back on board and carted back to France. In this atmosphere of tragic and squalid failure the Protestant Nation died, indeed voted itself out of existence in a bribed Irish parliament. But at the same time a new Protestant Nation, or perhaps more accurately a sub-nation, was being created in the province of Ulster.

CHAPTER NINE

The Diamond is a small village near Portadown in the County Armagh. Portadown itself lies on the Armagh-Belfast road, eleven miles from the one and twenty-seven from the other. This was among the most troubled areas in the 1790s. Portadown was then a new Scots-Irish settlement. In the villages Dissenters and Roman Catholics, or more accurately in the context Peep o' Day Boys and Defenders, were in direct confrontation and the same names constantly crop up in the chronicles of sectarian violence. Two of the major Protestant land-owning families in the district were the Copes (Jacobean settlers) of Loughgall and the Blackers (Cromwellians) of Carrickblacker, *anglice* Blacker's Rock, Church of Ireland gentry. The inn at the Diamond was run by a certain Dan Winter.

The reforms of 1793 were misunderstood by the peasantry. The Roman Catholics interpreted the extension of the franchise as the first step towards the expropriation of Protestant farms. The Protestant peasants saw that their value as voters to their landlords was automatically diminished and their hold on the land therefore less certain. True, the Protestant peasantry was still armed and a high proportion of them trained as Volunteers, while the Catholics were mostly disarmed. But in this atmosphere of reform, of dismantling the penal laws, would government continue to keep the Catholics defenceless? The more militant Dissenters set about disarming their armed Catholic neighbours themselves. The Roman Catholic response was to increase the strength of the Defenders, which became yet another secret society. This escalation was at grass-roots level. The Church of Ireland gentry and the leaders, lay or clerical, of the Roman Catholics were as yet scarcely involved and indeed regarded the brawling between Defenders and Peep o' Day Boys as little more than a normal, deplorable aspect of the Irish plebeian scene not unlike the present-day attitude of the British middle class towards the apparently pointless brawls that enliven English and Scottish soccer matches.*

The situation was, however, further escalated in 1793 by the creation of an Irish militia, in order to free British regiments for the French war. This meant, in most of Ireland, the arming— by the government—of Roman Catholic regiments, with Protestant officers it is true, but nevertheless the handing out of guns, officially, to those whom the Dissenters regarded as their mortal enemies. And soon enough the Defenders had their cells within many of the militia units. In Ulster it was, in 1794, government policy to create militia units containing both Protestants and Catholics. This, as has already been explained, failed and the Ulster militia and yeomanry units soon to be created rapidly got rid of unwanted Catholics to become a purely Protestant force. The Defenders reacted by forming illegal, quasi-military organizations of their own. All this was still at the grass-roots level, but others were beginning to watch developments with closer attention and growing disquiet. As early as 1793 a wealthy Presbyterian farmer in the County Tyrone by the name of Wilson set about forming a more responsible organization than that of the Peep o' Day Boys as a counterforce to the Defenders. Others must have been thinking as he was. The result was a new secret society, complete with signs, passwords and an oath to defend Protestantism and the Constitution. Wilson called his society the Orange Boys, but for the next two years it remained very small.

In the spring of 1795 a cock-fight was held in Dan Winter's inn at the Diamond. There was a brawl and a Defender was beaten up by Peep o' Day Boys. It is not hard to visualize the dreary pub, the blood lust aroused by the cruel sport, the tension mounting as the drinks were lowered. Among the Irish lower classes alcohol and violence go hand in hand, and petty incidents such as this have very frequently sparked off a long chain of tragedy. Nor do we know what this particular Catholic

---

* Nor is the parallel entirely fanciful, at least so far as Scottish football brawls are concerned. Glasgow is almost as Scots-Irish a city as is Belfast. The Presbyterians there hold Orange parades, and the brawls between the supporters of the two soccer clubs are, in some measure, sectarian in origin. The Glasgow Celtic team is traditionally supported by the Roman Catholics, Glasgow Rangers by the Presbyterians. Nowadays, of course, a lot of the bottle-throwing and drunken razor-slashing is mere hooliganism, as it is altogether among English 'soccer fans'.

was doing at the cock-fight. Perhaps he was a stranger, passing through, though few strangers would normally pass through the Diamond. If he was a local man he must either have been amazingly naïf, or so passionate an attendant at cock-fights that no danger to life and limb would keep him away. Or perhaps he was a coat-trailer: for Dan Winter was an extremist and his pub the meeting place for Peep o' Day Boys.

The reaction to the fight was not abnormal. The following day Protestant and Catholic bands assembled. Insults were shouted and occasionally shots exchanged, but as usual at extreme range. Then two weeks later two of these bands collided head on. The Defenders were returning from a wake, the Protestants from a dance. It is safe to assume that men in both groups had been drinking, some to excess. A free-for-all took place and there were casualties.

The County Armagh authorities immediately realized how serious the situation was, and moved in four companies of militia, Protestant militia of course, and a magistrate. The result was the arrest of fifty Defenders and two Peep o' Day Boys, a ratio not unknown in later attempts at peace-keeping in Ulster. A suggestion by the Armagh authorities that the entire working class be disarmed was not taken up, nor a proposal that Dan Winter's licence as an inn-keeper be revoked.

The Defenders, realizing once again that they could expect little if any justice or protection from the authorities, set about improving both their organization and their armaments. They established contact with other Defender groups in the border counties and further south (the Defenders were very active that July in Meath and Kildare) and a very vague sort of staff for this embryonic peasant army must have come into existence, but though we can trace its influence we know little about it. More important, the Defenders talked about an attack on Dan Winter's inn. For the moment gathering in the harvest kept the peasants in the fields. It was probably this talk of revenge, exaggerated as it passed from mouth to mouth, that reached Dublin Castle, on August 27th, as a report that a massacre of the Protestants in the North was planned for 'after the harvest'. That there was a plan is certain, but it was scarcely one for a rebellion, though no doubt it might have developed into this.

On September 14th, with the harvest gathered in, the Defenders began to assemble in the neighbourhood of Tentaraghan, not far from the Diamond, and started looting Protestant farms in the neighbourhood. Protestant bands assembled and attacked the homes of Defenders. By September 18th the rival forces faced each other from hilltops overlooking the Diamond, and shots were exchanged at very long range. At this point three Roman Catholic priests and two magistrates intervened and articles of reconciliation were drawn up, each side putting up a surety of £500—a very large sum indeed in the Ireland of the age—to keep the peace.

Meanwhile the news had spread and large bodies of Defenders were marching towards 'the battle'. A fairly formidable force from Tyrone was prevented from crossing the river Blackwater by James Verner, father of a future Orange Grand Master, and four (sic) members of the Mayo Militia. But other Defender bands reached the Diamond, did not consider themselves bound by the articles of reconciliation and insisted on attacking Dan Winter's inn. It has been estimated that the number of Defenders involved, including those turned back by Verner, amounted to 'several thousand', and that perhaps 400 took part in the assault on the pub.

This happened early on the morning of September 21st. The garrison, if that be the correct word, was a couple of dozen Protestants. The Defenders lost, in dead, figures that vary between 16 and 45: an eye-witness said 30. It was a Protestant victory, for the Defenders then faded away carrying with them their uncounted dead. But it was far more important than the normal skirmish. The Protestants were frightened by the emergence, inefficient as it had proved, of a Roman Catholic organization that could and would fight—the first such for a century. The reaction was at all levels. In Ulster the most important was the immediate formation, that same evening and at the Diamond, of the Orange Order.

The leading spirits were three local landowners and magistrates, Atkinson, Cope and Verner. They were high churchmen, and were interested that the Church of Ireland gentry should take and retain control of the new society. (The rich Presbyterian farmer, Wilson, from the County Tyrone who had created the Orange Boys two years before was present at the Diamond and at the meeting immediately after the battle, when the decision to form the Orange Order was taken. He did not, however, join the new movement, perhaps because his bid for its leadership was unacceptable to the squires on social grounds, possibly because they would not accept his rougher followers, probably for a combination of both reasons.) The formation of secret societies was of course strictly illegal, and of this the land-lord-magistrates were well aware. Their excuse for breaking the law they were supposed to enforce was both dual and banal: first that the Defenders were themselves an illegal society and had compounded the felony by breaking the articles of reconciliation: secondly that the Battle of the Diamond had shown the inability of the authorities to preserve law and order which in turn made it necessary for respectable Protestants to combine in self-defence.

The emphasis was very much on respectability. It was repeatedly stated that former Peep o' Day Boys were not acceptable as members of the new society, though it is certain that this exclusion was not and could not be enforced. However the cost of admission, £1.2.6, was high enough to keep out the poorest, and therefore presumably the roughest, Dissenter elements. Nor was Dan Winter's pub acceptable as a headquarters because of his and his inn's association with the more plebeian movement.

The society's first headquarters were therefore moved a few miles to an inn at Loughgall run by a certain James Sloan, who became the first titular head of the new movement. He himself seems to have been a shrewd publican who realized that this would bring him a lot of trade. He was also well thought of by the local gentry to whom he was no doubt suitably respectful. And Loughgall was, from their point of view, a very proper village, owned since the first plantation by the Cope family. In 1766 its Protestant population of 588 had contained the unusually high proportion of 464 Church of Ireland members, while the Catholics had then numbered 469. By 1795 the population must have increased, though not considerably. By then the Catholics probably outnumbered all the Protestants slightly. Thus though sectarian feeling was bitter, its overt manifestations were slightly less brutal and coarse than in places like the Diamond where Catholics and Dissenters, rather than Catholics and Episcopalians, lived cheek by jowl. Furthermore the latent animosity between the Dissenters and the Church of Ireland made it more difficult for the Peep o' Day Boys to take over the new society if it were centred in a place like James Sloan's pub in Loughgall, and correspondingly easier for the

Verners, Atkinsons, Blackers and Copes to control and even to take part in the new movement, though at first they did this somewhat gingerly.

One of the earliest to do so was a young man named Stewart Blacker, then an undergraduate on vacation from Trinity College Dublin. His memoirs, written many years later, now repose in the Armagh Museum. He had himself been present at the Diamond and he recorded in those memoirs: 'Very few of the resident gentry joined us in the first instance. Of those few were my old friend, Joseph Atkinson, the Rev. George Marshall of Dromore .... Captain Clarke of Summerisland and soon after the young Verner of Churchill. Old Mr Verner (the victor of the Blackwater) never joined us as an affiliated member though he took a great interest in the proceedings of the association.' He also mentions Lord Northland of Dungannon, and a Mr. Brownlow of Lurgan, as very early members though perhaps not as early as September, 1795.

It must not however be imagined that those members of the Ascendancy immediately assumed control of the Orange Society. Two weeks after the society's foundation a local gentleman by the name of Richard Jephson wrote to Lord Charlemont, the great Armagh magnate who combined the liberalism of the Enlightenment with the anti-Catholicism of the Ascendancy: 'It is impossible for the protestant gentry to keep up the farce of impartiality between the parties, or to disavow the absolute necessity of giving a considerable degree of support to the protestant party, who, from the activities of the two Copes, have got the name of "Orange Boys".'

If some of the Church of Ireland gentry were now looking towards an alliance with the more militant members of their own and the dissenting churches their attitude, for the time being, remained one of benevolent neutrality coupled with a scepticism based on class and religious distinctions. Some of them, eventually most of them, were prepared to use Orangeism against that other, increasingly Jacobin dominated and essentially working-class movement, the Society of United Irishmen. (We have here a fairly close parallel to the apparent but false community of interests that led many of the German upper middle class and a smaller proportion of the German aristocracy to support Hitler and his proletarian hordes in their fight for power with the Communists.) But few of the gentry, even in

Armagh, were at this time prepared to throw in their lot with the Orange Boys. The warrants that bestowed membership of the secret society on aspirants were signed by the publican, Sloan, not by some Atkinson or Cope. And the actual procedure of swearing the oath, with its direct reflection of Whiteboy, Defender and Peep o' Day methods must have been distasteful to a class in which even Free Masonry had then made only limited progress. I quote from Hereward Senior's *Orangeism in Ireland and Britain*, on which I have relied for much of the material in this chapter.

'The early meetings were secret with initiations and oaths administered on hilltops and behind hedges in the manner of any other agrarian secret society. Blacker described the first meetings of his lodge held in the frame wall of a partially constructed house at the crossroads of Tanderagee and Lurgan near the gate of Carrick. "An assemblage of men, young and old, collected upon these occasions as far as could be seen by the light of a few candles—some seated on heaps of sods or rude blocks of wood; most of them armed with guns of every age and calibre ... There was a stern solemnity in the reading of the scripture and administering the oath to the newly admitted brethren which was calculated to produce a deep impression and did so." The original oath ran, "I, ... do solemnly swear that I will, to the utmost of my power, support and defend the king and his heirs as long as he or they support the protestant ascendancy."'

Hardly the sort of pantomine and mumbo-jumbo to appeal to a Lord Charlemont or even a Mr. Cope. Yet the gentry needed the muscles of the Dissenters, or so they thought, and the peasants needed leaders. Thus were the two factions drawn together. For the next few years, indeed for the next two generations, the problem was how they should coalesce. In many respects this problem still bedevils the Orange Order, Unionism, call it what you will, in Ireland or at least in Ulster. A common enemy, be it Jacobinism, Roman Catholicism, Irish Republicanism, revolutionary Socialism, can produce some odd bed fellows in the Irish other room. And in this sense, the real sense, Orangeism has always been reactionary—since its very birth in 1795. But then it was itself a reaction against reaction, Defenderism, itself a reaction against the Peep o' Day Boys, themselves a reactionary force against Roman Catholic reaction to Plantation and so on.

But still the problem of this reactionary alliance between the Church of Ireland and the Dissenters remained one of respectability. If the thugs of Dan Winter's pub were to be discarded for the strong-arm men of James Sloan's, they still needed, in 1795 as Paisley's men need today, the lace curtain that only the gentry can provide in Ireland, or else become a straight revolutionary force in a country where they are in the minority, and where lace curtains are highly prized. And no sooner was the Orange Order created than its own little lace curtain, in Loughgall, was torn to shreds by what were called the Armagh outrages.

So long as they felt threatened by the Defenders the Protestant peasants had needed the support of the gentry, that is to say of the landlords who were also the magistrates and, through them, of the administration, the militia and ultimately of the military. For the peasantry, too, it was an alliance of convenience and of fear, for there was little love for their landlords among the Armagh Dissenters. Therefore as soon as their victory at the Diamond had removed the Catholic threat, they set about exploiting that victory in their traditional fashion, with the age-old intention of driving out the Catholics. 'Hell or Connaught' signs were nailed to Catholic cottages. Bands of Protestant peasants would set out at night, often from Dan Winter's or James Sloan's pubs, to terrorize those Catholics who refused to go, to loot their homes, destroy their furniture and smash their looms. They did not usually burn the cottages, for they intended to move into them when their present inhabitants had been driven out. However the Catholics sometimes burned them themselves before leaving, less out of spite than for the good reason that by laying the blame for the fire on their enemies they could claim compensation under the so-called Whiteboy Act, passed ironically enough to insure the property of Protestant landlords against Catholic agrarian crime in other parts of the island. How many Catholics were in fact forced to flee their homes during this period of outrage, which lasted for about a year, it is hard to say. Lord Altamount, a great landowner in Connaught, wrote to Dublin Castle in November of 1796 that some 4,000 refugees had reached Mayo from Armagh. This would indicate some 700 families in that county of Connaught alone. Another figure given is 1400 families in all. Blacker, an Orangeman, puts the figure as low as 130. He may well be right. When dealing with unauthenticated Irish statistics it is usually wiser to look for exaggeration rather than for underestimates. On the other hand when evaluating Blacker's figure the reverse applies, for obvious political reasons.

The Orangemen were quick to deny any complicity in these outrages. This is almost certainly true in that the Orange leaders, the Verners and Atkinsons, would surely not have ordered, organized, let alone have taken part in these nocturnal forays. On the other hand it is equally certain that just as many individual Peep o' Day Boys who had fought at the Diamond must have joined the new society, so many individual Orangemen must have taken part in the outrages. This got them a bad name with the gentry, for the sound economic reason that civil unrest in Armagh, as usual, sent down the rents. Furthermore the small shopkeepers who had joined the Orange Order for protection against the Defenders saw their profits decline as the county slid towards chaos. But neither class deserted the Orange cause, even though its claim to respectability was severely comprised, at least in the area controlled from James Sloan's pub.

Elsewhere it was spreading rapidly. Lord Northland formed a lodge of 'noblemen and gentlemen' in Dungannon, for example. Lodges were founded in Belfast and indeed all over Ulster. Military lodges were created within the militia units. Within a year there were probably close on 100 lodges in Ulster. The movement spread to Dublin and the Commander-in-Chief, Lord Carhampton, the officer who had despatched the Connaught Defenders to the Royal Navy, either joined the order or was an active sympathizer—to the very considerable annoyance of Clare and the Castle. In 1796 an Orange Lodge was formed by undergraduates at Trinity College.

The Irish government was opposed to the creation of the Orange Order for three good reasons, one political, one economic and one moral. Politically no government can tolerate the existence of an alternative military force, which is what this alliance of gentry and mob, with its infiltration of the militia and, soon enough, of the army, must inevitably tend to become. (Again there is a parallel with Nazi Germany. Once Hitler was head of the government, when it came to a choice between the army, which disliked him, and his irregular SA, who adored him, he chose the generals and murdered the SA leaders.) Furthermore the Irish government that then existed had been brought about by the action of the Volunteers only fifteen years before, and was therefore well aware of what Volunteers could do and did not wish to see a similar force, outside of its control, come into existence. Finally the French War, and the mounting threat of invasion, made tranquillity in Ireland a prime consideration.

Economically the spread of Orangeism outside Armagh was accompanied by a spread of Protestant atrocities in the North and counter-action by what must henceforth be called the United Irishmen in the South. These latter do not directly concern us here. In Armagh, the newspaper *The Northern Star* reported in November, 1795, that seventy-six peaceful inhabitants of that town were dragged from their beds by Orangemen led by two sergeants of the militia: in the following month a Portadown linen manufacturer's house was burned down by a Protestant mob: also in December a Catholic was murdered while seated by his fire. There were incidents in Belfast: a millowner named Magill was told to dismiss his Catholic workers, and when he did not do so his mill was burned. The economic damage caused by the Armagh outrages was spreading, and this was directly connected with the spread of militant Orangeism.

Finally, there was the basic moral issue, well summed up by Lord Gosford, who had recently succeeded Lord Charlemont as governor of Armagh, and who said, at the very end of 1795:

'The only crime which the wretched objects of this merciless persecution are charged with, is a crime of easy proof; it is simply a profession of the Roman Catholic faith. A lawless banditti have constituted themselves judges of this species of delinquency, and the sentence they pronounce is equally concise and terrible; it is nothing less than a confiscation of all property and immediate banishment.'

The men in the Castle, entirely behind the principle of Protestant Ascendancy, were also in general civilized gentlemen for whom such methods were not only most obnoxious but also threatened to undermine the whole morality on which the highly unstable state that they administered was based. They and their class had decided that the Penal Laws enforced by the State were both undesirable and unworkable and had repealed almost all of them: Penal Laws enforced by mob rule were far, far worse. As early as October, 1795, General Dalrymple, who commanded the troops in the Belfast area, had written to Dublin that he distrusted the Protestant gentry and that he feared lest their involvement with the fanatics might make for a permanent state of smothered civil war.

The government had already reacted with such means as were at its disposal. In late 1795 troops were moved into Armagh and this peace-keeping force undoubtedly served, in some degree, as a damper, even though the soldiers were usually raw recruits and were scattered about the countryside in small numbers, from a platoon to a company. Soon enough the Protestant extremists realized that these men were not only subject to propaganda but were also quite incapable of really enforcing the law. Furthermore, with all Ireland close to the boil, there were no reinforcements available for Ulster. Early in 1796 the outrages were resumed, not only now in Armagh but also in South Down and the other border counties.

The government also introduced an Insurrection Bill in February of 1796. Though directed primarily against the United Irishmen, it gave its officers powers to deal with Ulster. The military now had the authority to search houses for arms, to arrest strangers who could not account for their business, and a curfew from dusk to dawn was automatically imposed on any locality declared to be in a state of disturbance, which applied to large and soon larger areas of Ulster. The administration of secret oaths was also made an offence. In a debate on these measures in the Irish House of Commons Grattan, who was more qualified than anyone to speak for the Protestant nationalist liberals, maintained that the laws already in existence were being applied against the Roman Catholic and not against the Protestant rebels. The government spokesmen, including a Colonel Craddock who had been sent to Armagh to restore order there, explained that the intimidation of witnesses made it extremely difficult to secure the conviction of a Protestant criminal in an Ulster court of law. (This problem was endemic in all Ireland at that time and has remained so until today, at least so far as politically-motivated crime is concerned, in both parts of the island.) The government promised tougher action and were as good as their word. The Attorney-General himself, a man named Wolfe who was close to Clare both in office and in political allegiance, was sent to the Armagh spring assizes. He prosecuted most rigorously and announced his intention to prove to Irishmen that 'whatever their religious profession might be ... they might rely on receiving protection from every species of oppression.' Two Defenders and two Orangemen, described as such in the press, were sentenced to death. In view of what had happened over the previous six months the numerical equilibrium looks suspect, but at least Dan Winter's bullyboys could not now expect *invariably* to get away with their brutal 'Hell or Connaught' activities.

The respectable Orangemen, the Verners and Atkinsons and their like, now found themselves in opposition to both wings of the Protestant Ascendancy in Ireland, to Clare as to Grattan. The Viceroy, Lord Camden, who had only arrived in Ireland to succeed the liberal Lord Fitzwilliam in March of 1795, believed at this time, erroneously, that the landlord class in the North could at least control their own Protestant peasantry. Until the summer, the landlords were hesitant. Undoubtedly many of them felt betrayed by their co-religionists in Dublin but they were also sufficiently educated to realize that Dublin was pre-occupied with the threat posed by the Catholic United Irishmen, which was of course the ultimate and fatal threat not only to themselves but also to their Protestant tenantry. Thus was a further step taken in the psychological division between the Protestants of Ulster and other Irishmen, whether of the Protestant or Catholic faiths.

The discussion of historical might-have-beens is futile but interesting, and nowhere more so than in Ireland's tragic history. If Grouchy had landed his troops in Bantry Bay in that same year of 1796 . . . If, in the previous winter, the Irish government had encouraged, and not discouraged, the gentlemen in the North to take over the anti-Catholic Orange Order, might Ulster have become integrated into, rather than increasingly separated from, the rest of Ireland? Speculation, pure speculation. Nor are immediate political decisions taken *sub specie aeternitatis*, which no doubt is just as well. Dublin Castle did not, and probably for psychological reasons could not, embrace the Protestant extremists of the North: but being preoccupied with Catholic extremists in the South no more could it destroy them. Representing as it did a small minority of persons and a large majority of property that government could, faced by Jacobinism, only attempt to build dykes against a rising and fast-flowing tide. This meant that it could only rely on measures and not on men, for its primary purpose was to prevent the redistribution of property. Hence a hiatus, a lull, in the affairs of Ulster. This lasted only for a few months as the Orange bands realized how inefficient were the military and while the landlords and merchants took stock of their own position.

The Irish, wherever they may be, tend to fancy parades, to marching about, to commemorating remote events by so doing, and to the production thereby of strong political emotions. Even nowadays in the Republic of Ireland, in the Catholic areas of Belfast and abroad, St. Patrick's day, the saint's day of Ireland's apostle is celebrated by parades of a patriotic rather than of a religious nature, though that is not altogether absent. Amidst all the charming pageantry of Gaelic music, American bands led by very short skirted drum majorettes, and fanciful floats, there is an almost tangible element of force, of tough politicians, of armed men, even of tanks. In these years of grave potential crisis the annual celebration of the date on which St. Patrick is said to have lit the paschal fire on Slane Hill and thereby destroyed the ancient, pagan Ireland of Finn and Diarmaid and Cuchulainn, has become, and not for the first time, a celebration of that nationality which St. Patrick set out to convert.

This is indeed not new. The Glorious Twelfth, the annual celebration of Protestant victory at the Boyne, was celebrated with parades, bands, and drums, with especial emphasis in 1796. (To hear the drums and to see the hilltop bonfires, as did I in 1941 when a young soldier out on an exercise and under the impression that Ulster's like my own enemy was far away, is indeed an impressive lesson in the immutability of the historical conscience.) The parades, the speeches and perhaps above all the drums of July 12th, 1796, prevented the Orange Order from degeneration into yet another ephemeral organization of peasant hatred and agricultural crime. The phoenix is a tiresome, dirty bird, and perhaps nowhere more so than in its fiery Irish nest.

By June, 1796, Armagh was fairly quiet again and some of the Catholics driven out in the previous winter were beginning to return. The gentry, frightened away from the Orange Order by the government's hostility and particularly by the Insurrection Act, were beginning to have second, or rather third, thoughts. And for this there was a very good reason in another part of Ulster, the almost solidly Presbyterian counties of Antrim and northern Down, with between them the growing and prosperous Protestant city of Belfast.

Although the majority of the United Irishmen were by now

Irish-speaking Roman Catholic peasants in the southern counties, interested as always in the acquisition of land and the abolition of landlords and tithes, the movement's intellectual leadership remained in Belfast, where its principal journal, *The Northern Star*, was printed. Those Protestant or atheistical men —for they were increasingly tinged with Jacobinism—were a most interesting group. They looked both forwards and back, forward to an Irish democracy freed of all connection with England and hence without an Anglo-Irish aristocracy or landlord class which would presumably be guillotined or driven out, and without an established church: backwards to a romantic Ireland. For a generation the pagan or semi-pagan past had been fashionable in the Germanic lands, Ossian and Scottish ballads in Britain, the most primitive poetry and music in Germany. (It is interesting to note how small was the appeal of such artistic nostalgia to the French or Italians of the period, save that it did find an echo of a sort in Rousseau's nonsensical construction of the noble savage, not himself a Frenchman of course: for historical sustenance the Latins have almost always preferred to cast their imaginations back to the Empire of Rome. Nor did or do the Irish of more purely Gaelic stock attach as much importance as perhaps they should to the artistic achievements of their forebears, maybe because they take these for granted.) As early as the 1790s, therefore, Protestant intellectuals in Dublin but even more so in Belfast developed an ideology that contained an essential paradox. The present was to be a synthesis of the remote past and the immediate future, an Ireland in which religion was to be of no importance and a new social structure was to claim legitimacy from an ancient and mist-enshrouded system in which property was still almost unknown. This ideological dream, attractive and indeed seductive, has remained, *mutatis mutandis,* in Irish minds until today, in such diverse minds as those of Emmet and the early Fenians, of Yeats and Pearse, of some students at U.C.D., Trinity and Queen's University Belfast today. The fact that the social arrangements of ancient Ireland were at least as brutal as those of their descendants is irrelevant to historical myth-makers in Ireland, as to such fantasists everywhere else. It first attained political importance among the Belfast revolutionaries in the late eighteenth century, who desired both Jacobinism and 'to revive and perpetuate the ancient music and poetry of Ireland'. In other countries nostalgic, revolutionary

UNION IS STRENGTH.

Jn Bull. "HERE ARE A FEW THINGS TO GO ON WITH, BROTHER, AND I 'LL SOON PUT YOU IN A WAY TO EARN YOUR OWN LIVING."

Cartoon in *Punch* by the Irish artist Richard Doyle who designed the cover of *Punch* used for over a century.

'The Fort', Hillsborough, *c.* 1870.

Henry Cooke, 1788-1868.

romanticism, has, in the last century and this, provided the cultural and intellectual sap of many authoritarian régimes. In Ireland, perhaps because of the religious faith of the great majority of the populace, it has always been suspect, for it is essentially pagan. Yet it still has its appeal to a minority, particularly among the young. Though they may think of themselves as Communists, Trotskyites or Maoists, the appeal is that of the irrational to a group that believes it has eliminated from its thought what it regards as the irrationality of the Christian faith.

The Episcopalian landlords and merchants of Armagh and the other disturbed counties in 1796 were, we may assume, quite immune both to such ideological vagaries and to historical nostalgia. For them history began with the Plantations, reached its nadir in 1641, its zenith at the Battle of the Boyne and the present was to be seen not in terms of Jacobin Paris but in those of the Battle of the Diamond. Few can have cared about what the Belfast intellectuals were thinking: few unaware that the Dissenters of Antrim and Down were rapidly being armed with the old muskets that had belonged to the Volunteers and with new pikes, to act as the auxiliaries of French forces that were getting ready to invade all Ireland. In this fear of the revolutionary forces being created in the extreme Northeast they were in agreement with Dublin Castle. But since the British army was being drained away to fight the French in what was then a losing war, and since the militia was largely manned by their Catholic enemies, they looked to two means of self-defence, which were in many ways intertwined: the creation by the landlords of a yeomanry, consisting in principle of their own tenants whose reliability they knew: and the gain of control over the militant Protestant working class which might be provided by the Orange Order as it never could be by the drunken, undisciplined Peep o' Day Boys. To test the viability of this hypothesis, the organization of the annual parades on the Glorious Twelfth was of prime importance. That these parades were both massive and peaceful—a report to the Castle states that 'three or four thousand protestants and dissenters paraded and dispersed peacefully'—both shows that this massive demonstration, most of which involved a march to the Diamond, was well organized, presumably by the gentry, and also convinced those who were hesitant that here at hand was a most useful force to be used, when need arose, against their enemies both to the northeast, in the south, and preparing to march up the gangplanks in Brest and Lorient. That successful parade, even more than the Battle of the Diamond, marked the birth of the Orange Order as the political force in Northern Ireland which it has remained.

CHAPTER TEN

The decade or so that followed upon the Battle of the Diamond, and particularly the years between 1796 and 1801, are of the greatest importance in the history of Ulster, of Ireland, of the British Isles, and of all Europe. It is necessary, therefore, to return to the macrocosm in order to find out what pressure then—as now—international forces of the greatest power were exercising upon this small province at almost the extreme northwest of Europe. Continental Europe, as usual, twitched the rope. By the time the wave reached Ulster, via Paris, London and Dublin, it had been transmogrified not only by its intermediaries but also because time had passed and the initial twitch was part of history. It is much the same today. Despite modern systems of communications, and the very superior organizational abilities of the Russian Communists compared to those of the French Jacobins, what began or begins in Paris or Moscow assumes a very different form by the time it reaches Belfast. This delaying action in parts of the rope is detectable throughout its whole length.

As with the Spanish threat of a century and a half earlier, it took the English several years to grasp the perils of Jacobinism to their society, persons and property. By the time that they had done so not only was Jacobinism moribund, an ever smaller ingredient of French imperial expansion, but Britain's effective allies were being, if they had not already been, eliminated one by one by French revolutionary armies in Italy and, more important perhaps, in Northern and Central Europe. Britain found itself almost alone against a nascent imperialist power which still bore upon its banners a Jacobin image. This meant an ideological war. This in turn meant, on the one hand, that the British and Irish 'liberals'—who even at this early date belong in inverted commas—believed that their support of French imperialism could also be interpreted as an act of solidarity with the oppressed all over the world: on the other hand it led to a misapprehension of 'liberal' motives, which were coarsely con-

demned by anti-Jacobins as treason. The parallel with the
'liberals'' present day attitude towards the Communist-Im-
perialism of the Soviets and even of the Chinese is both obvious
and striking.

However neither Pitt's government in London, nor its ancillary government in Dublin over which Lord Camden presided
and Lord Clare controlled, were liberal in any sense of the word,
with or without inverted commas, once the Jacobin peril had
been recognized. As they have done several times in their history,
the English consolidated behind their leaders against the foreign
menace. Reform—and the younger Pitt was in essence a reformer
up to then—was put back in the cupboard. Tampering with
social and constitutional forms was too dangerous with the tiger
at the gate and was rendered even more unattractive by the
attraction, expressed or not, which French republicanism clearly
had for the more extreme among the reform party. Only in the
Royal Navy, with its high proportion of Irish seamen, did the
sailors, by the 1797 mutinies associated with Spithead and the
Nore, manage to wring concessions out of the authorities. The
ringleaders of the mutinies were hanged, it is true, but the
rest were given slightly better living and dying conditions. Those
conditions were still only a small improvement on what they
had been when Dr. Johnson wrote: 'Being in a ship is being in a
jail, with the chance of being drowned.... A man in a jail has
more room, better food and commonly better company.' Nevertheless the fleet did not again hoist the red flag and declare
itself the Floating Republic, but set about trouncing the French,
Dutch and Spaniards in a series of victories such as few navies,
if any, have ever emulated.

This decision to postpone all, or almost all, reforms in times
of national crisis until 'after victory' is not a uniquely British
phenomenon—the same promises were made in the Russian and
Austro-Hungarian empires during the First World War—but
in Britain the precedent established in the French War was to
become standard practice. The masses, in wartime, are to be told
that while nothing can be done for them so long as hostilities
continue, as soon as the foreign enemy has been defeated all
their grievances will speedily be met. The survivors of the 1914-
18 war were promised a land fit for heroes: those of 1939-45
were even given an immediate general election and the Labour
Party could declare, fatuously enough, that they were the masters

now, could nationalize the railways and mines and, even more fatuously, inform the proletariat that these were now *their* railways and *their* coalmines. The English have usually been most adept in their internal politics: such a combination of rigid wartime discipline with the promise of peacetime benefits requires great political skill, extreme patriotism on the part of the masses, and a high measure of self-deception or gullibility throughout all layers of society. At least until quite recently, and probably on future occasions as well, the British of all classes have shown great skill in mixing this particular, and hitherto war-winning, cocktail.

In their imperial days, and especially when the sun was setting on their empire, they even bottled it for export. Ireland was to be granted the Home Rule that was already on the statute book only *after* the First World War, India independence only *after* the Second. It was thus hoped that what Dr. Arnold Toynbee has termed 'the external proletariat' would be disciplined by the same mixture of threats and promises which experience had proved so satisfactory when dealing with the British internal proletariat in times of crisis. However, as history has shown, the bottled cocktail did not taste as good to foreign palates as did the one straight from the shaker to the British electorate.

As the eighteenth century neared its end, the British empire was once again on the verge of expanding, not retracting. Most of India and South Africa were still to be conquered, Canada ingested, Australia and New Zealand colonized. For the moment, however, with the American colonies gone virtually all that remained of the old empire was Ireland and the West Indies. Ireland, save for the Church of Ireland rooted garrison, was disloyal. Among the Presbyterians in the extreme northeast and the Roman Catholics in the south, the promise of sweet reform after the bitter medicine of wartime discipline was unlikely to bring about loyalty to the British cause. Indeed the reforms of 1793 had caused little more than confusion in simpler Irish minds, and had produced little if any gratitude to Britain among the faithful of any religion in Ireland. Grattan and his Enlightened Protestants were, by 1796, sulking in their tents: the Catholic peasantry was sharpening pikes in order to regain the farms: the only true effective force, effective other than by weight of numbers, was the Presbyterians and other Dissenters in the northeast, and these were now led by Jacobins. The game therefore had to be played with much rougher methods than those employed in England, if Ireland were not to fall to the French. Political jam tomorrow, in the pot of promised reform, made little or no sense to a population most of which had never tasted jam at all. It was no inducement to loyalty to Britain and was scrapped. (Later a vague promise of what came to be called Catholic Emancipation, i.e. full political rights as then given to Protestants of the Established Church, including the right to membership of Parliament, was held out as a minor incentive to support the Act of Union. Without basic electoral reform, which did not form part of the package, even this offer was of psychological importance only to the Roman Catholic upper and middle class rather than of political importance to the masses. The vague promise was dishonoured for a generation.)

In England, in that war as in later ones, the threat to the proletariat was largely, though not entirely, negative. If you do not do your patriotic duty we shall punish you and, even worse, those terrible foreigners will occupy our country, steal your land and money, rape the women and so on. The promise was wealth, happiness and greater freedom after victory.

Across the Irish Sea, in the weakest British-controlled territory, the alternatives took on a far more brutal form. Immediately, the Irish were to be disarmed and dragooned into impotence lest they help the French invader. And since neither happiness nor freedom could be offered to the natives, the only inducement was economic—a carrot that is still being offered to the inhabitants of the Six Counties of Ulster today, with some considerable measure of success. In those distant days it did not take the form of straight doles to the masses but of offers to the middle classes. And these offers were summarized in the proposals for an Act of Union that would give Irish merchants and manufacturers the freedom of the larger market, such as the Scots had enjoyed, and profited greatly from, for nearly a century. Such was the bribe, a poor one. The threat was put into force at once. Its first victims—and this is highly revealing of the minds in the Castle and their attitude towards the danger—were the Presbyterians of Ulster, for these would undoubtedly have provided the local storm troopers for the Jacobin invasion that was still feared. The Irish government had already arrested or expelled many of the leaders of the United Irishmen. In March of 1798 they arrested most of those still at liberty in Dublin. They then set about disarming their followers. But by 1797 they had already started on this rough and brutal process in Ulster.

It was of course quite logical that the systematic repression of the United Irishmen should begin in Ulster. Nor was the timing fortuitous. The build-up of the French expeditionary force and invasion fleet in Brest throughout the summer and autumn of 1796 did not escape the attention of the British secret service and there were sufficient garrulous men, both French and Irish, in Paris for its agents to establish that Ireland was its destination. (Wolfe Tone, not himself the most discreet of men, was shocked by the poor security surrounding the operation.) The best strategic plan was as obvious to British intelligence in London as it was to Tone himself in Paris. This was to land the French army in Connaught, overrun that province—which should be comparatively easy—and then with a firm bridgehead established west of the Shannon and using that river as a defence line, advance rapidly into Ulster to link up with the Presbyterian United Irishmen. They constituted the best organized, best led and by late 1796 the best armed republican force in Ireland. From Ulster and from Connaught a French-Ulster force could march quite easily on Dublin, collecting support, which would be more important from a numerical and moral point of view than from a purely military one, among the Roman Catholics, though mass desertions among the militia would obviously be of value.

Both London and Dublin Castle were relying in large measure, indeed almost entirely, on the Royal Navy to defeat the enemy by preventing the French from reaching the Irish shore at all. And then the weird expedition occurred. Three British fleets failed to prevent the French from sailing into Bantry Bay (which was in any case the wrong place) and the weather drove them, again almost unmolested, back to Brest. There was no rising in Ireland, as there would almost certainly have been had the French warships appeared in a northern or even a northwestern lough. And so everything was much as it had been before, with the French preparing a new expeditionary force but Dublin now badly frightened by the knowledge that the wooden walls were far from offering total security. They must look to their safety themselves. And the first place to which they looked was Ulster in general and Belfast in particular.

Throughout the winter of 1796-97 those United Irish leaders

still at large in Belfast were arrested almost to a man and the presses of their paper, *The Northern Star*, were later raided and wrecked. Republicanism in the province was virtually decapitated. Then in March of 1797 General Lake was given command in Belfast with extraordinary powers from the Lord Lieutenant, Camden, and the council. What amounted to martial law, though this was never legally proclaimed, was imposed, and armed with these powers he set about the destruction of the republican rank and file, with all the squeamish gentleness of an SS general dealing with partisans in German-occupied Russia during the Second World War.

General, later Viscount, Lake was a tough and successful soldier who had spent most of his military career abroad. He was then aged 52 and had gone into semi-retirement as governor of Limerick, though remaining on the active list as colonel of the 53rd Foot. His task was not an easy one, nor an attractive one to any soldier. Furthermore he had very few regular troops at his disposal, and had to rely on a raw and ill-disciplined force of militia and yeomanry. When first he took up his new appointment in Belfast, he wrote to Dublin Castle that he feared his militia regiments would have been much infiltrated by United Irishmen. Yet he was lucky in the timing of his appointment to his unpleasant task, for opinion had been moving fast in Ulster since the Battle of the Diamond.

Orange Lodges were springing up everywhere, and these were no longer peasant organizations run by publicans. The landowners and the Protestant urban middle class, traditionally hostile to the French, and alarmed by French atheism and egalitarianism, were moving in large numbers into the Orange Lodges, principally in Ulster but also in the other provinces. And the lodges thus took on a new, political significance. In Ulster, too, many of their tenants followed them, principally for religious reasons. This meant that the militia regiments in Ulster were not only officered but in increasing measure manned by the new Orange Order. Thus Lake had, in Ulster at least, a far more reliable force than he could have expected even three years earlier. The story of the Monaghan Militia in this period is indicative of a change of attitude in Ulster that has continued to affect the province and indeed all Ireland up to the present time, the forging of a union between Orange anti-catholicism and middle-class anti-republicanism. This, in due course, was to create a somewhat stranger alliance, never permanent, between the Catholics and the Republicans, though it must be emphasized that no such alliance existed in any real sense as early as 1797.

The Monaghan Militia had been stationed in Belfast since June of 1796, where the men were directly susceptible to United Irish propaganda. A fairly high proportion had joined that illegal organization. In May of 1797 their officers acted. The regiment was paraded and the United Irishmen ordered to declare themselves. Seventy men did so. Of these, four, who were regarded as ringleaders, were tried by courts martial and shot. The remainder were pardoned.

The outcome, at first glance, was surprising. In order to prove their loyalty the Monaghan Militia became excessively brutal in their treatment of the Belfast citizens. Without orders the militiamen, on May 19th, raided and destroyed the presses of *The Northern Star.* They were not punished for this, and indeed both their own officers and General Lake himself approved of this *razzia.* Furthermore they immediately formed a military Orange Lodge within the regiment, which in theory at least was as illegal as forming a United Irish cell. This however was tolerated as it was in the militia regiments from the other border counties of Cavan, Armagh and Fermanagh, all of which had lodges by the end of the year.

At second glance, however, this political *volte-face* is less surprising and indeed has historical parallels, notably in Germany in the 1930s when many ex-Communist street fighters joined the Nazi storm troops and also proved their loyalty to their new ideology by exceptional brutality. The process was reversed after 1945 in East Germany where ex-Nazis were among the most ferocious Communists. Indeed there is always a strong hooligan element in extremist para-military organizations, which is really all that the Irish militia regiments of the time amounted to. To this must be added the fact that many men of the Monaghan Militia were Roman Catholics and their new allegiance gave them the opportunity to indulge in hooliganism in their traditional fashion by bashing their hereditary enemy. The military and the yeomanry rampaged through Belfast, shooting and burning. This was not a police action, nor even a 'white terror' but rather a weird sort of civil war in which only one side was armed. The almost leaderless United Irishmen responded with the only means at their disposal, murder and an occasional burning. A horrid precedent was set, and seeds of bitterness and hatred sown in a country where the crop was already as abundant as potatoes.

Nor was the situation improved by the arrival of some regiments from across the Irish Sea. One of these bore the ridiculous name of Ancient Britons. These were Welsh fencibles, that is to say second-class, home-guard type infantry, little better trained or disciplined than the Irish militia and now let loose to 'pacify' an alien land.

They were first stationed in the Newtown-Hamilton area, County Armagh, where they intermingled with the local Orange yeomanry whose views and methods they rapidly adopted as their own. With the result that when sent to 'pacify' Newry in the County Down, an area predominantly United Irish, they introduced a veritable reign of terror. I quote again from Hereward Senior's *Orangeism in Ireland and Britain*:

'John Giffard, the Castle agent and journalist, generally considered to have been a loud and violent Orangemen, wrote to Cooke on 5 June 1797 that "the Welsh burned a great number of houses, and the object of emulation between them and the Orange Yeomen seems to be, who shall do the most mischief to the wretches who certainly may have seditious minds, but who are, at present, quiet and incapable of resistance". In describing a search for arms, he wrote: "I was directed by the smoke and flames of burning houses, and by the dead bodies of boys and old men slain by the Britons, though no opposition whatever had been given by them, and, as I shall answer to Almighty God I believe a single gun was not fired, but by the Britons and Yeomanry. I declare there was nothing to fire at, old men, women, and children excepted ... From ten to twenty were killed outright; many wounded, and eight houses burned."'

If the Ancient Britons were the most notorious terrorists in carrying out government policy for the disarming of Ulster, the yeomanry in the Dungannon area were perhaps equally savage, scouring the countryside, burning cottages and furniture, shooting and stabbing. In a village called Tantaraghan a crowd of Orange yeomen physically demolished a Roman Catholic chapel. In an attempt to restore a semblance of order the Castle ordered that the yeomanry was not to act without the presence of officers. In those areas where the local gentry were active in the Orange

Order these instructions were usually obeyed: in other areas, where the Orangemen were regarded as merely another sort of rebel, where in fact they were the old Peep o' Day Boys with a new orange sash, they were not controlled by the gentry at all. The 'Hell or Connaught' notices reappeared on Catholic homes, and the flight beyond the Shannon began again.

General Lake now extended his activities to the counties Antrim and Down. Flogging, torture and totally illegal drumhead courts martial which often passed death sentences were used to extract information about caches of guns and pikes. When terror is employed as policy, its principal lieutenant is rumour. The Presbyterian peasants in northeastern Ulster had heard tales, undoubtedly exaggerated, about the atrocities in the southern and western parts of the province. They rapidly surrendered their arms in large quantities. The operation was, in fact, a success in that Ulster was disarmed. Only comparatively few of the United Irishmen were brave or foolish enough to hide their weapons. And when they rose in 1798, under the leadership of obscure and hitherto unknown men such as Henry Joy McCracken, a Belfast cotton manufacturer, and Henry Munro, a Lisburn linen-draper, they were quite easily crushed, and their leaders executed, within a matter of a fortnight. The principal Irish auxiliary army on which Tone and the French were relying had ceased to exist in 1797.

Terrorization as a policy of government is misunderstood by the peoples of Britain and America principally because they hate it for themselves and have been fortunate never to be subjected to terror for any length of time without throwing off the yoke, and that long ago, in England not since Cromwell and in America, minority groups apart, not since Reconstruction after the Civil War. It is therefore commonly believed in the great Anglo-Saxon communities, and to a lesser extent in the other Western democracies, that terror is a self-defeating weapon only resorted to by desperate men at the end of their resources and bound, quite quickly, to produce an equally violent reaction that will sweep those men into history's limbo.

This attractive liberal view is, unfortunately, an illusion. Most societies have always and everywhere been based on terror (which does not mean a constant bloodbath, of course, but the constant threat of death or imprisonment to those who might resist the established order). Pharaonic Egypt lasted for thousands of years, the Ottoman Empire for many centuries, Sparta for several, while in historical terms democratic Athens came and went in the twinkling of an eye. In our own time Communist despots, using terror as their principal weapon, have preserved their power in Russia intact, despite civil war, world war, near defeat, and one of the most inefficient economic systems ever devised by man. Terror, in fact, comes to be accepted. As Manes Sperber has remarked, terror is not exercised by a million Russian policemen against two hundred million Soviet citizens: it is one citizen being terrorized by the twenty policemen in his small town multiplied to the geometrical power of eight in all Russia, and by his own knowledge that if he resists he will be utterly destroyed.

But what for the liberals must be even more depressing—so depressing indeed that they usually prefer to ignore it—is the fact that tyranny and its handmaiden, terror, are not invariably unacceptable to a people and are usually regarded as preferable to anarchy and social disorder. This is not a sort of political masochism, but rather a retreat from decision-making, from the world of 'ideas' into the world of 'reality,' from the political club back to the farm, the loom, the factory floor, the children's nursery. Thus did the Germans behave a generation ago. Though Hitler never won an absolute majority in any election, within three years his terroristic tyranny had gained the approval and loyalty of almost all the German people, a very highly educated people at that. The same was proved of the Soviet peoples who, in 1941, fought bravely for tyrants who had made their lives hell for a quarter of a century.

The reaction of the Ulster Presbyterians in 1797 and the following years falls into this same pattern. Whipped, beaten and tortured by an increasingly Orange-dominated militia and yeomanry, they first surrendered their means of self-defence, their weapons, and then enrolled in the Orange Order not in order to undermine it from within but to become loyal Orangemen, free to hate Irish Catholics, Church of Ireland landowners, Englishmen and all other foreigners according to choice, but above all free to stop thinking about politics and get on with their own lives. It has been estimated that by the time the Rebellion of 1798 broke out there were some two hundred thousand members of the Orange Order, all of them Protestants and therefore most of them in Ulster. It would scarcely be an exaggeration to say that General Lake's bullies had whipped a great many of them into the Order.

When a small conspiratorial or semi-conspiratorial political group is rapidly transformed into a mass movement, organizational problems immediately arise. The most important of these is the question of leadership, of how policy is made and how a measure of discipline is enforced. Even in our century, with the comparative ease of communications that permit the employment of totalitarian methods, both the Russian Communist Party and the German National Socialist Workers Party were confronted with this both before and after their seizure of power. In Russia it was only solved, and then not entirely, by the massive purges of the 1930s and early 1950s, huge terrorist actions directed not against the Party's enemies but against its own members at all levels. In Germany only Hitler's political skill, and perhaps the invocation of the *Fuehrerprinzip* or 'leadership principle' as an essential ingredient of the Nazi *Weltanschauung*, prevented fragmentation of his party during its period of rapid expansion before he seized power: and even with all the resources of the state at his disposal he still needed the 1934 purge to establish his absolute authority over his followers.

The Orange Order could not, for both technical and political reasons, turn itself into a monolithic organization: it was not until 1920 that it gained control, and that not absolute, of a mere six of Ireland's thirty-two counties. On the other hand its leaders could in the 1790s, and immediately did, set about creating a central controlling body to ensure continuity of purpose—the retention of Protestant control in all Ireland and therefore close anti-Republican links with Britain—and the maintenance or establishment of the leadership in the hands of the gentry, that is to say the exclusion from authoritative positions of the newly converted ex-United Irish Presbyterian peasantry and proletariat, this both for class reasons and because of the proven political unreliability of the Ulster workers.

As early as 1797 a secret society was set up within the technically secret Orange Order. Its members, originally called Orange Marksmen, soon took the name of Purplemen. Scattered among the Orange Lodges rapidly springing up in the north and within the militia and yeomanry, their primary task was to ensure that the Orange Order was not swamped by masses of dubious new recruits. They were sometimes, but not invariably, Lodge Masters, and usually, but again not always, members of the upper or middle class. They had their own secret passwords and recognition symbols, secrets far more carefully kept than those of the ordinary Orangeman. Just as in some Russian delegation or mission the chauffeur may be politically more important than its titular head, so in an Orange Lodge a simple grocer might be a Purpleman, the master not. This system, with changes, has persevered, which is one reason why the Orange Order in the Six Counties today is like the Ku Klux Klan essentially a 'grass roots' organization, in secret control of the politicians it has elected and not the other way about as in a normal democracy.

Almost immediately after the creation of this secret hard-core élite, which we would nowadays call a cadre, steps were taken to create a more rational command organization within the Orange Order as a whole. This never came to cover all Ireland, for reasons which will be shown below, but an Ulster Grand Lodge was created as the supreme official body within the province. Less than two years after the Battle of the Diamond the Orange Order was undoubtedly the most powerful force in Ulster apart from the military, and as the militia was becoming increasingly infiltrated and the yeomanry already almost taken over, by the end of 1797 only troops brought in from outside, from Britain, from Roman Catholic Ireland or from France, could have neutralized the new force. The British had no regiments to spare, the French did not arrive, and in Dublin while the Castle continued to oppose Orangeism as it opposed all secret societies, many men close to government or with authority among the Ascendancy class were either sympathetic to, or had actually joined, the Orange Order. A Dublin Lodge was founded in June of 1797 and soon included such figures as Sir Jonah Barrington, the well-known writer and judge, and Major Sirr, who was effectively what we would today term chief of the security services and who personally arrested most of the United Irish leaders still at large, in March, 1798. Many Church of Ireland clergymen also joined the Orange Order in Munster and Leinster, as did some of the clergy and gentry in Connaught.

In Ulster it remained, for the time being, strongest in the Armagh area, though spreading rapidly north and east. There was soon a lodge in Belfast itself, that fallen citadel of the United

Irishmen. Certain powerful local magnates who had inherited some of the tribal powers of their Gaelic predecessors were opposed to the new movement, such as Lord Blaney of Castle Blaney in County Monaghan and Sir George Hill of Derry, who announced that he would forbid the creation of an Orange lodge unless he received orders to the contrary from the government in Dublin. He did not, he said, trust Dissenters.

While a measure of discipline was imposed on the Orangemen in those districts where the Order was organized, in those where there was no organization the traditional attacks on the Catholic population continued, though diminishing in violence. By late 1797 the flight of refugees into Connaught had become a mere trickle, but many who had fled earlier had exhausted their few resources, dared not return, and had to rely on the pitiful public relief of the age. For them violent, murderous Protestantism had become identified with Orangeism, and this belief rapidly spread among the Roman Catholic peasantry of Munster and even Leinster.

In areas of southern Ireland where the Orange order scarcely existed if at all, such as the County Wexford, the Orange bogey-man most certainly did. Awful, armed Protestants, the ghosts of Cromwell's soldiers, were standing by to murder Catholic wives and mothers, and those demons were henceforth called Orange-men, with bloodshot eyes and fearful swords scarcely to be discerned among the majority of the Presbyterians in the north-eastern part of the island. When General Lake, now Commander-in-Chief, set about disarming Leinster and Munster early in 1798, and using even more brutal and beastly methods than he had employed in Ulster in the previous year, the fact that some of his officers were members of the Orange Order and that, very rarely, auxiliary units of Orangemen assisted the military in their tortures and outrages reinforced the rebels in their belief that this was a religious struggle. When they rebelled at last, ill-led or more often not led at all save by disaffected priests, the rebellion was not the one that had been planned by the Jacobin leaders of the United Irishmen, but rather an ill-armed Catholic rising against their Protestant oppressors. It was in fact a repetition of 1641, with less initial success for the Catholics who failed to synchronize the rebellion and were quite easily defeated in detail by the enemy they so vastly outnumbered. There was heroism, and there were atrocities on both sides which have never been forgotten. A stunned and horrified Protestant governing class accepted, albeit with reluctance, the Act of Union. For one hundred and twenty years Ireland as a country ceased to exist save as a dream in a few men's minds and a vague aspiration among the Roman Catholic majority. The life-span of the Protestant Nation, of 'Grattan's Ireland' was identical to that of Latvia, Lithuania and Esthonia in this century.

CHAPTER ELEVEN

Two years after the Union, that is to say in 1803, Robert Emmet, a Cork man and a Protestant, was trying to revive the United Irish in Dublin, while his brother Thomas was in correspondence with Napoleon urging another French expeditionary force for Ireland. The French were uninterested and when Robert Emmet attempted a rebellion in July it amounted to little more than a street brawl. He was arrested and executed in public, and with him died not only the United Irish movement but also Ireland's eighteenth century. In Belfast Thomas Russell also attempted a rising, but could only muster a dozen or so men, described by Maxwell in his *History of the Irish Rebellion in 1798* as being 'of the lowest rank and most desperate character'. For the next two generations the struggle for Irish independence was to be fought on a very different level. The new leader was a Kerryman, Daniel O'Connell, a constitutionalist, a quite unsentimental aristocrat, a Catholic, and almost certainly the greatest public orator, in a country of orators, that Ireland has ever produced.

In Ulster the Orangemen had split over the issue of the Union, but once it was on the statute book they coalesced again and indeed continued to gain in strength particularly since they now virtually controlled the yeomanry and the militia. On July 12th, 1801, they paraded in full strength, many of them in uniform, the civilians bedizened with Orange sashes and other emblems, accompanied by military bands with their great banners flapping overhead, singing their songs, 'Boyne Water' and 'The Protestant Boys'. With the brief Peace of Amiens in the following year, and with the Catholics now defeated, exhausted and sullen, it was possible to disband some of these irregular forces, but when war with France broke out again in May of 1803, and with French troops massing along the Channel Coast, the regular British regiments were needed in England, and the yeomanry and militia were once again activated and indeed enlarged. This delighted the Orange Lodges who sent the authorities fulsome expressions of their loyalty to the empire. The government in Dublin still did not care to have this private army—for that is what the Ulster regiments were—marching about, but it needed them again now. Already in 1801 the new Viceroy, Lord Hardwicke, had been the guest of honour at a yeomanry, that is to say predominantly Orange, dinner in Dublin. It is safe to say that his predecessor before the Union, Lord Cornwallis, would never have attended such a ceremony nor would Lord Clare have permitted him to do so. The president of the Yeomanry Association, that is to say the Viceroy's host, was John Claudius Beresford, notorious for atrocities committed during the '98. The Act of Union had brought about an immediate and marked decline in the public morals of the men who now ruled Ireland. Political emphasis had of course shifted to London where decisions were now made for the United Kingdom as a whole. To the drain of wealth from Ireland there was added a drain of talent and ambition which was to last throughout the next hundred and twenty years and which, indeed, has not ceased today.

From the economic point of view the Union, in its early years, appeared to bring a measure of increased prosperity to Ireland, as England's major wars have usually done in modern times, for then England becomes a ready and booming market for Irish-grown food. This was particularly so during the Napoleonic Wars and the years immediately after Waterloo with great fleets of sailing ships to be provisioned as close to their stations off Spain, the Mediterranean and the West Indies as possible. It has been estimated (J. C. Beckett: *The Making of Modern Ireland*) that between 1800 and 1826 the average annual value of Irish exports rose from £4 million to double that figure. On the other hand the commercially weak, though technically excellent, Irish crafts such as those of the silversmiths and the glass-blowers, could not withstand English competition, withered and died. The craftsmen emigrated. Furthermore even among the agricultural population the apparent boom in produce was of more benefit to the middlemen and landlords than to the peasantry, whose population explosion and absurd system of land tenure ate up any profits that might have come their way. (The population of Ireland increased from some five million in 1800 to nearly seven million in 1821 and by almost a further million in the decade that followed.) Only in Ulster did the peasantry, particularly the flax growers, prosper, as did the mill-owners and, to a lesser extent, the workers in the mills and the cottage labour, largely female labour. This was particularly true of Belfast, where ship building was beginning and the port facilities were being expanded. Belfast was growing fast, and was to become within a very few decades not only an important industrial centre but also one of Europe's major ports. The economic superiority of Ulster to the other provinces, which already existed, was to be accentuated, the religious division between the two parts of Ireland to be reinforced by economics. And in search of labour and a better wage, Catholics, particularly from the border counties, were to be sucked into Belfast. This in turn was to mean that the competition for farms in the countryside was slowly to be replaced by an equally, if not more, ferocious competition for houses and jobs in Belfast and, later, the other towns of Ulster as they grew in their turn. This is still one of the major issues: it is not and was not, however, the basic one.

Ghosts from the old Irish Parliament lingered on in both the Lords and Commons of the United Kingdom Parliament at Westminster. Grattan re-entered politics in 1805, being first elected for an English constituency, but soon becoming one of the members for Dublin, a seat he held until his death in 1820. He and various other liberal Irish Protestant M.P.s campaigned vigorously and not altogether unsuccessfully to persuade Parliament that the English promise of Catholic Emancipation, which had been linked vaguely with the Act of Union, should now become law. In the Lords Clare, who had never promised Catholic Emancipation, spoke against the measure shortly before his death in 1802. The violence of his rhetoric is said to have shocked William Pitt. Catholic Emancipation meant the final repeal of the remnants of the old penal laws, of which there were few and only one of any importance, the barring of Roman Catholics from Parliament: when the phrase is used it is this that is meant. Grattan and his friends made some converts, but in general the English were uninterested. Even if it had been possible to get an Emancipation Bill through the Commons, the Lords would certainly have thrown it out. Even if by some miracle of enlightenment the Lords had passed it, George III would with equal certainty have refused the royal assent, and so would the Prince Regent during the old King's insanity, for George III regarded Catholic Emancipation as a violation of his coronation oath. Grattan and his friends were in fact threshing straw, but nevertheless they had hit on the issue that Daniel O'Connell, using other methods, was to make predominant in Irish politics as soon as the Roman Catholic majority began to recover from the apathy induced by their latest defeat. With the meagre political means available to them destroyed by the Act of Union, and military methods a proven failure both internally and externally, the Irish longing for freedom from English rule had nothing to fall back on, in order to achieve unity, save the people's religion. (Just as the Irish looked to their Church, so did the otherwise leaderless Welsh look to their Chapels in the first half of the nineteenth century.) This injection of yet more religion into politics was to have a lasting effect in Ireland, and nowhere more so than in Ulster.

There, during the comparatively placid first two decades of the century, another eighteenth-century ghost—but one vulgarized and brutalized almost out of recognition—still walked, or rather marched. As stated in an earlier chapter, the Volunteers who helped bring about the constitution of 1782 had displayed in full the Irish passion for dressing up in fancy uniforms, having musket practice, holding parades and regimental dinners, and celebrating anniversaries—which is where the military training of the majority ended.

Orangemen from Derry to Down resumed this practice, but with a difference. While the old Volunteers had been a Protestant patriotic force which had included in 1782 nearly all the Irish gentry and middle class in all Ireland, the new Orange Order— its usefulness to that class apparently exhausted—was rougher material with motives closer to those of the Peep o' Day Boys. They too dressed up in Orange insignia and beat their Lambeg drums, huge seventeenth-century objects of early psychological warfare: three foot across and of equal depth, when heard from afar they sound like a cannonade. To this accompaniment they celebrated their anniversaries. And when they marched, the marches were more and more intended to provoke the hereditary enemy. Armed columns of these men would deliberately choose routes through Catholic villages and areas, would provoke the inhabitants by the singing of offensive songs and the shouting of anti-Catholic slogans, and then, when the inevitable temper was lost among the insulted, would fire 'in self-defence'. This sort of behaviour annoyed the authorities, principally it would seem because anarchical violence, or the constant threat of violence, as usual sent the rents down. Ireland, too, was beginning to move from the age of aristocracy into the age of *laissez-faire*: nothing must be allowed to disturb the market. The Act of Union had greatly reinforced the imposition of this English ideology upon the Irish, few of whom understood its virtues though very, very many were to suffer from its vices in the Great Famine of the '40s.

Daniel O'Connell was born in 1775 and brought up in the house of his uncle, Derrynane, in one of the wildest and most beautiful parts of County Kerry. Former Gaelic chieftains, the sept had been dispossessed of their territory, and many reduced to the status of tenants on what had been O'Connell land by English settlers, but the O'Connells were a shrewd lot and by smuggling and the French connection some had preserved a measure of wealth as well as of prestige. Another uncle of the same name as his own had joined the Irish Brigade in France under the monarchy and had risen to the rank of general before the Terror. (He subsequently, like many other Wild Geese, left Revolutionary France, joined the British Army, and for some years enjoyed the full pay of two generals in armies that were at war with one another.) Young Daniel, later to enjoy the monumental Victorian nickname of 'the Liberator', was visiting his uncle in Paris when some of the more repulsive aspects of republican revolution were on public display. These disgusting spectacles of atheistical sadism made the deepest impression upon his mind but did not destroy his inherited—so much in Ireland is inherited—hatred of the Protestant Ascendancy in his own country, of the treatment of his fellow-Catholics, and ultimately of the Union with England. To his excellent life of the Liberator, Sean O'Faolain has given the title *King of the Beggars*. It is hyperbole. O'Connell was a well-born Irish Catholic and, by the end, his followers were almost all the other Irish Catholics of every condition and class. He had nothing whatsoever in common with Wolfe Tone. This was a new century.

By the time he was thirty O'Connell was an immensely successful barrister, practising at the Dublin bar. It was during those years of political doldrum in Ireland that he began to play an active role on the various committees and boards that claimed to represent the Roman Catholic majority. The men who composed these committees were either bishops, members of the small Roman Catholic aristocracy or rich businessmen. They were not only intensely conservative but also very timid. They had been badly frightened by the French revolution and even more so by the leveller element among the United Irishmen. They were also frightened lest by offending the United Kingdom the few privileges that they had recently obtained be taken from them. Their attitude resembled, in some ways, that of certain rich German Jews in the first years of Nazi rule: if they kept absolutely clear of politics, save in the expression of complete loyalty to the state, maybe they would be left alone. Thus in 1808 the bishops rejected Grattan's emancipation bill on the grounds that, as a sop to the Protestants, the Crown would have the power of veto over the consecration of Roman Catholic bishops. A somewhat more broadly based Catholic Board, by then dominated by Daniel O'Connell, rejected a similar bill in 1812, and this despite a pronouncement that the Vatican was perfectly prepared to accept the veto. The argument against it was that the veto would destroy the independence of the last free Irish institution, namely the Church, in the interests of a partial democracy which, without a drastic reform bill, would not affect Protestant ascendancy and which, if such a reform bill were ever passed, would give power to a disaffected majority, with consequent dangers to property as well as the risk of even more direct English intervention. Such was the view of the Catholic upper class. It was not that of the rising middle class, who saw in emancipation the chance of sending men of their choice to Westminster. The lower class, who did not have a vote anyhow due to the property qualifications, were uninterested and listened to their parish priests who in turn were obedient to the bishops.

Over this issue the Catholic Board split—the fissiparous nature of Irish institutions is one of the constants—amidst acrimony and muted threats. Robert Peel, then Chief Secretary in Dublin Castle and therefore the most important political figure in Ireland, later Prime Minister, became alarmed and ordered the dissolution of the Board. It dissolved. The issue of emancipation languished in Ireland for nearly a decade, though an Emancipation Bill was passed by the House of Commons in 1821, together with a second bill introducing the veto, and these might well have been passed by the House of Lords, too, but for the energetic intervention of the Duke of York, George IV's corrupt and disreputable brother and heir. The Duke of York had close connections with the Orange Order, and though an extremely stupid man even by Hanoverian standards was the possible fount of immense patronage and therefore a man of great political power in the England of his day. It is a curious tale, but relevant, for together with Daniel O'Connell's emancipation campaign that was to come it shows the increasing injection of religious matters into Irish political issues.

Long before the foundation of the Orange Order there had existed anti-Jacobite societies within the officers' messes of certain British army regiments. One of these, in the Fourth of Foot or King William's Own, was called 'The Loyal Order of the Orange and Blew' and has been described by Hereward Senior as 'an exclusive officers' club unconnected with Irish affairs'. (The exclusive officers were presumably poor spellers.) In 1788 the Duke of York, perhaps after emulating his namesake by marching his men up the hill and down again, became a member of this society.

In 1796 the Orange Order, in its attempts at respectability, that is to say in the terms of the age aristocratic connections, was trying to establish a quite non-existent link with the Orange and Blew. This fraud was of particular interest to the new military lodges, and a man named Lavery was convicted for trying to induce a soldier to be 'true to the Duke of York and his committees'. (Senior: op. cit.) By 1812, when Grattan's second Emancipation Bill was under perfervid discussion in England though less so in Ireland, Orangeism had struck some roots among British army lodges, and straight anti-Catholic societies, quite illegally, had been formed within various regiments. These were called Orange Lodges, but had little to do with Ireland save that it was now a part of the United Kingdom. However, various Tory peers, including the Duke of York and his purple-faced brother the Duke of Cumberland, seem to have encouraged this development for they had inherited all, and more than all, of their dotty father's rabid anti-Catholicism.

In the following year, that is to say 1813, a certain Lord Yarmouth, the Marquis of Hertford's son, M.P. for the family's rotten borough in the County of Antrim and a keen Orangeman, apparently induced the Duke of York to attend an Orange dinner described as The Philanthropic Society, in London, under false pretences and, as the party drew to its close, to join the order. Indeed he appears to have accepted the appointment of Grand Master. On May 27th, 1813, Earl Grey, a Whig who was then

the equivalent of Leader of the Opposition and who had every
reason to dislike not only the Duke of York but also the entire
royal family, described a dinner conversation concerning the
Emancipation Bill at the Prince Regent's table (Fortescue
MSS—X.341-2):

'The Prince said publicly at his table a day or two before, that
nobody would vote for the question who did not wish to endanger his title to the Crown. And they say somebody has
really succeeded in putting this notion into his head, which is
only saying that he is as mad as his father. What do you think
of their having actually established an "Orange Club" *eo
nomine*, which is to meet today for the first time at Lord Yarmouth's, the Duke of York being announced President?'

Whether or not the Duke of York joined the Orange Order
as early as 1813 is not known, though it would seem probable.
The important fact is that an Orange Lodge was then created in
London by Lord Kenyon and others sufficiently aristocrat to
make it not incredible to Members of Parliament that the
Regent's brother should be its first Grand Master. This marked
the beginning, faint and extremely tentative, of what was to
become a tactical alliance between Orangeism and English
High Toryism, an alliance from which the Unionist Party was
to spring half a century later.

The Whig opposition made an issue of the Duke of York joining a secret organization, such political clubs having been prohibited by an Act of 1799 (39 George 3c.79), and if he was a member or even a Grand Master he would seem to have resigned. The
reaction of the English Orangemen was to pass new rules for
their order which ostensibly abolished its 'secret' nature, oaths
and so on. It was now supposed to be a simple, open, patriotic
association which, quite properly, swore loyalty to the Crown
and, rather illogically, to a non-existent British Constitution.
However this was mere camouflage, nor was so wise a man as
the Duke of Wellington gulled into joining. When asked to join
the Order in February of 1821 he wrote, very properly:

'I confess I object to belonging to a society professing attachment to the throne and constitution from which a large proportion of His Majesty's subjects are excluded.... The principal
objection which I have to belonging to this society, is, that
its members are bound to each other by an oath of secrecy. If
such an oath is legal, which I doubt, I can't swear it consistently

with my oath of allegiance and the oath which I have taken as one of His Majesty's Privy Council.' (Wellington, *Despatches, correspondence and memoranda,* 1819-1832.)

The Duke of York was less circumspect. In that same month he joined, or re-joined, the Order as Grand Master of the Royal Orange Institution. There was once again a rumpus in parliament, and four months later he felt obliged to resign, or re-resign, from the Order. However this fleeting brush with royalty had done the Order no harm, and no more had the attendant publicity. By then there were Orange Lodges in most of the great British industrial cities, as well as within many British regiments.

They appealed to the latent anti-Catholic bigotry of the English working man, particularly during a period when Catholic emancipation was a live political issue. We have a glimpse of them in Liverpool in 1819, parading on July 12th with effigies of the Pope and the Cardinal which they intended to burn outside the main doors of a Roman Catholic church, until forbidden by the mayor so to do. In that same year the Manchester Orangemen supported the authorities during the period of social unrest and nascent trade unionism that culminated in the so-called Peterloo massacre. A high proportion of the labourers flooding into the new city of Manchester, then little more than a vast and filthy shanty-town, were Irishmen. It is safe to assume that the support the Orangemen gave to the military was not another foreshadowing of future Unionist politics but was inspired by sectarian hatred transported from across the Irish Sea.

Thus when the third decade of the nineteenth century opened, the decade which in England was dominated by parliamentary reform culminating in the great Reform Bill of 1832 and in Ireland by the issue of Catholic emancipation culminating in the Act of 1829, there were at least five sorts of Orangemen united only in their determination to preserve the Protestant domination over the Catholics in both islands. In England there was a small and not particularly influential group of aristocrats and gentry, usually but not invariably High Tory, often with extensive Irish connections and property. They had little if anything to do with the Orange Lodges in the seething new slum-cities whose members were either expatriate Irish Protestant labourers or the English spiritual grandsons of the Gordon Rioters. This also

applies to the Lodges within the army, where a very high proportion of the recruits were Irishmen, both Catholics and Protestants. Once the issue of Catholic emancipation ceased to be
politically live, with the passage of the 1829 Act, English
Orangeism rapidly faded away. Even in those areas, such as
London, Glasgow, Liverpool and Manchester where there was
a constant influx of Irish labour, sectarian strife became little
more than an extension of what was to go on in Belfast, without any political significance in English or Scottish terms. The
great Chartist Movement of the 1840s, for instance, was not split
on religious issues, though many of the Chartists and a high
proportion of their leaders were Irish Catholics. Nor did anybody opposed to that movement for civil rights, a movement of
European origin and one in which Great Britain was almost the
only Western European power to be spared revolution and war,
attempt to 'play the Orange card'. Both as a sectarian and as a
direct political force, Orangeism in England had by then become
moribund. A vague anti-Catholicism lingered on among the
English working and middle class for a long time, perhaps until
today, but this emotion must be ascribed to English historical
memories and, so far as the Irish are concerned, to English
xenophobia rather than to past, present or future Irish situations.
This, incidentally, is one reason why the English were to find it
so difficult to understand Irish problems in the twentieth century.

In Ireland there were again two sorts of Orangemen. In the
three southern and western provinces there were so few Protestants, then as now perhaps 5% of the population, and those almost
all of the property-owning class even in Dublin, that the Orange
Order might be said to resemble an army of officers without
troops. And even among that class it never seems to have
attracted more than a comparatively small proportion of the
men of property, for it had a fairly formidable opponent in the
Free Masons who regarded the Orange Order as an upstart movement which had aped their customs for motives of which they
did not altogether approve. There has been little love lost between the two secret societies from that day to this. This situation also applied in the predominantly Catholic areas of Ulster:
plenty of leaders with nobody much to lead.

In Ulster the position was exactly reversed. Here, by 1820,
almost all the Protestants who were not actually members of the

Orange Order were usually favourably disposed towards it if they were members of the working or merchant class. The landlords on the other hand regarded this organization of their Dissenter tenants with a certain disquiet. With the end of the Napoleonic War, and the disbanding of the yeomanry and militia, their involvement rapidly declined, Duke of York or no Duke of York. Thus in northeastern Ireland there was, to continue the simile, a fairly massive army of men and precious few officers.

There were not many aristocrats and great landowners in Ulster—their number and even their names have remained almost unchanged for the last three hundred years—and they had never really favoured Orangeism. Now they more or less dropped out, at least temporarily. The Orange Order continued, of course, but with little real leadership. This was only to be revived in the second half of the nineteenth century, with the emergence of a powerful capitalist and mercantile class to provide the necessary leaders and with a fundamental political issue which would encourage them to take control. For the time being the Orange idea remained politically inchoate and its adherents socially low, descendants still of the Peep o' Day Boys.

Into this situation, in the early 1820s, came Daniel O'Connell, with the first and undoubtedly the greatest mass movement in Irish history. In the eighteenth century demagogic orators had mobilized, led and used mobs, quickly assembled and as quickly dispersed. Having seen such mobs in action in Paris, O'Connell wanted none of this in his own country. On the other hand long experience had proved to him that the timid middle-class Catholics, even in alliance with Grattan's Protestant liberals in the United Kingdom parliament, could achieve nothing against the entrenched Tories in England and the Ascendancy class in Ireland, who were together preponderant in the House of Lords.

In May, 1823, he set up a new Catholic Association the intention of which was to forward not only the political aspiration of the Roman Catholics but also other civil rights. Membership of the Association cost a guinea a year. Since few Irish peasants ever possessed a guinea that was not needed for basic, personal requirements, and since they were not really interested in an extension of the franchise that could not include themselves, few joined. It seemed for some months that O'Connell had merely revived the old ineffective organization. But then he had a stroke of genius. He changed the rules, and the cost of membership was reduced to one penny a week, a coin that any man could find. Furthermore he arranged that the Roman Catholic clergy collect the pennies, on Sunday, after mass. By the end of the year £1,000 a week was thus being collected and since there were other members, some paying a guinea a year, some like the members of the priesthood automatic members paying nothing, this meant a membership of well over a quarter of a million. Ghandi was to use not dissimilar techniques in India a century later.

Thus was a mass movement created and, since dues were paid, one in which a considerable measure of discipline could be exerted from the centre. Although he spoke, for hours on end, at the monster rallies which he organized—how can he have been heard by audiences of one or two hundred thousands in an age that knew no microphones? His words were repeated and indeed translated into Irish by others, on raised platforms, among his vast audiences—both for personal reasons and also owing to his close alliance with the priesthood he eschewed violent action. Legally, however, the famous barrister was beyond intimidation. When an alarmed Castle ordered the dissolution of his Catholic Association he immediately obeyed the law and immediately reformed it under another name, the Liberal Clubs. It continued as before, and the government realized that he could repeat this manoeuvre indefinitely. In the 1826 General Election his organization began to contest seats, with Protestant candidates pledged to emancipation and backed by the priesthood. Their efforts were remarkably successful in three southern and one border (Monaghan) counties where they made their greatest effort. Then, in May of 1828, O'Connell had a second inspiration of genius which also set a precedent that has been followed periodically in all Ireland until today.

A reshuffling of the Cabinet necessitated, by the electoral laws of the time, a by-election in the County Clare. The sitting member and now a Cabinet Minister, a Mr. Vesey Fitzgerald, was not only one of the most popular landlords in the county but also a known supporter of emancipation. His automatic re-election was assumed, until O'Connell decided personally to oppose him. O'Connell won and was elected, but as a Roman Catholic could not take his seat in the House of Commons without abjuring his religion. This of course he refused to do. And this in turn meant that the Clare electorate was effectively disfranchised at a most critical moment in English history when a movement for the extension rather than the diminution of democratic representation within parliament was very powerful. Since all legal measures against Dissenters, long obsolete in practice, had been abolished in the previous year, and now confronted with this massive threat from O'Connell's organization together with his personal spectacular victory and the constitutional implications that followed therefrom, the government saw no alternative to an immediate Emancipation Bill. It came on to the statute book in the spring of 1829.

A battle had been won. But whose battle and at what cost? In the first instance the victory went to the rich Catholics who could now not only vote but if elected could sit in Parliament. None of this benefited the poor Catholics, the vast majority whose massive support had enabled O'Connell to get the bill through. Indeed a corollary of the new act was a raising of the financial qualifications for voters in the counties. Hitherto limited to freeholders of a property rateable at £2, this figure was now raised to £10, thus effectively depriving many small farmers of the vote granted them in 1793. This of course was deliberate policy to ensure that very few Catholics would be elected to Parliament and therefore that an effective Catholic Party could not function in parliament. In pursuance of this same aim at the grass roots level O'Connell's Catholic Association was once again suppressed, and the Lord Lieutenant given special powers to make illegal any successor organization of the same sort. These conditional measures, though the first was modified by the 1832 Reform Bill, ensured that Irish representation remained almost entirely in Protestant hands, at least until the second Reform Bill of 1867 which did away with almost all property qualifications for adult males: indeed even after that Protestants continued for two generations to dominate Irish political life to an extent quite out of proportion to their numbers, though with the arrival on the scene of Isaac Butt and later of Parnell they too came to represent the national interest rather than the English connection.

On the other hand O'Connell's victory gave an immense boost to the morale of the Catholic majority. As pointed out earlier in this chapter, the disfranchised masses had never cared particularly as to whether they were to be governed by Irish Protestants or by English ones, by Dublin or by London. Indeed they had had occasion more than once to regard the more distant government as distinctly more favourable to the improvement of their wretched lot. They had therefore scarcely understood the real meaning of the reforms of 1793, slight enough, and had interpreted these as the beginning of sweeping changes. The result had been their total defeat in 1798. Now, however, that they had been governed directly from London for a generation and, in the last few years, had witnessed considerable, deliberate and repeated impoverishment of the Irish economy in the English interest as understood, incorrectly be it noted, by the ideological economists and the get-rich-quick English governing class, they had learned the folly of exchanging a government armed with whips for one equipped with scorpions. These lessons were being rammed home by the great potato famines: the century's first serious one occurred in 1827. Therefore the cry now was 'Repeal!', repeal of the Act of Union, and this was to be O'Connell's second great campaign.

But again repeal was interpreted not as an end in itself. The basic demands of the peasantry remained precisely what they had always been: the abolition of tithes and, if they could not regain the lost agricultural land, at least security of tenure from their landlords regardless of those landlords' religion. They believed, probably incorrectly, that a self-governing Ireland would bring these most desirable ends about now that Catholic emancipation was on the statute book. And they therefore continued to give their whole-hearted support to the Liberator. Revolution had failed, whereas his constitutional methods had succeeded. Until his death on his way to Rome in 1847 he remained the undisputed leader of the Catholic majority, even though—so far as Repeal went—he achieved nothing.

During the period of his first, emancipation, campaign O'Connell had expressed in violent terms his dislike of secret societies in general and of Orangemen in particular. In this he gave his full and very important support to the Castle, where the men in authority were thoroughly weary of the brawling in the North and of agrarian crime in the South perpetrated by White Boys and Ribbonmen. The government's attitude was that of a plague on both their houses, nor were they tempted by the suggestion that Orange yeomanry be brought south to enforce order in Munster. O'Connell was afraid that the activities of these agrarian secret societies would bring his association into

disrepute—many a countryman must have belonged to both—
and he therefore exerted all his great authority against them.
In February, 1825, he wrote an appeal to the people of Ireland
which was sent to every parish and read by the priest after the
celebration of the mass, at the time when the pennies were
collected. In it he said:

'In the name, then, of common sense, which forbids you to
seek foolish resources, by the hate you bear the Orangemen,
who are your natural enemies, by the confidence you repose in
the Catholic Association, who are your natural and zealous
friends ... we adjure you to abstain from all secret and illegal
societies, and White Boy disturbances and outrage.' (*Morning
Chronicle*, Feb. 11th, 1825.)

If these and similar remarks by Daniel O'Connell had some
effect on agrarian crime—and for a while they did—they produced a strong reaction in Ulster. An Orangeman, William
Saurin, had held the post of Attorney-General in the Dublin
government (it was he who had advocated the importation of
Ulster yeomen into Munster) until 1822. He had favoured his
fellow Orangemen and had indeed been among those who had
advocated the use of the Orange Yeomanry to 'pacify'—which
in this context means to terrorize—Munster. When Lord
Wellesley, the Duke of Wellington's elder brother and an Irishman, was appointed Viceroy by the new Whig government in
1821 he introduced new vigour into the Irish administration. He
saw his principal job as a dual one: the restoration of order by a
placation of the countryside, which meant in effect an appeasement of the Catholics, and the smashing of the secret societies.
He realized at once that these aims could not be achieved if
members of the Orange Order retained positions of influence in
Dublin Castle. He therefore immediately dismissed Saurin and
the other Orangemen in government. At the same time he
reorganized the whole system of law enforcement by creating
the Irish Constabulary, a force intended to be non-sectarian in
character, officered by former British army officers. This meant
that in the event of civil disturbances the government's first
line would no longer be the yeomanry, which indeed could be
dispensed with, for behind the Irish Constabulary stood the
British army. His first tenure of the Viceregency lasted for seven
years (he was Viceroy again in the years 1834 and 1835) and was
firm, friendly and fruitful. The fact that the Catholics knew that

the Viceroy was not their enemy made it both easier for O'Connell to lead them away from violence and for Wellesley to deal with agrarian crime.

However his dismissal of Saurin and the other Orangemen produced a markedly different effect in Ulster. It was now that the Orange Order in that province, while professing extreme loyalty to the Crown, began to realize that their form of loyalty to Church and State was not acceptable to government either in London or, now, in Dublin. As the Protestant extremists in the North observed the comparative toleration extended in the South to Daniel O'Connell's mass movement, they realized more and more that they must look to their own resources if they were to retain their dominant position even in their own province.

It took them a little time to understand this. On July 12th, 1825, the Dublin Orangemen were forbidden by the mayor to dress the statue of William III which then stood on College Green or to carry out their usual, provocative, anti-Catholic parade. This ban was on Wellesley's orders. When, in the following December, he attended a performance of *She Stoops to Conquer*, an Orange demonstration was mounted. The Viceroy was hissed in the streets on his way to the theatre and the performance was repeatedly interrupted with cries of 'No popery!' and other such slogans from Orangemen among the audience. Finally objects, including suitably enough a bottle, were hurled from the pit at the Viceregal box, where Wellesley stood rigidly to attention while other members of the audience applauded him. Such hooliganism was hardly likely to endear the Orange Order to the Iron Duke's elder brother, who in that same year had dissolved the Catholic Association. Behaviour of this sort was an indication of how far the gentry had lost control of the rowdy element within the order. Indeed by then the Grand Orange Lodge had been dissolved, and there was no effective leadership. (One of the earlier leaders from the heroic days of 1798 had recently died while, it is said, actually eating an orange.) In June of 1828 the Under Secretary at Dublin Castle wrote, of the Orangemen: 'The persons of rank who formerly had influence over them have lost it, and they are in the hands of inferior men, who are as violent as the lowest of their order.'

This was the year of O'Connell's Clare election which made emancipation inevitable. In a last ditch attempt to prevent it the Protestant nobility, headed by the Earl of Enniskillen, made a new attempt to mobilize the Ulstermen. They did not attempt to do this through the Orange Order but by a direct imitation of O'Connell's methods, forming an open society called the Brunswick Clubs, with a small subscription that made membership available to all. Almost all its members were Orangemen and at the inaugural dinner held on August 14th, 1828, Orange toasts were drunk and, we may presume, the usual no-popery rodomontade produced in the speeches that followed. Within two months almost all the male members of the working class in the Protestant areas, that is to say almost all Orangemen, had joined the movement, and in those areas it was as powerful as were O'Connell's Liberal Clubs in the rest of Ireland. The purpose of this mass movement—from which the middle class seems to have stood aloof—was a mirror image of O'Connell's own. The noblemen who led it wished to show London, and to a much lesser extent in view of the Union, Dublin, that there was also mass opposition to emancipation among Protestants. The noblemen in question must have been either extremely stupid, or extreme religious bigots, or possibly both. As already explained, emancipation at that time was, and was later proved to be, no threat to their own position. However, like the simpler Catholics, they probably regarded it as the thin edge of a wedge that would ultimately dislodge them from their role of Ascendancy. They were therefore prepared, not for the first or last time, to make a temporary alliance with the mass of Dissenters whom they really distrusted. The transmogrification of name, from Orangemen to Brunswick Club, deceived nobody anymore than had the change from Catholic Association to Liberal Clubs. But the lines of religious cleavage were further hardened. This alliance between the Church of Ireland nobility and the Dissenters could only reinforce the Irish Catholics in their growing belief that Orange and Protestant were synonyms.

O'Connell's reaction was both quick and foolish. He ordered a Belfast journalist, by the name of John Lawless, to lead a massive march of his now well-disciplined southern Catholics through Ulster, there to organize mass meetings of the Catholic minority and to preach the gospel of emancipation. He was courting violence, as he well knew, and he got it. Lawless claimed to have 10,000 men in his crusade or pilgrimage in September, but probably had less than a quarter of that number. The leaders of the new Brunswick organization could not control the anger of their followers at this invasion. The Orangemen, yeomanry out of uniform, mobilized once again under the leadership of an innkeeper this time named Sam Gray, and were perfectly prepared to fight Lawless's men should they attempt to enter the town of Armagh. Dedicated to non-violence as he was, and also faced with almost certain defeat, O'Connell called off Lawless and the march through Ulster was abandoned almost before it had begun, leaving only a couple of corpses in Ballybay but a great increment of hatred behind this particular non-happening. In Protestant Ulster, the siege mentality was accentuated. The external enemy might march in at any time. Meanwhile the internal enemy, the traitors within the gates, the traitors who had so nearly surrendered Derry and thus the whole province but for the bravery of the Apprentice Boys in 1689, must be eliminated. Rapidly, and particularly after Catholic emancipation, the nobility of Ulster assumed a more tolerant, even a friendly, attitude towards the Orange Order and some of their number actually joined it. And in 1835 the first sectarian riots occurred in Belfast where, as recently as 1825, the Roman Catholic bishop of Down and Connor invited the Protestant notables to attend a dinner to celebrate his inauguration and was given, by them, a dinner in return. Ten years later this ecumenical spirit was dead, and in a century and a half no attempt to revive it has succeeded in any way that could be described as more than ephemeral. Henceforth the Protestants of northeastern Ireland were on their own, armed and not least with the determination: 'What we have we hold.'

It has been argued, most recently by Senator Ernest Blythe in the 1970 issue of *Everyman*, an Irish annual religio-cultural review published by the Order of the Servites, that O'Connell's emancipation campaign was a disaster for Ireland, a disaster played out for nearly a hundred years in the south and for a further half century in the northeast where the tragedy is far from resolved. The basis of this argument is that O'Connell, advocating first and successively emancipation and only then, unsuccessfully, repeal, had reversed the real priorities. According to his critics, freedom to enjoy full civil rights would automatically have followed upon repeal in all Ireland, whereas his campaign for emancipation alienated the Protestant north forever. It is an interesting argument, but not, I think, a valid one. In order to achieve repeal, O'Connell had first to create a power base.

Though the United Irish ideal lingered on (no Irish ideal ever seems to die completely) and though O'Connell himself even toyed with it, his disastrous excursions into the northeast—which undoubtedly did his country no good and probably much harm—proved to him that sectarian bitterness had reached a point where the only possible power base was Catholic power. Though he never altogether abandoned his search for Protestant support his main mission was the education, both political and linguistic, of the Catholic masses. This inevitably frightened the Protestant minority and exacerbated those sectarian feelings which O'Connell, like every other Irish patriot before and since, was anxious to see vanish. However politics, they say, are the art of the possible. In the 1820s emancipation was a possibility, repeal not, and this not merely because no United Kingdom parliament would then have accepted a Repeal Bill but also because it would not have then been possible to mobilize the mass of Irish opinion behind a movement that merely offered them a return to the miserable *status quo ante* the Act of Union. He achieved something, though not much, but still enough to become a great national hero, for he snatched at least a semblance of Irish victory from total defeat and thus gave his countrymen back their courage. How much harm he did it is impossible to estimate: it was also and certainly, considerable. By the end of his life he appears to have regarded his long, spectacular career as a failure. With the Irish people dying of hunger in the Great Famine, he left no political heir.

The Marxist interpretation of this critical period of Ireland's and Ulster's history is as usual interesting but also, and as usual, misleading. This is because the purely economic or, in their jargon, class analysis is valid but inadequate. Nowhere is the Communists' conspiratorial view of history less applicable than in Ireland, north or south, in modern times. That O'Connell was on occasion irritated by the peasants he enrolled in his Liberal Clubs is true: the great Ulster landowners felt much the same, we may be sure, about most of the members of the Brunswick Clubs: but that there was any sort of alliance by the leaders against the workers is the purest fantasy. The only emotion which they had in common was one which all Communist thinkers and leaders have adopted since the invention of that ideology: a fear and hatred of anarchy, of those anti-social forces exemplified among Ribbonmen and other agrarian criminal organizations in the south and among some of the Orangemen in the north. Like most peoples, everywhere and at all times, most of the Irish in the first half of the nineteenth century wished to preserve an ordered society in which they could do their work, bring up their children, and go safely to their beds while alive and peacefully to their graves in the church of their Faith after a natural death. Yet it was so artificial a society, split so deeply by historical issues of religion and language, of resentment and pride—words that have no place in the Marxist vocabulary—that the economic overtones became and have remained distorted. The unfolding Irish, and particularly Ulster, history of the past century and a half sounds extremely odd if the record is played upon a Marxist gramophone, for when the needle is not stuck in a repetitive groove half the notes and many whole bars of the music are inaudible. Though far from deficient in their desire for material prosperity, that is to say possessions and above all land, it would still seem that the theory of historical materialism is even less applicable in an Irish setting than perhaps anywhere else in Europe. Everywhere, in this writer's opinion, dialectical materialism is too facile: but in Ireland, once the ancient Irish social arrangements had been totally destroyed even beyond dreams of recreation, it has only added a further, foreign confusion to a social imbroglio created by other old foreign importations.

CHAPTER TWELVE

The Irish scene, during the period of the generation before the Famine, is as usual peculiar, at least to foreigners of the age and perhaps equally to Irishmen of a later time. It is also, and within the Ireland of the 1830s and 1840s, diverse. Stendhal, who visited Ireland during this period, described it as the worst governed country in Europe, not excluding Sicily. Walter Scott and Thackeray had similar, though less strong, reactions: to them it was a British colony, badly run perhaps but fortunate to be the protectorate of an enlightened nation. Carlyle found the poverty, misery and squalor sickening beyond belief, but then he visited Ireland in 1849, at the height of the famine. As early as April 8th, 1824, however, Lord Darnley, speaking in the House of Lords, had said: 'That the peasantry of Ireland are generally speaking in a miserable state, cannot, I fear, be doubted; and I forbear to dwell upon the painful description. Let us rather investigate the causes, and seek the remedies, if any can be found. It may perhaps excite some surprise when I state, that among the most prominent causes of the wretched state of the Irish peasant, I shall place the introduction of that vegetable which now constitutes almost the only food of the population of Ireland—the potato. The richness of the soil, and the mildness of the climate, have contributed in the first instance to promote the cultivation of this root more in Ireland than elsewhere; and the temptation afforded to the inherent indolence of human nature, to prefer a food more easily obtained and prepared for use than any other; a food, the nutritious (and I may add the prolific) qualities of which, together with the facility of its production, have tended materially to spread over the face of that island a superabundant population, satisfied to exist without comfort, and without employment, except that which arises from the wretched cultivation of the soil necessary to produce this their only food. From hence arises among the peasantry of Ireland an eager competition for land, which is necessary for their existence. For it is not in that country as in England, where the labourer is almost certain of obtaining a day's work, and payment for it in money, with which he goes to market for his food. In Ireland the poorest man is a sort of small farmer, renting a portion of land for his subsistence.'

Be it noted that these words were spoken three years before the first, major failure of the potato crop in the nineteenth century. There had been failures of the crop in the previous century, and great distress in consequence, but in part because of the smaller population, in part due to a greater diversification of agriculture, maybe because the landlords were then more closely tied to their peasantry, and perhaps due to the general level of callousness and the comparative absence of communication, the misery caused by famine was then taken far more as an 'act of God' than it was to be in the nineteenth. The attitude of the Victorians was no longer that of their grandparents nor that of their contemporaries in, say, India or China. They were to feel guilt and, its corollary, dislike or even hatred sometimes directed against their own society, more often against its 'rooted garrison' of their own stock and faith in Ireland, and generally against the Irish as such for being a burden on their conscience. As Irish misery increased, an increase which will be explained, English resentment against the Irish, all the Irish, grew. Until eventually with the Great Famine a great many Englishmen, particularly those in powerful places in government and the civil service, managed to convince themselves that their ideology of the free market would have saved the natives had not those natives, that is to say the remnants of a once proud civilization, deliberately starved themselves to death in order to discredit the God-ordained doctrine of *laissez-faire*. During the famine the Irish were to become as dangerous, being disease-carriers, and as repulsive—being dying men, women and children—as the inhabitants of German concentration camps a century later. Both had been reduced, by a stupid ideology and by personal greed, to the status of sub-humans.

And when the Famine was ending, the English governing class, unable to understand Irish bitterness from that day to this, might well have echoed Heinrich Himmler's remark to Norbert Masur, director of the Swedish section of the World Jewish Congress, and delivered by way of Himmler's physiotherapist, Felix Kersten (*The Kersten Memoirs*) on April 21st,

1945: 'I want to bury the hatchet between us and the Jews.' All well-meaning Englishmen, whether politicians or not, have wished for many generations now to 'bury the hatchet' with the Irish. Their deeds, however, have not invariably tended towards that laudable end.

In the half-century preceding the Great Famine there had been great changes in Irish society, both in Ulster, to a lesser extent in Leinster, but particularly in the other two provinces. Eastern Ulster, above all Belfast, was becoming industrialized. On the other hand Ulster west of the river Bann, that is to say rural and largely Catholic Ulster apart from such Protestant enclaves as Londonderry and Enniskillen, was involved in the same social process that was affecting the rest of the Irish countryside. In Leinster, or to be precise in that area once known as the Pale, two apparently contradictory trends were in operation. On the one hand there was a measure of industrial growth (though nothing like on the scale of Belfast) in the Dublin area and indeed in the other seaports even down to Cork: on the other, the political effects of the Act of Union had both deprived Ireland of a true capital city and had encouraged the leaders of the Protestant nation to seek fame and fortune abroad. As a city with a rising population, Dublin steadily decayed throughout the whole nineteenth century. Georgian town houses in once elegant squares, such as Mountjoy Square, were slowly turned into teeming tenement slums, for there was little in Dublin now to attract the aristocracy who tended to make their 'town residence' a house in Mayfair or Belgravia, a process facilitated by the advent of the railroads. This also affected the growing urban middle class who for reasons not only of comfort but also of health were moving out of the city centre into the suburbs where new housing followed the new railway lines. The 'dear, dirty Dublin' of song and legend, that fair city where the girls are so pretty, was a tumbledown, overcrowded place of rats and filth and fever. Poverty was acute and almost unrelieved. Beggars swarmed. Before Queen Victoria visited Dublin, in 1849, an operation worthy of Prince Potemkin was mounted to hide the true condition of her capital city from the Queen of Ireland's eyes. Those buildings where she would dine or sleep or receive her subjects were refurbished at very considerable expense, although by then the Treasury could find no funds to feed those numerous Irish subjects of hers then dying of starvation in ditches. The streets of Dublin through which she must drive were cleaned, refuse collected, broken windows repaired. Since there was no time to extend this operation to side streets, it was proposed that large screens be put up to hide the true condition of her second city from the young monarch. In those side streets, if the girls were as pretty as they had been in the eighteenth century, and were to be in the twentieth, large numbers of them could only live by selling their charms in Dublin's countless brothels.

All this squalor was true, in some measure, of other European cities of the age, of London and Paris and the Manchester that Engels observed so closely. In Ireland, however, the Act of Union had ruled out any political solution to economic and social problems other than repeal through either constitutional or revolutionary methods. And during the first half of the century neither method appeared practical. Not only was Ireland the principal recruiting ground for the British Army, it was also that army's major training area. British troops abounded, and most particularly in and about Dublin.

Dublin was perhaps in a situation not dissimilar to that of other enemy-occupied cities with a historic past, such as Venice or Warsaw, but rural Ireland in the years before the Famine of 1846-49 was unique. Here, and particularly in the wildest and poorest parts of the west and southwest, the population explosion had got completely out of control to the extent that society, in any sense of that word, whether ancient Irish, Anglo-Norman feudal, or capitalist modern, had broken down almost completely. The population of Ireland doubled between 1801 and 1846. (See Appendix A.)

Cecil Woodham Smith, in her book *The Great Hunger*, admits that this vast increase in human life is not readily comprehensible. True, in England and most of Western Europe population had been increasing, with growing momentum, since the early eighteenth century and on the Continent this growth was only briefly halted by the terrible casualties of the Revolutionary and Napoleonic Wars. Demographers are generally, however, agreed that this was due not to an increase in the birthrate but to a decrease in the deathrate and especially in infant mortality. And this in turn is ascribed to progress in the medical sciences, the provision of some form of medical facilities for the poor, and an increase in food production resulting from the rationalization of agriculture and better communications. None of these factors existed in such counties as Mayo, Sligo, Donegal, Clare, Kerry or West Cork, yet it is precisely here that the population explosion was most violent. Without roads, without shops, without doctors or hospitals, almost without agriculture, huge populations of boys and girls grew up among the grey rocks and brown bogs of mountainy Ireland, married at fifteen, and had enormous families themselves most of whom also survived, illiterate, Irish-speaking peasants, some of whom had apparently never seen a tree, most of whom had never spoken to an educated man save perhaps their local priest. To give but one example, by the time of the Great Famine Mayo had a population of close on 400,000 (its population according to the latest census, 1966, was in that year 115,547) and only a single dispensary. And these people lived on two commodities, turf and the potato.

Turf is quite easy to cut, is abundant almost everywhere in Ireland and when dried makes a most satisfactory fuel for heating. Thus the dwellings of the poor were at least warm. This is conducive both to procreation and to health. Often the turf fire, in the centre of the cabin's single room where the family lived together perhaps with a pig or a few chickens or more rarely a cow had not gone out for decades. Sometimes the cabins themselves were built of turf. On the turf fire a large iron cauldron would be constantly boiling potatoes. It has been estimated that the consumption of potatoes when the crop did not fail was 14 lbs. per person per day. The potato skins fed the animals. Potatoes were illegally distilled, as grain had been in olden times, and poteen was the result. Potatoes eaten in these quantities provide a perfectly adequate balanced diet and visitors constantly noted how strong and healthy were the inmates of these hovels, bigger and better-looking men and women than the English farm labourer with his slightly more variegated diet based on bread and cheese.

Virtually all other produce went to the landlord, where there were landlords, or were sold to the hated merchant-usurer, the gombeen man, to buy the very few other necessities, such as salt or more rarely clothes. The peasantry were half-naked, often entirely so in their cabins where furniture was a rarity. The method of growing the potato in Ireland was primitive, simple trenching for drainage, the soil from the trenches being used to earth up the seed potatoes on 'lazy beds' between the trenches. This earthing up was repeated when the seed began to sprout. An acre and a half would feed a family of five or six for a year, if the crop was normal. The Irish quite quickly forgot how to cook anything else. Turf cutting and drying and the cultivation of the potato crop involved a few weeks' work in the year. Where there was landlord or agent, always armed with the dreaded eviction order, more work had to be done for him, resentfully and sullenly. In the wilder parts rents were simply not paid at all in any form. (Such social generalizations are dangerous, particularly in a country where communications are as poor as they were in most of mid-nineteenth century Ireland, and where regional variations were therefore great. Nevertheless there were large areas where poverty was total.)

Complete poverty, a total absence of possessions, if food and warmth are provided, can produce a sort of happiness. Such is the appeal of the monastery, an appeal to which the Irish have always responded strongly. Total absence of personal responsibilities also exists, or at least existed until quite recently, for private soldiers.* To this, too, the Irish have responded generation after generation, though as pointed out earlier other motives sent the Wild Geese overseas and it was economic pressures in Ireland as in the Scottish Highlands that provided so much manpower for Britain's armies throughout the last century. To dismiss all this as Irish fecklessness or laziness, as the English and the Scots-Irish of Ulster tended and tend to do, is to mis-understand both the Irish view of life's purpose and the attitude induced by centuries of misrule and exploitation by alien land-lords. And it is not irrelevant to point out that the Irish abroad, both in England and in America, provided a labour force of the greatest importance. It was Irish unskilled labour in those lands that in large measure built the railroads, the canals, the port installations and the roads. They have done useful, exhausting

---

* Such an attitude is admirably described in Alexander Solzhenitsyn's work of semi-fiction *The First Circle* (Collins, 1968). Russian political prisoners in the less brutal concentration camps of the Soviet Union—men employed on scientific work for the Soviet government and therefore given a subsistence diet, adequate sleep, and seldom physically maltreated—can in some cases achieve a strange sense of well-being, of something approaching a monastic freedom from the cares of mankind, of possessions and decisions. We know, too, from the writings of Moltke, Bonhoeffer and others that men of very strong convictions and beliefs could even on occasion achieve a sense of serene detachment in the Nazi camps and prisons.

and often unpleasant work in hospitals, running saloons, working down the mines. Only the land seems to have been surprisingly unattractive to most of the emigrants so land-hungry before they left home. This may have been because of Jungian memories of landlordism in Ireland or, more simply, because so many of the emigrants had almost no knowledge of agriculture beyond the planting of potatoes in the moist Irish climate, and knew no tool save the spade.

Life on the wild and crowded mountains of the west, in what any economist must describe as huge rural slums, seems to have been surprisingly happy, a sort of anarchy, with much singing, dancing, story-telling and above all gossip. This mass of people, usually descended from those expelled by the English or Scots-Irish from the theoretically more prosperous areas, had no bosses, no class-distinctions and, for most of the year, nothing to do save amuse themselves and one another from their own resources, for the Irish are very gregarious and therefore like to entertain. Only the direst tragedy could drive them from their little cabins, their friends and neighbours. Countless ballads of the last century tell of the misery that such an uprooting caused both to those who went and to those who stayed behind. Even though their tiny plots, their potato-patches, were divided and subdivided again they clung to the soil. A happy people in a miserable land, there was as yet no tradition of emigration to America from Munster and Connaught such as had sprung up in Ulster in the previous century. And when they went to England this was usually for seasonal work or with the intention of saving enough money to return home and buy a plot of land.

In the less wild country of the east, midlands, and southeast, and in the border counties, this pullulating population of paupers was a menace to the landlord class. There were, quite simply, too many labourers, occupying too much land with their cabins and their potatoes. There were, of course, good and humane landlords. Some of these began to pay their tenants to go away, booking whole families and even villages passages to America and even sometimes giving them a little money with which to make a start on the other side. Thus the landlords could rationalize their landed property with a smaller and more manageable tenantry. But other landowners, and particularly the agents and sub-tenants of the absentees, were less squeamish in their methods. They rackrented their tenant peasantry not only to extort the maximum rents in the minimum time—and so great was the population pressure and the land hunger that new tenants could always be found prepared to mortgage their entire future for just enough land to feed their families potatoes while growing corn or tending livestock for the boss to sell—but also and ultimately to drive them off the land. Non-payment usually meant instant eviction. Often the tenants refused to leave. The constabulary and the military would then demolish the cabin and drive them off the land to starve. Even so they would often creep back to live in holes in the ground. This, of course, was perfectly in accord with the liberal ideology of the day. *Laissez-faire* economics laid down that if there was no work for the people, then those people should go somewhere else where there was work. At this time the French bourgeois king, Louis-Philippe, was advising his people: '*Enrichissez-vous!*' There was no need to tender such advice to the landlord class in Ireland.

As for their tenantry, even if fully versed in the economic theories of Adam Smith and not merely inspired by a passionate longing to live on the land of their ancestors, where could they go? There was almost no industry left in the three southern provinces of Ireland to give them jobs, for the English had systematically destroyed it in the interest of their own industries. Even if the Irish had wished to move, permanently and *en masse*, to England, the English had no wish to see them do so. Owing to their habits of occasionally shooting landlords and agents, particularly after eviction, and of periodical rebellion on a larger scale, the English governing class regarded them as turbulent and dangerous second-class citizens within the United Kingdom. The English working class, on the other hand, cherished strong anti-Irish prejudices comparable to their anti-coloured prejudices of today and based on the same rationale. The Irish workers would accept a lower wage even than the ill-paid English workers and in the economic system of the day this could only force down the Englishmen's standard of living to the Irish level. These immigrants were only acceptable if they took jobs so menial and so transient, such as building roads and railways, that no Englishman with a home and family would wish to uproot himself to compete. Only in the big new cities that were springing up in the Midlands and more so in the

North of England was there such a demand for labour that the Irish could and did establish large colonies among an English working class largely also drawn from the land and therefore almost as rootless in the new cities as the Irish themselves. But even here there was the same animosity that is directed against Pakistanis and West Indians today. The newly arrived Irish would crowd into the very worst, and therefore cheapest, accommodation. They were dirty and immoral and spread disease. They either spoke a weird sort of English or sometimes none at all. They were clannish, stuck together, could never be assimilated because of their religion and for the same reason were disloyal since they owed their loyalty to the Pope, not the Queen. There was a danger that eventually they would quite simply take over the cities by force of numbers. After all, they breed like rabbits, don't they? When, during the Great Famine, they began to arrive in large numbers, starving and indeed frequently diseased, the poor wretches were greeted with dislike by the workers and with fear by the authorities, who sometimes transported whole shiploads straight back to Ireland there to die. So much for United Kingdom citizenship in those days, scarcely more valuable to an Irishman then than a British passport is to a Kenya Asian at the time of writing.

According to Cecil Woodham Smith even in good years, during the period just before the new potato crop came in, some two and a half million people in Ireland, that is to say approximately one quarter of the entire population, was living at or below starvation level, drawing what limited relief was available, filling the workhouses, some of them engaged on public works specially created for the purpose particularly in the bad years, many of these quite unnecessary (in parts of Ireland there were soon far more roads than were ever needed, in other parts almost none) and on private works provided by the more benevolent or intimidated magnates (it was now that the great demesne walls went up around the huge estates, hundreds and hundreds of miles of them, not infrequently ten or more feet high, designed not merely to give work but also to protect the inmates from starving or infuriated mobs), but most of them to make their way, on foot of course, into the cities there to beg and perhaps to steal. Hark, hark, the dogs do bark, the beggars are coming to town. This annual invasion was as intimidating to the authorities, even though they could now rely on a constabularly as well as on the military, as it was unpleasant for the ordinary inhabitants of Cork or Dublin. It frightened the middle class and further debased the already low standards of the urban proletariat. Dear, dirty Dublin had little to learn from their contemporary *lazzaroni* in Naples. And, as in the American cities today, those who could afford to do so tended even more to move their families out of the city centre into the new suburbs springing up north, west and south of the defunct capital.

It was worse when the potato crop failed. It failed periodically and with increasing frequency in the years before the Great Famine. I quote from Cecil Woodham Smith: 'The potato of the mid-nineteenth century, not yet even partially immunized against disease by scientific breeding, was singularly liable to failure.

'Twenty-four failures of the potato crop were listed by the Census of Ireland Commissioners of 1851. In 1728 there had been "such a scarcity that on the 26th of February there was a great rising of the populace of Cork"; in 1739 the crop was "entirely destroyed"; in 1740 "entire failure" was reported; in 1770 the crop largely failed owing to curl; 1800 brought another "general" failure; in 1807 half the crop was lost through frost. In 1821 and 1822 the potato failed completely in Munster and Connaught; distress, "horrible beyond description", was reported in and near Skibbereen, and subscriptions were raised for relief, £115,000 in London and £18,000 in Dublin. 1830 and 1831 were years of failure in Mayo, Donegal and Galway; in 1832, 1833, 1834 and 1836 a large number of districts suffered serious loss from dry rot and the curl; in 1835 the potato failed in Ulster, and 1836 and 1837 brought "extensive" failure throughout Ireland.

'In 1839 failure was again universal throughout Ireland, from Bantry Bay to Lough Swilly; famine conditions followed. Government relief works were started and a Treasury grant made. In 1841 the potato crop failed in many districts, and in 1844 the early crop was widely lost.

'Thus the unreliability of the potato was an accepted fact in Ireland, ranking with the vagaries of the weather, and in 1845 the possibility of yet another failure caused no particular alarm.'

Yet for those who did not accept periods of starvation as

inevitable as the weather, where was there to go in order to live and work and eat? The obvious and easiest answer would have been Belfast, a fast growing and comparatively prosperous city comparable to Manchester or Birmingham, where labour was in short supply and which was within easy reach of the hungry Roman Catholic countrymen of the border counties and of most of Connaught. But here they came up not against the sour apathy and dislike that they met in England but against hatred and violent hostility on the part of the Scots-Irish inherited down the centuries and now organized and led not only by officers of the Orange Order but also by fanatical Dissenting clergymen. Yet so great was the pressure behind them of population, landlordism and hunger that they came to Belfast nonetheless, even though the first of the anti-Catholic riots in that city had occurred as early as 1835.

In 1784, when the first Catholic Church, St. Mary's in Chapel Lane, was consecrated, the population of Belfast was estimated at 15,000 of whom some 8% were Roman Catholics. By 1798 the Catholic population had trebled, though the Protestant population had also grown. The ratio remained tolerable, all the more so since the republican and egalitarian, not to mention the fraternal, ideals of the United Irishmen encouraged a natural alliance between the Presbyterian and Catholic members of the working and lower middle class against the Church of Ireland, aristocratic landowners and the emergent professional and mercantile upper middle class which, though usually Dissenters by family origin, sought increasingly to identify themselves with their 'betters'. The non-sectarian spirit of Belfast even survived the disasters of 1798 for some years, but crumbled under the pressures of the 1820s, of the dual and interconnected political campaigns for Catholic emancipation and electoral reform. By 1840, when the population of Belfast amounted to 70,000, of whom one third were Catholics, that spirit had vanished, apparently forever.

There can clearly be no statistical correlation between the size of a religious, racial or linguistic minority and the moment at which the emotions of the majority turn from indifference or contempt to trepidation and dislike and the second, more critical, moment when these in turn are transformed into hatred, violence and ultimately genocide. There are other co-efficients that have to taken into account. Economics is one, brains another and each of these two can work both ways. The minority can, in the eyes of the majority, be too good at making money: such was the case in France at the time of the Dreyfus Affair, such in Turkey the basis for the Armenian atrocities. Or they can be, in the eyes of the majority, too poor, too ready to accept poverty, and thus constitute a threat to the majority's own view of a proper standard of living. That was one reason behind Polish anti-semitism and was imported by Polish Jews into a hitherto only vaguely anti-semitic Germany after the First World War. It was this that drove the 'poor white trash' of the southern United States into the Ku Klux Klan. When the minority are too clever in the eyes of the majority, as was the case with the thoroughly assimilated and extremely patriotic German Jews of two generations ago, of the Levantine Greeks, of the Ibo in Nigeria, the fact that they do well in the professions, in business and even in government is ascribed by their stupider compatriots to conspiracy. On the other hand if they are culturally retarded or perhaps actually stupid, like the Ainu in Japan, the aborigines in Australia or some of the Red Indian tribes in America, they become in the eyes of their persecutors little, if any, better than two-legged animals fit only to be domesticated, that is to say enslaved, or exterminated. Xenophobia is, of course, always present. It is reinforced when the majority comes to believe, or can be persuaded to believe, that the minority has loyalties beyond their own local patriotism, to real or even to imaginary forces and organizations elsewhere. Russian and Polish anti-semitism today is justified, if that be the correct word, by the invocation of Zionism, anti-negro racialism in the United States sometimes by a similar invocation of International Communism, anti-Catholicism in England by the Papacy. Nor are these fears always as ridiculous and imaginary as those examples, let alone the spectre created by the Nazis of an International Jewry in control both of Wall Street and the Kremlin with powerful tentacles inside the City of London and even the Vatican, a truly fantastic and terrifying beast worthy of whichever forgotten Greek invented the chimaera and the basilisk, of the forgotten Teuton who invented those horrifying two-headed, man-eating giants and fire-belching dragons with which to send the children screaming to bed. The foreign allegiance may be quite real. In their country's first incarnation the Czechoslovak authorities were quite right in believing that the loyalty of most Sudeten Germans belonged to Germany, not to Czecho-slovakia: the Italians of today are not so foolish as to believe that the South Tyrolese do not regard themselves as Austrians: and Stormont, today, quite correctly believes that an increasing number of Ulster Catholics regard Dublin, not Belfast, as their capital, a belief that is reinforced whenever the Irish tricolour is raised in Derry's Bogside or the Falls Road area of Belfast.

There are, of course, countries, both in Europe and elsewhere, where majorities and minorities have lived happily side by side for long periods of time. So far as I know Finland has never accused its Swede-Finns of conspiring with Stockholm. Switzer-land is an even more spectacular example. Even at the zenith of Nazi conquest the German-Swiss Nazi party was so small as to be negligible, while the French-speaking Swiss, having once ex-perienced the joys of Revolutionary and Napoleonic conquest and occupation, have never looked to Paris again, or if they have it is to the Paris of the Bourse and the Louvre and the Folies Bergères, not to the politicians and the soldiers.

Meanwhile there are also other, unhappier, countries in which minorities and majorities clash without apparently any external loyalties whatsoever, and without much visible economic cause. Walloons and Flemings bash each other because the one group speaks a patois of French, the other a language akin to Low German or Dutch. In the Indian sub-continent, Muslims and Hindus massacre each other when freed of British rule, and go to war within a decade or so of forming their own national states, for no apparent reason other than a hatred of one another's religion, a hatred rapidly extended to other religions and religious variants such as those of the Sikhs and the Parsees and the Indians Christianized by the Portuguese. It is essentially in this category that the sectarian riots, murders and pogroms of pre-Partition Belfast belong, particularly in the first three quar-ters of the century before the great Catholic Irish emigration to America could enable the Irish to call on the American-Irish as allies in their struggle to throw off English rule and therefore before the Ulster extremists could hoist their Union Jacks as a super-patriotic, anti-Catholic gesture of defiance aimed at their Irish compatriots.

The catalyst was, and has remained, land, transmuted by Bel-fast's industrial revolution into houses and jobs. And just as Nazism had one first begetter in the person of Adolf Hitler, and died with him, so can we pinpoint in time and place the man who created sectarian hatred in Belfast. It was a Presbyterian minister, a certain Rev. Dr. Henry Cooke, who imported violent anti-Catholicism from his native Derry into Belfast in the early 1820s, much as Hitler was to import violent anti-semitism from his youthful home in the Vienna slums into Weimar Germany. Hitler was destroyed by war, and we hope left no heirs. Cooke died, full of years and honours, in 1868 and has left a succession. The current occupant is Mr. Ian Paisley, who also styles himself Reverend (without having been ordained by any Church save perhaps the one which he himself invented) and indeed Doctor too, though what he is a Doctor of or where he received his doctorate is also a mystery. By the time these words are printed he will be able to put M.P. behind his name twice, for he is already a member of the Northern Ireland parliament and will by then have taken his seat in the Chamber of the House of Commons at Westminster.

A political priest is almost invariably either a bad politician or a bad priest or, not infrequently, both. Cooke, was, however, a very competent administrator, an orator whose hot-gospelling, Bible-thumping style appealed to Ulster audiences, and he fulfilled his personal political ambitions, which were considerable. When John Milton in his *On the New Forces of Conscience under the Long Parliament* wrote: 'New Presbyter is but old Priest writ large,' he was referring to the highhanded authoritarianism, both in theology and in politics, of the Scots Kirk. The Irish Presbyterian church into which Cooke was ordained early in the nineteenth century was a far looser organization. The leader of its liberal wing, the Rev. Henry Montgomery, born like Cooke in 1788, wrote many years later: 'I am proud to say that during the last forty years I have found by best, my clearest-minded and my warmest-hearted friends among the United Irishmen of 1798.' He believed, in true Protestant fashion, that the first duty of a Christian was to obey his own conscience. And he objected to his church's *Westminster Confession of Faith* describing the Pope as 'the anti-Christ'.

Such opinions were anathema to Cooke, who, though not himself a member of the Orange Order, quacked like a very orange duck indeed. It was over this matter of the *Westminster Confession* that he and Montgomery collided. If ever there was a priest writ large, it was Cooke and he wished to make sure that he adorned a church at least as authoritarian as the Church of Rome. Therefore he insisted that all ministers and aspirants to the ministry must not only accept the *Confession* in toto but also a tight discipline and a conformity of views as imposed by the Moderator and the Synod. He fought a long battle on many fronts with Montgomery, the final and most violent being about Catholic emancipation, which Montgomery favoured. But in Ulster the tide was flowing for Cooke during those years. More and more of the Presbyterian ministers, bowing perhaps as much to the growing Orangeism of their own congregations as to Cooke's arguments and oratory, rallied to him. In 1829, the year of emancipation, Montgomery and his followers left the parent church and formed their own Non-subscribing Presbyterian Church, which still exists and can still be counted as distinctly liberal, by Ulster standards. Cooke then turned his attention to the other Dissenting churches, the Methodists, Baptists and so on, and quite rapidly achieved a considerable degree of authority among their ministers and members too. By 1832, the year of the first Reform Bill, he was not only the unofficial leader of almost all the Dissenters in Ireland, which means in effect in Ulster, but had turned his attention to bigger game, namely the land-owning aristocracy and the established Church of Ireland itself. His aim now was no less than the creation of an anti-Catholic bloc, to include all Protestants of every denomination and every class, a monolithic grouping based on religious bigotry among the masses and on class interest among the richer classes, with the purpose of ensuring perpetual domination by the Protestants, in all Ireland if possible, but certainly in Ulster.

Again he had chosen his time well. The great landowners, in Ireland even more than in England, were usually extreme Tories. They had fought against, and hated, the 1832 Reform Bill. They were even more frightened by Daniel O'Connell's new campaign for the repeal of the Union. By no measure were they all stupid men and some of them were extremely acute politically. These saw that the Reform Bill's first, hesitant steps towards democracy must, sooner or later, be followed by others and ultimately by the overthrow of their class and its privileges. For them, from the viewpoint of their age, democracy did not mean the form of government that now exists in the United States, Britain and the Republic of Ireland: it meant what they had seen in France in the 1790s and might well soon see there again after the latest revolution of 1830 that expelled the reactionary Bourbons in favour of the regicide-tainted House of Orléans.

The English aristocracy had, at last and reluctantly, accepted reform. With luck the transformation there from oligarchic to democratic control would be slow, as indeed it was, for it is even now not entirely complete. In Ireland on the other hand, and particularly perhaps in Ulster, the magnates were faced simultaneously with O'Connell's campaign for repeal. Ireland still remembered '98, land-hungry peasants and landowners alike. If O'Connell were to win this new campaign—which must have seemed not impossible: he had won emancipation—democracy, in their eyes, must surely make very rapid progress in a self-governing Ireland. And this in turn, again in their eyes, could only mean the expropriation of Protestant estates by a brutal Catholic peasantry. Therefore the noblemen who were quick to adjust to new political situations, realizing both the implications of reform and the dangers of repeal, looked about them for allies among the classes and the faiths that they had previously despised. In Ulster what immediately met those eyes was the Orange Order and the Rev. Dr. Henry Cooke who could talk, as they could not, to the masses. They were, in fact, prepared to invoke the Dissenting devil to drive out the Catholic beelzebub, to use the votes and if need be the muskets of the Protestant mob against the Catholic mob. Again, and from their own point of view, they were quite right. The descendants of most of those noblemen and gentlemen who attended a most important mass demonstration at Hillsborough, in County Down on October 30th, 1834, are still living on their ancestral estates. The guest of honour on that occasion, and principal speaker, was the Rev. Dr. Henry Cooke.

His, and his hosts', more sectarian aims had been aided by another minor, though to them all important, straw in the wind of change that blew nowadays from Westminster. Second only to land the major grievance of the Irish majority was the compulsory payment of tithes to the Church of Ireland to support the vastly inflated hierarchy and priesthood of a faith which almost all Irishmen regarded not only as heretical but also as hostile and oppressive. The clever gentlemen of the government in London, which was now subsidizing though not very generously both the Dissenting ministers and the Roman Catholic priesthood in Ireland, were inclined to agree. The first very tentative steps towards the eventual disestablishment of the Church of Ireland were being taken, under the pressure of the Tithe War.

It is not proposed to discuss this issue in any detail. Briefly, the Church of Ireland had completely failed in its missionary intent, which was to convert the Catholics and Dissenters. It served, at this time, perhaps 5% of the Irish population. It was extremely expensive to run, and that expense was not only raised from the Catholic majority but also badly distributed. There were parishes where the incumbent received almost no money, others where he was grossly overpaid, while plurality was commonplace. The constabulary and even on occasion the military were used to collect the tithes, which were not infrequently paid in kind, for cash was rare, a hen perhaps or some potatoes or a garment of clothing. In 1832 this ridiculous and expensive system was changed by the Tithe Composition Act to a cash payment only. This tithe many of the poor simply refused to pay and tithe collectors were occasionally shot at. This has been called the Tithe War. (In 1838 the charge for supporting the Church of Ireland was nominally transferred from the Catholic tenantry to their usually Church of Ireland landlords, but in most cases it went back straight to the tenants in the form of increased rent.) As seen from London, the situation of the Church of Ireland was therefore most unsatisfactory. The Irish bishops were, of course, aware of how the current of opinion was running.

A second and subsidiary purpose of the state church had been to pack the old Irish House of Lords with Irish bishops, often Englishmen appointed to Irish sees, who would vote the way London wished. Since the Act of Union this service had become redundant and the Church Temporalities Act of 1833 suppressed ten bishoprics and two archbishoprics. Thus, in the age of Reform, the Church of Ireland, like the land-owners whose spiritual needs it served, could feel a chilly wind rising from England, and no matter how cold it might be such a wind must surely blow up the embers of the Tithe War. Many of the Church of Ireland clergy were devout, holy and a-political men. Some were not. And the Church as an institution, like the aristocracy as a class, began to look for allies. (It is not coincidence that the Church of Ireland was disestablished in 1870, a mere two years after the Second Reform Bill that created the first real British democracy.) The obvious ally was not then, as it is now, the Irish Roman Catholic hierarchy but rather that suave leader of the Dissenters, who was already dining in the houses of the aristocracy, the Rev. Dr. Henry Cooke.

The consummation of this somewhat unnatural union took place in 1834. I cannot do better than describe this Orange *fête champêtre* or jamboree by quoting at length the anonymous 'Member of the Order' who compiled two enormous volumes entitled *Orangeism in Ireland and Throughout the Empire*, published by Thynne and Co., London, undated, but probably vintage 1939. I would, however, draw the reader's attention to the repetition of names, among the gentry rather than among the nobility, which we have already encountered and particularly in 1795. Like so many Irish concerns, the Orange Order was becoming a family affair, for which the aristocracy were then making a takeover bid which has never quite succeeded but never entirely failed. 'The Member' writes: 'Of all the gatherings in Ireland at this time, the meeting at Hillsborough, in the County of Down, was the largest and most attractive. It was held on the 30th of October, 1834, and it was in many respects a remarkable demonstration. The number present, estimated at 60,000, thoroughly represented the Orange and Protestant sentiments of the Province of Ulster.

'Early in the morning one hundred stalwart tenants of the Downshire Estate were sworn in as special constables to keep order among the multitude expected to arrive. The platform was erected in a field of six acres, north of the historic town, and large signposts indicated the routes for pedestrians, equestrians and carriages. The vehicles were occupied by the ladies of the county. According to appointment, the great landed proprietors met their tenantry on the several estates and marched at their head to the place of assembly. The first body on the ground was composed of a dense mass of manly yeoman, headed by the Rev. Holt Waring, whose carriage was drawn by the people. Other splendid bodies came in succession, led by the Marquis of Downshire, the Marquis of Londonderry, Lord Clanwilliam, Sir Robert Bateson, Colonel Forde, Colonel Blacker, Lord Castlereagh, and Lord Roden. The last named was at the head of 15,000 men. One contingent had marched from Warrenpoint, twenty-five miles distant. Altogether it was a glorious display, in delighful autumn weather, of Protestant strength and solidarity, owners and occupiers of the soil standing shoulder to shoulder, one in thought and feeling to defend the Constitution. Stern men they were all; modest in demeanour; and resolute in purpose. Having right upon their side, they believed that success would reward their efforts, but their hopes were blasted by subsequent events, the evil of which time made manifest.

'Shortly after noon the Earl of Hillsborough, High Sheriff of the County, was called to the chair, and occupying seats on the platform with him were Viscountess Mandeville, the Countess of Roden, Lady Elizabeth Jocelyn, the Countess of Clanwilliam, Lady Bateson, Mrs. James Reilly, the Misses Reilly, Mrs. and Miss Hill, Mrs. James, the Misses Blackwood, Mrs. Stackpoole, Mrs. Hunt, the Marquisès of Donegall, Downshire and Londonderry; Earls of Roden, Clanwilliam and Hillsborough; Lords Castlereagh and Dufferin; Sir Robert Bateson, Colonel Forde, Colonel Blacker; Very Rev. Dean Stanus, Very Rev. Dean Carter; Archdeacon Saurin; Colonel Verner, M.P.; John Ward, Patrick Savage and John Moore; James Watson (Commodore), J. Waring Maxwell, M.P., Roger Hall, James Corry, Fortescue Gregg, Henry Hardman, David Lucas, William Storey, Needham Thompson, G. Burgess, William H. Quin, Francis Forde, Esquires; Revs. Holt Waring, James Blacker, E. Boyd, W. B. Dolling, W. H. Wynne, Robert Daly, Hamilton Madden, and F. Gervaise. These were of the Established Church. The other clergy present were the Rev. Dr. Cooke, the Rev. Mr. Moorhead, the Rev. Mr. Little, the Rev. Mr. McCullagh, the Rev. Mr. Anderson, the Rev. Mr. Crory, and the Rev. George Moffit.

'The earl briefly addressed the large concourse, and other great men present similarly expressed their sentiments. Reference may be made to their remarks for the benefit of those who have not had the opportunity of reading any of the reports published.

The Marquis of Downshire. 'In moving the first resolution, which disapproved of the doctrines propagated in parts of the country respecting property the Marquis of Downshire, who was cheered for several minutes, said the conduct of the Protestants of County Down and of the other counties in the North of Ireland, had merited and received the approbation of the King and of the King's Government. It had also received the approbation of the Lord Lieutenant of Ireland, who had borne testimony to the peaceful behaviour, the loyalty and the spirit of obedience to the laws evinced by the inhabitants of that part of his Majesty's dominions. Having been once the advocate of Liberal opinions, he felt the more imperatively called upon as a landed proprietor to come forward and state that there were limits beyond which concession should not go. He considered himself bound to make that declaration when he saw measures advocated and when he heard the advocates of those measures state that the minds of the people would not be satisfied till they were carried. the ultimate effect of which he did in his heart and soul believe would be the separation of Ireland from England, the destruction of all kinds of property, and finally of the Protestant religion in Ireland.

The Marquis of Londonderry. 'One of the speakers who had the best opportunity of knowing the leading objects of the Act of Union—the Marquis of Londonderry—said in the same proportion as he valued that Act must be his condemnation of every effort for its repeal. Why was it that the Legislative Union had been established? With what object had it been carried into effect? It was to give to the Roman Catholics the rights to which it had been deemed they were entitled; it was to enable them to receive the boon of emancipation. It had been thought that if they could succeed in connecting themselves with Great Britain, there would be no danger in permitting the Roman Catholic people—that immense body of their fellow countrymen—to partake of those rights to which all were deemed to be equally entitled. But had their Roman Catholic brethren made any adequate return for the boon conferred upon them? Had they been tranquil and content, and had they ceased from agitation? No. He was sorry, deeply sorry, to say they had not. They had raised a cry of "Repeal of the Union" from one end of the country to the other.

'Lord Castlereagh, Lord Arthur Hill, Lord Clanwilliam and Sir Robert Bateson followed. The worthy Baronet said they had tried conciliation in vain. The more that was conceded the more was demanded. Protestants had been called upon by their Sovereign to support their religion, and they would obey the call, their universal cry in one voice of thunder being, "No surrender!" The next speaker, Lord Castlereagh, said it was really the eleventh hour with them; their properties and their very lives were in danger. They felt that under the Government of the day they had no protection. The Bible had been banished from their schools and in effect, an interdict had been put upon the reading of that Book. Their Protestant Yeomanry had been banished, and the means of preserving the peace of the country and their lives had been taken from their hands. When they looked to the unprotected state of the Protestant magistracy, and the growing violence of the effects and exertions of a powerful party, could they wonder that the Protestant peasant, returning to his home at night, frequently found that that home had been burned and his property otherwise destroyed. Could they wonder that any clergyman of their faith could hardly with safety be a dweller in the country? But it was not by emigration alone that their Protestant population was reduced. Let them look to the burnings, the murders and the slaughters that were committed.

'Excellent speeches were also delivered by Mr. Ker, the Rev. Holt Waring, Mr. Roger Hall and Lord Roden. While his Lordship was speaking, Mr. N. D. Crommelin, G.M., of the Orangemen of Down, arrived at the head of a large body of men who were greeted with loud cheers and the waving of hats.

Rev. Dr. Cooke. 'The Rev. Dr. Cooke at this stage spoke with powerful effect, explaining why, as a Presbyterian, he sympathized with the clergy of the Established Church, and was prepared to co-operate with them to avert the dangers with which they were threatened. He proclaimed himself neither Whig nor Tory, but a Conservative; denounced the existing system of national education—"the system which secured and promoted national popery", which excluded the Bible during school hours, which prohibited prayer and which substituted a figment of the Board for the Bible; and ably exposed what he called "the horrors of the policy" which gave such large powers to priestly ex-officers. But the great attraction in Dr. Cooke's speech was not in his invective against the national system, nor his proclamation of sympathy with the clergy of the Established Church, nor his unfurling of the Blue Banner of his own Presbyterianism. The point which gave vitality to his Hillsborough utterances was his publication of the banns between the Irish and the Presbyterian Churches.

' "I trust," said the great orator, "I see more in this meeting than a mere eliciting of public opinion or a mere gathering of the clans. I trust I see in it the pledge of Protestant Union and co-operation. Between the divided Churches I publish the banns of a second marriage of christian forbearance where they differ, of christian love where they agree, and of christian co-operation in all matters where their common safety is concerned. Who forbids the banns? None. Then I trust our Union, for these holy purposes, is indissoluble and that the God who has bound us in christian affection, and by the ties of a common faith, will never allow the recollections of the past, or the temptations of the present, to sever those whom he has united." These utterances were worthy of the great Presbyterian divine. Dr. Cooke never became an Orangeman. On this occasion, however, he declared a fundamental principle of Orangeism.

'The members of the Orange Society do not encourage sectarianism. Their organization was begun and continues to promote Protestantism, and every evangelical form of that faith can command its sympathy and assistance. The strong bond of union among Orangemen exists in the fact that their Society is "exclusively Protestant". Various changes have occurred in the Orange constitution, but its Protestantism has never changed. Officers have been shrifted (sic) scores of times, laws and ordinances have varied, ceremonials have altered, signs and passwords have been renewed and superseded; but the Protestantism of Orangeism is inimitable. Orange Episcopalians, Presbyterians, Methodists, and Independents had already been married in the sense alluded by Dr. Cooke. Nevertheless, the wholesome counsel he offered was pertinent to non-Orangemen; and the misfortune was that it did not commend itself generally. The Rev. William McClure, Moderator of the General Synod of Ulster, addressed a communication to a Dublin newspaper, taking exception to Dr. Cooke's attitude at Hillsborough. The letter was dated, "Londonderry, November 6, 1834," and contained these words: "I beg to state that Dr. Cooke is not the Moderator of the Synod of Ulster; that he had no authority from that body to appear at the meeting in question; and that, for whatever sentiments he may have there expressed, he alone is individually responsible." The Moderator, who seems to have felt some personal jealousy about the position taken up by Dr. Cooke, was too late in forbidding the banns; the ceremony was over; and it would have been well if the catholicity of the man who published them had prevailed more widely than it did among both Episcopalians and Presbyterians. Still, good was done by Dr. Cooke. The flame of loyalty spread from Hillsborough and great meetings were promoted in every other county in Ulster.'

The whole spectacle, as described by this devout Orange historian, recalls descriptions of the great Nuremberg rallies by the Nazi journalists of the 1930s. Nor was the result so dissimilar. The great flames of loyalty enkindled by this clerico-aristocratic but also proletarian rally had their first little bonfire in the Belfast slums on July 12th of the following year. In September of 1969 an English friend of mine, on holiday upon the western coast of Scotland, could see the flames of Belfast burning reflected by the clouds above the Northern Channel.

In 1555 an earlier Protestant divine but martyr, paraphrasing the apocryphal book of Esdras, had said to his fellow martyr at the stake: 'Be of good comfort, Master Ridley ... we shall this day light such a candle by God's grace in England as I trust shall never be put out.' On that sunny afternoon, surrounded by the Lords this and the Misses that, the Rev. Dr. Cooke—to whom Bishop Latimer's words must have been infinitely familiar—also lit a candle which in Ulster has not yet been put out.

CHAPTER THIRTEEN

During the 1820s, Lord Wellesley not only initiated the Irish Constabulary but also introduced stipendiary magistrates, salaried law officers exercising judicial functions similar to those of the unpaid Justices of the Peace. This innovation was developed much further by Thomas Drummond who was Under-Secretary in Dublin Castle from 1835 to 1840. Drummond was a tough, resolute and fairminded Scot, who rapidly became the most powerful man in Ireland. He disliked the landlord class and won their hatred by reminding them that 'property has its duties as well as its rights', words which would have appealed to the ghost of Lord Clare. Nor did he care for the Orange Order. He used all the powers at his disposal to smash it. In this he did not succeed, though he weakened its aristocrat wing. He also dismissed many Orange magistrates in Orange trouble spots. All this made him intensely unpopular with most of the Protestants, and correspondingly popular with the Catholics who began to feel, for the first time in years, that Dublin Castle existed to govern all Ireland and not merely to oppress the Catholic majority.

The introduction of the stipendiary magistrates was an essential and very sensible move on the part of the Irish government to put down agrarian crime, the Ribbonmen as they were generally called, in the south and west, and to curb sectarian strife in the northeastern part of the island. The J.P.s remained, and indeed still remain in all the United Kingdom including Ulster, but from 1825 on their powers declined, and the cases with which they dealt became increasingly trivial: poaching, trespassing and other such misdemeanours. They could and did still handle criminal cases but these became more and more within the jurisdiction of the magistrates who would pass sentences in minor cases while more important ones were indicted for trial by judge and jury at the assizes.

In England this replacement of what was still basically the feudal system of law enforcement—the lord of the manor acting as J.P., his trusted retainers as yeomen—by the modern system of a police force bringing delinquents before a trained magistrate had become imperative with industrialization and the rise of the cities. In England, however, some elements of the old system remained and are, indeed, still in existence. The police, for instance, have never been nationalized, each county retaining its own force, as is also the case with the police forces in the United States, where each State, being in theory sovereign, has its own apparatus for law enforcement. In England, Scotland and Wales, though counties have no claim to sovereignty but only to limited self-administration, the county police is recruited, paid and administered by the county authorities. In theory its functions cease at the county's borders. Although this has become much eroded by time and by the need for a centralized force to deal with major crime, the theory still remains: thus only in very exceptional circumstances can the Dorset police carry out a search or an arrest in, say, Hampshire; usually the matter is then passed to the Hampshire police who must obtain a warrant from a Hampshire magistrate. In America the autonomy of the State police force is much greater. The justification of this system is that it safeguards the liberty of the subject by making the creation of a 'police state' that much more difficult. A national police could, and in other countries has, become a state within the state, obeying its own officers for their own ends, in fact a rival to the armed forces which, as stated in an earlier chapter, should be unique in any well-run country no matter whether its political system be democratic or not. In effect this devolution of police powers makes life slightly easier for the criminal element, but in the last century there was a general consensus of opinion in Britain and America that this was a price worth paying to safeguard the liberty of the subject. (One of the early acts of the British and American Occupation authorities in Germany after the Second World War was to break up the German police on their own patterns, creating a separate police force for each *Land* or province: some have ascribed the increase of ordinary crime in Germany, and the escape of many 'war criminals' from justice, to this innovation.)

In Ireland none of this applied. This, too, Drummond realized when he created a national police force which Catholics were encouraged to join. What slight roots feudalism had struck in Ireland had been blasted by the Elizabethan Wars, by 1641

and Cromwell, by the Williamite reconquest, and finally by the
'98. In most of Ireland the landowner was not the lord of the
manor to whom the peasantry owed a traditional obedience in
peace and allegiance in time of trouble and who, in theory at
least, would as J.P. guard their interests and protect them against
robbers and marauders. Rather was he the expropriator of their
land, the prime enemy. There were, of course, popular landlords, though these were rare, and there was very strong local
feeling, though this was seldom channelled into trust for the
rich and affection for the rural scene. It was an Englishman,
Thomas Grey, who wrote the bitter-sweet *Elegy written in a
Country Churchyard,* for generations one of the most popular
and nostalgic descriptions of a way of life that lingered on, where
each knew his place and filled it as best he could, and not un-
happily. It was an Irish contemporary of his, Oliver Goldsmith,
who wrote a poem almost as famous, *The Deserted Village,* in
which a bitterness near despair replaces Grey's nostalgia and
sweetness is only a memory of a happy past brutally destroyed
by 'the tyrant's hand'.

> 'And trembling, shrinking from the spoiler's hand,
> Far, far away thy children leave the land.'

Quite apart from the fact that several hundreds of years had
shown the English the folly of trusting Irishmen, or the Irish
descendants of English and Scots, to enforce the English writ in
their own districts, there were very immediate reasons why both
the police and the magistrature should be a national rather than
a local force. Family feeling remained and remains very strong
in Ireland, particularly in the country areas. Constable Rooney
in West Cork would hesitate to arrest a Ribbonman who happened to be his wife's third cousin by marriage once removed,
unless he had some motive of personal animosity, and that is no
basis for sensible police activity. On the other hand, living the
life of a disciplined member of the Force in the County West-
meath it would be some time before he had struck sufficiently
deep roots there to forget his duty to his officers. And if those
officers feared that his involvement with Katie O'Leary was
likely to influence his attitude to her brother, suspected of moon-
shining, he could always be moved to Kilkenny or Antrim.
That is the advantage of a 'barracks police'. It worked quite well

for a century and replaced the yeomanry which had provided the basic military manpower for the eighteenth century's 'rooted garrison' of Protestant landlords, a system which the '98 and now the Ribbonmen and Orangemen had proved an anachronism.

The magistracy, by the same argument, had also to be professional, or at least stiffened by a trained and centralized backbone. In the south and west, the old J.P.s, being local landlords, were subject to intimidation by the local Ribbonmen and other 'disaffected' elements. Their reaction to this could be one of timidity or it could be one of revenge. There were many J.P.s who stooped to neither such emotion, but there were others who did, and this was therefore no longer an administrative device with which to enforce that respect for English law which Wellesley was determined to impose upon his Irish compatriots. In Ulster, on the other hand, the landed J.P.s were likely to be Orangemen. Again many were not or, if they were, looked beyond their secrets and their oaths to justice in the English sense, and were prepared to risk physical danger and social ostracism in enforcing English laws by punishing the Orange extremists. But again, justice in English eyes must not only be done but be seen to be done. In a country the size of Ireland, and among a people so given to gossip and exaggeration, one act of injustice that is seen to be done by the English authorities will wipe out ninety-nine acts of justice in Irish eyes: one partial J.P. or judge will undo the work of nine fair ones. Hence the need for a centralized police and magistracy responsible directly to Dublin. It was a good reform, because the intention was to produce a placid, pacific Ireland content with British rule.

Protestant fanaticism in the northeastern, or indeed in any other, part of the island was hardly conducive to helping bring this about. Attempts were therefore made during the critical years of emancipation and repeal to forbid Orange marches and other forms of provocative, anti-Catholic display. There had been a riot in Maghera, County Derry, in 1823. This took place at a cattle fair and the provocation on this occasion seems to have come from the Catholics who attacked a force of Yeoman, twelve of whom were Orangemen, driving them into the barracks whence they emerged, armed, and fired on the crowd, killing several and wounding many more. In 1829, despite the ban imposed by the Party Processions Act, there were more than twenty

Orange processions to mark the anniversary of the Battle of the Boyne. There were clashes and casualties at Armagh, Newry, Belfast and Strabane. At Glenoe, in County Tyrone, a pitched battle took place between Orangemen and Ribbonmen, in which two Orangemen and perhaps as many as forty Ribbonmen were killed. In Fermanagh the Earl of Enniskillen, later Grand Master of the Orange Lodge of Ireland, was celebrating 'the immortal memory' with a banquet in his home. Ribbonmen gathered outside and attacked the Orangemen when they left, killing three. It is not clear whether it was before or after this incident that drunken Orangemen fixed bayonets and attacked their enemies, killing an undisclosed number. On July 20th the Viceroy, now the Duke of Northumberland, issued yet another proclamation forbidding processions.

This proclamation was repeated before July 12th, 1830, copies being posted on churches and public buildings, and the Ulster magistrates informed that they must pay particular attention to the problem of sectarian violence. To preserve order this year in Maghera and other perennial trouble-spots, British troops were moved in. It was to no avail. Approximately the same number of Orangemen paraded as in the previous year, perhaps 5,000. In Maghera the troops marched about the little town, alternately dispersing bodies of Ribbonmen and Orangemen. Magistrates attempting to read the riot act without the support of troops were fired on by both factions. That evening the military stopped a battle in which several Catholic homes had been burned and arrested two dozen Orangemen. When these appeared in court next day the court house was rushed by other Orangemen, and the prisoners rescued: the magistrates ordered the police not to intervene. Law enforcement, even with British troops in support, was no easier in the border counties then than it is now.

Though the summer months, particularly July and August, provided an almost open season for riots, and the two best anniversaries to celebrate, that of the Boyne battle on July 12th and of the Derry siege on August 12th, there was no close season. In November of 1830 a concert was held in the village of Marghery (a place in the County Armagh where the Verner family continued to dominate the Orange Order). It seems to have started as an amiable social event, despite the fact that the musicians were Orangemen and the audience mixed but predominantly Catholic. The Orangemen, however, could not resist playing their sectarian songs. Infuriated Catholics thereupon beat up the musicians and smashed their instruments, particularly their drums. The Orangemen fled but were soon back, with supporters. Colonel William Verner tried, but failed, to halt them. The little village was wrecked and pillaged. Curiously enough, when an attempt was made to bring the wreckers to justice, Colonel Verner was unable to identify a single one of them, though he had harangued them, many of whom must have been his own tenants, for some time on the road outside the doomed village. Incidents of this sort could be multiplied many times over.

The attitude and actions of Colonel Verner are and have remained typical of Orangemen of his class. It is to be assumed he did not wish to see Marghery burned down, just as Orange landlords and brewers in Belfast do not today enjoy the spectacle of their property going up in flames. On the other hand only seldom do they act as leaders to prevent such violence. It is even more seldom that the gentry personally take part in riots, but since they then controlled and still largely control the administration of the law, and since they were increasingly sympathetic to the Orange cause and anti-pathetic to the Roman Catholics, they served the Orange Order by giving a very high measure of legal immunity to its thugs and bravos. It was in this way, rather than in actual leadership, that Lord Hillsborough's mass meeting in 1834 marked such an accretion of strength for the Orangemen.

The so-called Tithe War which was going on at this time also strengthened the hand of the Orangemen in two ways. Briefly, the Catholic population, led by Daniel O'Connell, had decided to stop paying tithes to support the Church of Ireland clergy. The tithes had to be collected by force. The new Irish Constabulary was quite inadequate for this task, and Ireland was once again in a state of smothered rebellion. To use troops in order to collect tithes from indigent peasants was not only ridiculous but also—which was far more important to the United Kingdom government—grotesquely expensive. In December 1830, that is to say a month after the wrecking of Marghery, it was the troubles in the Catholic areas that were worrying the Prime Minister, Lord Melbourne. During the emancipation troubles Peel had quite deliberately resisted demands that he re-arm the yeomanry. But Melbourne was a Whig, and the Whigs have, on the whole, an even worse, because more dishonest, record in Irish affairs than the Tories. Melbourne now wrote to Lord Anglesey, the Viceroy, saying: 'If this really becomes serious remember there is no body in Ireland like the Protestant yeomanry in the North ... They must be won to the support of the government, if possible. Nothing would have so much effect in doing this as the calling them out and showing a disposition to encourage them.'*

In the following year the Yeomanry were indeed rearmed with modern weapons, called out on active service, and used to collect tithes from Catholics in the border counties. This was taken, not surprisingly, as the government's endorsement of the Orange Order. This, combined with the fact that the Duke of Cumberland was now the Royal Grand Master of the Order, seemed to give it that respectability for which it had yearned so long. It even led to a revival of some lodges in the South, where Orangeism had become moribund. Furthermore without this apparent benediction from the highest in the land it is unlikely that all those aristocrats and magnates would have assembled to listen to the Rev. Dr. Henry Cooke, nor that an increasing number of establishment clergymen would have enrolled beneath a banner held aloft by a man whom their fathers would have dismissed as a canting hypocrite. However the aristocrats and magnates, and the Church of Ireland clergy too, were premature. If Melbourne was prepared to invoke the Orange yeomanry in the Tithe War—and also, incidentally, to prevent any rebirth of that nationalist spirit which O'Connell was then attempting to revive—this did not mean that he or the government he headed, or the quasi-government in Dublin, liked that secret society. They did not. Indeed in 1835 they decided to set up a Parliamentary Select Committee to enquire into the affairs of the Orange Order. During the summer it submitted no less than four long reports, three dealing with Irish affairs and the fourth with Orangeism in Britain. They were on the whole unfavourable, pointing out the perversion of justice in Ulster and the illegality of Orange Lodges within the army. (These were thereupon dissolved.) The involvement of that arch-reactionary, the Duke of Cumberland, with the Order was regarded as extremely distasteful by the majority who did not share his views. In England the law against secret societies had been invoked in 1834 against

* Melbourne to Anglesey, 22 Dec. 1830 (ibid. 619/VI/7).

six Dorset men, the so-called Tolpuddle Martyrs, who had combined to form the prototype of an agricultural trade union. They were transported to Australia. The radicals and some of the liberals now proposed that similar action be taken against the reactionary leaders of the Orange Order, but since these were now either aristocrats or under aristocratic patronage nothing of course was done. However when a hare-brained conspiracy was hatched by some Orangemen in England, to set aside the rightful claims of Princess Victoria as successor to her uncle, King William IV, and to put the Duke of Cumberland on the throne instead, both Melbourne and Cumberland had had enough. On February 25th, 1836, it was announced that measures would be taken against secret societies generally. A few days later the Duke of Cumberland dissolved the Orange Lodges. Henceforth the Order continued on two levels. There was an open Orange Order and this was controlled by a secret society which had gone underground. Nothing, in fact, was changed.

According to various authorities there were sectarian riots in Belfast in 1835, 1843, 1857, 1864, 1872, 1880, 1884, 1886, and 1894, or approximately one every seven years throughout the last two thirds of the century. These were, of course, major riots, and since our ancestors were less squeamish than ourselves in their terminology a riot really was a riot, usually with gun play, fatal casualties and the destruction of property, not a mere punch-up. Punch-ups were of regular occurrence, and particularly, in the words of *The Old Orange Flute* 'on the twelfth of July, as it yearly did come.' To describe all these riots in detail would be tedious. The reader who would care to know more about them is referred to Andrew Boyd's *Holy War in Belfast*, Anvil Books, 1969, from which the descriptions that follow later are largely taken.

Like most of the cities built in the nineteenth century to provide the manpower needed by the industrial revolution, working-class Belfast did not degenerate into a slum. It was built as one, a congeries of narrow, noisome streets and courts and alleyways, back-to-back houses usually without sanitation designed to hold the maximum number of people, and thus provide maximum rents for the landlords in return for a minimum capital outlay. (Belfast was slightly less revolting than the equivalent English cities of the Industrial Revolution, being built a generation later, by which time some very rudimentary legislation concerning hygiene and building standards was on the statute book. For instance the back-to-backs in the Belfast slums were not usually so, as in Manchester, but were often separated by a tiny yard. However the population, particularly the Catholic population, was even poorer than its English equivalent and overcrowding in the worst areas therefore even greater.) There were crowds everywhere and this was accentuated by the habit of the country people, who flocked into Belfast from the overpopulated countryside, of bringing their domestic animals with them. Pigs and chickens rooted and pecked among the filth and garbage: there were even cows. And because the houses were so crowded—whole families living in a single room —the populace developed the habit, more suitable to the climate of Southern Italy than that of Northern Ireland, of living in the streets. When the pubs were closed, or the wages spent or jobs not available, groups of youths and men would collect at street corners to talk and grumble, exchanging silly rumours and the foolish half-ideas of the uneducated, while around them, playing in disgusting gutters or climbing upon heaps of refuse among the animals were crowds of what Ezra Pound once called 'the filthy, sturdy, unkillable infants of the very poor'. They are still there today, the corner-boys and the children, in the winter with shoddy coat-collars turned up against the drizzle and the sleet, in the summer nerves irritated by heat and smells and thirst, thirst for alcohol first, for excitement second. In their drab and dreary lives a procession was and is an event, a riot a real treat.

This wretched, rootless proletariat should, at first glance, have given corporeal reality to the spectre which, according to Karl Marx, then haunted all Europe, the spectre of revolution. Yet the slum-dwellers of Belfast were even less inclined to revolution than were their equivalents in Manchester, whom Engels observed so closely, or in the other English cities. For one thing, like proletarians almost everywhere and at almost all times, they were leaderless, or if they had any leaders then it was their clergy, Dissenters or Roman Catholics. The ministers of these churches could not possibly combine, in the last century or indeed in this, to produce any form of revolutionary leadership. Therefore, and in defiance of their more enlightened priests and preachers, the bitterness of Belfast's wretched proletariat was channelled into sectarian rather than class hatred. This was not a conspiracy by the wealthy—certainly not in its inception—but was a product of circumstances, mounting intolerance as the Victorian religious revival moved into full gear, and basic ignorance.

By 1835 the tendency of the Belfast proletariat to live, more or less, in different streets and even areas according to their religious affiliations was already underway. By this time, for instance, Sandy Row was almost entirely Protestant: an area of waste land, which was to be a perennial battlefield, separated it from the district known as The Pound, where most of the population were Catholics. There were other areas, such as Smithfield, which had a Catholic majority, others again with a Protestant one in a mixed area. Thus the situation that had existed for so long in the border counties was repeated, but physically telescoped, in the Belfast streets. And the gangs of corner-boys, hanging about outside the pubs, assumed more and more a sectarian quality not at all dissimilar to the racial qualities and loyalties revealed by proletarian minority gangs in the slums of New York: Puerto Ricans, Italians, Negroes, Jews. The *West Side Story* situation was foreshadowed in Belfast in 1835, the only common enemy to them all being the police. In Belfast, however, each side had only one real enemy. And each has only one enemy today, apart from the British army sent now, as then, with the initial purpose of being impartial dispensers of pacification.

On July 12th, 1835, the Orange celebrations ended in a riot. The military intervened, including, it would seem, heavy cavalry for there were many sabre wounds reported. One man and one woman were shot dead. At the same time in Smithfield Roman Catholics were marching about, waving green flags. They wrecked and looted Protestant-owned shops and pubs.

In 1843 the *Northern Whig* reported on the civil disturbances that July:

'... one corner of our town, including a part of Sandy Row and Barrack Street, has been the theatre of much excitement and rioting, the contending parties being Catholics and Protestants of a low description.'

The horrors and tragedy of the Famine, to which in Belfast was added an epidemic of typhus in 1847 and of Asiatic cholera in 1848, had a temporary stunning effect. In the midst of all this

misery a small group of Irish patriots, led by William Smith
O'Brien, attempted to raise a rebellion. It must surely rank
among the most futile insurrectionary revolts in all history.
Theoretically Young Ireland, as it was called, tried to revive
the ideals of the United Irishmen in opposition to the constitutional methods of Daniel O'Connell whose policy had died
with him in 1847: but Young Ireland had no appeal at all for
the Protestants in Ulster, and if it had any effect in the Northeast
it was only to harden the hearts of the Dissenters against their
Catholic fellow-citizens. In the South Smith O'Brien was hoping
for a *levée en masse* by a rural population that was starving and
sick unto death. This did not of course occur. The leaders were
arrested, sentenced to death, but finally transported for their
folly. They were, in their youth, attractive romantics in an age
that created Mazzini in Italy and saw the poet, Alphonse de
Lamartine, a senior member of the government of the short-
lived Second French Republic: as revolutionaries they were quite
useless.

Indeed as failed revolutionaries they were positively harmful
to their starving, fever-ridden compatriots. The English, particularly the English Whigs, were already wearied by this huge increment of impoverished citizens to the United Kingdom. With
the famine this emotion hardened: they simply did not know
what to do. A man named Nassau Senior, perhaps the most distinguished living English political economist of the day and an
economic adviser to the British government, remarked to the
great Benjamin Jowett, Master of Balliol College, Oxford, in
1848 that he 'feared the famine in Ireland would not kill more
than a million people, and that would scarcely be enough to do
much good.' Few expressed themselves quite so bluntly in public.
Nor was this government policy. Faced with an unprecedented
problem, and bound by the economic theories of the age, the
men who formed that government did attempt to feed the Irish
and support them by ordering the building of public works.
Millions of pounds were squeezed from a reluctant Treasury,
some £13 million in all. Unfortunately the gentlemen in London
had very little knowledge of social and economic conditions in
Ireland, while the men sent over to administer this relief operation, vast by the standards of the age, were often inefficient and
not infrequently corrupt. Much public money thus went to
waste. After 1848 relief measures to feed the starving Irish were

cut back drastically and in the end virtually abolished. Trevelyan, permanent head of the Treasury, justified this on brutal
economic-ideological grounds: to feed or clothe the dying would
be to interfere with the free market. The Prime Minister preferred a political justification for government's failure within
an intrinsic part of the United Kingdom. Because Smith O'Brien
with a few dozen followers had attempted a rebellion that turned
out to be a complete fiasco, causing no damage and very few lives,
all Ireland must be made to suffer. Lord John Russell spoke for
the majority in England, or so he imagined and probably correctly, when he aired his petulant views to the Viceroy in Dublin,
Lord Clarendon, in a communication dated February 24th,
1849: 'We have subscribed, worked, visited, clothed, for the
Irish,' wrote Lord John, 'millions of money, years of debate,
etc., etc., etc. The only return is rebellion and calumny. Let us
not grant, lend, clothe, etc., any more, and see what that will
do. This is the great difficulty today—British people think this.'

The result of the famine, of the evictions, of the epidemics
and even more, but resulting from these, of the massive emigration to Britain, Canada and the United States was a basic
alteration to the demography of Ireland. The Protestants had
suffered in the famine and the epidemics, but nothing like the
Catholics. Many emigrated, but again there was no massive
flight from the land. In the Northeast the system of land tenure,
and a more variegated diet, kept the yeomanry on their farms.
Even in cholera-ridden Belfast rapid industrialization gave jobs,
food and low-grade housing to the excess farm population. In the
South and West the property owners were almost all Protestants
and there was almost no Protestant proletariat: property owners
seldom emigrate, save under the most extreme political pressure
which usually and perhaps invariably involves the confiscation
of their property by brute force, as in seventeenth and early
eighteenth century Ireland, as in the Communist countries or,
for the Jews, in Germany a generation ago, as has been done by
fiscal means in England in recent years.

Had there been no Great Famine and no quasi-genocide and
no mass emigration, it would seem probable that by 1861 the
population of Ireland would have amounted to between eleven
and twelve millions, or approximately one third of the population of the whole United Kingdom. A little over one million
Irishmen would have been Protestants, most of them Northern

nonconformists, some 10% of the Irish population. As it was the Protestant element remained, and has remained, at about the million mark, while for a hundred years after the Famine the Catholic population shrank, rapidly at first but still steadily thereafter. The Irish Republic was declared in 1949, an ironic centenary to the worst year of the Famine and to the first massive emigration. The census of 1966 shows that in the intervening century the proportion of Protestants, by then even more concentrated in the Six Counties of Ulster, had risen from some 10% to some 30% while within those Six Counties it was some 60% and, in the four most densely Protestant areas it was 80% or more. The native Catholic Irish were smashed, embittered, and their numbers more than halved. Three generations were to pass before they had regained the vigour and courage to attack their conquerors again, this time with partial success, but by then the conqueror had changed too.

In the Northeast, on the other hand, the genocide to the West and South seemed to offer the possibility of a 'final solution' to their own, provincial problem, that is to say the murder or expulsion of the entire Roman Catholic population. As the Protestants in Ulster also began to recover from the horrors of the Famine they found themselves in a far stronger position than ever before. Simultaneously they found themselves increasingly threatened, particularly in Belfast, by a greater influx of Catholic Irish labourers. Belfast became, as it has remained, a city of hatred. And Andrew Boyd dates the first of the really vicious, modern, sectarian riots to the year 1857. The corner-boys still hung about the corners, and the pubs were still crowded with ignorant men, even as they are today. The social arrangements in Belfast were hardening, not relaxing. It was of great significance that the clerico-demagogic leadership had, by 1857, passed— at least temporarily—from the hands of Dissenting outsiders into those of an ordained minister of the established church who once again put all the respectable abbreviations in front of his name, the Rev. Dr. Thomas Drew. I cannot do better than quote a long passage from Andrew Boyd (op. cit.) about what happened on July 12th, 1857, and the days that followed.

'Like most Victorian Sundays, Sunday 12th July 1857 was a quiet day in Belfast. The sun shone. The town lay apparently at peace amid the mountains and green fields that surround it.

That morning Sub-Inspector Harris Bindon, who commanded
the Belfast garrison of the Irish Constabulary, had remarked
to Samuel Tracy, the resident magistrate, that it looked like
being a quiet Twelfth of July. Tracy was not so optimistic. He
had been in Belfast since 1849 and could not remember a July
when there had not been trouble of some sort. He told Bindon,
who had been stationed only ten months in the town, that he
would never forget 1852. The Orangemen stoned him in York
Street that year. He was lucky to escape alive.

Soon after six o'clock in the evening Bindon was returning
to the constabulary barracks in Durham Street. His way was
through Sandy Row and as he strolled along he came upon a
large number of people going in the same direction as himself.
They were walking in what he, an ex-military officer, later
described as file-marching.

There must have been about 400 of them, nearly all men, some
accompanied by their womenfolk. All were respectably dressed
in their Sunday suits. They wore white gloves, carried Bibles and
had orange-coloured flowers in their hats.

Bindon hurried past these people and reached the barracks before they crossed the Saltwater Bridge. From an upstairs window he watched them assemble in a side-street near Christ
Church, where Thomas Drew, the Vicar, preached every Sunday.
Drew, Doctor of Divinity, was also Grand Chaplain of the Grand
Orange Lodge of Ireland. It was likely, thought Bindon, that a
special service had been arranged to mark the Orange anniversary.

Christ Church is built in a place which was then on the exact
line dividing Sandy Row from the Pound. "It was infelicitously
situated," wrote the commissioners who reported on the riots
of 1857, "to be selected as the place for a great and unusual
celebration of the festival of the 12th of July."

At a few minutes to seven o'clock the people in the side-street
walked towards Christ Church and Bindon noted that, once
they were within an area enclosed by iron railings, the men took
Orange sashes from their pockets and draped them over their
shoulders. He knew they dare not wear the sashes in the public
street, because Orange parades and the displaying of Orange
regalia and emblems in public were forbidden by the Party
Processions Act.

The news that Dr. Drew was to preach a special sermon for

Orangemen that day had spread throughout Belfast. It reached the Catholics who lived in the Pound, and a man named John Hackett heard it there. The police suspected that Hackett, a labouring man, was a member of the illegal Ribbon Society, a Catholic organization. They could get no evidence to support their suspicion but they knew that Hackett was noted for his antipathy to Orangeism. He lived near a man who had been shot and permanently disabled by Orange terrorists in 1853. On occasions he had helped to carry victims of Orange gunmen to hospital.

On the evening of 12th July 1857 John Hackett was on his way to visit the president of a labourers' friendly society but, when he came to Christ Church and saw the Orangemen, he decided to enter and hear for himself what Drew had to say.

Thomas Drew was a controversial preacher, a well-known "denouncer of popery". He had sermons for every Protestant centenary and celebration. He could preach as easily on the birth of Luther as on the death of Latymer, and could talk for hours about the massacre of St. Bartholomew or the Battle of the Boyne. He built chapels of prayer in many parts of Belfast and dedicated them to great Protestants of history—Wycliffe, Luther and Huss.

Drew also wrote Orange songs and pamphlets. One, his *Twenty Reasons for Being an Orangeman,* includes such sentiments: "I learn by the doctrines, history and daily practises of the Church of Rome that the lives of Protestants are endangered, that the laws of England set at nought, and the Crown of England subordinated to the dictates of an Italian bishop."

Drew was an able orator. His skill in the pulpit was an advantage in an age when lecturers and preachers were held in great respect and could influence public opinion.

Born in Limerick, in 1800, he graduated Bachelor of Arts from Trinity College, Dublin, in 1826, and was ordained a priest of the Church of Ireland the following year. He came to Belfast, in 1833, as first rector of the newly-built Christ Church and for many years exercised a remarkable, though not always a Christian, influence on the Protestant working people. Sandy Row was within his parish.

One of his daughters married William Johnston, a well-known Orangeman who, in 1867 and in defiance of the law, organized an Orange procession at a place called Ballykilbeg. Johnston was sent to prison and imprisonment brought him fame, a place in Orange history and election to Parliament as one of the Conservative members for Belfast. When in Parliament he fought successfully for the repeal of the Party Processions Act.

When Drew, dressed in the plain vestments of an Episcopalian priest, mounted the pulpit that day in Christ Church his congregation fell silent. The people had come from many parts of Belfast and were estimated at more than 2,000. The first, carefully-chosen words of his sermon were intended to flatter them:

"Matthew five, (he intoned) verses thirteen, fourteen, fifteen and sixteen ... Ye are the salt of the earth. Ye are the light of the world. Let your light so shine before men that they may see your good works and glorify your Father which is in heaven....

"... The Sermon on the Mount is an everlasting rebuke to all intolerance.... Of old time lords of high degree, with their own hands, strained on the rack the limbs of the delicate Protestant women, prelates dabbled in the gore of their helpless victims. The cells of the Pope's prisons were paved with the calcined bones of men and cemented with human gore and human hair...."

The sermon was a long fanatical tirade against the Catholic Church. For example:

"The Word of God makes all plain; puts to eternal shame the practices of persecutors, and stigmatizes with enduring reprobation the arrogant pretences of Popes and the outrageous dogmata of their blood-stained religion."

Then, as was fitting on 12 July, Drew dealt with the plight of Ireland's Protestants during the reign of James II:

"The fierce Tyrconnell was sent over, a man of ready blasphemy and merciless bigotry. Then did the Protestants feel intensely their oppression. Then were the Protestant churches nailed up and the congregations ordered to forgo their assemblies. Then were the lives and property of the Protestants of Ireland a prey to the despoiling priests. Then, at the great hour of extremity, the Deliverer landed at Carrickfergus."

The "deliverer" was William, Prince of Orange, whom the bankers and Whiggish businessmen of London brought from the Netherlands, in 1688, to overthrow the Stuart autocrats. Today, long after the City of London ceased to regard this event as a glorious revolution, the Protestants of Ireland remember William in their churches, their Orange lodges and their Conservative politics.

Drew's sermon was not unusual. It was the kind that many Protestant clergymen in Ulster were in the habit of preaching until fairly recent times. He denounced "the pernicious doctrines which we call popery" and recalled the deeds of "gallant William, world-famed Schomberg and fearless George Walker."

The Orangemen and their wives, nearly all uneducated working-class poor, believed every word spoken by their pastor. To them the appalling image of the Pope's prisons and torture-chambers was real, the awful warnings of oppression to come were genuine.

John Hackett found the sermon frightening. Halfway through it, when the congregation had reached a near-hysterical state in which they were cheering every time they heard the name "William" and howling when the Pope and Rome were mentioned, he thought there would be violence and decided to leave.

By then a crowd of Catholics had gathered in the streets around Christ Church and were being held back by a party of the Town Police Force of Belfast.

These policemen did not belong to the Irish Constabulary whom Bindon commanded. They were members of a local force which had been set up by an Act of Parliament, in 1845, and were under the direct control of the town council's police committee.

As the police committee consisted entirely of Protestants, membership of the Orange Order or a letter from a Protestant clergyman seems to have been the most effective qualification for anyone who wanted to join the force. Not surprisingly, all but five of the 160 men in the Town Police Force of Belfast, in 1857, were Protestants. Several were Orangemen who walked, despite the law, in Twelfth of July processions outside Belfast.

In his evidence to the commissioners who inquired into the 1857 riots, Samuel Tracy, RM, described the town police as "sympathizers with the Sandy Row mob and enemies to those in the Pound".

"Accordingly," commented the commissioners, "during the riots they could safely appear in Sandy Row but their appearance in the Pound was the sign for attack. Consequently, instead of being a help they became a hindrance to the constabulary during the riots."

The commissioners also noted that as the town police had no

firearms and were supplied only with light walking sticks they were "plainly insufficient for the protection of life and property".

The commissioners of 1857 and also those who inquired into "the magisterial and police jurisdiction of Belfast," in 1864, found that many of the town policemen had other sources of income, apart from their police pay. Some were greengrocers, others kept lodging-houses, reared pigs and poultry, or plied cars for hire.

The fact that twelve town policemen were registered as burgesses and could, therefore, vote in elections for the town council, and that eight of the twelve also had the parliamentary vote was considered by the commissioners to be "very objectionable".

The Catholics of Belfast detested the town police and called them "hornies" and "bulkies," while the more liberal Protestants thought of them as being "undisciplined, partisan and suspected by all decent inhabitants".

The superintendent in charge of the town police, an Orange veteran named Adam Hill, had been appointed, in 1852, when he was 72 years of age. Hill drew £200 a year for doing almost nothing, his duties consisting of going occasionally to the Police Office and making sure that the constable on duty made the correct entries in the day-book.

Hill was a member of the no-popery party, and the no-popery policy, he found, paid him well throughout his long life. Before he became a superintendent of police he had been Belfast Town Council's Under-Treasurer, for which his salary was also £200 a year. He had been an original member of the Orange Order and often recalled how, when he was a yeoman in the government's service, he had helped to crush the rebellion of United Irishmen in 1798.

Adam Hill had close associations with John Bates, a disreputable politician who, for many years, was both Town Clerk and Town Solicitor in Belfast. In the general election of 1841 Hill and Bates were in charge of the Conservative Party's campaign in Belfast, but they used such manifest corruption to get their men elected that Parliament felt compelled to set up a court of inquiry which unseated the Conservatives and ordered a new election.

Under the control of men such as Hill and Bates, the Town Police Force of Belfast was bound to be corrupt and partisan. In June 1865 Parliament passed an act abolishing it for all time.

This Act declared that Belfast was a distinct district of the Irish Constabulary; it provided for a police force of at least 130 constables, with officers, to be stationed in the town. Before the 1865 Act the Irish Constabulary garrison in Belfast was merely part of the contingent allocated by law to the whole of the county of Antrim. Belfast, unlike Cork and Limerick, was not entitled to a constabulary force in its own right.

While Thomas Drew was preaching, on that Twelfth of July 1857, two young post-office workers, Francis Holland and William Burton, went out for an evening stroll. They walked through the centre of the town, then towards Christ Church and eventually turned in a direction that took them into the middle of the Catholic crowd that had gathered near the church. There they were recognized as Protestants and surrounded by several angry youths. Holland was struck on the head. Burton was pulled to the ground and kicked as he fell.

News of this assault reached Bindon within a few minutes. He ordered one of his subordinate officers, Head-Constable Henderson, to take three men to the scene of the trouble. Henderson found Burton badly injured and covered with blood. Francis Holland had escaped from the mob. He fled along Castle Street to the safety of the town centre.

That same evening, Brigid Kane, an inoffensive Catholic who lived in Tea Lane in the heart of Sandy Row, heard prolonged cheering outside her house and, on looking out, saw a crowd of people waving flags and bunches of orange flowers and dancing around an immense effigy that was supposed to represent Dan O'Connell, the Catholic leader, who was dead since 1847. She saw them carry the effigy up and down Tea Lane, then set it alight outside her front door and dance while it blazed.

Brigid Kane accepted the burning of the effigy as a warning. Next day, when a friendly neighbour advised her to leave, she packed her belongings and found herself another house in English Street, within the safety of the Pound.

Earlier in the day two Catholic curates had been obstructed and jeered when they attended a funeral in Sandy Row, and in the evening a drunk shouted Orange slogans as he drove into the Catholic crowd outside Christ Church. This man was later identified as a young Catholic named Loughran, and fined forty shillings for riotous behaviour.

Loughran's escapade was played up by the newspaper editors,

some of whom tried to blame him for causing the riots. The court of inquiry, however, dismissed the incident as "slight and unimportant".

Apart from these incidents, nothing very serious happened on Sunday night. On Monday morning, however, reports of the attack on the two young postmen, of the interference with the funeral and of Dr. Drew's sermon spread through the town. Alarming rumours were invented and, as they circulated, tempers began to rise.

When Drew finished his sermon, the Orangemen left the church without any interference from the Catholics. Towards midnight, however, the police heard gunfire, but were not sure whether the guns were being fired in the Pound or Sandy Row. The firing of guns during the month of July was nothing new in Belfast. It happened every year. Shots would be fired in Sandy Row and answered in the Pound.

In July 1857 the shots awakened Jonathan Jones, a young English technician who was working in Belfast. He also heard the thunder of drums, like a distant cannonade, he thought, apparently coming from the farthest part of Sandy Row. Jones, who lived in the Pound, was to be a witness before the commission of inquiry into the 1857 riots.

The drums also disturbed Sub-Inspector Bindon as he was having late supper and getting ready for bed. He went out to investigate and, in Sandy Row, came upon a crowd of men and women gathered around a fat man who was beating a mighty instrument known, in the north of Ireland, as the Lambeg drum.

Drumming and sectarian music, as well as party processions, were forbidden by law because they usually led to serious disturbances. One such disturbance was the riot on Dolly's Brae, which Bindon had witnessed because he was there with the constabulary. He had seen the numerous deaths and the destruction of property that resulted.

It happened on 12 July 1849 when the Orangemen, protected by strong forces of police and military, were returning from a rally in Tullymore Park, estate of the Earl of Roden, near Castlewellan in County Down. On Dolly's Brae, in the townland of Magheramayo, the Orange procession was met by a party of Catholics. Both sides were armed and for several hours they fought a bloody battle that was long remembered in Orange ballads.

The Battle of Dolly's Brae happened at a time when the Party Processions Act was relaxed. Among other things it brought about a re-enactment of the restrictions as well as the disgrace of the Earl of Roden and many of the other Orange landowners of County Down.

With all this at the back of his mind, Bindon seized the fat drummer by the arm and told him to stop. This made the drummer's audience angry. They shouted insults and threats, but Bindon stood firm and told them that if they did not go home he would send for the Mayor. And the Mayor, he reminded them, would order out the police and the military. This seemed to subdue the crowd, though Bindon waited until the last of them had trailed off behind the fat drummer before he, too, went home to bed.

In those times, just as today, the people who lived in Sandy Row and the Pound were mostly of the working class. "People of the humbler orders" as they used to be described. They were mill hands, unskilled labourers, skilled workmen, with a sprinkling, as in every community, of self-employed people such as shopkeepers, cabmen and others only a little better off than the industrial workers.

At five o'clock on Monday morning 13 July James Carolan, a young newspaper worker, saw several men stringing Orange arches across Albert Street, within sight of the Pound. The arches were made of nothing more than a few orange-coloured flowers and pieces of cloth, but even such pathetic displays as these were unlawful. Carolan noticed and reported that six members of the town police stood under the arches and had apparently given their consent to these illegal manifestations of Orange militancy. Normally the police were expected to pull down such arches and were often ordered to do so during July.

Later that morning some Orangemen formed a procession in which at least two members of the town police joined. They marched to a public house at Ligoneill, several miles outside the town. That afternoon many of the Orange lodges held meetings in private houses and church halls. Indoor meetings were lawful, but public processions, like the one to Ligoneill, were unlawful.

There was not much rioting on that Monday evening, though large crowds of Catholics and Protestants, excited by the gunfire of the previous night and by the rumours that had been circulating all day, gathered in a field of wasteland that lay

alongside Albert Street and separated the Pound from Sandy
Row. The wasteland stretched to the south until it merged with
a vast swamp, the remaining parts of which are known today as
the Bog Meadows. Lying, as it did, between the Pound and
Sandy Row, this wasteland was a place where gangs from both
sides often fought on Saturday nights. In 1857 it became a
battlefield.

Jonathan Jones, a stranger in Belfast, was fascinated by the
sight of the mobs which gathered on Monday night. He could
have seen them from where he lived in Quadrant Street, but, to
get a better view, he walked out and stood in the doorway of a
shop owned by a man named McIlhone, little realizing that, if
there would be gunplay, he was in a very dangerous place. The
Orangemen often aimed their fire at McIlhone's house. They
were convinced that it was an arsenal in which were stored the
guns and ammunition of the Catholics.

Jones, out of natural curiosity, observed everything that
went on and, months later, recalled it all in detail when he gave
evidence to the commissioners who inquired into the disturbances. The mob from Sandy Row, he said, were taunting the
Catholics and screaming insults about the Pope. The Catholics
were equally abusive; they sang songs which Jones admitted
he could not understand, though he did remember one line,
something about "to hell with Sandy Row".

In the words of the commissioners' report, "the aspect of those
localities was that of the camp of two armies, waiting only for a
convenient time of actual battle."

While the mobs on the wasteland did little more than shout
insults and hurl sods of earth at one another, there was action
not far away when a Catholic crowd, from the lanes of Millfield,
Smithfield and Carrick Hill, attacked a spiritgrocer's shop owned
by a Protestant named Watts. The shop was known to be a
house-of-call for the town police. Watts welcomed them with
drinks and pipes at any hour of the day or night.

The mob arrived in the vicinity of Watts's place about nine
o'clock. Soon they saw a town policeman, Constable Blair, making his way towards the shop and they stoned him as he tried to
find refuge behind a brick wall. Watts saw them coming and
managed to get his front door bolted and his windows shuttered
in time, but these precautions were no use.

Within minutes the mob had pulled the shutters off their

hinges and broken every pane of glass in the shop. As Constable
Blair ran for help, they threw Watts's entire stock-in-trade into
the street, and by the time help arrived, in the form of Bindon
and a party of the constabulary who had been stationed nearby,
all the attackers had disappeared, leaving the unfortunate Watts
to clean up the mess and count the damage.

A few minutes later, two Wesleyan pastors on their way
through Millfield walked into the mob that had wrecked Watts's
shop and, on being recognized as Protestants, were beaten with
sticks and stones. One of the pastors was knocked to the ground
and kicked. The other was so badly injured that he was lame for
a long time afterwards. Both escaped from their assailants, however, and reached the safety of a Protestant house in Brown
Square. From there they were escorted to their homes on Shank-
hill Road.

Next day, Tuesday 14th July, Head-Constable Henderson saw
Protestant millworkers being jeered and hissed as they made
their way along Cullingtree Road, within the Pound. He saw
Catholics getting the same treatment in Sandy Row. It rained
heavily that day but patrols of police, their heavy uniforms
soaked, kept on the move through the disturbed districts. Rain
was still falling in the evening when the mobs again assembled
on the wasteland. John McLaughlin, proprietor of *The Ulsterman*, a Belfast Catholic newspaper, saw some of them for-
gathering in the side-streets as he passed through Sandy Row
on the way to his office. He was recognized, called a papist and
pelted with stones as he went by.

For about an hour the mobs on the wasteland exchanged
insults and slogans, as they had done the previous evening, and
all the time they were watched by a group of town policemen
who did nothing to break up the assemblies. Eventually stones
and sods of earth began to fly through the air, and suddenly the
Sandy Row mob cut loose and charged across the roadway towards Brook Street and Quadrant Street.

The houses in these streets, which are occupied to the present
day, were new in 1857. They had been built three years earlier,
at a cost of £9,000, by William Watson, who was one of the
very few wealthy Catholics then in Belfast. He hoped to get
good-class tenants and, in fact, drew a substantial income from
the property. Jonathan Jones and Head-Constable Henderson
lived in two of his houses.

As the mob rushed towards Quadrant Street, Henderson was in Durham Street barracks trying to reassure a Catholic woman who had asked for police protection. She was a widow named Betty Donoghue and she occupied a house on the wasteland with her four children and an old woman. There she kept cows and poultry and made a living selling eggs and milk. The gossips said she also kept a house-of-call and sold liquor to the fowlers who shot over the Bog Meadows at week-ends.

Betty Donoghue's garden, which lay between the Pound and Sandy Row, was often the Saturday night battleground of the rival mobs, but when she complained to the police about this they merely advised her to move to another place. This was what she had to do eventually.

No less frightened than Betty Donoghue was Hopewell Kelly, wife of a man who owned a small bakery. The Kellys rented one of Watson's houses and could afford to keep two housemaids, one of whom, Brigid Trainor, was watching from a bedroom window when the mob charged. A few seconds later, a shower of stones broke every window in Kelly's house and sent a baby in one of the bedrooms into hysterics. No harm came to the child that evening, but he was to die a few weeks later because of the riots.

The people who swept towards Quadrant Street, with the obvious intention of taking the Catholics in the rear, carried long poles which they used to smash the upstairs windows of houses as they ran past. Like unruly mobs everywhere, they revelled in the crash of breaking glass and the fierce leap of flames. They were to enjoy plenty of both before the riots of 1857 had run their course.

Anticipating the Protestants' plan of attack, the Catholics charged from the opposite end of Quadrant Street and, according to Jonathan Jones who was watching this time from the vantage point of his bedroom window, they drove their enemies back across the road and into the wasteland.

As the Protestants retreated across the fields they suddenly took up the pursuit of a Catholic woman who was running for her life towards Donoghue's house. Betty Donoghue had just returned from the police barracks and was helping the old woman to bed when a brick came crashing through the window and landed at her feet. Then a wild-looking man, all covered with mud, climbed in, yelling for "the papist from the Pound".

The old woman became terrified at the sight of this man. The rioters, whom he led, had already broken open Donoghue's gates and would have wrecked her house if the police had not then arrived on the scene. The police were advancing from two sides of the wasteland with the intention of surrounding the mob. Armed with carbines and bayonets and led by Harris Bindon, the constabulary came from the direction of Albert Street. The town police, brandishing their walking sticks and led by their senior officer, Chief-Constable Thomas Lindsay, had entered the wasteground from Durham Street.

At the sight of the police the mob scattered. Lindsay, running hard to intercept them, managed to grab the man who had climbed through Donoghue's window. Just as he thought he had his prisoner secure, Lindsay slipped in the mud and the man escaped into a maze of little streets near the wasteland.

Lindsay's men pursued the mob through the fields without taking any prisoners, but the constabulary captured five, among them a 14-year-old boy who complained that a constable had bayoneted him in the back. Meanwhile Betty Donoghue's house was a shambles of tangled fences, broken gates and smashed windows. The rain was still pelting down on the sodden, muddy wasteland.

The constables were securing their prisoners and bringing them to the barracks when some of the rioters returned and attempted a rescue. They would have succeeded, too, but for Harris Bindon. On foot and brandishing a naked sword, he charged them, as he must often have charged the enemy when a soldier in the Crimean War. At the sight of this fearsome figure, in the dark, tight-fitting uniform of an officer of the Irish Constabulary, the rioters again fled into the side-streets.

Then a detachment of hussars arrived under the command of Major Hood and they completely cleared the wasteland. The hussars were followed by two companies of the 54th Infantry, led by Samuel Geddes, Mayor of Belfast; William McGee, local surgeon and Justice of the Peace, and Samuel Tracy, RM. For the remainder of that night the infantry occupied positions along Durham Street and Albert Street while the hussars patrolled the Pound and Sandy Row.

A favourite trick of the rioters was to extinguish the street-lamps, thus making it impossible for the police or military to pursue them through the streets and narrow lanes after nightfall. Chief-Constable Lindsay said he could not cope with this stratagem nor could he provide protection for the lamp-lighters. When the lamps were extinguished nobody tried to light them again.

On one occasion in the Pound, Lindsay saw a man come out of a house with a little boy seated high on his shoulders. The man walked coolly towards the nearest street-lamp, and suddenly the boy reached and turned the lamp out. Man and boy had vanished in the darkness before Lindsay realized what had happened.

When John McLaughlin got clear of the crowds in Sandy Row he went straight to Durham Street police barracks and was there, having a parley with Tracy, when the constables brought in the five prisoners. McLaughlin told Tracy that a party of Sandy Row gunmen had barricaded themselves in a nearby house. Tracy refused to believe him. He wanted proof, and asked McLaughlin to bring him to the gunmen.

In fact, McLaughlin was telling the truth. Later in the evening McGee and Tracy were summoned to a house which had been riddled with bullets. On their way to this house they saw the place McLaughlin had described. It was a partly-built house with one wall loop-holed and fitted with a platform from which the gunmen fired across the wasteland towards McIlhone's corner.

The riots commissioners mentioned this and other barricaded houses in their report. "In the Sandy Row district," they stated, "preparations were made for the conflict; a building in the course of erection was loopholed for the occasion, and bricks were placed behind the walls of some of the backyards to give an easy means of firing." The firing continued every day from these positions yet the police were unable to capture the gunmen responsible.

As Tracy and McGee were inspecting the bedrooms of the bullet-riddled house, a party of town policemen were fleeing along Cullingtree Road before a Catholic mob that had already extinguished the street-lamps and wrecked several houses. Three of the policemen, Constables Cairns, Bingham and Gourley, were trapped and forced to seek refuge in the house of a man named John Heyburn.

Heyburn refused to deliver up the policemen when called upon to do so. At this the Catholics rushed the house, broke down the front door and dragged out the three constables. The policemen remembered nothing more for some time. Tracy and Lindsay came upon them as they lay motionless in the gutter with a group of wailing women around them. Meanwhile the mob had vanished in the darkness and, despite subsequent searching investigations by the police, not one of them was ever identified.

At first, Tracy thought the three policemen had been killed, but when a lamp was brought he could see they were all alive. Cairns was not very badly injured but Gourley was bleeding from the mouth and Bingham had severe head wounds. All three were detained in the General Hospital for a month. During the first week, Samuel Browne, the house surgeon, feared that Gourley and Bingham were not going to recover.

The attack on the three policemen struck terror into the Town Police Force of Belfast. Thereafter they would not go on duty unless protected by the armed constabulary or the military.

All this time the terrorizing of innocent individuals continued. Protestants were attacked in the Pound and driven from their homes. Catholic houses were wrecked in Sandy Row. Ellen Crawford, an elderly widow who kept a shop in Stanley Street, and her daughter, Catherine, were victims of this terror. These inoffensive women were Catholics and for this reason were regarded as a menace by the Orangemen of Sandy Row.

Disturbed by the shooting on Tuesday night, Ellen Crawford and her daughter had gone to bed early. When they retired the riots seemed to have died down, but in the small hours of the morning they were awakened by loud shouting and singing and, as this noise grew louder, they realized that a mob was advancing on their house.

Ellen Crawford was too terrified to move, but her daughter pulled aside the heavy bedroom curtain and could see a crowd of people down in the street. They were singing Orange songs, cursing the Pope and Dan O'Connell and calling on all papists to get out of Sandy Row.

Then a barrage of heavy stones hit the house. One came crashing through the bedroom window and struck Ellen Crawford on the face, leaving a deep, bloody gash. After this it seemed that the mob had withdrawn some distance, but soon they were back. They tore the shutters from the downstairs windows and scattered the stock of the shop about the street. Again they withdrew, then returned a third time and unleashed another barrage of stones. Catherine Crawford could hear them calling for the place to be burned down.

Then, for no apparent reason, they ran away, still shouting threats at the papists and cursing the Pope. They left two terrified women and a bedroom littered with stones, broken glass and even some of the stock which they had thrown back into the house. When she was sure it was safe to venture out, Ellen Crawford wrapped a bedsheet around herself and went for police protection.

One disgusting feature of this outrage was that the Durham Street constabulary barracks was only a few hundred yards away from Crawford's house and for most of the night had been full of policemen. Catherine Crawford said she saw several mounted police as she ran along Albert Street to the barracks.

The constable who opened the door to the barefooted girl showed little interest in her plight. Impatiently he told her to go home and that someone would be round to see what damage had been done. But it was not until after daybreak that two policemen took the trouble to walk to the damaged house, and then they merely sauntered along the street without inquiring if any of the mob had been seen since or recognized.

It would probably have been useless for them to inquire, anyhow. The tactics of the mobs consisted of launching sudden attacks and then vanishing at the first sight of the police. This made it almost impossible for them to be caught. And in the case of the attack on Ellen Crawford's house several hours had elapsed between the activity of the mob and the appearance of the police.

That same morning Ellen and Catherine Crawford packed their belongings on a handcart and left Stanley Street, never to return. They went to live with a friend in North Queen Street.

On Wednesday morning, when he examined the damage that had been done to his property, Watson found that about 400 panes of glass had been broken and that the doors and window-shutters had been ripped from many of the houses. Nineteen of his tenants, most of them Protestants, had left their homes in Quadrant Street, Brook Street and Albert Crescent, taking their belongings with them and telling neither Watson nor his agent where they intended to go. Arthur Boyle, a pawnbroker, told Watson he would have left also but he could not get a carter to carry away his extensive stock.

Watson, anxious to hold his remaining tenants, ordered all damage to be repaired immediately. He must have wondered, however, if he was not wasting his workmen's time as well as his own money and materials, especially when a glazier who was renewing the windows in Boyle's pawnshop was told by three youths that he need not bother because they intended to return that night and smash them again. The youths had come across the wasteland from Sandy Row and were throwing stones and shouting abuse at people whom they believed to be Catholics.

Jonathan Jones stayed indoors that Wednesday evening to read his favourite magazine, *Cassell's Illustrated Penny Weekly*, but he had not been reading for more than a few minutes when he heard gunfire and shouting and the crash of glass. He heard also the thunder of horses' hooves and it seemed to him that a squadron of cavalry was charging somewhere at the back of his house. He put away his magazine, hurried his wife and their baby son to the safety of the kitchen and went out to see what was happening.

When Jones reached the junction of Quadrant Street and Cullingtree Road he saw the hussars gallop past. Led by Major Hood and followed by a party of the town police, they had charged right through the Pound. The town police brandished their walking sticks as they ran closely behind the horsemen. People scattered into doorways before the hussars but emerged to kick and stone the police as they went past.

At the corner of Quadrant Street, Jones observed two well-dressed young men who, he said, looked like newspaper reporters. The men stepped aside, as the hussars galloped straight ahead and then swerved into Albert Street. Then the town police came up and for no apparent reason grabbed the two men and beat them about the heads and shoulders with their sticks. Jones watched as the astonished men, having had more than enough for one night, took to their heels as soon as they got free of the police.

During this time Bindon and Tracy, together with Robert Thompson, a magistrate who had come from Antrim that day to assist the authorities in Belfast, were face-to-face with a mob of people on Saltwater (later Boyne) Bridge. These people had assembled on the Sandy Row side of the bridge and were threatening to invade the Pound, but their way was blocked by a force of armed constables and a company of infantry. Tracy had read the Riot Act but the mob refused to disperse and became more unruly.

Bindon then decided, after a consultation with the officer commanding the infantry, that the most effective way of breaking up the crowd was to press forward steadily with the police and military, instead of the usual sudden charge. As the soldiers and the policemen advanced at a slow steady pace, the mob gave ground and most of them retreated, step-by-step, across the bridge towards their own quarters in Sandy Row.

But one group broke away and ran down College Street, then a wealthy, residential thoroughfare. There they took cover behind hedges and garden walls and hurled insults and defiance at the police, particularly at Bindon, whom they remembered as the officer who had stopped the drumming on Sunday night.

Infuriated by the taunts, Bindon jumped over a hedge and hauled out one of the mob but, to his great embarrassment, he found that his prisoner was a little girl. When the other rioters saw her in Bindon's grip they yelled madly and pelted the police with stones and sods of wet earth.

That evening the lamps were again extinguished in the Pound. There, in the pitch-black maze of narrow streets, courts and lanes, Tracy said he could see people only when they were outlined against the horizon at the top of certain steeply-rising streets. The whole place resounded to the crackle of gunfire and the crash of breaking glass, and all the while men and women, many of them fortified with whiskey and gin, kept up an endless din of singing, shouting, cursing and screaming.

It was very dangerous for even the police and military to be in these streets. Like their enemies in Sandy Row the people of the Pound had firearms and were determined to use them. The police and the soldiers knew that in addition to the danger of being shot, stabbed, stoned, bludgeoned or sliced by broken glass there was the risk of being pushed down an open manhole.

Sandy Row was not any safer, even in comparatively peaceful times. "It was not without at least a momentary trepidation," wrote O'Hanlon, the Congregationalist investigator, "that we penetrated into this region. I had heard of its bludgeon-men and, even though on a peaceful mission, I thought it just possible that we might fare ill among men of blood."

On the afternoon of Wednesday 15th July, Tracy and William

Thomas Briscoe Lyons, JP, a prominent Belfast politician, were fired upon as they rode along Albert Street. Neither was hit, but an infantryman, whom Tracy had sent in pursuit of a group of men who might have fired the shots, was struck on the forehead by a paving stone and very badly injured. Some time after this, a man whom the police had arrested on the wasteground was found to possess a bagful of ammunition and a mould for making soft-lead bullets.

That evening, according to the report of the riots commissioners, the Mayor of Belfast was struck by a paving stone, the pavements were torn up, house-wreckings occurred, and "sallies were made out of the respective districts to destroy the properties of their opponents."

The climax of the 1857 riots was not reached until the night of Saturday 18 July, but for several days before that date both sides were preparing. On Thursday police officers who visited the gunsmiths' shops in High Street learned that many people had been buying arms and ammunition; those who could not afford to pay ready cash were getting weapons on hire purchase.

On hearing this news, Tracy asked Major Hood to have as many troops as possible ready for action, and at eight o'clock on Thursday evening he called a council of war in Durham Street constabulary barracks. Those who attended were Hood, Chief-Constable Lindsay, Robert Thompson, RM, Sub-Inspector Bindon and Lindsay's second-in-command, Chief-Constable Thomas Green.

It was Tracy's opinion that, if the rioting was to be brought to an end, the police would have to arrest the ringleaders. Bindon explained to him that it was not easy to make arrests. As soon as the police appeared, the mobs, especially in the Pound, often fled with astonishing speed and vanished within a few seconds. Eventually the council of war decided that Bindon should select a squad of his youngest and fittest constables who would lay aside their heavy equipment and thus be able to pursue the mobs and make arrests. The other constables were to carry loaded carbines and provide cover for these younger men.

Meanwhile the people in the Pound had been piling up ammunition in the form of paving stones which they prised from the streets. Heaps of stones lay about on the roadways and outside the front doors of many houses, yet policemen who tried to remove the stones were truculently told not to interfere with private property. Not only did these people dig up the pavements for stones, they also knocked down walls that extended along the rear of their houses, to get bricks. The magistrates saw many of the demolished walls when they made a tour of the area in search for concealed arms, on the Friday afternoon of that week.

When the meeting in Durham Street barracks was over, Tracy and the police went out to where the mobs had again gathered. He read the Riot Act to the Protestants at Stanley Street, then crossed the road with the intention of reading it to the Catholics in the Pound. The second reading had no sooner been commenced than the mob in Stanley Street opened fire. The Pound retaliated. Then Tracy, furious at being ignored, called on Major Hood to clear the streets. When the hussars charged, the mobs scattered, as Bindon knew they would, and disappeared into open doorways and along narrow lanes. The police runners ran as fast as they could but they caught nobody.

Saturday was the most dangerous day of that week. The mills and factories closed at two o'clock in the afternoon, thus giving the rioters plenty of time to get ready for fighting. Many rioters and wreckers were, in fact, looking forward to an exciting week-end, especially those who had secured firearms and were eager to use them. To make matters worse, garbled accounts of the rioting had spread to some of the strongly Protestant towns and villages near Belfast and, on Saturday, Sandy Row got reinforcements from Lisburn, Ballynafeigh, Newtownbreda and other nearby places. Encouraged by this support the Protestants were first to gather. They were on the wasteground between the Pound and Sandy Row at five o'clock in the afternoon.

The first victims of the gunmen that day were two little boys, Adam Ward and Pat Murphy. They were playing marbles in the Pound Loaning with other boys when suddenly four men rose from behind a hedge on the wasteland. One of the four shouted to attract the boys' attention and, as the children looked up, two shots rang out. Adam Ward was struck on the left leg about six inches below the knee. The bullet passed clean through his calf, shattered bones and carried away a large piece of flesh. Pat Murphy was also wounded but not so seriously as Ward.

The screams of the wounded boys drew a crowd of people, one of whom secured a cart and had them taken to hospital. Surgeon

Browne amputated Ward's leg at the knee.

From the corner of Cullingtree Road twenty members of the Town Police Force of Belfast saw the gunmen fire, yet, instead of making an arrest, they tried to drive away the people who had gathered to help the boys.

Tracy did not get home until three o'clock on Saturday morning, and from then until breakfast time he was kept awake by the noise of gunfire. Nevertheless fatigued though he must have been, he toured the disturbed districts that afternoon and also held another meeting of the police and military officers. He told them it was obviously futile to read the Riot Act, but he had thought of a new plan. The police and the military, he suggested, were not to interfere unless the mobs were violent.

Bindon agreed with this plan because neither he nor any of his men wanted to get to grips with the mobsters. He realized that his small force of 32 constables was no match for thousands of violent men and women, many of whom would be armed with guns. He knew, too, that the brunt of the fighting was being borne by the constabulary. The town policemen were unreliable and, of course, unarmed; the soldiers were hampered by army regulations.

In accordance with Tracy's plan, the constabulary did their best to keep the Protestant and Catholic mobs apart that Saturday afternoon, but by seven o'clock the situation had become so dangerous that Head-Constable Henderson sent word to Bindon that he could not hold out much longer—the mobs were becoming excited and violent. Scarcely had this message been despatched than the Protestant mob on the wasteland cut loose and charged towards the Pound, scattering Henderson and his constables in confusion.

Bernard Kelly, who gave evidence before the riots commission, testified that this attack was encouraged by a party of town policemen. "They waved their sticks over their heads," said Kelly, "and urged the Protestants to attack the Pound."

From his bedroom window Jonathan Jones saw the mob burst into Quadrant Street. According to him, a Protestant woman who lived in the street tried to direct them to Catholic houses, but no one bothered about her directions. The mob wrecked indiscriminately, without troubling to ascertain whether the houses belonged to Catholics or Protestants. They tore off window-frames and shutters, pulled doors off their hinges and dragged furniture into the street. They heaped this debris into a great mound and set it on fire.

Hopewell Kelly, fearing that they would massacre her little child and herself, told Brigid Trainor to take the infant to the house of a washerwoman who lived in the Pound. In her haste, the housemaid neglected to clothe the baby properly. He caught a chill, developed pneumonia and died a few weeks later.

When Bindon and a force of armed constables arrived at Quadrant Street, the rioters were still wrecking and burning; yet, for nearly fifteen minutes, the police stood at a safe distance and did nothing. Their inaction infuriated Head-Constable James McIntyre of Ballymacarrett. He told Bindon it was monstrous that the forces of the Crown should stand by and watch a lawless mob destroy the homes and property of peaceful people. Bindon admitted he was afraid that, if he attacked, some of the constables might be killed. McIntyre's reply was that he had often faced larger mobs in Ballymacarrett without any fear of danger to his men. And this was no idle boast. With a small force of seven constables he kept law and order in that part of the town for which he was responsible. At the first sign of disturbance he always acted swiftly and ruthlessly and on every 12 July he toured the Protestant streets to pull down any Orange arches that had been erected. In 1854 an Orange lodge complained about his methods but a subsequent public inquiry upheld his actions.

Bindon's conduct before the wreckers in Quadrant Street was also to be the subject of an inquiry. Allegations of cowardice, bias against the Catholics and partiality to the Protestants were made against him when the riots commissioners came to Belfast in September 1857. The outcome of the allegations was the setting up of a special "Inquiry into the Conduct of the Constabulary". The inquiry was conducted by two magistrates, George J. Goold, RM, and George Fitzmaurice, RM. When they reported to the Lord Lieutenant of Ireland, on 11 February 1858, they found that "ample testimony had been borne to the courage, decision and coolness of Mr. Bindon".

Nonetheless, when Tracy arrived at Quadrant Street on the night of 18 July and saw the wreckers and their bonfire he wanted to know "what the hell Bindon was doing" and ordered him to disperse the wreckers immediately, using firearms if necessary. In fact, there was no need for the police to fire; the mob was not nearly as dangerous as Bindon feared. They watched expectantly as the constables loaded their carbines, and, as the police started a slow, deliberate advance, they turned and fled from Quadrant Street. Within a few minutes most of them had disappeared across the wasteland and were back in Sandy Row.

Early on Sunday morning the magistrates, Tracy and McGee, rode through the disturbed districts. They had given orders for pickets of police to be placed at street corners and, as they rode by, they inspected these pickets and checked that their guns were loaded. There was little disturbance that morning and by midday most of the police pickets had been withdrawn. No doubt the constables needed rest. Few of them had had much sleep since the riots started. They had been on duty until nearly dawn every day and frequently they had to attend the magistrates' court in the mid-mornings as well, to give evidence against prisoners charged with riotous behaviour.

But once the pickets were withdrawn the gunmen emerged and soon their fire was raking the Pound from one side and Sandy Row from the other. Their shots "came so fast and were aimed so low" that Head-Constable Henderson, though needed at Durham Street barracks, was unable to leave his own house. From his front parlour window, screened behind curtains, he could see the edge of the wasteland and a ditch which he later described as "closely lined with men, having guns levelled, firing without intermission". This firing continued for two hours.

Other gunmen had taken up positions in the partly-built house about which McLoughlin, the newspaper proprietor, had warned Tracy. To the mobs of Sandy Row this place became known as the Malakoff, after the fortifications of Sebastopol during the Crimean War. It remained a fortification throughout the riots, in an excellent position from which the gunmen behind its walls could observe every movement of the police over a considerable distance. And none of the gunmen was caught. Whenever the police succeeded in entering the place they found nobody there.

The number of people wounded or killed in the shooting that Sunday afternoon of 18 July will never be known; it was impossible, even at the time, to estimate the casualties. The families of victims, fearing arrest and prosecution for being in riotous assemblies, told the authorities nothing. Doctors, magistrates and police suspected that the deaths of riot victims were often ascribed to other causes, or concealed and the dead buried secretly.

It was late on the Sunday afternoon before the gunfire ceased and Henderson was able to make his way to the constabulary barracks. There he found Watson, whose houses in Quadrant Street had been wrecked, insisting that the police be given orders immediately to disperse the gunmen on the wasteground. Watson told Tracy that at Mass that morning many people had urged him to arm his tenants so that they would be able to defend themselves against attacks from Sandy Row. Tracy replied that he hoped the police would do their duty and that it would not be necessary for Watson, or anyone else, to arm civilians for the protection of life and property.

Watson then accused Tracy and the other magistrates of hostility towards the Catholics and of favouring the Orange party. And the Orangemen, he insisted, were the aggressors in all the riots. The verbal exchanges continued for some time before it was decided that, if Watson would speak to the people in the Pound and advise them to go home quietly, the police would disperse the gunmen on the wasteland.

Watson was a Poor Law Guardian, a position which gave him much influence among the poorer classes, and so he had little difficulty in persuading the Catholics to go home and remain indoors. His advice, simple as it was, seemed to bring the first phase of the riots of 1857 to an end. Within thirty minutes the streets of the Pound were empty.

When Watson surveyed the damage done to his property he found that eighty of his houses had been wrecked and many of his tenants had disappeared. But other people, less able to bear the burden of loss, had suffered also. They had been driven from their homes, in Sandy Row as well as in the Pound. Many had lost their jobs and an unknown number had been injured and maimed.'

I have quoted this long description of this first, major Belfast riot for two reasons. One is that there was a Commission of Enquiry called almost at once which supplied the massive, first-hand report on which Andrew Boyd principally bases his account. No other riot until very modern times is so fully reported. Secondly it would seem to this writer typical of all such riots in that city, up to and including the ones that have been taking place in Belfast, Derry and elsewhere since 1968. (The terrorist activities of the Irish Republican Army Provisionals comes into another category: though brought about by the riots these activities, in the eyes of the activists at least, are a pseudo-military campaign launched in late 1970 and designed to destroy the Northern Irish government at Stormont as a first step towards enforcing British withdrawal from the Six Counties and the incorporation of the province into the Republic of Ireland. Defence of the Roman Catholic enclaves against Protestant activists, against the Royal Ulster Constabulary and latterly against the British army is only incidental to this major objective, though of course the I.R.A. gunmen find refuge, support and recruits within those enclaves.) The riots follow a simple pattern.

First comes the emotion usually connected with an anniversary. Into this there is injected the religious element, in 1857 the Rev. Dr. Drew's sermon to his orange-sashed congregation. The anonymous author of *Orangeism in Ireland and Throughout the Empire* (op. cit.) points out quite correctly that the Roman Catholic crowd which collected outside Christ Church neither heard his sermon nor can have read it until it was published in a newspaper called *The Down Protestant* nearly a week later, on July 17th. By then the rioting was nearing its peak. But they did not need to hear it or, if they were literate, to read it. They knew it all by heart already: they had been insulted, in their religion and their race, for years, and were to go on being so insulted for many generations. Furthermore the anonymous Orange author is almost certainly quite correct when he says that the respectable Orangemen who listened to the Rev. Dr. Drew, easily whipped up to hysteria by his demagogy though they might be and apparently were, by their own lights were law-abiding citizens. If they did not don their Orange sashes until within the precincts of Christ Church, they were hardly likely to crouch in ditches or try to murder small Catholic boys playing marbles on wasteland. No more do Unionist M.P.s and industrialists toss petrol bombs through the windows of Catholics and loot Catholic pubs today: and no more do middle-class Catholics rampage through Ballymurphy or stone the British Army. Those activities are left to the two mobs, nearly but not quite leaderless, quick to assemble and quick to fade away when

Hugh Hanna, 1824-1892.

Lord Randolph Churchill
(*BBC Radio Times Picture
Library*).

Leading Unionists at the House Party at Mount Stewart, Co. Down, on the occasion of the visit of Mr. Bonar Law M.P. on 9th April 1912.

Sir Edward Carson, in a fiery attitude.

faced by almost any form of organized, disciplined opposition. This is particularly true of the Protestant mob. The Catholics, being in the minority and therefore more frightened, do tend to be more susceptible to some measure of organization. They know that they need leadership. This was as true in 1857 as it was in Londonderry in 1969 and is in Belfast today. The Protestant mob, on the other hand, knew then as they know now that they have leaders, even though the powerful men within the Orange Order and, nowadays, in the Unionist Party may, for tactical reasons, temporarily disown their rougher co-religionists. When this happens, rabble-rousing clergymen take over.

Both these reactions occurred immediately after the first week of rioting in 1857. The Catholics then, as now, wanted guns, primarily for self-defence but also and undoubtedly for more aggressive purposes. The owner of a Catholic newspaper, *The Ulsterman*, set about creating an organization modelled both on Daniel O'Connell's mass movement and on the Orange Lodges. This was called the Catholic Gun Club. Membership was to be sixpence a week, and the money was to be used for the purchase of 'beautiful new guns' which were to be distributed among the members by a form of lottery. The newspaper proprietor, a Mr. McLoughlin, also proposed to use some of the money collected in order to promote propaganda in favour of the Enquiry that the Catholics demanded, and to pay legal fees for members of his organization facing trial for involvement in sectarian troubles. How much money was collected, and how many guns bought and distributed, is not known for certain, but the evidence is that it was very little of the one and very few of the other. The police had persuaded the chosen gunsmith not to honour his contract with the Club.

The reaction of the Protestant mob and its clerical leaders was, with the advantage of hindsight, equally predictable. Being much stronger than their enemies, and much better armed, they could expect victory in any major engagement in the streets. They therefore set about, once again, provoking their fellow citizens so that when the clash came they could, as usual, claim that they were only acting in self-defence. Since they posed as a counter-revolutionary and not a revolutionary force they could not afford to alienate the authorities beyond a certain point. Those authorities, as the Commission of Enquiry was

to show, still looked on the Protestant mob, and indeed the
Orange Order, with very considerable disfavour. Religion on
the other hand, in this high noon of Victorianism and of the
religious revival in England, was, if I may play on words, sacro-
sanct. Therefore the best and safest way to infuriate the Catholics was by public, ostentatious 'missionary' effort on the part
of Protestant clergymen, both establishment and Dissenting
ministers. So, while the Catholics tried to get guns, the Protestants organized open-air religious services. Furthermore, and in
order all the more to confuse the authorities, an even greater
emphasis was placed on wrapping the Orange drum in the red,
white and blue of the Union Jack thus playing on the general
English dislike of most Irish Catholics as rebels and traitors.
This combination of super-patriotism and super-Protestantism
is well summarized by a quotation from some remarks made at
this time by the Rev. Dr. Henry Cooke, he who had organized
that seminal gathering on Lord Hillsborough's estate nearly a
quarter of a century earlier. 'The right of Ulster to the laws and
religion of England must be once and for all resolutely, deter-
minedly, unflinchingly maintained. The resolution of our fore-
fathers when the forces of bigotry threatened their annihilation
in this same Ulster not two centuries ago is the beacon which
we must hold before us in asserting our liberties today.'

Such sentiments were aimed not only at the Protestant mob
but also, and over the heads of the Irish authorities in Belfast
and in Dublin, at the powerful men who controlled policy for
the whole United Kingdom at Westminster and in Whitehall.
The Irish authorities were, on the whole, hostile. They disbanded the Belfast Police and brought in the Irish Constabulary,
just as 122 years later the British were to disband the B-Specials,
an auxiliary armed police force manned almost exclusively by
Orangemen, and attempt to create a non-partisan force called
the Ulster Defence Regiment. The authorities brought pressure
to bear on the Church of Ireland and on the Bishop of Belfast,
Bishop Knox, to cease the provocative actions of his Parochial
Mission, and were again successful. The bishop refused, however and regretfully, to ban categorically all open-air preaching
in the town.

There were some formidable preachers at large, not only the
veteran Cooke, the famous Drew, but also an orator named the
Rev. Roe and, perhaps most famous of all, the Rev. (later also

Dr.) Hugh Hanna, whose nickname 'Roaring Hanna' is evidence of his rhetorical style. He was a Presbyterian and therefore not bound, like his Church of Ireland colleagues, to pay any attention to the timid wishes of Bishop Knox.

For many years clergymen of the Parochial Mission and others, at least one of them unfrocked, had preached from the steps of the Customs House. Only recently had the Church of Ireland clergy demeaned themselves to this form of revivalism. The business had in fact been called off during and immediately after the July riots. It was soon resumed, but without noticeable disturbances, early in August. However the temperature was rising again and rapidly. A Catholic mill-girl of sixteen, who had gone to McIlhone's shop in the Pound to buy a ha'penny's worth of gooseberries was shot through the head by an unknown man while eating them on her way home. It was assumed that the man, who had stalked her, and blown out one of her eyes, was a Protestant fanatic: he was never arrested. There were other such atrocities. Catholic animosity to the Protestant preachers rose and on September 6th it exploded. It was, once again, a miserable and confused affair, though the Protestants were as usual better organized and better led than the Catholics. Public preaching had by then become the prime issue of the day. This was because it was treated by the authorities with the same uncertainty which they adopt towards provocative Orange processions today. Discouraged but not forbidden, then as now it is only when violence breaks out that the police and troops move in to disperse the rioters, the fire brigade to douse down burning houses, the ambulances to collect the wounded, and the mortuary vans to pick up the corpses.

On Saturday, September 5th, the rumour had reached McLoughlin, part-owner of *The Ulsterman,* and his partner and editor, Denis Holland, that the Rev. Dr. Thomas Drew was to preach on the steps of the Customs House the following afternoon. They immediately printed posters and, it would seem, leaflets urging the Catholics to assemble *en masse* there. A clearer call to sectarian violence would be hard to imagine. They were, however, misinformed. Drew, presumably in obedience to the wishes of Bishop Knox, had declined to preach. Hanna, however, quickly and willingly took up the challenge. And he mounted what can only be called a battle plan. Again I cannot do better than quote Andrew Boyd:

'By three o'clock a crowd had gathered in front of the Customs House, awaiting the arrival of the "evangelical ranters". But they waited in vain. Hanna had decided to hold his meeting, not at the Customs House but outside the Seamen's Church in Corporation Square.

This was some distance along the quayside from the Customs House but near to a storeyard owned by the Harbour Board. There, behind a line of ornamental chain, he set up his platform. The harbour storeyard was locked, but the key was in the pocket of a harbour constable who was one of Hanna's followers. This was part of the strategy which Hanna had made known to his men on the previous day.

The Mayor and nine magistrates, the police officers—Bindon, Lindsay and Green—the entire Town Police Force of Belfast and most of the men of the Irish Constabulary were already at Corporation Square. Crowds of civilians were gathering there also, despite the rain and a heavy dull sky. The decks of ships in the harbour were crowded with spectators.

At three o'clock precisely, Hanna mounted the platform, but, before he could start speaking, John Clarke, a former Mayor of Belfast, asked him not to preach and pointed out that the crowds were already excited. Hanna glared at Clarke, who was known to be a liberal, and said that he had come there to assert his Protestant rights and that if the police and magistrates were doing their duty they would make sure he was protected. He then turned abruptly away from Clarke, faced the crowd and opened his large, leather-bound Bible at Psalm 119.

Heavily-built and tall, this 33-year-old clerical agitator presented an aggressive figure in his black ministerial garb. He was to spend all his pastoral life in Belfast. As the years passed his name became known throughout the United Kingdom as a symbol of Protestant intolerance. His sermons, both within his church and on the open highway, his pamphlets and many of his other activities were to be the cause of numerous disturbances. Despite this, he was made chaplain to the army garrison in Belfast and, in later years, appointed a commissioner of national education.

As Hanna preached his congregation remained attentive and apparently well-behaved, though it was observed that one rather irreverent character near the platform was puffing a pipe. Hanna gave the smoker a sour look but did nothing more about him.

Meanwhile the Catholics at the Customs House, realizing that the meeting was not to be held there, were about to disperse when someone told them where Hanna was preaching. They rushed immediately towards Corporation Square.

From his platform Hanna could see the hostile crowd coming, but he knew he was safe. Between him and the infuriated Catholics was the entire Town Police Force of Belfast, the Irish Constabulary and thousands of his own followers. In any event, it had not been his intention to have a long meeting, fifteen or twenty minutes at the most. Furthermore, the state of the weather, for by this time it was raining heavily, was reason enough for bringing the meeting to an early close.

Some of the Catholics were coming down Tomb Street, heading straight towards Hanna's platform. Others were running along Donegall Quay while a third group was rushing down Corporation Street. When they saw Tomb Street fill with people, Hanna's supporters knew exactly what to do. They acted according to the plan that had been prepared the previous day.

The harbour constable who held the key to the storeyard unlocked the gate when given the word. Stored in the yard were hundreds of sharp-edged staves, iron crowbars, oars, pieces of ship's gear, pulleys, blocks and deadly sharp marlin-spikes—all effective weapons.

Immediately the gate was opened, fifty of Hanna's men, all shipwrights who worked in Edward Harland's shipyard on the Lagan, rushed in and armed themselves with whatever implements they could lay hands on. Most of them were not natives of Belfast at all, but immigrants from Greenock and Glasgow; they had brought to Ireland not merely their skill as shipbuilders but also a deeply-ingrained Calvinistic antipathy to the Catholic Church.

As the Catholics and the shipwrights clashed, Corporation Square became a battlefield. The noise was deafening as the mobs screamed and attacked one another with their improvized weapons. With hundreds locked together in furious combat and at least as many others throwing paving stones in every direction, Hanna decided to close the meeting. Raising his voice above the turmoil, he pronounced the following benediction to the mob: "Please go home now, my good people. We have asserted our right to preach the Gospel in public, but let your conduct for the rest of the day be worthy of Christians. Don't linger in the streets; afford no opportunity for tumult and disorder. I believe the good work we have been engaged in today will be pregnant with a mighty influence. God bless you, one and all."

With that he stepped down from his platform and swaggered off to where a carriage awaited him at the corner of the Seamen's Church. He drove rapidly to his home in Donegall Pass, leaving behind the very tumult and disorder he had asked his followers to avoid, and leaving the task of restoring the peace to the magistrates and the police.

As Hanna was driving away from the scene of conflict, Bindon was dashing through a barrage of paving stones to the rescue of a boy who was being beaten on the quayside by three shipwrights. He could see Thomas Briscoe Lyons, the magistrate, on horseback, driving another group of shipwrights into a side-street.

Then Lyons rode with all speed to the military barracks where he urged Captain Adair of the hussars to send a force immediately to the quayside. Adair summoned his fellow-officers, Major Hood and Captains Birmingham, Seager and Nicholls, and mustered the hussars and infantry. Then minutes later, the cavalry were galloping along Donegall Quay, with the mobs fleeing before them. The nimble military horses, trained for rough uneven ground, found the going difficult over the smooth wet paving stones of the quayside.

The fighting mobsters, driven from the quayside, assembled again in the business centres of the town. Soon Waring Street, High Street and Donegall Street were crowded with people, many sheltering in the doorways of banks, shops and offices, not only from the rain but from the fury of the mobs as well.

So many of the mobsters were loose in that part of the town that it was highly dangerous for unprotected people to be about. One gang assaulted a Catholic youth and left him unconscious in Donegall Street. Not far distant, in Waring Street, a Catholic mob chased a man and two little girls because "they looked like Protestants".

In Durham Street that night a boy was carried into a doctor's surgery with a gunshot wound in his face. The bullet had entered the back of his head and made an exit through his jaw.

He lived but was hideously disfigured for the remainder of his life.

A few days after these events Hanna published the first of his letters to the Protestants of Belfast. He wrote: "Men and Brethren: Your blood-bought and cherished rights have been imperilled by the audacious and savage outrages of a Romish mob.... But you were not to be bullied or cajoled out of your rights. They are not to be surrendered, and they are to be strenuously maintained. That you have unmistakenly shown on the past Sabbath. Then you arose, calm but powerful, as the thunder reposing in the cloud."

Continuing, Hanna announced his intention of preaching again on Sunday 13 September. "A few Sabbaths like the last will achieve a permanent good," he wrote, and went on to express his determination to defy not only "the Romish mobs" but also the magistrates and the police.'

And so it went on, year in year out, exhaustion producing lulls but never destroying the endemic hatred and fear that seethed and simmered and always at last boiled over again. The Irish Constabulary did its best as the problems yearly came round, and were given the prefix 'Royal'. It is as the Royal Irish Constabulary that they have gone down to history, and their heirs are the Royal Ulster Constabulary of today.

Into this dangerous and inflammable situation there was injected the explosive fuel of Fenianism and Home Rule. In the next chapter, therefore, we must draw back from the little streets of Belfast and the personalities of clergymen, from boys shot while playing marbles or girls while eating gooseberries, and examine the political developments of the late nineteenth century as they affected that corner of Ireland with which we are here concerned.

CHAPTER FOURTEEN

The decades of the 1850s and 1860s have been described as a period of lull in Ireland as a whole. This is only conditionally true. The Irish were physically exhausted, as a race, by the Famine and even more weakened by the steady haemorrhage of massive emigration, particularly to the United States. Although Irish rural society recovered, in altered conditions, quite rapidly from the atrocious tragedy—already, by 1860, living conditions were generally better than they had been before 1854—the Famine, the plagues and the coffin ships were not forgotten. They never have been. The very strong family, indeed tribal, feeling that has always been so marked among the Irish now sent tentacles back across the Atlantic. Those who prospered, even modestly, in the new country, and many did so with surprising speed, sent money to their relations at home. Often these remittances were used to pay for new passages to America.

On one occasion, during the Second World War, General George S. Patton, United States Army, issued a curious order of the day to the men of the U.S. Seventh Army which he commanded. This was on the eve of the first major Anglo-American invasion of the European continent, via Sicily, in 1943. Patton then informed his troops that they were about to meet a somewhat inferior species of human being, for all Europe's real fighting blood had gone to America long ago. This strange view of history, which did not particularly please his British and French allies and which can only have amused the Germans and the Russians, contained perhaps a tiny grain of truth, tiny both in historical time and in geographic space. The massive flight from Ireland during and after the Famine had been in large measure inspired by a desperate wish for naked survival: many died in the attempt, many more went under in the incredibly harsh circumstances that they found in the new country, but the toughest and cleverest did survive, and profited. At the height of the Famine an altogether different type of emigrant had appeared upon the Irish roads leading to the ports.

These were not the sick, starving, illiterate refugees, but more substantial farmers with their immediate families and some cash in their pockets who had sold up and were going to farm elsewhere rather than continue living in an accursed, ill-run land. They were a loss, as the Irish government realized, that Ireland could ill afford, for their numbers in Ireland were few. Their departure was a real and lasting damage to the Irish nation. They were a positive asset to the United States. They came from the less disaster-ridden Eastern provinces rather than from the chaotic west where yeomen were, in any event, even fewer in numbers. Cecil Woodham Smith estimates the immediate net loss in population during the famine years as follows: Connaught, 28.6%; Munster, 23.5%; Ulster, 16%; and Leinster, 15.5%.

It was they, together with those who had risen quickest from the abject poverty of the Irish ghettoes in New York, Boston and elsewhere, that were first able to provide passage money for friends and relations left behind. Since these were likely to be, in effect, of the best or at least the toughest stock, it would not be a gross oversimplification to say that the men and women Ireland lost to America throughout the second half of the nineteenth century were those she could least afford to see go. And this, combined with the very powerful influence of American ethos and mores and perhaps even climate, may account for the marked divergence of general attitudes to be discerned to this day between Irish-Americans and the Irish in their own country. (So perhaps George Patton was not being, in this context, quite as stupid as he sounds. It would be an interesting study for a social anthropologist, but one largely though not entirely irrelevant to the theme of this book. Be it noted that Tom Moore, the poet and composer, had remarked long before the Famine that the Irish can neither fight nor write in their own country. One sees his first point, in comparison to the skill of Irish soldiers elsewhere: but perhaps he would have done better to say 'unite' rather than 'fight', for they have certainly given every evidence of the latter. As to his second point I, an Irishman writing in Ireland, can only take the gravest personal exception, but I see what he meant.)

To this haemorrhage—I must repeat the word—of courage and talent and indeed manpower from Catholic Ireland in the years after the Famine there was added a basic re-arrangement

of property which had a profound social effect. The policy, if that
be the word, of the landlords to evict unwanted tenants in order
to rationalize their estates was not only brutally facilitated by
the Famine but was continued throughout it and in some three
decades that followed, with at least the tacit approval of the
United Kingdom government. J. C. Beckett (op. cit.) quotes the
following statistics for land holdings in all Ireland that reveal
the change between 1841 and 1851, a process that was to
continue:

Holdings	1841	1851
1— 5 acres	310,436	88,083
5—15 acres	252,799	191,854
15—30 acres	79,342	141,311
above 30 acres	48,625	149,090

The quarter of a million small farmers who had vanished from
the smaller holdings probably represent, together with their
families, a million and a half souls, close to the approximation of
those who, according to Cecil Woodham Smith, died of famine
and fever during the second half of that period, though the
mortality rate is largely guesswork.

The increase in the larger holdings was not only accompanied
by a comprehensible distrust in the potato as a sole means of
support but also by a basic change in the type of agriculture
by which the rural population lived. Hitherto tillage, that is to
say the growing of cereal crops, had been the means by which
the peasantry paid their landlord's rent. The Repeal of the Corn
Laws in 1846 had opened the British market to foreign wheat
in order to give cheaper bread to the growing cities. In the
archaic, inefficient, strife-ridden state of Irish country life, Ireland could not compete with the Great Plains and the Prairies
once they were exploited and put down to corn. Tillage therefore
gradually ceased to be viable as an export crop. On the other
hand there were in those days no refrigeration ships; the English wanted to eat beef, and could pay for it. Therefore and
increasingly land that had been previously tilled was put down
to pasture. This in turn meant that far less labour was needed
on the land. A farmer and his family could handle the cows
and sheep on quite a large farm. (This was one of the motives behind the evictions. Another is: the larger a ranch the bigger the

profit per acre.) The stubborn determination of the Irish countryman not to let his country be treated like Texas prevented the
true pastoralization of Ireland, with the concurrent disappearance
of its population, but nevertheless the larger farms added to
the momentum of famine and emigration in decreasing the
number of Irishmen in Ireland. The old social structure was
destroyed: it was no longer the extended family unit that controlled, or at least in historical imagination might once again
control, the ancestral herds. The new herds belonged on the new
farms: the farmer rented the farm, and subdivision according to
English property laws was not economically possible as with
the old potato patches: therefore the younger sons when they
had reached man's estate emigrated, for there was no other work
for them in Ireland: the eldest son remained and only when the
father had died could he, as heir, marry and bring home a wife.
Before the Famine the Irish had married, and had had children,
early and from the English viewpoint fecklessly. This tendency
was now drastically, and with dramatic speed, reversed. They
courted for years: their priests, now second or third generation
clerics trained by Maynooth Jansenists, continued to use their
full and very great authority to curtail and usually to prevent
extra-marital sexuality: and in consequence the population further declined. And, for this reason among others, the huge singing, dancing, easy-going population of Ireland before the famine
became, in the second half of the century, a far more timid,
close-lipped, even sour and often embittered peasantry. From
the records that exist it would seem that the Connaught of 1860
was as different from that province in 1840 as was Stalin's
Ukraine from that of Nicholas II. In both cases policies that
almost look like genocide, though not complete, had done their
evil. Since it was not complete, in neither territory were its
effects permanent. Only, the memory became a part of the
national trauma.

This 'rationalization' of Irish agriculture in the years immediately succeeding the famine had, as might be expected,
marked social consequences. The process of change was slow and
was certainly not to be completed for many years, if indeed
it has been finished yet, for relics, increasingly fossilized, of any
older society always linger on into its successor. In general,
however, it may be said that the nineteenth-century mercantile
and capitalist society now reached Ireland, including rural

Ireland. Money assumed a far greater importance than before. The landlord class, almost exclusively of Anglo-Saxon descent and members of the Church of Ireland, became less the officer class of the rooted garrison—though this role they also preserved *diminuendo*—and more and more became agricultural *entrepreneurs*. The riproaring, often drunken, fighting squire of the eighteenth century was an anachronism in the late nineteenth. The more profligate, or more unfortunate, members of this class were given the opportunity of realizing the value of their estates under the terms of the Encumbered Estates Act of 1849. An 'encumbered estate' was, briefly, one so heavily in debt or so heavily mortgaged that it could no longer show a profit after payment of interest and other charges. The 'encumbrancer' was the one who owned the mortgage or other charges. If the landlord refused to sell, but could not pay the interest on his debts, then the encumbrancer could go to the Encumbered Estates Court and a forced sale by the court would result. When the charges against the estate had been paid off the residue of the purchase price, if any, went to the original landlord. This affected all Ireland, including Ulster, though in that province there were more encumbered estates in the western and southern counties than in the more prosperous and better farmed northeast. In all Ireland some five million acres, or approximately one quarter of all cultivated land, was disposed of to new owners by 1871. Almost immediately the Land War began, in which the tenants simply refused to pay rent, made life as difficult as possible for their landlords by boycott and not infrequent violence, and this further weakened the landlord class. The various Land Acts, starting with that of 1881, which enabled the tenants to purchase their farms on favourable terms and with the assistance of the State, finally destroyed the economic basis of the Protestant Ascendancy, the rooted garrison. The United Kingdom government in effect sold out its own people, the Protestant minority, to the Catholic majority, in the name, quite a correct name, of good government and of democracy. This was noted in the northeast where the Protestant Ascendancy, dependent upon a largely Protestant tenantry, was far less vulnerable. Up there most of the big houses are still surrounded by large estates and inhabited by the families that have owned those estates for three centuries. In the South, many of them that are not now hotels are ruins.

In most of Ireland this might be termed the equivalent, at landlord level, of those evictions intended to rationalize, that is to say anglicize, agriculture at the cottier's level. Indeed the one served to expedite the other. A landlord who could not or would not re-organize his estate on modern lines was likely to find himself encumbered. On the other hand the new purchaser had not even those tenuous links with his tenantry that the old landlord, whose family might have owned the land for generations, not infrequently preserved. Land-owning in Ireland was thus thrown into the full competition of the Victorian market during the high noon of early capitalism when *laissez-faire* knew almost no restrictions. Just as the Statutes of Kilkenny of 1366 had attempted, and failed, to prevent the Anglo-Normans from becoming 'mere Irish', so the unexpressed motive behind the Encumbered Estates Act was to impose the English liberal ideology of the age on an alien society. It was only partly successful, as the novels of Somerville and Ross show, for even the new, more efficient landlords soon found that methods which worked well with the peasantry of Gloucestershire or Lincolnshire were far less effective in the counties Clare or Tyrone. (The Germans who bought Irish estates, and attempted to farm them efficiently, after the Second World War, soon made the same discovery. In general the Irish countryman is simply not amenable to Teutonic discipline. Most of the Germans soon enough departed in despair.) Evictions were commonplace in the 1850s and 1860s. They did not produce a smiling, hard-working peasantry but rather a sullen, rural proletariat which, determined to hang on to the land, reached for the gun, not out of choice but because there was, in its eyes, no alternative to Land War save emigration. Agrarian crime was rife in the 1850s and 1860s. In Ulster the 'new men' even tried to abrogate the Ulster custom, but here they came up against even tougher resistance and were usually defeated. Only the very richest estates, Digby, Devonshire, Dufferin, Londonderry, Dunraven to name but a few—those in fact with great English capital resources behind them—could afford to 'improve' their estates by gentler and more gradual methods. It is curious how many of those estates still remain, while most of the encumbrancers have been blown away, and their mansions burned down, vanished like the seventeenth century undertakers.

At the next social level the tenant farmers with the larger

holdings profited during the first twenty years after the famine. This was a period of comparative agricultural boom. Both beef and butter were in demand in Britain where there was a considerable degree of prosperity after the slump of the Hungry Forties. Even tillage was still a viable activity. The breweries, especially that of Arthur Guinness and Son, and the distilleries were expanding rapidly and bought all the barley that the Irish farmers could grow. For some years the American Civil War held up the expansion of the corn belt over there and, even more, the export of its products. Though the acreage of oats declined in Ireland and that of wheat even more so, this was not as yet disastrous. The bigger farmers were still making enough money to pay their rents and their labourers.

But it was at this, the labourers', level that this rationalization of agriculture brought misery and bitterness. The farmers now had no time for a peasantry that grew its own food on its own plots and paid its rent in the form of part-time work. The Victorian market demanded of a man, whether an industrial or an agricultural worker, that his labour be a simple commodity the value of which was calculable in simple monetary terms. Their little plots of land were in the way of even medium-sized farming and were taken away from them, not always but frequently enough to change the countryman's way of life. Instead he received a cash wage, which in most of Ireland rose from about 6d. to about 9d. a day during the period here under consideration. Out of this he had to buy the food for himself and his family which previously he had grown. Since during this period food prices rose as fast as wages, the simple countryman not only felt himself, quite correctly, to be uprooted but also bewildered by a way of life he scarcely understood. Furthermore those cottage industries, in particular weaving, were no longer economically competitive with the new factories of Belfast and Derry where textiles were mass-produced in increasing numbers. Finally, for a very large proportion of farm labourers their employment on the farm was seasonal. With the sowing done or the harvest in, large quantities of men would be laid off. Since there was no other work whatsoever available in the countryside those men would have to trudge many miles of road to find casual, manual work in the cities, or on the railroad buildings, or even in England, in order to earn the few shillings that might just keep their families at home alive. (In Miss Bernadette Devlin's account of her childhood, *The Price of My Soul*, we read of her father doing just this as late as the early 1950s: unable to earn a living in Cookstown, North Tyrone, he worked in England and only occasionally came home to his wife and family.) The tensions and hatreds created by such a system, particularly among a people with such strong, traditional family ties as the rural Irish, are not difficult to envisage.

Before the famine there was only a very small middle class, mostly Protestant and mostly urban. Apart from the Presbyterians of Ulster, the population was basically divided on a religious issue which was only incidentally, indeed coincidentally, due to conquest, a class issue in so far as class can be identified with wealth (which in Ireland is far from universal). The Protestants and the Catholics worshipped their God in different ways, lived their lives according to different social conventions and quite frequently spoke a different language. (About half the population were monoglot Irish speakers at the beginning of the nineteenth century: only a quarter fifty years later, while only some 5% had by then no knowledge whatsoever of the English language.) They were two nations, each in its own way attached to the land, sometimes hostile, less often friendly, usually with very little contact, two societies, both in its own form of decay, sharing a single country.

Now, superimposed as it were upon this comparatively simple duality famine and evictions brought the English three-class system, for a permanent, landless rural proletariat was created. And a proportion of this new proletariat inevitably drifted into the cities of which only three were expanding with sufficient speed to absorb comparatively large numbers of totally unskilled labourers: Dublin, Belfast and Derry.

If the cities, not only of Ireland but also of Britain and America, could take a high proportion of this unwanted, rural proletariat, many more tried to cling to their own countryside. For generations there had been an excess male population, living in near idleness and extreme poverty or driven forth from their own society by sheer penury to try and earn a living, as soldier or labourer, elsewhere. Now the very society, long moribund, was itself in ruins. Yet as bees will continue to buzz about the burned out hive, as if hoping that some miracle may bring it back to life, so did these landless men cling to Ireland, even to the fields and demolished hovels from which they had been evicted, more in bitterness than in hope. It was to men of this sort above all that Fenianism made its greatest appeal. Throughout most of Europe the nineteenth century saw the destruction of the old, classical relationship between master and man, between aristocrat and peasant, between owner and producer, a relationship that could engender every form of emotion but which was always present and which ensured a certain continuity, even a form of security. This relationship was smashed, quickly in the new cities by industrialization, more slowly on the land by the rationalization of agriculture. It was, in some measure, replaced by a new, romantic relationship, a revolutionary relationship between the alienated proletariat and what for lack of a better word may be called 'the intellectuals', themselves a very small minority who distrusted and came increasingly to hate the brutal, ever more materialistic middle and upper class from which they were almost always sprung. Dostoievsky and Kropotkin in Russia, Marx and Nietzsche in Germany, Verlaine and Zola in France, Samuel Butler and Wiliam Morris in England, the men behind these names, taken more or less at random, had little in common save a profound distrust of their society and a desire to see it changed by revolutionary or other means. Yet when they looked about them, the only class of men other than themselves not identified with that society were elements of the proletariat, what Wolfe Tone many years before had called 'that respectable class ... the men of no property': and which was to be echoed many years later by George Orwell in his *1984*, 'if there is any hope it is with the proles'. This somewhat naif search for a sort of spiritual purity in the mere absence of possessions, harking backwards to an idealized Christianity and forwards to an idealized Communism, was far more attractive to the intellectuals than to the post-Famine masses whom in Ireland they aspired to lead. Men of no property have seldom regarded their condition as respectable, unless they have chosen it voluntarily, while the hope of the proles is usually to cease being proles and with all speed. The number of men who, given any alternative, would deliberately choose the life of a monk, a private soldier or an inmate of the most 'comfortable' Nazi or Soviet concentration camp was always very small and with the increase of general materialism through the last and present centuries has grown smaller yet.

However there have been circumstances, usually of a revolutionary or quasi-revolutionary nature, when the proletariat, deprived for one reason or another of its 'natural' leaders, its aristocrats, its clergy, its own political leaders, its trade union officials, its professional fascists or its professional communists, will for a short while accept 'intellectual' leadership and sometimes will respond as romantically to a d'Annuzzio, a Toller or a Lorca as they to it. Thus in the 1860s did the Fenians acquire a very considerable hold over the Irish dispossessed.

The Irish had then no temporal leaders. O'Connell was long dead. Politically a great gap separated them from their spiritual leaders, for the Roman Catholic hierarchy, led by the primate, Archbishop Cullen, was firmly, indeed almost violently, anti-revolutionary, partly as a result of Cullen's experience in Rome during the Risorgimento. Although the franchise had been much expanded by an Act of 1850, from 61,000 to 165,000, the Irish M.P.s at Westminster were a singularly ineffective lot and in any case only represented the men of property in Ireland. The Young Ireland movement had ceased to exist. Only one member of that group was still politically active: Charles Gavan Duffy. In 1850 he attempted to create an all-Irish tenants' league, the principal intention of which was to legalize the Ulster custom and extend it to all Ireland. Since both Protestants and Catholics attended a conference in Dublin Duffy, promptly and prematurely, attempted to re-create the United Irish movement in the form of a League of North and South. The Protestants immediately took fright: that League collapsed and the Irish Tenant League soon followed it into limbo with nothing achieved. Duffy despaired and emigrated to Australia in 1855, where he was to have a moderately distinguished political career.

His successor as editor of the *Nation*, A. M. Sullivan, described the condition of Ireland at that time in the following words: 'Repeal was buried. Disaffection had disappeared. Nationality was unmentioned. Not a shout was raised. Not even a village tenant-right club survived. The people no longer interested themselves in politics. Who went into or who went out of parliament concerned them not ... All was silence.'

In the Northeast, and particularly in Belfast, the Catholic mob was as leaderless as was the rest of the Catholic population of Ireland, indeed perhaps even more so. The Protestants there had at least their ranting clergymen, their Rev. Dr. Demagogues to tell them when and sometimes how—as in the 1857 riots described in the previous chapter—to bash the Catholics and thus assure, and be assured of, their conquerors' superiority over the Papish sub-men, while behind them, in local administration, in the forces of law and order and in the courts lay the security of the long arm of the Orange Order. From that day, indeed from long before that day, to this, the Protestant mob has almost always defeated the Catholic mob in the street battles that recur with such monotony throughout the history of the province. The Protestants may ascribe this to superior courage and divine protection. Others may assume that even the most rudimentary form of organization in such brawls is better than none. The sense of superiority, of divine right to rule, was steadily reinforced by these riots among the Protestants of Ulster: their alienation from the local Catholics and thus from the majority of Irishmen steadily increased. At no point between the Famine and today would it have been possible to re-create a United Irish movement, yet as will be seen the dream lingered and lingers on.

The Fenians, being in no sense a sectarian force and indeed often on very bad terms with the Church, aspired, as all Irish revolutionary associations have done, to create a purely secular organization. Also known, later almost invariably so, as the Irish Republican Brotherhood or I.R.B., it counted many Protestants, including Ulstermen, among its more important and active members: one of these, for instance, was to be Sir Roger Casement. Nor was its membership limited to Irishmen living in Ireland. The Irish diaspora had led, and continued to lead, to the establishment of large Irish minorities in Britain, the United States, Canada and even Australia. In these countries too the Fenians were active, and from the foundation of 'the Organization' until the Anglo-Irish Treaty of 1922 and even beyond the Irish-Americans were a major, often the major, source of finance for revolutionary activity in the old country.

It was founded in 1858 by two emigré survivors of the abortive Smith O'Brien revolt of 1848 who had been living in Paris with so many other emigrés from other lands, forced to flee their homes after 1848, the Year of Revolution. It is not hard to envisage the endless conversation in the cafés and cheap lodging houses that produced, as their most significant document, *The Communist Manifesto*, in the very year that the two Irishmen arrived there. James Stephens and John O'Mahony were not, however, Communists. Nor did Fenianism ever have any clearly formulated policy of economic and social reform, though it was always willing to exploit discontent in these fields for its own revolutionary purposes, reserving the right to decide on the forms to be adopted only after the English should have been driven out of Ireland by force. It is significant that O'Mahony should have been an enthusiastic, though it is said not very erudite, Gaelic scholar. It was he who gave the movement the name of Fenians, derived from the *fianna* or host led, according to legend, by Finn MacCool in pre-historic times. This harping, in every sense of the word, back to the Gaelic past, real or imaginary, rather than planning for the future has always been an important element in Irish nationalism and now became a major strand in Irish revolutionary aspirations. It created and continues to create a rift with the Scots-Irish of Ulster whose own mythology is firmly anchored in the seventeenth century, the Plantations, Enniskillen, the Walls of Londonderry, the Boyne and so on.

Stephens and O'Mahony must have heard much, in Paris, about conspiratorial secret societies in Italy, Russia and elsewhere. With their own knowledge of the less directly political or even a-political secret societies of Ireland, Whiteboys, Ribbonmen, the Orange Order and all the rest of it, they realized that this form of activity, if skilfully applied in much tougher fashion in their own country, could provide a most powerful lever. Having lived through the fiasco of 1848 they did not intend to try to woo the masses, but rather to give those masses the effective, disciplined leadership that Smith O'Brien had been unable to provide and that had also been missing in 1798. (The Fenians or I.R.B. published periodicals and newspapers which were suppressed with monotonous regularity by the authorities. These, however, never appeared as products of 'the Organization' but more or less pseudonymously. Their purpose was to educate the public against the Day of Revolution rather than to attract supporters for a society which, being secret, could not seek open support.)

It was organized on the now classical basis. The number of Fenians known to any individual was in theory strictly limited. It was also pyramidal, with a high command of greater or lesser efficiency at various periods of its development. It set about infiltrating, and when possible controlling, all patriotic organizations, from those dealing with Gaelic matters and even sport to straight political, even party political, groupings, and this inevitably won it a measure of unpopularity, for its activities in these fields could not be kept entirely secret. The British had less quick success than usual in breaking through its curtain of secrecy, with its elaborate and effective system of passwords and the rest, though they did infiltrate the Organization with quite a few secret agents. It would seem probable that it was quite ruthless in the execution of traitors, though of this almost nothing is known. To the British, even the British authorities in Ireland, it rapidly became and remained a bogeyman. Every manifestation of anti-British activity was soon ascribed to 'the Fenians'.

Having seen the failure of Daniel O'Connell and of Young Ireland to achieve Irish freedom by constitutional means, it was dedicated to liberation through selective violence to be followed, when the time was ripe and the English enemy sufficiently demoralized, by a national uprising. Just as no plans were made for a future Ireland after victory, so little account was taken of the views of the Dissenters in Ulster and none of the Protestant minority in Ireland as a whole: these presumably would simply disappear, in one way or another.

For the sixty years following the Famine the Irish liberation movement was usually to be split between two wings: the constitutional wing and the physical force wing. Sometimes one was predominant, as during the Parnell period towards the end of the century when Fenianism almost, but not quite, disappeared, or during the Anglo-Irish war of 1918-1922 when the I.R.B., led by Michael Collins, had the support of the overwhelming majority of Irishmen. Not all the members of the I.R.B. were men of the sword (one has only to mention W. B. Yeats) nor all the constitutionalists utterly opposed to the use of violence (one has only to mention Arthur Griffith), but such was the basic dichotomy. At times the two main groupings were at loggerheads, and this even led to Civil War in 1922: at times they worked together, indeed in some slight measure coalesced, as was tht case when Parnell was the 'Uncrowned King'. But they were fundamentally opposed, not only politically but also psychologically.

It is not really curious that this dichotomy has survived and is visible in the Ulster crisis today, both among the Catholics and the Protestants. The respectable Unionists and the Paisleyites have nothing in common, save that neither is Roman Catholic and both wings believe that it can use and control the other. The same is true of the Roman Catholics who desire reform and those who lust after revolution. And just as in the past the attitude of the Churches further confused the situation, so today the importation of Marxist issues and the consequent *simpliste* Marxist interpretations of current history (whether Russian, Chinese, Trotskyite or old-fashioned Democratic Socialist) make a nonsense of any sort of political spectrum. There is no dualism in Irish affairs, but only a multiplicity of dualisms, no right or left but a Medusa-like head of dangerous snakes. This has perhaps always been the case, but its modern form was first cast by and through the Fenians.

Fenian propaganda appealed not only to the rural proletariat. Despite massive emigration to England and America the flight from the land had greatly increased the unskilled labour forces in the few Irish cities, from 31,000 in 1841 to 144,000 in 1871. The fastest growing, both as a port and an industrial centre, was Belfast. The men laid off from the farms were, invariably, given the most menial and worst paid jobs in the construction and similar industries, such as port enlargement, road building and so on. Skilled and semi-skilled men, particularly in the growing ship-building industry, were almost invariably Dissenters. Indeed this state of affairs became, as it were, institutionalized, the better paid Protestant workers being determined to preserve the differentials both in status and in pay, which meant in effect to crush by all the crude means at their disposal any attempt by the Catholic workers to obtain better jobs. During the sectarian riots we find, with remarkable regularity, the workers in the shipyards fighting and on occasion murdering the construction workers, and vice-versa. More important, perhaps, they interfered with the employment of Catholic workers in the yards. The owners and managers, not wishing to see production held up by strife, usually bowed to this form of intimidation, even though it ran counter to the purest theories of *laissez-faire*. Belfast's Catholic *Lumpenproletariat*, in so far as it was capable of mastering any political ideas at all, inevitably looked to the Fenians who had already sided with the landless or very small peasantry in the countryside. This in turn alienated the middle classes, both Catholic and Protestant, rural and urban. In Belfast, Derry and the other towns of Ulster it brought about a tacit, and sometimes not so tacit, alliance between the *entrepreneurs* and the Protestant working class with the object of 'keeping the

Papists down'. The leadership in this campaign, which has endured until today, was and is provided by the Orange Order. Its effect, then as now, was to prevent the birth of any real working-class movement, such as the Labour Party in Britain or the various Socialist and Communist parties on the European continent. Just as immigrant pressures and resultant hostilities in the vast United States—Irish, Italians, Jews—prevented the creation of a Labour movement over there during the period, roughly 1870-1920, most propitious to such phenomena, so in Ulster sectarian fear and sectarian hatred had a similar effect in the minute mixed community of Ulster. It even delayed for many years the creation of an effective trade union organization. This, needless to say, did not displease the owning and managerial class, many of whom were not above exploiting these emotions of ignorance and fear for their own purposes of financial gain and when, as they usually were, important members of the Orange Order for increasing and consolidating their power in that corner of Ireland.

One of the fundamental beliefs of the Marxist Second International was the solidarity of the international working class. Such a solidarity, accepted as dogma in Paris and in Berlin, in Brussels and even in London, led to the logical conclusion that a European war was henceforth an impossibility, since vast conscript armies must consist primarily of workers who would of course refuse to fire on one another. Indeed, they said, even to conscript and arm the workers would be extremely dangerous if not actually fatal for the capitalists and their militarist allies in every industrialized European country. August, 1914, proved and forever the complete folly of this Marxist error. If any of those theoreticians of revolution had taken the trouble to examine Belfast at any date after the convening of the First International he should have been forewarned that the economic motive, important as it is, can almost always be stifled or at least diverted by other, even more powerful and perhaps more primitive, emotions. At the time of writing, despite the Marxist theorists and the attempt of home-grown and imported Communists to get in on the act, what is happening in Belfast's shame and misery has no explanation to be found in the Marxist dialectic acceptable to any objective observer.

Fenianism, in Ireland, was in practical terms a failure. By 1865 James Stephens and the other I.R.B. leaders had constructed a powerful secret society pledged to an armed uprising at the earliest possible opportunity. The Organization was deeply involved in the land struggle, though this had not yet reached its most acute form since the comparative boom in agricultural prices did not collapse for another decade. It had also acquired great strength among the large Irish minority groups, still very closely knit, in England and America. (American Fenians, many of them very experienced soldiers trained in the Civil War, raided into Canada and also carried out assassinations there.) In Ireland, however, the forces of the Crown were closing in on the Fenians. In 1865 many of the Fenian leaders were arrested and sentenced to long terms of imprisonment under the somewhat dubious Felony-treason Act. Stephens himself escaped and was urged by the other I.R.B. leaders to order an immediate rising. He hesitated until March of 1867, and the rising, when it came, was even more of a fiasco than that of 1848, a mere scuffle extinguished within twenty-four hours. That was the end of Stephens, but not of the I.R.B., for he had laid its foundations surely and well. However the government's secret agents were not eliminated.

It became more active in England, rescuing two Fenians from Manchester gaol (a policeman was shot in the process) and carryout similar raids—atrocities to the English—in other parts of England, sometimes involving the loss of innocent lives. These activities, copied by the I.R.A. in England in 1939-40, aroused great hatred of the Irish, an emotion never difficult to distil from the guilt the English were then beginning to feel for their miserable, half-starving colony. The *Punch* cartoons of the period reveal the combination of hatred and contempt that the English bourgeoisie felt for the inhabitants of John Bull's other island: a hideous, stunted scarecrow figure, with nostrils like drain pipes and tousled hair starting immediately above the eyebrows, sometimes fawning on his English betters in a quaint mishmash of the English language, at others planning their murder, a blackthorn club clasped in his simian hand. Yet soon enough there came a reaction. The English Victorians, when educated, were a rational people and by the general standards of most societies a decent people too. They began to ask, or at least some of them did, the eminently Victorian question: why? Why were the Irish, that is to say by then approximately one sixth or seventh of the inhabitants of the United Kingdom, so miserable, so desperate that only in the murder of landlords and landlords' agents, only in the bludgeoning of tithe collectors and in almost indiscriminate dynamite explosions in English cities could they see hope or at least find a measure of surcease to the hopelessness of their conditions? Gladstone denied that it was the Fenian outrages which had caused him to embark on his Irish policy. He had been thinking about Ireland for years, but certainly the Fenians must have caused him to concentrate England's most powerful political mind on 'the Irish problem' and it can hardly be coincidence that when he formed his first ministry, in 1868, and Fenian activity together with agrarian crime were greatly on the increase, that he announced his mission: to pacify Ireland. The greatest of liberals was to devote an immense part of his immense energies to this end, and for the rest of his long life. If he failed, and he only just failed, it was not for lack of purpose, let alone of compassionate intelligence. Meanwhile he set about, immediately, disestablishing the Church of Ireland against powerful and deeply entrenched opposition. And in 1870 he pushed through a Land Act: intended to ease the lot of the Irish countrymen, it failed, largely because of an atrocious agricultural slump. This did not deter him from pushing through another and successful Land Act in 1881 which was intended to give, and ultimately succeeded in giving, the land of Ireland to the men who worked it. Many Irishmen, perhaps naively but not altogether so, attributed this change of heart at Whitehall to the direct actions, the policy of physical force, employed by the Fenians. What, after all, had Daniel O'Connell and his peaceful mass meetings ever achieved for Ireland? Of what political use was the Church? Bombs were obviously better, the gunman a heroic figure. 'Who fears to speak of Ninety-eight' wrote the Fenian romantic poet, John Kelly Ingram, and thus was another myth born, looking as usual in Ireland both backwards to an Ireland that no longer existed and forwards to a country still to be conceived.

> They rose in dark and evil days
> To right their native land;
> They kindled here a living blaze
> That nothing shall withstand....

Myth had transformed, not for the first or last time, a

bungled, miserable, murderous Irish peasants' failure into a
glorious page of patriotic history. Precisely the same mythopoesis
was to illuminate for future generations the features and failures
of the Fenian themselves. The Irish need for *dead* heroes is
insatiable: with their living ones they tend to be far less satisfied.

The first Fenian terrorist campaign had virtually no direct
influence on Irish political developments. It frightened and horrified the English: it united the Irish-Americans into a powerful
lobby which in due course was able to exercise considerable
pressure on London: but in Ireland itself it became little more
than the activist wing of the peasant forces fighting the so-called
Land War, and with the passage of the Land Act of 1881 and
subsequent such acts (which encouraged the tenant farmers to
buy their farms on very advantageous terms with government
loans) the Organization gradually became redundant. It did not
die, but it hibernated, as it were, for a generation. The Irish
pendulum swung back to constitutional methods. The man immediately responsible for this was Isaac Butt.

A barrister, the son of a Church of Ireland cleric, and a man
of some means, he had been an opponent of Daniel O'Connell's
during the repeal campaign and had even debated against the
great man. He had however represented Harwich and later
Youghal in the United Kingdom parliament from 1852 to 1865
and Limerick after 1871 and had learned at first hand how neglected and misunderstood Irish affairs were in the British House
of Commons. As a barrister he defended several of the Fenian
leaders when they faced trial, and is said to have been deeply
impressed by their personal sincerity, honesty and patriotism.
He did not agree with their politics or methods: appealing as
they did to the poor and the dispossessed they had what would
nowadays be called a very definite 'left-wing' taint, which was
most unattractive to Butt, even though they never formulated
any clear social policy of the Leveller, Jacobin or Communist
variety. Isaac Butt, on the other hand, had very clear political
views: he was, in social affairs, an extreme conservative who believed that the 'natural leaders' of the politically non-existent
Irish nation were the nobility, the land-owners, the clergy and
the emergent middle classes. Like Disraeli in England, who
greatly extended the franchise with his Reform Bill of 1867, he
believed that the masses would automatically vote for and fol-

low their 'natural leaders'. On the other hand, as an Irish patriot he could only agree with the Fenians that Ireland was being very badly run from Whitehall. The man who had been O'Connell's opponent on repeal thus became the father of Home Rule. In 1870 he said: 'I have long since had the conviction forced upon me that it is equally essential to the safety of England and to the happiness and tranquillity of Ireland, that the right of self-government should be restored to this country.' Once again the most prominent of Irishmen, for such he rapidly became, was looking to the past for a model for the future, in his case to Grattan's Parliament. As the quotation just given shows, he was not seeking an Irish state but only a measure of Irish independence in the interest both of Ireland and of England. To achieve this he did not adopt O'Connell's methods. With the great extension of the franchise after 1867 the mass meeting was no longer necessary. The majority could now express its wishes through the ballot box. In 1869 he had set about organizing an Irish nationalist party. This was to function through Irish Nationalist M.P.s elected to the United Kingdom parliament, men whose loyalty was not to either of the great British political parties, but to the Irish people through their own party. He was almost immediately successful in this and after the 1874 election the Irish Party was a real force in being. However it achieved little, and a most reasoned speech by Butt in favour of Home Rule, delivered in that year to the House of Commons, achieved nothing at all. The forensic talents of even the most brilliant barrister are not enough for the leader of a political party. His star was in eclipse, and soon enough was to be outshone by perhaps the most brilliant political orb ever to shine in the cloudy, Irish sky. From 1877 until his fall in 1890 the mind of Charles Stewart Parnell, as cold and clear and inflexible as the Polar star itself, was to dominate Irish politics absolutely. This Protestant landowner, 31 years old in 1877, was of the very essence of the enlightened Ascendancy on his paternal side. His grandfather had been a close colleague of O'Connell's and an M.P. His great-grandfather had been the last Irish Chancellor of the Exchequer before the Union and an opponent of Clare's on the Union issue. Behind him there were eighteenth century judges and other public men. His mother was an American, the daughter of a Commodore in the United States Navy that had, marginally at least, helped defeat the British. It is perhaps from her that this Irish patrician, steeped in Irish politics, inherited or imbibed a measure of contempt for the mounting vulgarity of Victorian England—an emotion not uncommon among well-born Americans of the age—together with a comprehension and a measure of respect for British constitutional methods, which he proceeded to use in his attempt to defeat British aims in his own country. He was a most formidable figure.

This icy aristocrat was also far more ruthless than the bourgeois Butt. Butt treated the mother of Parliaments with a filial respect and was distressed when one of the members for Cavan, a Belfast provision merchant by the name of J. G. Biggar, initiated the policy of 'obstruction'. This policy, similar to the type of strike action called 'working to rule', meant the abuse of parliamentary practice, by the filibuster and other means, to prevent the transaction of normal business in the House of Commons and thus to draw attention to Irish grievances and Irish demands. Parnell immediately accepted, and as leader perfected, this essentially undemocratic method of political warfare, which became a standard tactic of the Irish Party when he became that party's leader. His party always sat with, but did not always vote with, the Opposition. He knew that the day would come when the government, whether Liberal or Conservative, would have so narrow a majority that it must rely on the bloc vote of the Irish Party in order to press through legislation it regarded as essential, or indeed to survive. The price of that vote was always plainly marked: Home Rule. Such cynical bargaining, amounting at times almost to blackmail, was of course not unknown in the House of Commons, though never before nor since has it been quite so blatant. It showed the disdain that Parnell felt for the United Kingdom legislature, and was accepted by many of the English legislators as an insult. The Tories in particular displayed a marked reluctance to play the parliamentary game according to Parnellite rules, after the failure of their single attempt in 1885. Nor need they do so again, since until 1912 they had the backing of an overwhelmingly Tory House of Lords. It was really only the Liberals—and only a portion of them, but the most important so long as Gladstone led the party—who were prepared to accept an occasional, shifting alliance with the Irish Party. Yet even this was enacted in the cloud-cuckoo land of humbug and self-deceit or, for

those who prefer a more dignified metaphor, amidst the obfusca-
tions of a Druid's mist, that have so often engulfed Irish political issues. The Liberals knew, and the Parnellites also knew, that
so long as the House of Lords could and would throw out legislation that had passed through the Commons, Home Rule would
never reach the statute book. It was this absence of realism in
its handling of Irish affairs that, as much as anything else,
prompted Parnell and his followers to try and make a farce of
the House of Commons in its handling of English affairs too.

Nor was he any more scrupulously democratic in his dealings
with the Fenians. He was perfectly prepared to use them, and
particularly their powerful American wing called Clan na Gael,
as allies in his own form of guerilla warfare against the United
Kingdom administration. However he was determined that they
should not use him and his organization for their ends. He
played this very difficult game with exceeding skill. Everybody
knew that there were comings and goings between the Brotherhood and the Parnellites, in Ireland, in England and in America,
but Parnell saw to it that no firm evidence, valid in a court of
law, linked him with the terrorists. His arrest under the Coercion
Act in 1881, on the grounds that he was encouraging agrarian
crime in the Land War because of his opposition to the Land
Act of that year, boomeranged in his favour and made him even
more popular in most of Ireland though much less with the
I.R.B., whom he disowned publicly. Later in that same year a
terrorist group called the Invincibles (quite unconnected with
the I.R.B. or any other secret organization with which Parnell
had any links) carried out a cold-blooded, double assassination
in the Phoenix Park, Dublin's great and fashionable park, the
site of the Vice-regal Lodge. The victims were the newly appointed Irish Secretary, Lord Frederick Cavendish, and the
Under-Secretary, T. H. Burke. Attempts were made by his
enemies to tie Parnell's name to this atrocity. In fact so distressed
was he by the crime that he seriously considered retiring from
public life. His emotions were so strong, and so obviously
genuine, that it needed not only the pleas of his followers but
also the persuasion of Gladstone and Chamberlain before he
agreed to remain in politics. As late as 1887 *The Times* published
a letter purporting to show his involvement in the Phoenix Park
murders. He sued for libel, won his case, and the letter was
proved a forgery. Nevertheless, and throughout his whole public

career, his discreet contacts with the 'physical force' elements, whether of the I.R.B. or, with much less discretion and sometimes none, of Davitt's Land League with its campaigns of Boycott and No Rent, meant that he, as a parliamentarian, was skating on very thin ice. He was an expert skater, at least so far as his public life went. Still, his contacts with illegal, or semilegal organizations made him many enemies though most of these held their peace until the thin ice of his private life gave way and his former friend, Captain O'Shea, cited him as corespondent in a divorce action in 1890. Then all those enemies came out against him. To the Tories and many of the English Liberals, whose great institution he had mocked and tried to undermine, to the Irish Unionists and the Orangemen, were now added more than half of his own parliamentary party, which he had ruled with so iron a fist for a dozen years, the majority of the Catholic priesthood, which distrusted him not only as a Protestant but also as a politician prepared to traffic with the physical force men, a proportion of the I.R.B. who felt that his overwhelming influence had led directly to the decline of their own organization, that he had achieved nothing for Ireland while preventing them from attempting to achieve anything at all. With his crash Irish nationalism was stunned, and for nearly twenty years. Furthermore, and this is of the highest relevance to this work, the Orangemen were reinforced in their prejudice and belief that all Irish nationalism, indeed all Irish patriotism, no matter how constitutional, how democratic its face may be, is merely a mask to conceal its real features, vice, popery and tyranny.

He married Kitty O'Shea and attempted a political come-back. The crowds, who had worshipped him two years ago now howled him down. On one occasion his audience attempted to blind him by throwing lime in his face. He never gave up, but within a year he was dead, at the age of forty-five.

The Ireland of 1891 was as embittered and as exhausted, though for quite different reasons, as the country whose legislators had voted their nation out of existence after the '98, as the Ireland from which men had stampeded abroad after the Famine. It was a comparatively prosperous Ireland but for twenty years it was in the grip of a torpor, soon enough compounded by shame for its betrayal of the lost leader, nowhere better described than in James Joyce's *Portrait of the Artist as a Young Man.* None of this, of course, affected the Protestant northeast where tribal solidarity was strengthened by an apparent, if vicarious, victory manifested by the obvious discomfiture and disarray of what the Orangemen now, more than ever, had come to regard as the hereditary enemy. It is therefore necessary, in the next chapter, to examine the post-famine and Parnellite period from their point of view.

CHAPTER FIFTEEN

The Union between Great Britain and Ireland, that is to say the
United Kingdom as it existed between 1801 and 1922, was, like
every form of colonization, an unnatural political compromise.
The political logic for its existence, as advanced by Unionists at
the time of its creation, was that two governments within 'one
Empire' were 'as absurd and monstrous as two heads on one
pair of shoulders'. Professor Mansergh, in the final sentence of
his essays on some aspects of that Union, asks tartly whether
'it was not more absurd and even more monstrous to conceive of
two pairs of shoulders with only one head?'* In fact, and certainly from 1886 if not before, the Imperial Parliament contained the representatives of at least three bodies directly and
personally concerned in Anglo-Irish affairs, for by then the
Calvinists of the northeast had been injected into the Imperial
equation, forcibly, ruthlessly and in a manner and for a purpose
that was ultimately destructive to the whole concept of the
British Empire, as I shall hope to show later in the book, owing
to the consequent insistence on the constitutional and legal
morality of colonialism and of the rights of colonizers permanently to preserve ascendancy status. (By one of the many paradoxes that flicker through Irish history, the English attempt
to solve 'the Irish question' in 1920 was once again to put two
heads on what was theoretically one pair of shoulders. The
United Kingdom was, and to this day still does, contain two
governments, the one at Westminster, the other governing the
rump of the old, much larger Irish colony from Stormont.)

In rural Ireland, that is to say almost all of the southern and
western parts of the island, the power of the old colonists was
being steadily whittled away, by government and economic
pressure, throughout the third quarter of the nineteenth century, a process which was to continue in the years that followed.
The colonists' descendants were everywhere on the retreat, spiri-

* The Irish Question 1840-1921, Nicholas Mansergh, Allen and Unwin, 1965
edition.

tually, economically and politically. Gladstone's disestablishment of the Church of Ireland in 1869 was construed by many as an essential denial of the Act of Union, for Clause Five of that bill had united, indissolubly and forever, the Churches of England and Ireland into one Protestant Episcopalian Church. Some Protestants in Ireland regarded disestablishment as sacrilege, others as political surrender, but in England it went through with remarkable ease. The English electorate was uninterested in backing this alien Church: the English taxpayer, indeed, was becoming wearied by his expensive, dangerous and unhappy colony, by what had now become the Irish question, a lack of interest and a weariness that are very much in evidence in Britain today. Vast quantities of cash were still flowing out of Ireland, principally in the form of revenue and rents—the economists' figures are so loaded politically as to be almost irrelevant —but vast sums of the taxpayers' money were also going back into Ireland in attempts, not always effectual, to preserve law and order there. In effect, and speaking very generally, this meant that the mass of the population throughout the whole United Kingdom was paying golden sovereigns to ensure the incomes of the land-owners in Ireland, Irishmen and Englishmen alike. And this the mass of the new middle-class taxpayers (ever larger in number) and their supreme accountant, the greatest of all Chancellors, Mr. Gladstone himself, did not appreciate. Furthermore the landed gentry were in disarray both economically and politically. The long drawn out (with brief intervals) agricultural depression, together with the introduction of more modern methods of food distribution, had deprived them of their semi-feudal base. The conditions that led to the Encumbered Estates Courts had deprived them of their social supremacy. The massive sale of Church of Ireland lands was an unmistakable portent of what would happen to the many vast 'demesnes' which were now ill cultivated and on which hungry Irish eyes were fixed. And, finally, the supremacy of the Royal Navy in the second half of the nineteenth century—which to many appeared permanent —made the 'rooted garrison' seem an anachronism not only in Liberal but also in Imperialist eyes. The British two-navy and later three-navy fleets (that is to say a marine arm capable of defeating two or three of the strongest alien navies that might, in any circumstances, be allied against it in time of war) hardly needed the support, so acceptable in 1800, of the Cork Militia or

F. E. Smith speaking at a
U.V.P. meeting, Dromore.

Ulster Volunteers in training, 1912.

Sir Edward Carson signing the Ulster Covenant, Belfast City Hall. On hi: left Captain J. Craig (Lord Craigavon); on his right the Marquis of Londor derry. Also in the picture are Alderman R. J. M. Mordie (Lord Mayor o Belfast), Viscount Castlereagh (later Marquis of Londonderry), Earl of Erne Sir James H. Campbell (later first Lord Glenavy), and Dr. William Gibso) (honorary secretary of the Ulster Unionist Council).

the Monaghan Fencibles when iron-clads and the later dread-
noughts controlled all the seas around Ireland. So far as Great
Britain was concerned, by the 1870s the Anglo-Irish gentry had
fulfilled their function, and a long series of Land Acts, which
facilitated the distribution of their estates to small farmers or
peasant-proprietors, saw to it that they slowly withered away.
Some remained, of course, and still do, the hardest working or
most resourceful of their class, usually accepting with greater
or lesser reluctance a democracy which, from the time of Isaac
Butt, expressed by votes a steady determination that Ireland
should be in some measure, or in all, a sovereign state.

With the eclipse, gradual but steady, of the Anglo-Irish
gentry in most of Ireland as a political and economic—though
not for some time as a social—force, the English interest in the
country fell, briefly, into the hands of the aristocracy, of those
great families with Irish estates, seats in the House of Lords and
very important relationships with the United Kingdom government when not actually members thereof. Until 1886, the year
of Gladstone's first Home Rule Bill, a high proportion of these
great land-owners were Whigs, the party which had fathered
Gladstone's Liberals, and therefore usually voted with their
political heirs. Others, indeed most, were Unionists of Tory
heritage: Disraeli's Conservative Party became almost, and at
time of Irish crisis almost entirely, dominated by its preoccupa-
tion with, and acceptance of, Unionism, the head-stone of the
Victorian imperialist structure.

None of this affected, or need (except geographically) have
affected, the nonconformist population of northeastern Ireland.
Industrialization continued, particularly in and about Belfast
and Londonderry, and in consequence those two cities went on
growing with the resultant pressure on housing and the creation
of ever larger 'ghettoes' where the Roman Catholics lived. Indeed in Derry, and in certain other towns of the west such as
Strabane, this situation was eventually almost reversed, the
Protestant inhabitants living in their own, hereditary areas surrounded by steadily increasing numbers of Catholics in shanty
towns that progressed to the status of slum and thence into
urban districts. Meanwhile in the countryside the change of
ownership was less marked than in the rest of Ireland. This was
due in part to the traditional 'Ulster custom' which made drastic redistribution of land less necessary and often not even

desirable to the tenants, in part to a superior agricultural technology and administration, which led to far fewer encumbered
estates. In proportion few of the big estates were broken up, and
those that went were generally in the west and south. In northeastern Ulster the Presbyterian farmers worked hard, prospered
in good times and survived in bad, put on their black suits and
their best dresses for church on Sundays, the boys joining their
local Orange Lodge as they reached man's estate, marching on
summer days with sashes and drums to celebrate their ancient,
tribal victories over the old Irish, convinced by their own clean-
living, non-swearing, hard-working and industrious rectitude
that they were the master race, the *Herrenvolk*, because they
were the Lord's Anointed. His strong arm would protect them
from their enemies, and as they oiled their muskets and made
sure that their powder kept dry they knew that they were acting
not selfishly but as His agents, to ensure that His will be done.

It would be rash to say that sectarian bitterness increased in
all Ulster between the riot of 1857, described in an earlier chapter by a long quotation from Andrew Boyd, and the great Home
Rule riots of 1886 and subsequent years. It would however seem
fair to say that like much else during those thirty years sectarian hatred, most especially in Belfast, had become institutionalized by tradition, just as class hatred was then becoming
'institutionalized' elsewhere in a rapidly industrialized Europe.
While emotions remained basically unchanged, their political
expression was becoming both more formal and more dangerous to all.

In 1864, that is to say some three years before the so-called
Fenian Rebellion and a year before most of the arrests of the
Fenian leaders began, there was a most violent and protracted
anti-Catholic riot in Belfast. The reason for this, however, was
an event in Dublin. On August 8th of that year Dublin's Lord
Mayor laid the foundation stone for the monument to Daniel
O'Connell that graces, as best it can, the street now re-named
after the Liberator and in those days called Sackville Street. The
Irish Nationalists, renascent after the torpor that had followed
the Famine and with new and purposeful leaders in the I.R.B.,
made this small ceremony into a great patriotic celebration. A
trainload of similarly minded men, with some women, came
down from Belfast for the day. Much advance publicity had
been given to the occasion. All this infuriated the Belfast Pro-

testant mob, which had of course remained at home, but not in idleness. O'Connell to them, then, typified Irish Catholicism, which had become, and was increasingly to become, merged with their vision of Irish nationalism. They therefore constructed an enormous effigy of the dread, dead man which they stuffed with fireworks and other combustible materials. (Would that there had been a photographer to preserve an idea of what it can have looked like!) First the mob tried to scrag the inmates of the train returning from Dublin. They were foiled by the Irish Constabulary. The rest of the day they spent lugging their effigy around Belfast, attempting to penetrate the Catholic areas in order there to set it alight. Again they were foiled, by Catholics, the police and the military. Finally they put fire to it on the river bank and tipped the charred remains into what was in those days an open, slow-running drain half choked with sewage, garbage and the carcasses of dead dogs. It was the most insulting gesture they were allowed to make, and it resulted in days of rioting in which many lives were lost and much property destroyed.

The historical importance of this long protracted Belfast riot is that it was the first one that would seem to have been directed, at least initially, against Dublin and Irish nationalism, rather than against Irish Catholic immigrants into what had once, long ago, been a Protestant enclave, though of course it was the citizens of Belfast who suffered from the after effects. It would seem that better communications—in this case the arrival of the railway—did not (as is frequently claimed of all such inventions) unite people but rather created further divisions between them, and hardened prejudices. What had been an 'Ulster problem' was about to become the 'Irish question' and, sooner than most people then realized, grow into the most divisive and decisive political issue not only for the United Kingdom as a whole but for the brand-new still uncompleted British Empire. If the Englishmen and Scots and Irish Unionists then training themselves for future triumphs in Asia and Africa had envisaged their own Triumphs—they all knew Roman history— would they have realized that the whispering slave in the triumphal car was not to be an African or an Indian but an Irishman, maybe a Papist Fenian murderer but more probably a God-fearing Protestant who worked, usually well, in one of the new Belfast shipyards?

The attempted revolution by the Fenians was foiled, in large measure by the Irish Constabulary. In 1867 Queen Victoria awarded them the privilege of adding the prefix 'Royal' to their name: and when it was disbanded in 1922 its heirs in the Six Counties of Ulster retained both the prefix and many of the old R.I.C.'s traditions and methods. From then until the time of writing the Royal Ulster Constabulary, or R.U.C., was the old R.I.C. in localized miniature, as the problems and forces with which it has had to deal in the truncated province were in large measure those with which its parent organization had had to deal in all Ireland.

With most of the Fenian leaders in jail, the Church of Ireland quietly disestablished and the first reforming Land Act of 1870 on the statute book, the United Kingdom government had reason to believe that at last a measure of pacification in Ireland had been achieved and that more might be expected to follow. True, the Land War continued but the Coercion Acts of 1870 and 1871, which gave the authorities in Ireland powers of arrest without warrant and detention without trial quite unacceptable in any other part of the United Kingdom, were believed to provide the Crown with adequate means to put down agrarian crime wherever outbursts of hostility against landlords should get beyond the control of the R.I.C. acting with and through the more normal processes of law. In these, apparently tranquil, circumstances Gladstone's Liberal Government felt safe to repeal the Party Processions Act, which had forbidden parades, and in 1872 the Orangemen were permitted to march openly once again. They immediately availed themselves of this and there were many, massive parades on July 12th of that year. These passed without disorder, in part perhaps because the rain in Belfast was so heavy that large parts of the roughest Protestant area, Sandy Row, were under water on that day.

However a month later the Roman Catholic Nationalists (the two terms had become by now almost synonymous) decided that they too would hold a parade, on August 15th, the day dedicated to the Assumption of the Blessed Virgin Mary, commonly called Lady's Day. This would seem to be the first such Catholic procession or parade of the century and was obviously political both in motive and in organization. One of its principal leaders, both in the preparation and on the march itself, was that same Joe Biggar, then a local Nationalist politician but soon to go to Westminster, there to become the 'Father of Obstruction-ism', the teacher who was to become the follower of Parnell in constitutional sabotage. For this parade he and his followers, having no precedents of their own, merely aped their Orange enemies. Huge banners were constructed, portraying Sarsfield instead of King Billy, green sashes were stitched with crown-less harps, and it would seem that banners demanded both the release of the Fenian prisoners and Home Rule. Only in the matter of drums do they appear not to have copied their Orange neighbours: accounts of the march do not mention drums.

Protestant reaction, even before the parade took place, was instantaneous, massive and hysterical. The Rev. Dr. Hanna had recently built himself a new church, called St. Enoch's, which was close to the five-mile route of the march. 'Roaring Hanna' therefore informed the Protestant workers in the shipyards and elsewhere that they must be prepared to defend St. Enoch's against the attack that he anticipated on his church. They res-ponded, and by the time the march took place there were in existence Catholic and Protestant mobs armed with every weapon from the most modern rifles of the day to wooden cud-gels. The authorities, anticipating the inevitable trouble, moved in foot and horse constables and troops.

The authorities were right, only they underestimated the chaos that was about to descend on large areas of Belfast. The rioting, in Winston Churchill's phrase, was 'savage, repeated and prolonged'. The two mobs were soon looting almost with-out discrimination. Pubs were their first objective, at first the pubs owned or patronized by members of the other faith, then, when the authorities tried to halt the resultant mass drunken-ness by closing them, any pub. After the pubs came the looting of the shops and the wanton destruction of private property. Sectarian hatred, the excuse for this orgy of drunken wreckage and ordinary theft, continued and reached its climax in the so-called Battle of the Brickfield, when, in pouring rain, Catholics and Protestants pelted one another with broken bricks, collected for the men in the aprons of screaming women, while an occa-sional rifle, shotgun or revolver provided a lethal *obbligato*. More and more police and military were brought in, finally some 4,000, some of whom were killed, many more wounded. Cavalry charges, with sabres drawn, were the only really effec-tive method of dispersing the more violent, drunken rioters and even then it was like dispersing quicksilver. They would run away up sidestreets, often in darkness with the street lights extinguished, to re-assemble as quickly elsewhere and continue their orgy of looting, burning and terrorization. Even funerals were considered suitable occasions for hatred, violence and murder. Both murderers and murdered included children. Nor were the very old spared, even when bedridden. The bestialization of some elements of the Belfast working class, and their slightly better educated leaders, was shown to the world, first, in 1872. As rats grow sleek and fat, huge and increasingly dangerous in the sewers of Paris or New York, so did the evil instincts of Peep o' Day Boys or Defenders luxuriate in the fetid, filthy, crowded, drunken Belfast slums.

And among their betters, the concept of justice declined. Andrew Boyd believes that all those killed in the 1872 riots, and most of those forced to flee their burned homes, were Catholics. However both factions tended to carry away their dead—incriminating evidence—often to bury them like animals in waste land. Be that as it may, when justice came to be done, which was in general at the Assizes of the following year, 1873, it certainly was not seen to be done. The courts, dominated by the Orange Order, took the opportunity to carry the understandable anti-Fenian political motives of the British government into the sewers of Belfast. The sabres of the Highland cavalrymen had not discriminated between drunken rioters of rival faiths: the lawyers did. The vast, ponderous and pompous apparatus of British law, so much admired by the English and by many Americans, has not always looked so handsome to foreigners. When manipulated in Ireland, for purposes of preserving British domination, it has on occasion looked very strange indeed, and seldom more so than when administered by judges, magistrates and juries in Ulster whose prime loyalty was to their own semi-legal, semi-secret Orange Order. One contributory factor to the Irish distrust in English legality was the fact that the trials resulting from the 1872 riots were, quite obviously, retribution against the Catholic minority in that part of Ireland. It was then that the Orange courts delivered a blow, perhaps the first and mortal one, against the British Imperial concept which, from its Roman model, could only be based on justice—or naked force: and only with peril and briefly upon a combination of both. Yet it was on this slippery path, an alternation of coercion and conciliation, that successive English governments were henceforth to base their rule in Ireland. The old Roman precept of *civis Romanus sum*, which Palmerston had attempted to re-create in British terms and which the French copied far more successfully in their empire, was and is applied only in a half-hearted, compromising manner in Ireland.

Once upon a time, many years ago, I found myself on a New Year's Eve in that huge Munich beer palace called the *Hofbrauehaus*. There were thousands seated, drinking and talking, in the principal hall and at either end, installed if I remember correctly behind raised balustrades, were brass bands, for so great was the crowd that the music from a single band would have been inaudible to the more distant beer-drinkers. I and my friends were, as it happened, near the middle of the great hall, where both brass bands were plainly audible even above the conversational din, the one playing Wagnerian airs, the other Strauss waltzes. The resultant cacophony was curious and memorable. Suddenly one band would outblast the other, and a rational, recognizable tune be discerned above the chatter: quite rapidly the process would be reversed. Occasionally the musical mixture even appeared to make sense, to produce a fortuitous co-ordination. The reason I give this memory, so remote from Irish affairs, is that it seems to me to provide a rough simile. Over the howling, drunken, murderous mobs of Belfast two political brass bands were playing at full blast. The one in London and the other in Roman Catholic Ireland. In the 1870s and 1880, like my two Bavarian bands, both worked for the same management, the United Kingdom, but their scores were quite different. Should one attempt to dance to such music, as the Irish and the English did politically, it could only be a *danse macabre*, clumsy, awkward, even hideous and finally lethal to the dancers, all the dancers.

Throughout the Parnellite period, and indeed for half a generation after Parnell's fall, the principal economic problem in Ireland as a whole, including most of Ulster, was the redistribution of land, the dismantling of the old landlord-tenant apparatus and the substitution therefor of ownership by the farmers themselves. There was little if any parallel to this process in England, though there were echoes in Wales and in parts of Scotland. It impinged on United Kingdom political economy, however, through the fact that a proportion of the Irish landlords were in fact Englishmen and usually noblemen at that, by right of inheritance legislators in the United Kingdom House of Lords (Irish peers were not there represented unless they also held a United Kingdom title or were elected, by themselves and from their own number, as remains the custom in Scotland). These were, however, a minority, though a powerful one, even in the Lords, and they with their supporters an almost negligible element among the enlarged United Kingdom electorate as a whole. With what seemed to Irish countrymen of the time infinite slowness, British governments, both Liberal and Conservative, steered a series of bills through Commons and Lords, culminating during the period of British rule with the so-called Wyndham Act of 1903, which enabled the cultivator with the support of public funds to buy the land he tilled or grazed. It was perhaps one of the most enlightened acts of self-interest by the British during their brief period of imperial grandeur, and it created a new and almost certainly happier Irish countryside. Land had always been the great grievance. The so-called Land War had merely been another expression of this grievance not so very different though much better organized than that expressed by Whiteboys and Ribbonmen, Oakboys and Steelboys, in generations long past. Its quietus (though echoes linger on even today after further legislation by the successive Free State and Irish Republican governments) produced modern, rural Ireland, a country of medium sized or small farms, not run with any particular efficiency but breeding a race of patriotic, more-or-less contented and therefore on the whole conservative men and women. One description of this sensible, basically benevolent development was 'killing Home Rule through kindness'. It was certainly the best aspect of the conciliation part of British policy. It did not of course apply to northeastern Ulster, let alone to an ever more industrialized Belfast.

Politically the main Irish issue that a policy of kindness was intended to kill was indeed Home Rule itself. Parnell, though in close alliance with the Land League and committed to its leaders' economic aims, was really interested in nothing else, or at least nothing else to begin with. He had virtually no social or economic policy (apart from land) save the transfer of power, in Ireland, from English to Irish hands. Men knowledgeable in history—and Victorian politicians were more knowledgeable than most—saw that the Irish would hardly be satisfied for long with the measure of devolution (the panacea advanced by the Radical Liberal Imperialist, Joseph Chamberlain, for the United Kingdom and indeed the British Empire) and, once this were granted, must in due course press on to a severance of all umbilical links other perhaps than economic ones (and though they knew much history, most of the Victorians bothered comparatively little about economics) with what the English were now beginning to call 'the mother country'. This in turn implied a great military danger to Britain. The publicists of the age called global international politics 'the great game' as Russia seemed to threaten the Empire from the ill-defined borders of northwestern India, as an expansive and increasingly hostile France was close to collision with an expansive Britain in central Africa, as imperial Germany flexed its very considerable muscles with a Kaiser who was soon enough to announce that Germany's future lay on the blue waters of the great oceans. A potentially neutral, let alone a hostile, Ireland was a nightmare to cause any Victorian imperialist to tear his nightcap from his head and to determine that such a thing must never be. Within living memory we heard the same sentiments uttered in 1938, and later written and printed, by the last of the great English Victorian statesmen, Sir Winston Churchill. It would seem probable that the ghost of this concept has survived two World Wars, and the loss of Empire, to influence those British politicians reluctantly called upon to deal with the Ulster problem of the 1970s.

All this was foreshadowed by the activities of the Parnellites, and English reactions thereto, which culminated in Gladstone's first Home Rule Bill of 1886. With, usually, some eighty-six well-drilled supporters in the House of Commons, roughly 15% of the elected members, representing virtually the entire Irish electorate save the Northern Irish Nonconformists and the Church of Ireland members regularly sent by Trinity College Dublin, Parnell was a formidable force, his strategy destructive to Empire, his tactics soon equally dangerous to the House of Commons itself. His arrogance was, to many Englishmen, distasteful in the extreme and his followers, such as Joe Biggar, foreign oafs. His contemptuous and open methods of making deals with either of the two major parties seemed to endanger the reduction of the Mother of Parliaments to the status of Tammany Hall. Yet himself they could not dismiss, either as a man or as a political force. The Conservatives accepted his alliance, well aware of his single aim, in 1885, the Liberals in the following year. Both needed those eighty-six votes.

Yet his tactics were at fault. His was, by his own wish and that of his electorate, essentially an alien party, representing in reality a foreign if then non-existent country, much as the Communist parties in Western European legislative assemblies today represent a foreign power. These can often do great mischief: they can and have toppled governments: they cannot govern without the presence of the Red Army. Parnell could do such mischief, could and did topple governments, could almost wreck the parliamentary institution, but he had no Green Army. He could only impede government, but could never force through legislation in Ireland's interest. And soon enough his intrusion into Imperial affairs was answered by an action the effect of which is still with us, instigated by Lord Randolph Churchill.

Such were the Irish airs being produced at one end of the enormous room, at least in a very abbreviated notation. At the other end the larger, far more powerful and noisier English brass band was engaged upon a totally different, and perhaps superficially at least far more complicated, contrapuntal arrangement, unrehearsed as all political disputes must almost invariably be, but as strident and violent as they usually are. In its simplest terms, in those of the *Punch* cartoons of the period, it was a sort of gladiatorial conflict between Gladstone and Disraeli. Yet it was of far greater depth even than the conflict between the new Liberal party, which Gladstone was creating, and the new Conservative party, which was Disraeli's contribution to British democracy. To say that it was a struggle between the old England of the squires and the new society of the urban industrialists would also be an over-simplification. Marx and Engels saw it as a sublimation of their basic dichotomy between the labouring class and that other class which exploits the value of the labourer. None of these simple explanations is true, but none is irrelevant to English history. What was, or should have been, quite irrelevant in a period when the English were bitterly antagonistic about the sort of society that they wished to create, for Englishmen, was 'the Irish question'. Yet because of the Act of Union, because of those eighty-six Irish M.P.s, it became at times almost, and for brief periods entirely, the primary and in some ways most intractable problem facing the administrators of the largest empire the world has even seen. And even now, in an utterly changed world, a splinter of the Irish bone remains in the English throat. Who would have thought that in August 1970 Scottish Highlanders in British uniforms would be confronted by crowds of furious Irishwomen in the slums of Belfast? Were it not tragic, and tragic for so long, it would be almost comical. On, on it went: on, on it goes. Winston Churchill, intimately involved in Irish affairs since his birth, writing about the permanence of this issue in his book *The World Crisis* (written nearly fifty years ago) said: 'Great Empires have been overturned. The whole map of Europe has been changed.... The mode and thought of men, the whole outlook on affairs, the grouping of parties, all have encountered violent and tremendous changes in the deluge of the world, but as the deluge subsides and the waters fall we see the dreary steeples of Fermanagh and Tyrone emerging once again. The integrity of their quarrel is one of the few institutions that have been unaltered in the cataclysm which has swept the world.'

It has still not been altered. It would not even be fair to say that it was Winston Churchill's father who created it, though Lord Randolph's hatred of Gladstonian liberalism in 1886 was certainly a contributory factor to the condition of Belfast in the 1970s. They gambled in those days, most of the gentlemen who controlled policy at Westminster or in Whitehall. The cards with which they played were usually, on the tables of Brooks's or White's or even the Reform, red or black: in 'the great game' red, white and blue. The green cards, and the orange ones, did not really belong in the cardrooms of gentlemen's clubs. When inserted into the pack they made for very bad hands.

Benjamin Disraeli died, out of office, in 1881. He had never shown much interest in Irish affairs—in his long political life he never bothered to visit Ireland—nor indeed in any form of nationalism other than what he would have called English, not British, nationalism. He did not regard it as the moral duty of Englishmen to hasten to the defence of small, oppressed peoples such as Armenians or Bulgarians, let alone Irishmen. He had spoken against Gladstone's Church and Land reforms, warning that these were the first steps towards Home Rule. Despite the great complexity of his mind, and his extreme political skill in defending British interests against even such formidable persons as Bismarck, his patriotism shows a curiously simple, even romantic quality, visible in his relationship with his Queen and surely emphasized by the fact that he was a Jew. He epitomized and implemented imperialism in its first, that is to say its political as opposed to its later economic, period. In general the more areas of the map that could be re-printed in red, the addition of the title empress to that of queen, the panoply of great navies patrolling the oceans of the world, of contented, loyal maharajahs and African chieftains jingling on horseback behind the Royal Coach as it carried the ageing monarch along the Mall, the determination that no foreigner who was not insane would challenge such power and the near certainty that this maniac could be destroyed, such was in simple terms the basis of Disraeli's imperialism. This form of wellnigh contemptuous xenophobia appealed also to the new electorate, enfranchised by his Reform Bill of 1867, and was to ensure a Conservative Party majority in one government after another from the time of his death until today. (Apart from the Coalition governments of 1916-18, the National Government of 1931-1940 and the Second Coalition Government of 1940-1945, all of which were in effect Conservative governments, the Liberal and Labour parties have only held office in Britain in some thirty-three years of the one hundred and four since the Second Reform Bill.) This new Conservative Party, which was already the Conservative and Unionist Party by the time Disraeli died, was by its very genesis opposed to the granting of political rights to subject nations, and particularly to the Irish. Disraeli had drawn a large part of the urban proletariat to support a party which had hitherto been based upon the country gentlemen and their tenants. None of these groups had any interest, and the land-owners at least a marked counter-interest, in allowing the Irish self-government. This does not mean that they were necessarily hostile to Irish economic and social aspirations, though on the whole they were tepid about these too. It was the son-in-law of Disraeli's successor as leader of the Conservative Party, Arthur Balfour who had married Lord Salisbury's daughter, who was sent by his father-in-law to Dublin as Chief Secretary, and who was himself to lead the Party and be Conservative Prime Minister, who coined the phrase and announced that his intention was 'to kill Home Rule through kindness'. He did his best too, for he was a kind

and gentle man. There was, however, little that Irish national-
ists could hope to win politically from the Conservative and
Unionist Party, all the more since its usual majority in the
Commons was to have an almost solid backing in the United
Kingdom House of Lords, at least until 1912 as a branch of the
legislature, and morally thereafter.

Their great rivals, the Liberals, split over Home Rule in three
directions in 1886. The old Whigs, headed by Lord Hartington,
later Duke of Devonshire, himself Gladstone's Chief Secretary in
Ireland during the 1874 riots, took his part of the Liberal Party
—that is to say, roughly, the English owners of Irish land—into
the opposition within the House of Lords. The old Whig-Liberal
coalition was over never to be reunited. The class division between the two major British parties became accentuated with the
departure of the Whig magnates. At the same time, and for
quite different reasons, the radical wing of Gladstone's followers
decided against Home Rule, and Joseph Chamberlain resigned
from his government. For a brief period they called themselves
Liberal Unionists, described by an Irish opponent, John
O'Connor Power, as 'the mules of politics: without pride of
ancestry, or hope of posterity'. Gladstone's Home Rule was
defeated in the Commons and his government fell. The Liberal
Party survived, and was indeed to triumph briefly in 1892 and
again early in the following century, but as English politics became increasingly dominated by class conflict its nature had to
change, if it were not to become redundant. Such a change was
indeed attempted by Lloyd George in his early, socialistic period.
(Lady Violet Bonham-Carter once remarked to this writer that
Lloyd George was never a Liberal: he started life, she said, as a
Socialist and turned his coat to become a Conservative, with no
Liberal phase between.) But even by 1910 it was certainly too
late for the Liberal Party to prevent the creation of a new party
that really represented the working class. Its eclipse by the
Labour Party as the only party capable of providing an alterna-
tive government to the Conservatives was completed in 1931
when many of the Liberal leaders styled themselves National
Liberals, another of history's mules, and accepted office in an
essentially Conservative government.

No prophet of course could have foreseen these developments,
not even Gladstone himself, when, after pondering the matter
deeply, he decided at last to commit the Liberal Party to the

issue of Home Rule. According to Philip Magnus, in his biography of the great man, it was while cruising on Sir Thomas
Brassey's yacht, *Sunbeam*, through the Norwegian fiords in
August of 1885 that he made his momentous decision. He had
long pondered on the miserable condition of Ireland and had
already done much to right Irish wrongs. The happy condition
of Norway and the Norwegians, who though still citizens of
Sweden enjoyed a considerable measure of Home Rule, convinced him, it would seem, that a measure of independence
might produce similar effects in Ireland. However he was not
quite so pure an idealist as he appeared. He was then out of
office, his government having fallen two months earlier as a
direct result of Parnell's switching his eighty-six votes to the
support of Lord Salisbury's Conservatives. Gladstone had repeatedly expressed his distaste for competitive bargaining by
the two great English parties to gain this bloc of Irish votes in
the House of Commons. He had indeed uttered rather vague
hopes that the Conservatives would themselves introduce some
measure of constitutional reform for Ireland, or even that there
be a party truce while a solution was worked out. Now, however,
with a General Election due at the end of the year, it would be
surprising if Gladstone had not meditated on those eighty-six
Irish Home Rulers in the Commons, all the more so as he was
well aware of Parnell's disillusion with his fruitless and politically unnatural alliance with the Unionists. Gladstone, however,
played his cards with his usual care and caution. It was not
until immediately before the election that his son, Herbert Gladstone, leaked the news to the press that the G.O.M. ('The Grand
Old Man') had been converted to Home Rule. This not only
gained for his Liberal candidates the now very considerable
Irish vote in the English constituencies but also assured him the
support of the Parnellites in the new parliament. In fact historians are generally agreed that Gladstone's 'conversion' won
him that election.

It was, as we have seen, a Pyrrhic victory. It was also evidence
of how ineffective, in fact, Parnell's tactics were. At the lowest
level his obstructionist methods did little more than create ill-
will and increase anti-Irish feeling in the House. These methods,
combined with the mounting disorders in Ireland itself as the
Land War pursued its painful course despite the new Land Acts
now on the statute book, only hardened many an English legis-

lator (and the English press and public generally) in the conviction that the Irish were a savage, backward people, quite unfitted for even partial self-government and more fittingly typified in Fenian terrorists than in ill-mannered Members of Parliament. Parnell's grander strategy, of playing off the English parties against one another, was equally unacceptable at Westminster. In English eyes it revealed a cold-blooded cynicism, highly repugnant to the moralistic Victorians. Practically it achieved nothing, and for a very obvious reason. When the balance of Liberal and Conservative M.P.s was nice enough, Parnell's bloc of votes could topple the government in office. It could not, however, get constitutional legislature passed so long as the House of Lords retained its powers. And as 1886 was to show, it could not even keep the party with which he was allied in office when any great issue—and particularly the Irish issue—was made the centre of policy. This was true in 1886, and it is true today. Any English party that accepted or accepts an Irish alliance is donning a shirt that is, more often than not, a shirt of Nessus. The same is true, in reverse, since the Anglo-Irish truce of 1921 and the Treaty that followed: any Irish politician who visits London to try and heal old wounds by negotiation is placing his political, sometimes even his physical, life in jeopardy should he fail to achieve his mission.

Talleyrand once remarked that the greatness of a man can better be assessed by the weight and stature of his enemies than of his friends. Gladstone was already a much hated man, before his conversion to Home Rule, and that hatred came from many of the most powerful in the land, led by the Queen herself. His enemies immediately dismissed his new found favour for Home Rule as a despicable, if not actually treasonable, political trick. Yet this was certainly not true: for the rest of his life it remained the lodestar of his policy, a cause to which he adhered with such passionate intensity as to make one wonder whether he did not in fact doubt his own judgment in this matter, and was determined to stifle such doubts. His political enemies were determined, immediately and permanently, to exploit the Home Rule issue against him to the full.

On February 13th, 1886, Lord Randolph Churchill celebrated his thirty-seventh birthday. Three days later he was writing from London to his friend Lord Justice Fitzgibbon (no relation of this writer) in Dublin: 'I decided some time ago that if the

G.O.M. went for Home Rule, the Orange card would be the one to play. Pray God it may turn out the ace of trumps and not the two.' Within a week he was on his way to Ulster and on landing at Larne, in the County Antrim, he first uttered (though possibly not in the precise words he was later to use) his famous slogan: 'Ulster will fight, and Ulster will be right.' He then made rabble-rousing speeches of extreme violence in Belfast's Ulster Hall and elsewhere and returned home. The Ulster Unionists, by now entirely dominated by the Orange Order, made their preparations. On June 7th, 1886, Gladstone's Home Rule Bill was defeated in the House of Commons and his government in ruins. By then Belfast had been gripped, for three days already, in the worst and bloodiest sectarian riots that that unfortunate city had so far experienced. These riots were directly concerned with the Home Rule issue. Even if Lord Randolph had not made his inflammatory speeches earlier in the year such rioting and bloodshed would probably have taken place, but it was he who placed the problem of Ulster in the forefront, or rather the cockpit, of British party politics. From that unfortunate situation no politician in the last eighty-five years has permanently succeeded in extracting them.

This was precisely Lord Randolph's intention. A younger son of the Duke of Marlborough he was the leader of a new and highly aggressive form of Conservatism, as remote from the staid old Tory country gentlemen who formed the backbone of his party as the radical Joe Chamberlain was from the Whig aristocracy which had long been the backbone of his. Like his more famous son, Lord Randolph as a youth was of only limited academic ability but as a young M.P. he soon won fame, which many called notoriety, for the violence of his oratory, not sparing his own, elderly front bench but infuriating his opponents even more. He defeated the old fashioned Tories at the Conservative Conference in 1884 and became chairman of the Central Union of Conservative Associations. In 1885 Lord Salisbury, who does not seem to have cared for him personally, saw no alternative but to give him an important post in the new administration. As Secretary of State for India during the few months of that government's lifetime he proved his efficiency in high office, an office, be it noted, directly connected with imperial expansion on a massive scale. It was thus as a senior ex-Cabinet Minister, despite his young age, that he played the Orange card.

After the defeat of the Home Rule Bill, the fall of the Gladstone government following a general election, and the return
of Lord Salisbury as Prime Minister, Lord Randolph once again
held high office, this time as Chancellor of the Exchequer. Again
he was a conscientious administrator, but an excessively difficult
colleague. He was quarrelsome in cabinet, and in December he
resigned, apparently under the impression that the government
would fall apart as a result, and that he could then return, on
his own terms, to a cabinet of his own devising. He was wrong,
and though his political career was not quite over he never
again held office. In 1893 his mind became clouded, and in 1895
he was dead. The cause of death was given as G.P.I., or general
paralysis of the insane. He is said to have been the last prominent man ever to have died explicitly of that malady, for almost
immediately after his death it was identified by the medical
profession as tertiary syphillis.

I am told, by medical opinion, that one of the course of symptoms that can be produced by advanced syphillis is violence of
manner culminating in megalomania and cut short by rapid
mental decay. All these symptoms are detectable in the behaviour of Lord Randolph Churchill. It may well be that the
man who played the Orange card was neither evil nor stupid
but was slowly going out of his mind.

It was not an altogether original card. As early as 1883 Lord
Salisbury, writing anonymously in *The Quarterly Review*, had
brought the sectarian issue into the forefront of Irish politics:
'The highest interests of the Empire, as well as the most sacred
obligations of honour, forbid us to solve this (Irish) question by
conceding any species of independence to Ireland; or in other
words, any licence to the majority in that country to govern the
rest of Irishmen as they please. To the minority, to those who
have trusted us ... it would be a sentence of exile or of ruin. All
that is Protestant—nay, all that is loyal—all who have land or
money to lose ... would be at the mercy of the adventurers who
have led the Land League, if not of the darker counsellors by
whom the Invincibles have been inspired.' And during the
Home Rule debate of 1886 Lord Salisbury again gave his blessing
to Lord Randolph's incitements to violence in Ulster ('Now
may be the time,' he had said in Belfast, 'to show whether all
those ceremonies and forms which are practised in the Orange
Lodges are only idle meaningless ceremonies') by publicly specu-

lating whether Ireland should not in fact be regarded as two nations rather than one. Thus was partition, too, conceived during the bitter Home Rule campaign of 1886.

Lord Randolph, be it remarked, had little interest in and less affection for the men who controlled the Orange Order, referring to them, in late 1885, as these 'abominable Ulster Tories' and remarking that 'these foul Ulster Tories have always ruined our party'. Yet this was the genie that he, chairman of the party that has always proclaimed itself the party of law and order, was prepared to conjure up with the short term objective of destroying Gladstone's government. The sorry spectacle of using Ulster's misery for English political aims at Westminster was repeated in 1914 and again in 1920. The genie are the mobs of Belfast hooligans, and particularly the Protestant hooligans mobilized by demagogic clergymen and manipulated by Orange Unionists in the interests of English politicians who really, and sometimes openly, despise them all.

In view of the tense emotions created by the Home Rule issue, and perhaps even more important by Belfast's history and sociology, it would seem probable that there would have been rioting there during the summer of 1886. However without Lord Randolph's incitement, and remarks made during the debate by Joseph Chamberlain, Lord Hartington and others, construed by leading Orangemen as encouragement for the Protestant cause, they might have been both less violent and less protracted, for they lasted, with brief lulls, well into September. Many lives were lost and vast damage done.

Even more important for the future perhaps than this pouring of oratorial gasoline on old fires was the fact that the Orange Order had been led to believe that at last it had that 'respectable' backing for which it had yearned so long, that it could rely on the English, or at least on the English Conservatives, in its perpetual struggle (through the Ulster Unionist Party which it now fully controlled) against Irish Nationalism, both within Ulster and in Ireland as a whole. The Union Jack, as its name implied, was supposed to be the flag of the whole United Kingdom and since 1801 had included the cross of St. Patrick added to those of St. George and St. Andrew. Now, in Ulster, it became the symbol of anti-Catholic, anti-Nationalist hatred and has remained such until today. Within Ireland, and particularly within Ulster itself, a state of perpetual if intermittent and smothered civil war was created. This institutionalization of what had hitherto been a far more chaotic and spontaneous tragedy can be traced directly to the events of 1886. Lord Randolph's speeches in Belfast made Protestant sedition respectable and thus undermined, in the long run, the moral authority both of the country and of the empire which he believed he loved and served. It is perhaps only charitable to infer that the powers of his mind were already impaired by illness, far earlier than has been generally recognized. On the other hand, he was not the only one, neither quite the first and certainly not the last....

CHAPTER SIXTEEN

For over twenty-five years after the defeat of Gladstone's first Home Rule bill the Irish issue was, in some measure, in abeyance, though never out of sight, both in Westminster and in Ireland itself. True, Gladstone clung to Home Rule, almost obsessively so in his old age, and his last administration foundered over it. When he formed his last government in 1892, the Liberal Party was pledged to Home Rule by the so-called Newcastle Declaration of the previous year, while the Liberal Unionists were rapidly being ingurgitated into the Conservative Party. Furthermore Gladstone's majority in the House of Commons was dependent on the eighty-one Irish Home Rulers, though these were themselves divided since the Parnell divorce and the death of the 'Uncrowned King', into a majority of anti-Parnellites, led by Justin McCarthy and a sizeable minority, led by John Redmond. On the Home Rule issue, however, they were all prepared to support the G.O.M., and when he introduced his second bill, in 1893, it passed through the Commons only to be defeated in the Lords by 419 votes to 41, statistically the greatest defeat that any major bill sent there by any British government has ever suffered in the House of Lords. For nearly twenty years, that is to say until the powers of the Lords could be drastically curtailed, Home Rule became almost a dead issue so far as parliamentary policies and tactics were concerned, though it remained, in theory at least, on the Liberal Party agenda during its long years of opposition after the Conservatives had regained office in 1895. This ensured them the general support of the Irish Nationalists, more or less valueless in the division lobbies, in view of the size of the Conservative majorities for the next eleven years. Nor could the Nationalists sell themselves to the Conservatives, as Parnell had attempted and failed to do in 1885, in return for Home Rule. Finally, when the Liberals were at last returned, with a massive majority, in 1906, they too did not need the Irish vote, nor could the small Conservative opposition have profited by the support of the Irish M.P.s. The

Liberals therefore postponed the Home Rule issue in effect until after the election of 1910, when the margin between the successful Liberals and the defeated Conservatives was so narrow that the Irish vote once again became of great importance. By then much had happened and, which is perhaps more important, much had not.

This long alliance of the Nationalists, representing Roman Catholic Ireland in its desire for at least a measure of self-government, with the Liberal Party, which increasingly represented a greater measure of social justice within an imperial framework, caused the Orange-dominated Unionists of Ulster, and perhaps of all Ireland, to tie their cause to that of the English Conservatives. It would, however, be as wrong to identify Belfast Unionism with British Conservatism as to make such an identification between Irish Nationalism and British Liberalism in that imperialist epoch. Both of these alliances were essentially unnatural, though that of the Ulstermen with the Tories perhaps the less so of the two. As the English Conservatives became, increasingly throughout this period, the party that represented money (or at least class in monetary terms) rather than class itself (still in England largely represented by land), so it approximated to the mercantile class in Northern Ireland that controlled the Orange Order and, through it, the Unionist Party there. Yet at the same time a marked division was also appearing.

By the early years of the twentieth century official Christianity, that is to say the Church of England, was moving into decadence, both as a religion and even more so as a political force. Even hypocrisy, that greatest of Victorian England's virtues, was falling into disrepute. In 1890 Gladstone—who according to Roy Jenkins's life of *Asquith* had known of Parnell's liaison with Mrs. O'Shea for many years—could not come to his defence when the scandal became public, because of the English, Welsh and Scottish nonconformist vote. Although this moralistic bogeyman has been repeatedly produced, and almost to the present day, to justify tiresome and petty pieces of British legislation (such as the licensing laws), it is highly doubtful if, by 1910, a statesman such as Gladstone would have sacrificed a statesman and an ally of Parnell's, not Profumo's, stature to retain the bogeyman's approval of his own moral values. Such progress, if that be the word, did not however apply in Ireland then, and probably not in Ulster now. In Britain, though Welsh preachers might thunder against sin in their chapels and Scots Presbyterian ministers in their kirks, the political power of those Men of God was on the wane, as that of the Trade Union leaders increased. In Ireland it was not yet so.

Many of the Protestants, and most of those in Ulster, delighted in Parnell's fall because he was an Irish Nationalist: most of the Roman Catholic clergy also came out against him, from their pulpits to their congregations crowded into their new and usually ugly churches, as the Protestant adulterer. Their voices still carried great weight with the people. The treatment of Parnell by the clergy reinforced the spirit of anti-clericalism in Catholic Ireland which has always existed in every Catholic country, but which in Ireland had definite political overtones, for the hierarchy and most of the priesthood had been hostile both to the Young Ireland movement and to the Fenians. Furthermore it also reinforced the determination of Ulster Protestants never to allow themselves, or their descendants, to be ruled by any bigots other than their own.

In Ireland as a whole many factors, some advantageous to the people, some less so, contributed to the state of superficial political torpor that seems, in retrospect, to have prevailed at the turn of the century. Fenianism seemed then to be dead, though a handful of ageing men, of whom Tom Clarke was to achieve the greatest fame because of his personal involvement in the Easter Rising of 1916 and his subsequent execution, kept the flame burning, though it burned low until the turn of the century, as low as a smouldering turf fire, even in the little newsvendor's shop that he kept in Dublin after release from his long years in English prisons. The parliamentarian patriots, split over the Parnell divorce, only slowly coalesced, to find as they did that their English Liberal allies were themselves split on many issues between the Little Englanders (of whom Campbell-Bannerman was the most famous and who became Prime Minister in 1906) and the Liberal Imperialists, whose leader was to be H. H. Asquith, and who succeeded Campbell-Bannerman as Prime Minister on the latter's retirement in 1908. This was an alliance based indeed on shifting sands. Throughout the last decade of the nineteenth century and the first of the twentieth the rivalries, essentially imperial rivalries, of the great powers had come so often and so close to open warfare, had teetered for so long on what we now call the brink, that it was beginning to seem that 'the great game' could be played, harmlessly, forever. In this atmosphere it began to appear, also, as if the Irish could constantly demand Home Rule, the English steadily alternate between promises and refusal, and nothing would happen. The very great improvement brought about slowly by the Irish Land Acts calmed the countrymen too. It seemed that the Irish might, after all, become West Britons, as it had seemed equally briefly and far less distinctly during the Grattan period. And the Anglo-Irish renaissance in literature and the theatre at this time, the so-called 'Celtic revival', gave the *status quo* a measure of intellectual and artistic respectability, though its 'Celtic' element was, simultaneously, over- and under-estimated.

Over estimated in that even such writers as Synge, Lady Gregory and at times Yeats sought their nourishment in the language and legends of the Old Irish as represented by the Irish countryman. Their forms of expression nevertheless placed them in the great, overpowering tradition of English literature: underestimated in that such writers as Wilde, Shaw and for most of his life Moore, who had little explicit interest in their own 'Irishness', are yet unmistakably Irish writers who could have been produced by no other country. This great artistic revival, which did not extend to the plastic arts nor save marginally to music, scarcely affected Ulster, and its Presbyterian core not at all. Belfast continued to express itself as a great industrial city and port, but did not even produce the cultural manifestations of a Manchester: there was no Belfast equivalent to the Hallé Orchestra, for example. In the long run this has been a further divisive influence, if not in Ireland as a whole (for culturally there was not and is not a great deal to choose between Limerick and Cork on the one hand and Belfast on the other), it did underline the distinction between Belfast and Dublin. The merchants and businessmen of the North might well not give a hoot, in general, for culture, but they or perhaps their wives could not help suspecting that in this respect at least their's was an inferior city to Dublin, and their eyes must have told them that though a richer it was a far uglier one. And this in turn increased the sort of communal inferiority complex, with its usual symptoms of aggression, that have contributed over the centuries to the sectarian hatreds of Ulster Protestants, to the siege mentality discussed earlier in this book.

Another social matter, usually described as cultural and of the greatest importance in all the Western world over the past century and more, was education, or more precisely the control of the formation of young people's views. Traditionally this had lain in the hands of the priesthood, whether Catholic, Protestant or Jewish. Indeed some might say that it was the last real function and therefore the last source of power left to the Churches. But all over Europe the State was casting jealous eyes on this privileged position of the Church or Churches, fundamentally for socio-political reasons. One of the heritages of the French Revolution was that young citizens should be brought up as citizens, not as members of a particular church. (This in turn dates back to such distant events as the Counter-reformation, the Edict of Nantes in France, the Clarendon Code in England, and the Penal Laws in Ireland.) In the age of high imperialism, which can be roughly dated from 1870 to 1920, the rulers of most of Western Europe wished to turn its citizens' nationality into nationalism and it was basically on this issue that Bismarck fought and won his *Kulturkampf* against the German churches. In France, and to a lesser extent in Italy, *laïcization* led to the arousal of more or less violent pro- and anti-clerical opinion, expressed in political terms. In England the process was slow, once Oxford and Cambridge had ceased to be almost entirely in the control of the Anglican Church, and both students and teachers limited to those who professed its faith. In England the educational structure remained divided on class, i.e. wealth, and not on sectarian lines when the various Education Acts of the nineteenth and early twentieth centuries had made free education a right for all children while paid education remained the accepted privilege of the few. (Only quite recently have English socialist or socialistic governments attempted to use Bismarckian methods in this field to realize an egalitarian ideology. In time, though not in purpose, this corresponds with the even more Bismarckian efforts of successive American governments to produce a homogeneous United States citizenry by 'de-segregation'.)

Now as usual this whole process became distorted in its passage across the Irish Sea. Here the *Kulturkampf* was fought not between the acknowledged leaders of a national state and its clerics, who might at times be called turbulent, determined to defend ancient rights, but between administrators ordered to impose English solutions on Irish problems and a priesthood that represented the majority of the Irish population. The confrontation was long, bitter and, I fear, excessively boring. I shall spare the reader the details. The outcome of the battle, which indeed is not yet over and certainly not in Northern Ireland, is that the Roman Catholic hierarchy appears to have won, as it has won nowhere else in Europe save in Spain and hence in Portugal, but there at the cost of bloody civil war. In Ireland the children of Roman Catholics are, with a tiny exception, educated by priests, nuns, lay brothers, and lay teachers, but in any event under the closest supervision of the Church. (Protestant schools have been equally well treated, and subsidized, however, by the State both before and after the Treaty of 1922.) And that is equally true, if not even more true, of Ulster today than it was of Munster seventy years ago. In Ireland, the British state rapidly and gracefully accepted defeat in this version of the *Kulturkampf*, and subsidized Catholic schools just as it, through the Northern Ireland government, subsidizes them in the Six Counties today. From an English, Protestant point of view this was and is a very fair and generous solution to a problem that has caused immense ill-feeling elsewhere. But from an Irish point of view? And particularly in Ulster now, where the Roman Catholic Church guards its educational powers with the greatest jealousy? Though it must be remembered that the Protestant minority in the South is almost equally determined that Protestant children be taught in Protestant schools.

Liberal Unionists—I am not here referring to those mules who vanished long ago, but to Ulster Unionists of liberal views who may well soon go the same way—often maintain that sectarian segregation at school age is at the root of the troubles that constantly afflict their unhappy province. Since the Roman Catholic minority is, in general, composed of the poorer classes, and since they insist on being within walking distance both of their church and of their children's school, the creation of Catholic ghettoes in the larger towns becomes inevitable. This however ignores the fact that for reasons of mutual self-protection such ghettoes, or enclaves to use a less emotive noun, existed long before the Education Acts and would continue to exist, particularly after the events of the past few years, for any foreseeable future. We have recently seen many Catholic families living in mixed areas of Belfast or the other cities, driven from their homes by arson, threats or fear, seeking refuge in such enclaves. I myself happen to be a Protestant, but if I were an Ulster Catholic, and since I happen to have small children, I should certainly attempt to live in such an enclave where neither my wife nor my children would face the daily dangers of walking through potentially hostile and occasionally murderous streets.

Another liberal argument against denominational schools is that it enables any extremist Orange employer to discover the religion of a man or woman applying for a job without direct enquiry. Where did you go to school? is all he needs to ask. In a community as small as the one under discussion, he can immediately, if he has not already done so, detect a Papist and declare that the job is filled. But this argument is again almost totally invalid. In the old days such employers used to ask: 'Which foot do you dig with?' for it was generally believed that a Catholic put his left foot to the spade, a Protestant his right, or maybe the other way about. In the Six Counties of Ulster any sectarian employer who does not wish to employ a man of the other faith does not need to enquire about his schooling, even though this may be, at the moment, a quick and convenient way of finding out. There is no reason to believe that de-segregation, even if it included some system of taking children by bus to de-segregated schools as attempted in the United States, would break down the ghetto or enclave society—let alone destroy job discrimination.

Yet should not the Roman Catholic hierarchy relax its very tight grasp on education? Is it really a sin for a Catholic father to send his child to a Protestant school, provided he ensures that that child receive elsewhere the religious instruction demanded by his priest? Or is bigotry so endemic in that part of Ireland, so deeply rooted in history, that even so small a gesture would be interpreted, and exploited, as surrender? The slogan of the Londonderry Apprentice Boys, those old men in bowler hats who march each year on August 12th and often hurl insults at their Catholic co-citizens, is 'No surrender!' It was revived by Lord Randolph Churchill and repeated by Carson and by Craig. It is probably the only useful slogan during the supreme crisis of a siege. But is it really relevant in Belfast or Derry today? For who can possibly surrender to whom in the province? Lenin's repulsive *Realpolitik* remark—'Who, whom?'—is surely quite inapplicable to a dual society wherein both parts are as deeply rooted as the three hundred-year-old trees which they have already outlived.

When Lord Randolph played the Orange card he was deliberately playing Irish politics for English party-political ends, in his case the destruction of the third Gladstone administration. When Parnell adopted obstructionist tactics and an opportunist strategy in the House of Commons he was playing the same game, with other cards, exploiting British party politics in the interests of Irish nationalism. Nobody in 1886 and the generation that followed was, at their high level, primarily concerned with the welfare of Ulster, which in London's eyes became little more than a bargaining counter, a card that might on occasion be the ace, sometimes the two, usually somewhere about the middle of the pack, but always, like all cards, one that is ultimately expendable if its loss is essential to the winning of the game. This was apparent in Ulster, too, and was to produce the new crop of Unionist politicians, of whom Sir James Craig, later Lord Craigavon, was to be the most prominent, men who saw that they must, ultimately, protect the interests of their province, as they understood those interests to be, against other nationalists whether from Dublin or even from London. In this respect the Ulster Unionist leaders were more the political heirs of Parnell than of Lord Randolph with almost no inheritance from Roaring Hanna or the Peep o' Day Boys, for this legacy passed to other hands, the latest being the Rev. Dr. Ian Paisley's. By gaining almost complete control of the Unionist Party in Ulster the Orange Order had, in fact and at last, achieved a considerable measure of political respectability. During the final decade of the last century and the first of this it consolidated its position, not only in Ulster's commerce, industry and politics but also in the folk traditions of the province. On every possible anniversary, and on some that many would regard as quite impossible, the Orangemen marched, 'to the sound of the flute and the beat of the drum', to assure their fellow-citizens and reassure themselves that they were and are the masters.

It was at this time that their marching clothes became a sort of uniform or sacerdotal garb. The flamboyant sash shrank to become the coloured 'collarette' worn over the jacket of the black or perhaps navy-blue best suit that also clothed the Orangeman when he attended his religious service each Sunday. Upon his head was his bowler hat, known in America as a Derby because first made popular by a Conservative Prime Minister of that name in the 1860s, and in his right hand he carried a rolled, black umbrella, another symbol of middle-class respectability. Just as the Englishman's most formal dress, the tailcoat worn black at night and grey at weddings, Ascot and royal garden parties was a petrification of Regency fashion, as the knee-breeches and silk stockings English aristocrats used to wear to royal balls date back to an earlier style, so the very dark suit, embellished by a collarette as the evening tails often were by medals, the bowler and the umbrella of the late Victorian managerial class became and have remained the uniform of the Orangeman when celebrating his tribal rite of marching beneath his flapping banners to the beat of his band and its Lambeg drum. Other European and American governing classes copied, more or less successfully, the formal Regency clothes chosen by Englishmen of their sort. Formal Orange attire had no such sartorial imitators save perhaps among successful socialists, themselves also anxious to show social respectability while retaining visible identification with the more sober-minded elements of the working class. They, however, tended quite rapidly to dispense with the umbrella—a sword symbol of less practical use in most countries than in Ireland—and, soon enough, the bowler hat, to Orangemen perhaps reminiscent of Cromwellian steel helmets but to English, Irish and Continental socialists infinitely less symbolic of their loyalties than the proletarian's cloth cap.

Thus attired did they, and do they, march about Ulster. Many of these marches, with or without music, are very small in numbers and short in length, while a few of them are enormous in both respects. I have read that in the Six Counties there are some eight hundred such marches each year. Always military in intent, to show who is master and not infrequently to insult the Catholic minority, they are also military in design. The design is itself as much a period piece, a late Victorian or Edwardian period piece, as is the marchers' costume, arms swinging, the 'officers' in front, keeping in step, the men supposed never to glance to right nor left, imitation soldiers. Thus did the soldiers they still imitate, the Kaiser's huge army, the Czar's Preobajenski Guard, the infantry of the French Third Republic, the British Brigade of Guards, march into the mincing machine of 1914. Except on rare ceremonial occasions few soldiers ever march about that way, in public, today. In the Red Square, to commemorate May Day or the October Revolution: in Washington on the occasion of a presidential funeral: in London for the ceremony called the Trooping of the Colour. In Belfast, Newry, Dungannon, Strabane and the other cities and villages of Ulster amateur military groups of men—some of them exsoldiers, it is true—indulge in this historic pageantry some eight hundred times a year. The Orange Order has acquired for itself, in nineteenth-century bourgeois dress and with the methods of the period, the role that was once given, with ultimate failure, to the 'rooted garrison' in all Ireland a hundred and fifty years before Lord Derby donned his first bowler hat. Yet they have been, are, and almost certainly will remain tough and determined men, not to be trifled with, then or now, despite their antiquated garb and oppressive tactics. These were the men whom the new leaders in Ulster were to forge into a formidable force while other leaders were parading the armies, and the nationalist emotions, that were soon to march to the Marne, Tannenberg, Verdun and Passchendaele. Ulster hardened, as Europe prepared for suicide.

The general quality of the men responsible for Europe's destiny during the decades before the holocaust was proved not only by the holocaust itself but by their inability to prevent it, master it, or indeed even to conclude it. Germans and Englishmen, Frenchmen and Russians, had learned so little from the horrors of 1914-1918 that they permitted an even more monstrous and suicidal war to take place less than twenty-one years after the First World War was over. Millions of young corpses were buried, monuments to the unknown dead sprouted like mushrooms in October, yet when at last an exhausted continent began to rebuild its devastated cities and replant its poisoned fields it was not only the dreary steeples of Tyrone and Fermanagh that re-appeared from out the flood, but the same, or almost the same, self-satisfied though perhaps less self-confident faces and voices of the politicians who must bear the major responsibility for the horrors of the first half of this horrible century. Their ineptitude in dealing with Anglo-Irish relations, in finding an answer to 'the Irish question', is only a microcosmic example of what was happening all over Europe before the lights went out.

Much nostalgia has been penned, and doubtless more felt, about the *belle époque*, the doomed pomp of Wilhelmine Germany, the elegant, easy manners of the Edwardian upper class playing croquet beneath stately elms on the shaven lawns about their stately homes. Only in Russia and America, the two great nations that were eventually to inherit (if only briefly) a near hegemony of power as the direct result of Europe's suicide, do we seldom hear these diminished sevenths of lament for *les neiges d'antan*, while the Europeans themselves who had lived through the period, and perhaps in particular those close to the centres of power, have usually adopted a far more sceptical tone. Few have echoed the Frenchman's famous apothegm that those who knew not France before the Revolution had never experienced *la douceur de vivre*. However sweet that sweetness of living may have been in certain social and intellectual circles in eighteenth-century France, however awful must have seemed its destruction by the iron men of the Revolution and the Empire, there is precious little parallel with the lives lived by the governing class in the United Kingdom throughout the two decades before 1914, where boredom or more precisely *ennui* seems to have been among the leading emotions of many. As the old moral certitudes or doubts and the old intellectual vigour of the Victorians declined, we find men, with the destinies of great nations in their hands, spending an almost incredible amount of time playing card games, shooting or watching birds, holidaying for weeks or even months on end, often at fashionable spas there to rid their bodies of the toxic poisons created by overeating and, not infrequently, overdrinking as well, and sometimes treating politics as little more than a superior form of gossip.

Perhaps among no group of men was this decadence more manifest, and more disastrous, than among the leaders of the Liberal Party once Gladstone had gone. (The Conservatives were little if any better served when Lord Salisbury left the scene.) Lord Rosebery, who succeeded Gladstone as Prime Minister in 1893, was a sexually eccentric, extremely rich race-horse owner who cherished a sort of hero-worship for the ghost of Napoleon Bonaparte. He was much given to sulking, to insulting his colleagues sometimes to their face but more often behind their backs, and might not unfairly be described as the worst leader that any great English political party has ever been burdened with. Once he had vanished the Liberal Party, quite simply, split. The leader, a rich merchant named Campbell-Bannerman, was a Little Englander and thus an heir to Gladstonian anti-Imperialism, while the most powerful member in his party, both in opposition and in government when the Liberals won the 1906 election, was H. H. Asquith who was, and admitted to being, a Liberal Imperialist, as were Sir Edward Grey, Augustine Birrell and other prominent Liberals, soon to be joined by Winston Churchill when first he crossed the floor of the House. Lloyd George, on the other hand, was the most outspoken anti-Imperialist of the rising Liberals and had been branded, not at all unfairly, as a pro-Boer during the war at the turn of the century. When the Liberal Party was swept at last into office with an enormous majority in 1906 its leadership was therefore a weird amalgam of men, with very differing political views, social backgrounds and intellectual methods. In retrospect it is astonishing that they managed to retain authority and maintain government for the next ten catastrophic years. It is perhaps less astonishing that they were the last Liberals to do so. Only on one point of policy, apart from the usual desire of successful politicians to retain office, were they united after their triumph in 1906, and this was that the hitherto disastrous issue to their party of Home Rule for Ireland, while remaining a part of their programme, should be as near as possible at the bottom, preferably linked with the traditional ending to all English dramatic and imperial programmes: 'God Save the King!'

In Ireland the political scene, as viewed from London and indeed from Dublin Castle, was placid and, by Irish standards, easy-going. John Redmond, a stout, amiable and well-mannered man was re-uniting the Irish Nationalists in alliance with a Liberal Party which at the moment did not need their support and which therefore need not attempt to legislate on their behalf. Ulster was prosperous, in particular Belfast where naval expansion brought ample work to the shipyards, and thus also as a result quiescent. In the Irish countryside the re-distribution of land had ended the Land War. In Dublin a rather tawdry Vice-regal Court gave rather tawdry satisfaction to what was left of the Protestant Ascendancy and to the Catholic rich who wished to identify themselves with it. Emigration, to America and even more so to England, dispersed the young men who might have been subversive had they remained. (Michael Collins went to London, in 1906, at the age of fifteen. It was ten years before he returned to fight in Ireland.) When, at the same time, 1906, Campbell-Bannerman decided to send an amiable writer of *belles lettres* who had failed as a reforming President of the Board of Education to Ireland as Chief Secretary, Augustine Birrell viewed this promotion without disquiet. It was a promotion to something not unlike a sinecure and he treated it as such, establishing friendly relations with Redmond, the literary great and members of the Protestant Ascendancy class. Nor did he, the leading English political officer directly responsible for Irish affairs, regard it as lax on his part to spend a very great deal of his time in the more comfortable and amusing circle of his London friends. After all, was he not also a member of the British Cabinet? And there was really nothing whatever to worry about in Ireland. Or, perhaps, anywhere else. He held the post until 1916. By then Michael Collins had become a leader of the I.R.B. and had fought as a staff officer at the General Post Office in the Rebellion of Easter Week, an event that seems to have taken the bland and amiable Chief Secretary completely by surprise.

For the apparent tranquillity of the period was entirely deceptive. In all Europe a better educated urban proletariat was turning to one form or other of socialism or syndicalism, as Socialist Parties grew and their industrial allies, the Trade Union movements, became better organized and more aware of their strength. The great emotive force invoked, more or less unconsciously, by the old landed governing class in alliance with the still comparatively new industrial plutocracy was nationalism. As stated in an earlier chapter, the events of 1914 saw, in metropolitan Europe and Britain, the almost complete victory of nationalism over the alleged internationalism of the various workers' movements, a phenomenon that was to be repeated in the Second World War and which will almost certainly be once again the case if we are ever so unfortunate and so stupid as to indulge in a Third.

This was true also in Ireland, though here of course nationalism took on a very different and confused meaning. On the one hand there was the British nationalism of the Unionists, that is to say of the old 'rooted garrison's' remnants, of the Orangemen in the North, and of many members of the now comparatively prosperous Catholic middle class in all parts of Ireland. Into this false alliance Redmond and the other parliamentarians were sliding. Home Rule was still their first and most vocal demand, but not the disruption of the Empire through methods which they regarded as treasonable, that is to say by reliance on help from sources hostile to Britain. The slide became precipitate in 1914 when Redmond and most of his followers swore complete loyalty to the British cause in that war and many scores of thousands of Irishmen, of both faiths, volunteered for the British forces, a high proportion to fight with the greatest gallantry and, like Redmond's own brother, to be killed in action before it was over.

On the other hand there was Irish nationalism. A few hundred Irishmen had already volunteered for the South African war and had fought and been defeated with the Boers. The total failure of parliamentary tactics to achieve Home Rule, combined with increasing awareness of Parnell's betrayal, caused the Irish pendulum to swing once again. It was beginning to swing back from constitutional to revolutionary ideas. Early in the century the moribund Fenian organization was given an injection of new blood when a handful of young men of ability, both Catholics and Protestants, joined a revivified I.R.B. dedicated not to the stale idea of Home Rule but to the creation of a Republic of Ireland and fortified by the strength of the Irish cultural, and even of the Irish sporting, revival. These men, among whom Padraic Pearse was to achieve the greatest fame, were national, not social, revolutionaries. Except for a wish to expedite the transference of land ownership already underway, their ambitions seem, in retrospect, comparatively modest, the transfer of power from English to Irish hands, the creation of a modern Irish state, the citizens of which should be encouraged to speak the Irish language and develop a pride in their ancient, national heritage. And, though there had been no state Church in Ireland since Disestablishment, the majority must inevitably be Roman Catholic and a special role was therefore foreseen, rather vaguely, for the Roman hierarchy and priesthood. All this, and particularly the last item, was viewed with emotions easily whipped up into horror by the Presbyterians of the northeastern corner.

There were, in the years before the First World War, other tides running. A measure of industrialization had reached beyond Belfast to create an urban proletariat in other Irish cities, particularly the Dublin area. In 1909 and 1910 there was a great Dublin strike and lock-out and, as elsewhere in all Europe and

America at that time, the police backed by the military were used against the workers. This produced the usual, immediate counter-response. The Dublin workers reacted, under the leadership of James Connolly, by tightening their organization and even by the creation of a small, voluntary, paramilitary force called the Citizen Army. Connolly was a Marxist and, as such, uninterested in the nationalists' bourgeois ideals. Though claimed by Irish Communists today, even by Maoists, as a father-figure, in Russian terms he would—to judge by his writings—be more accurately defined as an Irish Menschevik. Had his revolution succeeded, it would seem probable that Bolshevik successors would quite quickly have cut off his head. However in those distant days he was quite enough of a revolutionary to cause the utmost anxiety among the capitalists who controlled the Irish economy, not least among leaders of the Orangemen, for he wished to see not merely an Irish Republic but an Irish Socialist Republic. Furthermore, being a revolutionary and therefore in the Irish conditions of his time almost inadvertently a patriot, he soon found himself in uneasy, but self-respecting, alliance with the bourgeois revolutionaries controlled by the I.R.B. and backed by Irish-American finance. This, in turn, provided a weapon for the Belfast managerial class to divert violent emotions among their workers from themselves against their Catholic fellow-workers. 'Home rule means Rome rule!' became their slogan, though what they undoubtedly meant was that Home Rule could be the first step towards an Irish Socialist Republic and their own expropriation.

Thus did the Unionist leaders in the North ensure that there was not only no solidarity between the workers of Belfast and those of Dublin during the industrial crises of the early twentieth century, but also that in Belfast itself those violent emotions endemic in any population, compelled by habit and economics to live in the hideous, boring towns that industrialization has created, remained sectarian and implosive. It is one way, if not a particularly satisfactory way, of running a multiple society, as the inhabitants of several northern American cities have recently discovered.

And into this apparently quiet situation there was once more injected, in 1910, the now antiquated, by then almost pointless, but still highly explosive issue of Home Rule for all Ireland.

CHAPTER SEVENTEEN

Personality has always played a very important part in Irish political history, more so, I think, than in the history of most other European countries. This is in part due to the smallness of Ireland, in part to the veritable passion of the Irish people for gossip, from village pump and the creamery to the vagaries and affairs of prominent men. With the Irish, more so than with most peoples, men are frequently more important than measures. And for centuries the only measure that really interested the majority of the population was how to get rid of the English, their landlords, their Episcopalian Church, their administration and their soldiers. Any leader who showed any prospect of attaining such ends, whether using the constitutional methods of a Grattan, an O'Connell or a Parnell or the revolutionary methods of a Tone, Young Ireland or the early Fenians became a hero in the eyes of his countrymen, of most of his countrymen that is, for the Irish are much given to envy and with no tradition of national leadership are prone to pulling their great men to bits. Yet when he has actually been pulled down, as with the death of Parnell or later of Michael Collins, the Irish seem to be almost stunned until a new leader appears upon the scene.

It was so during the last decade of the nineteenth century and the first of this. Slowly Redmond put the fractured pieces of Parnell's Irish Party together again, though he had not completed this process before his party was blown out of existence by the executions which followed the Easter Rising of 1916. Nevertheless until that happened he was the most prominent public man in Ireland. This amiable, portly figure was highly regarded as a parliamentarian by his fellow M.P.s at Westminster and had many friends among the English upper classes. Indeed it might be fairly said that he was neither significant nor dangerous enough to create bitter enmity either in England or in Ireland. Only in parts of Ulster was he hated, but as the leader of the Home Rule party rather than as a man. Orange fanatics did not burn him in effigy when celebrating their tribal rites. Had the United Kingdom granted Ireland Home Rule at an earlier date he would certainly have been the first Irish Prime Minister and might have been the best man to try to heal the rupture between Catholics and Protestants. Whether he would have succeeded is another matter, and a fruitless speculation.

His 'opposite number' during this period was for most of the time Augustine Birrell, the Chief Secretary, of whom I have written earlier. And for a large part of the period the titular head of the Irish government was Lord Aberdeen. This was his second appointment as Viceroy. It was also his second during a Home Rule crisis, for Gladstone had also sent him to Dublin in 1886. He and his wife were well disposed towards the Irish and their modest aspirations for Home Rule, and were in consequence popular, though regarded with a measure of ridicule for their alleged meanness. It was said that tea with the Aberdeens was one cup and one biscuit. Thus the men who held the stage, or appeared to hold stage, during these years were well-meaning, unexciting persons, and Ireland was calm as the Land Acts brought a measure of prosperity to the countryside and some industrialization came to the cities. There were however far too few jobs, so that emigration remained heavy and the population continued to shrink.

There were other forces at work. H. H. Asquith, who had long been a leading figure in the Liberal Party and who became Prime Minister when Campbell-Bannerman retired in 1908, had inherited Home Rule as part of Gladstone's legacy, but was never particularly keen on that plank of Liberal policy. As early as 1901 he wrote:

'If we are honest, we must ask ourselves this practical question. Is it to be part of the policy and programme that, if returned to power, [a Liberal government] will introduce into the House of Commons a bill for Irish Home Rule? The answer, in my judgment, is No....'

The Irish vote was still needed by the Liberals but Home Rule was much played down in the election campaign of 1905 which resulted in the great Liberal landslide of 1906. In November of 1905 the Liberal leaders, Asquith, Campbell-Bannerman and Grey met and decided on the party's Irish policy. Roy Jenkins in his *Asquith* writes:

'At this meeting a compromise solution to Home Rule was worked out, to which Campbell-Bannerman gave expression in a speech at Stirling on November 23rd. Full self-government for Ireland remained the objective of the Liberal Party, but the Nationalists were given clear notice that in the next Parliament Home Rule would not be given the priority of 1886 and 1892. It would have to wait its turn, and in the meantime the Irish were advised to accept any degree of devolution they could get "Provided it was consistent with and led up to (the) larger policy".'

Even so the previous Liberal Prime Minister, Lord Rosebery, was so opposed by now to Home Rule that he said in a speech a few days later that he could no longer serve a party committed to throwing even these crumbs to the Irish.

The policy platform of the Liberals was, in fact, disingenuous. They wanted the Irish vote, but they wanted the English vote more, and the English were heartily sick of the 'Irish question' and twenty years' talk about Home Rule. The Liberals had great plans for reform, and did not relish yet another mammoth debate, that would consume valuable parliamentary time, about a bill that even if passed in the House of Commons would certainly be thrown out in the Lords. Nor was any such bill introduced in this parliament, for with their huge majority the Liberals had no need to woo the Irish members. Home Rule was put back in cold storage, in the phrase of T. M. Healy who was to be the first Governor-General of the Irish Free State. Campbell-Bannerman toyed with reform of the House of Lords, but for English, not Irish, purposes, and in the event did nothing about this either. Thus Irish aspirations for a measure of independence through peaceful means seemed caught in a maze of English party politics and constitutional formulae.

Ireland remained quiet, but not all Irishmen were content that this should continue. The old Fenian Brotherhood was dormant but not dead. Old Tom Clarke, who had served fifteen years in English jails for Fenian activities, was the most famous of those who passed this particular torch to younger men, among them most of the leaders in the Easter Rising. There were others who blew upon the embers of revolutionary patriotism. Among the first members of this new I.R.B. was Padraic Pearse, who was to lead the Rising. Other, older men were to teach their juniors conspiratorial methods. Other, younger men joined this secret society, committed to the use of physical force at the earliest opportunity. Among them were Michael Collins and, a little later, Eamonn de Valera, though the latter did not attend

I.R.B. meetings. Indeed virtually all the leaders of the Irish revolution, both in the Rising and in the War of Independence, were members of the I.R.B. before the First World War.

According to Batt O'Connor in his *Life with Michael Collins* the main sources of recruitment for this secret society, in which the men had to be of high quality, were the linguistic Gaelic League, dedicated to the revival and survival of the Irish language, and the Gaelic Athletic Association, which promoted the playing of Irish games as opposed to the imported games of the Ascendancy such as cricket and Rugby football. There was nothing whatsoever sectarian about the I.R.B. Such very different Protestants as Douglas Hyde, W. B. Yeats and Sir Roger Casement were members of the Organization, the last indeed an Ulsterman. However it could not but be predominantly Catholic. For its finances it relied very largely on Catholic Irish-Americans, the Clan na Gael. Its method of recruitment was simple. Batt O'Connor has described how, while watching an Irish sporting event, he was asked by a friend if he would care to become a member of a secret political organization dedicated to the freeing of Ireland from English rule. He agreed and attended a small meeting where he found that almost all the members of this branch were friends or acquaintances from the sports ground or the language school that he also attended. He swore an oath of allegiance and also an oath of secrecy. His cell was some ten men strong. Only one of them had contact with a higher echelon. They were men of all classes—O'Connor was then a speculative builder with a small business—and there were therefore no social distinctions. Thus was a pyramidal secret society created with built-in safeguards to protect both the members and the leadership from the British whose agents had so skilfully infiltrated the earlier Fenian movement. It was to prove remarkably successful in keeping its identity, indeed almost its existence, hidden until the Day. The Irish may have a deserved reputation for garrulity, but when serious matters are at stake they can be remarkably tight-lipped. Throughout this quiet period they laid their plans and made their preparations against the Day of Rebellion.

That it was coming soon they did not doubt. Great Britain was still a most formidable power, with a vast Empire, but the first evidences of decline were already perceptible to those with cold eyes. As a great mercantile and industrial power Britain was no longer predominant in global terms, having been surpassed both by Germany and the United States. When the century started the British Empire had no allies and few friends of any stature. In military, and soon in naval, strength Imperial Germany was a very major threat. War was coming, probably more or less by accident as was indeed to be the case, and the sorry story of British inefficiency in the Boer War against a numerically insignificant force of Dutch farmers was a prognosis of worse to come if the British were to be pitted against one or more major powers. And such a situation would be, once again, Ireland's opportunity. The I.R.B. intended to exploit it, on the assumption that Redmond's staid political party either would not or, more probably, could not do so.

How much of this secret planning trickled through to Northern ears? Probably very little, but perhaps enough to reinforce their fears of being swallowed whole by a Roman Catholic Republic, and this fear was as usual directed against any form of Home Rule, no matter how watered down and tepid this compromise might be. For had not Asquith himself spoken of gradualism as the answer to Ireland's woes? *C'est le premier pas qui coûte*, and even an Asquithian form of Home Rule, of devolution, would in the eyes of Orange extremists be a dangerous first step which they were determined to prevent lest it lead to a second and a third, as Asquith had implied.

The situation in Ulster, and particularly in Belfast, Londonderry and the other towns did not suffer any fundamental change between 1886 and 1912, indeed some might say it has not changed today. The existence of Protestant mobs determined to terrorize or expel their Catholic fellow-citizens continued, as did the Catholic mobs ready to fight, if need be, to protect their homes and families while refusing to surrender their allegiance to their Church or to the idea of a free Ireland. There were, however, considerable modifications, more to the Orange Order than to the Catholic resistance. During the terrible Home Rule riots of 1886 even harder lines were drawn between the Catholics and Protestants. That crisis brought about the creation of the Unionist Party, in that same year. In close alliance with Lord Randolph Churchill's wing of the Conservative Party, and in more flexible alliance with the Unionists in the rest of Ireland, in Ulster it was and has remained entirely dominated by the Orange Order. This meant that virtually the whole Protestant population of Northeastern Ireland, whether Church of Ireland or Dissenters, rapidly came under the more or less direct control of the Orange Lodges. During the present crisis a Unionist M.P. who resigned from the Orange Order in an attempt to promote better feelings in the province was expelled from the Unionist Party by his local constituency, another for attending an ecumenical church service at which Roman Catholic divines were also present.

But what is perhaps more important, at least politically, is that with the whole of Protestant Ulster now united in the Unionist Party under the control of the Orange Order, that semi-secret society could call upon a whole new class of leadership. The rabble-rousing priests remained and remain, but policy, even in times of grave civil disobedience, was not now in their hands but in the hands of moderately well educated members of the middle class, even of the upper class, Unionists who could, did and do use the primitive methods of shipyard workers and peasants to forward their own interests as members of a reactionary political party prepared, seldom cynically for they believe in their cause, to use violent sectarian emotions for their own reactionary purposes. After 1886 the Protestant mob had leaders and has been manipulated by them ever since.

Thus in the North the Unionist Party, created around the armature of the Orange Order, became perhaps the first monolithic political party of modern Europe. Embracing as it soon did virtually all the Protestants of all denominations in Ulster, from shipyard workers, factory hands and farm labourers to industrialists, great landowners, professional men and shopkeepers, as well as clergymen of all sorts, it could hardly have a positive policy. Nor did it, and in this it foreshadowed some aspects of Nazism. Just as the only really unifying forces among the Nazis were patriotism and anti-semitism, so the Unionist Party beat the Orange Drum, expressed itself in violently anti-Catholic terms, and periodically persecuted, on occasion murdered, the Roman Catholic minority.

In 1892 a parliamentary branch of this movement called 'Young Ulster' was created by a certain Fred Crawford, of whom more later. In his book *Not an Inch* Dr. Hugh Shearman, a Unionist moderate by Ulster standards, writes:

'... A condition for membership of this society was the possession of one or another of three weapons, a revolver, a Martini-Henry rifle or a cavalry Winchester carbine, together with a hundred rounds of ammunition. As the Arms Act was in force the members had to prepare their ammunition secretly, melting their lead into bullet moulds in the heating furnaces of certain Presbyterian churches....'

In 1893 there were riots in Belfast, directly connected with the Home Rule debate, and Catholic workers were driven out of the Belfast shipyards. Since the new Labour Party in Britain identified itself in some measure with the oppressed minority in Northern Ireland, partly for reasons of conscience, partly because of close alliance and eventual merger of the Conservative and Unionist parties, and partly to steal the Irish vote from the Liberals, the Orange leaders had little difficulty in persuading the Protestant workers that the Labour Party was part of the monstrous 'Papish' plot to drive them from their jobs and homes and farms, though at that time few members of the small Labour party were Roman Catholics. Keir Hardie and Burns voted for Home Rule in 1893. When the Trades Union Congress met in Belfast later that year shots were fired at a Labour procession, and when Burns tried to address a Labour meeting in Ormeau Park an infuriated Orange mob threatened to drown him in the River Lagan. Once again Catholic workers were expelled, by their workmates, from their jobs in the yards and the mills. A profound distrust of Socialism and Socialists was added to the siege mentality of the Ulstermen embattled, as they thought, to defend their 'freedom, religion and laws'. And this has in some measure persisted until today. A vague alliance between the Nationalists and the various Socialist parties that spring up and wither away in the North has never yet produced what might be called an opposition. Yet another attempt at the creation of such a party was recently made by Mr. Gerry Fitt, M.P. The immediate result was the resignation or even expulsion of several men from the various left-wing or nationalist parties or groups who favoured such a coalition. Meanwhile the Unionist M.P.s who continued to be returned with huge majorities to Westminster, and after partition in 1922 to Stormont as well, are usually extreme reactionaries. Any hint of moderation, as was the case with Captain Terence, now Lord, O'Neill is immediately interpreted as an abandonment of the 'No surrender!' mentality and usually leads to political limbo after political death. In what other country, which was not an authoritarian or totalitarian state, could that staunch Orangeman, Major Chichester-Clarke,

be described as a moderate? Yet compelled by the last Labour
government to accept a measure of electoral and other reforms,
which are very slowly being carried out, that is what he became
in the eyes of many Ulster Protestants. Caught between the in-
transigence of the Orange Order and the pressure for reforms
from London—reforms of the police, housing and the electoral
system, which in the eyes of many Orangemen are equivalent
to the foiled attempt by its commander to surrender Londonderry in 1689—he felt that he had no choice but to resign in
March of 1971.

One would have thought that since the British Labour Party
became 'respectable' and governed the United Kingdom, not
without success, for almost one third of the last forty-three years,
it would have produced an offshoot in the North. Why should
there not be a Socialist Unionist Party? The answer is the
Nationalist-Left Wing alliance which itself is highly artificial.
The Nationalists look to Dublin, where two essentially right
wing political parties have alternated for some fifty years. The
wish of the Nationalists, or their expressed wish at least, is that
of the Sudeten Germans under Czech rule: *Heim ins Reich*!
Though they benefit from the Welfare State, which is usually
though not altogether correctly credited to successive Socialist
governments, they cannot at present accept any form of Unionism. Meanwhile the majority of the Protestant working class,
well aware that the Labour Party has almost always been profoundly anti-colonialist, and they themselves are long-established
colonists, cannot accept any form of socialism except possibly
in a Northern Ireland that had severed, or had had severed, its
constitutional links with the rest of the United Kingdom and
had none with the Republic of Ireland. During recent years
there has been a certain amount of loose talk about a possible
Unilateral Declaration of Independence, on the Rhodesian
model, by Ulster extremists. Even if so improbable an event were
to occur, it seems unlikely that socialism would follow, or at
least not for many years, and probably not until after a civil war
that would shatter or utterly transform the Orange Order and
the political party it has controlled for nearly one hundred years.

After this long digression reference must be made to one more
major nineteenth century riot. I quote again from Andrew Boyd
(op. cit.)

'There was another major outbreak of rioting in June 1898

when the Nationalists commemorated the centenary of the rebellion of the United Irishmen. On the eve of the commemoration, R. R. Kane of Christ Church, Grand Master of the Orangemen, published a pamphlet in which he sneeringly threatened that, if the Nationalists had the courage to rebel like the men of '98, loyal Belfast would know how to deal with them. To protect himself against a charge of incitement, however, he advised the Orangemen "not to interfere with the rebel procession".

'On 6 June, the day of the procession, 2,000 shipyardmen ignored a warning from their employers that absence from work would mean dismissal. They assembled near Falls Road to stone the Nationalists. But the route of the procession was heavily guarded; at the request of the Belfast magistrates, Dublin Castle had sent 300 armed constables to reinforce the police garrison in the city.

'Nevertheless, there were several serious incidents. When a mob from Sandy Row stoned the procession near the Bog Meadows it seemed that Belfast was on the verge of another "1886". Later that day crowds of rioters, frustrated in their design to break up the Nationalist procession, gathered on Shankill Road to wreck public houses and attack police.

'Police casualties were heavy. Upwards of 100 constables were unfit for duty next day, and the authorities, as in 1886, were compelled to withdraw the constabulary from Shankill Road and put the district under military control.

'The 1898 riots were marked by the customary persecution and expulsion of Catholic workpeople. Seven hundred Catholics were driven from shipyards, linen mills and other places of employment where Protestants were predominant.'

This was far from the last occasion on which rival mobs were to collide on the ill-defined borders of their ghettoes, scream insults and taunts and hurl rocks at one another, loot the pubs and then exact revenge on their enemies by burnings and occasional shootings. But it was perhaps the last major riot which leading politicians both in England and Ireland might more or less ignore, deplorable though they found the antics of the Rev. R. R. Kane and his breed of clerics. Important figures were moving, or perhaps it would be more accurate to say reluctantly stumbling, on to the Irish stage off which so many of their predecessors, of all parties, had been booed into oblivion. For in 1910 the Liberals won a general election by so small a majority that they could not remain in office without the support of the 84 Irish members and the 42 Labour M.P.s.

No Liberal leader was particularly enthusiastic about Home Rule and certainly none had inherited Gladstone's crusader fervour for this cause. Asquith, as we have seen, was decidedly tepid, and the two brilliant young members of his Cabinet, Lloyd George at the Exchequer and Winston Churchill, Home Secretary until 1911—that is to say the two senior members most directly involved—were expressing doubts about Ulster as early as 1910. Yet even to mention the possibility of partition to Redmond's Irish Nationalists would probably have driven them into Parnellite sabotage of parliament during the highly critical session ahead, or have cost Redmond the leadership, both most undesirable from the Liberal point of view. Therefore in the second and more bitter election of 1910, fought principally over the issue of Lords Reform, the Liberals promised categorically that once that issue was resolved they would introduce a Home Rule Bill giving a considerable measure of self-government to the Irish, which might be roughly described as Dominion status, but retaining Defence and Foreign Affairs in Whitehall. No mention was made of Ulster. So convinced were the Irish leaders, both in Ulster and in the other provinces, of this offer's genuine nature that the North began looking to its own defence and Redmond's moderate Nationalists set about discussing the details of the transfer of power, finance and so on, from Westminster to the new and future parliament in Dublin. The more extreme Republicans of the I.R.B. regarded the whole deal with a scepticism which future events were to justify. Arthur Griffith, who had recently created a small party called Sinn Fein ('ourselves alone' is a convenient translation but 'we ourselves' with its active implications, though less elegant, is closer to the sentiment intended), occupied a position somewhere between Redmond and the I.R.B. He did not believe in physical force, unless this were absolutely necessary, but he did believe that the Irish must work out their own salvation rather than plead at Westminster. He believed that the policy of boycott— applied to unpopular landlords—could be used against all English institutions, from Parliament to tax collectors. This, as the reader will remember, was merely an extension of an old and tried Irish tactic, and it was to prove remarkably successful in 1918 and the years of rebellion that followed.

During the four years immediately preceding the First World War, that is to say the period of the second and third Liberal governments of that age, political disagreement between the two major parties reached a peak of bitterness such as England has seldom known. In the previous century successive reforms of the franchise had deprived the upper and upper middle classes of automatic control in the House of Commons, yet they could throw out bills in the Lords, though by a centuries old tradition not money bills.

Lloyd George therefore, and deliberately, sent them a budget in 1910 which must be unacceptable to the landed interest, indeed to the rich in general, since its manifest intention was to create the basis of the Welfare State by fiscal means, by taxing the rich heavily in order to subsidize the poor. This the Lords interpreted, quite correctly, as the first step towards levelling, to the creation of an egalitarian society, and as a precedent that has indeed been followed by all Labour and some Conservative governments, and so they voted it out. They, however, lost the constitutional crisis that followed, with equal bitterness, and their powers were clipped. They could no longer tamper with money bills and they could only postpone all other legislation passed through the House of Commons by some two years unless there were to be a change of government during that period. They thus found themselves almost entirely deprived of real political power and penalized, from their view at that time, by unjust taxation and perhaps more important by death duties which many of them construed as aimed at the destruction of their class.

And then, on top of this political and economic defeat, was piled the Irish Home Rule Bill. Many of the Lords had estates, usually large estates, in Ireland. Those who did were well aware that a self-governing Ireland would not and indeed could not protect those estates from the hungry peasantry whom their ancestors had dispossessed long ago, but who had never forgotten. Their motives were not always as despicable as the Marxists would depict. Many of course were merely against Home Rule in order to hang on to land and money, but the Encumbered Estates Act had relieved Ireland of a good proportion of its bad landlords. And many of those who remained were conscientious men who seriously believed that they could do more for their tenants than those tenants could do for themselves. Their leader in the House of Lords was Lord Lansdowne, the owner of large estates in County Kerry and in many respects a most admirable man. What they forgot, or at least seldom mentioned, was that the Irish countrymen of the time wanted land, land of his own, rather than materialistic progress in the form of a better tied cottage with better drainage, though of course he wanted the cottage and the drainage too. However an alliance was struck up between the embittered English Conservatives, the land-owners in the South and West of Ireland, and the Protestant population of the Northeast.

This alliance was led by two most remarkable men, Carson and Craig. Their statues, on a heroic scale, now dominate the huge imperial palace at Stormont which houses the Northern Irish parliament and many of its executives' offices; the one gazes down the long avenue which leads up to this great building, the other, from the top of the first flight of steps, presides im-placably over the politicians and civil servants whose footsteps echo through the great entrance hall. At first glance, before driv-ing up the long, steep, straight avenue, Stormont on its hilltop seems as big as Versailles which it resembles in that it, too, is well away from the city and the Belfast mobs. On closer in-spection, however, it is not only smaller and considerably shabbier than it appears from below, while its ostentatious pro-portions are more reminiscent of the edifices Mussolini was put-ting up in Italy at the same time that Stormont was built, and that Hitler was to build in Germany a few years later. But this parallel, too, is misleading. The buildings and monuments erected in the twenties and thirties by the Fascist, Nazi and Communist governments were intended to be proof in stone that man is puny, the state an irresistible power. The building over which Carson and Craig preside strikes, by its very tawdri-ness within (Cabinet Ministers lunch in a most dreary restaur-ant, served by slow-motion waitresses, off dishes that no French mayor of the smallest town would touch) and its external Vic-torian architectural malapropisms suggest, far more through diminuendo, the failed pomp and circumstance of New Delhi or Canberra. There is, in fact, a human note, as in most buildings, no matter how ugly, that the British Empire constructed to its own greater glory. And it was, indeed, the last of them all. It is right that Carson and Craig should be honoured by such a palace, since the Northern Irish state was their creation as much

as anybody's. In historical perspective, tough and iron-willed
as they appeared to their contemporaries, they bore a certain
resemblance to the little Dutch boy with his fist in the hole of
the dyke while the rising storm battered at the Empire. They
created, or at least saved from the engulfing disaster, this little
state, the first and now almost the last of Britain's many colonies,
certainly the last of any importance. They were men of very
different character and motive, and perhaps had only two qualities in common—courage of a very high order and ruthless
determination.

Their family background, however, was not dissimilar. On his
father's side Carson was of Scots Presbyterian descent, while his
mother came from Galway where her forebears had long been
settled. His Carson grandfather had come to Dublin from
Dumfries early in the nineteenth century, had set himself up
as a merchant, selling imported hats as his principal line, and did
well enough to be elected to the Dublin Corporation. Two of his
sons became Church of Ireland clergymen, the third, Edward
Carson's father, was an architect and did well in his profession.
His wife, Carson's mother, was neé Lambert and was directly
descended from Cromwell's major-general of that name. The
Lamberts were competent, capable landowners and managed to
preserve their large estate unencumbered. The Carsons' second
son, Edward, was born in 1854 in his parents' Dublin home, 4
Harcourt Street, just off Stephen's Green, the site of what is now
an hotel, a good address in those days. As more children
arrived they moved to a larger house, at No. 43, in the same
street. The architect and his clerks worked in the back part of
the house while his six children were brought up by the usual
nannies, nursemaids and parlourmaids of the period. The Carsons had no aristocratic pretensions. They were well off, but not
rich, the epitome of the Victorian upper-middle class, the Irish
equivalent of Galsworthy's Forsytes or Thomas Mann's Budden-
brooks. Edward Carson *père*, the architect, could not however
afford the fashionable luxury of educating his large family in
England, but he saw to it that they went to good Irish Protestant
schools and then, the boys that is, to Trinity College. Needless
to say they were brought up as devout members of the Church
of Ireland and convinced Unionists. It was the father who decided that young Ted should be a barrister, and this paternal
decision the son seems to have accepted without demur, though

he would have preferred to be an architect himself. As a young man he was no sort of rebel, working hard at his studies but far outshone at Trinity by his contemporary, Oscar Wilde. Indeed his scholastic record was good but not brilliant. He won an exhibition but not a scholarship to Trinity: in his final law examination he came seventh out of the ten successful candidates, and in 1877 was called to the Irish bar, where in due course he joined the Leinster Circuit. He was slow in making either a name for himself, or a decent income. In 1879 he married, on virtually no income, the equally poor daughter of a retired County Inspector of the R.I.C. This seems to have been the one rash action of this sober, hard-working young man. He had no connection with Ulster and, according to H. Montgomery Hyde in his biography, *Carson*, he preserved to the end of his life the light and easy accent and manner of speech of the Dublin in which he was born and brought up.

James Craig was seventeen years younger than Edward Carson. His father came of a Presbyterian family living in the County Down: of the purest Scots-Irish stock, they had been settled in that county for several hundred years, his mother's family much the same, though according to St. John Irvine in his biography, *Craigavon Ulsterman*, there may have been some remote admixture of Spanish blood far back. The father, also called James, was the younger son of a County Down farmer of small but not insignificant means. He became a clerk and eventually what would nowadays be called the advertising manager with Dunville's, the whiskey distillers. So successful was he that he was soon on the board of the distillery and a millionaire by the time he was fifty. With the hard-headed, and some might say the hard-hearted, logic of the selfmade man, he was determined that his sons should make their own way too, that is to say fight and suffer as he had done. Nor was he prepared to waste good money on such frills as an expensive education. As soon as young James left his Ulster school at the age of seventeen he was apprenticed as a clerk to a Belfast firm of general agents and brokers, then moved by his father's orders to a similar job in London, and finally brought back to Belfast where he became a moderately successful stockbroker on his own account, no doubt helped by his formidable father's status as a local magnate and by his own membership of the Orange Order. He returned to live in the parental home, Craigavon, where he and his brothers were kept under the strictest supervision by the millionaire distiller.

Only one anecdote is told about him by his biographer during this period of his life. In 1893 or 1894 he, together with a brother and a sister, took a holiday in Iceland, a most respectable, if scarcely exciting, island for a young man to visit. Its only attraction then, as now, were its curious, bubbling springs of steaming hot water called geysers. James Craig agreed to buy a few of these from an elderly Icelandic acquaintance for £100, and on his return to Belfast did so. The old tyrant was furious. After all, nobody in Belfast had ever bought an Icelandic geyser before, and there was certainly no money in them. People would talk! James Craig, then aged twenty-six or twenty-seven, obediently and immediately sold his geysers. His solitary youthful act of rebellion was over. When the Boer War broke out in 1899 he immediately volunteered for the army. It must be assumed that his expressed motive was that of the super-patriotism towards the British Empire to which his class of Orangemen were so sturdily and noisily loyal. It may be guessed that he was heartily glad to be given the only acceptable excuse for an escape from Craigavon.

His military career was sad rather than spectacular. As a junior officer he behaved with commendable bravery in the few engagements in which the 3rd (Militia) Battalion of the Royal Irish Rifles was involved, but within a matter of weeks after his arrival in South Africa he was taken prisoner, which he regarded as a most humiliating experience. He had been rendered partly deaf in his last engagement, and the Boers chivalrously released him to the neutral Portuguese. He remained hard of hearing for the rest of his life. Back with the British army, he was given a lines of communication job. (But surely he must have signed some sort of parole, when the Boers released him for the medical treatment that they could not supply?) He returned to Belfast and was demobilized as soon as the war was over, in 1901, with the rank of Captain. Though not a regular soldier, he clung to this rather insignificant rank, as a civilian, until ennobled many years later. Many Ulster politicians have done, and still do, the same. Among the more fastidious British ex-officers the retention of wartime ranks, unless they be at least as exalted as Colonel and among the most fastidious not even then, is regarded as an expression of vulgarity. In Ulster, on the other hand, and among some of the Unionists in the rest of Ireland, a military rank is a badge, a proof of past loyalty to the Crown and of a right to leadership over those who never achieved officer rank but who can yet express their own loyalty by waving Union Jacks and stringing red-white-and-blue bunting across slum streets.

If one were to judge Carson and Craig by their early lives, it would be hard to imagine two men less likely to lead a most dangerous insurrection against the government of the United Kingdom, one that nearly led to civil war and most certainly contributed greatly to the destruction of the British Empire.

During the second general election campaign of 1910, in his inaugural speech to a vast audience in the Albert Hall, Asquith promised that in the new parliament the Liberals would regard themselves as freed from the so-called 'self-denying ordinance' not to raise Home Rule, which the Party had imposed upon itself in 1906. This was in fact a direct appeal for the Irish vote. Nor could a new Liberal administration have been formed without the support of the 82 Irish Nationalist M.P.s (70 of them followers of Redmond, the other 12 more extreme and distrustful of Redmond's faith in Asquith's promises) for the Unionists had won 273 seats, the Liberals 275 and Labour 40. Home Rule thus became, once again, a very live issue. With Lords reform out of the way, Home Rule came to fill the very centre of the English political stage. Asquith introduced the third Home Rule Bill on April 11th, 1912, and after interminable debates in the House of Commons it was passed on January 16th, 1913. Two weeks later it was rejected by the House of Lords, only 69 peers voting for it and 326 against. However, with the new constitutional arrangements now in force, it seemed that it must become law not later than early 1915. It then seemed that Redmond and the constitutionalists had triumphed. But the crisis was only beginning.

In June of 1912, that is to say during the Home Rule debate, the Liberal member of the St. Austell division in Cornwall, a man named Agar-Robartes, had proposed that Home Rule be not applied to the four counties of Ulster with a clear Protestant majority, Antrim, Down, Londonderry and Armagh. The Unionists were consistently demanding the exclusion of the mixed counties, Tyrone and Fermanagh, and at this early stage of the crisis were also asking for the exclusion of the remaining three, Catholic Ulster counties, Cavan, Monaghan and Donegal. Asquith on the other hand, speaking in Dublin in July of 1912, answered both Agar-Robartes and his Unionist opponents very firmly. 'Ireland', he said, 'is a nation, not two nations but one nation.' However other members of his cabinet, in particular Lloyd George and Winston Churchill, were becoming increasingly favourable to the concept of partition. This was totally unacceptable to the Catholic majority of the Irish people and Redmond knew that his Party could not survive were he to accept it. Asquith, on the other hand, was well aware that without the support of Redmond's Irish Nationalists his government must fall. It is probably not fortuitous that he made his remarks about the indivisibility of the Irish nation in Dublin. It is also clear that his subtle mind had not altogether dismissed the idea of partition, if that were to be the only alternative to civil war in Ireland. And in Ulster the Orangemen were mobilizing.

The Ulster situation in the immediate pre-war years has been described, with admirable clarity and commendable brevity, by A. T. Q. Stewart in his book, *The Ulster Crisis* (Faber and Faber, 1967). The Unionist members from Ulster did not then, and do not now, constitute a bloc comparable to the old Irish Nationalist Party. They were, in effect, simply Conservative-Unionist M.P.s, usually of fairly extreme right wing tendencies, who voted with the Tories whether in government or in opposition. However they did, for obvious reasons, meet from time to time to discuss their own mutual local interests. And though they had no appointed leader a formidable Orangeman by the name of Colonel Saunderson had long filled that quite unofficial function. He died in 1906, and was succeeded by Walter Long, who was to achieve great prominence in the Conservative Party. In 1910, however, Long was returned for a London constituency. In the gathering storm of the Home Rule issue Ulster's leaders turned to Carson to lead the Irish Unionists, both in the north and in the south, and to James Craig—an M.P. since 1906—to be the leader of the specifically Ulster M.P.s at Westminster.

Initially the motives of these two founding fathers were not identical. Carson wished to preserve the Act of Union so that all Ireland might remain a part of the United Kingdom. For this purpose the tough, determined Protestants of the Northeast must provide his shock troops. Craig, on the other hand, was determined that in the event of Home Rule being granted to

Ireland, his Ulstermen would be excluded. He, and the Orange leaders he represented, had no wish that Ulster, or part of Ulster, be given Home Rule, which is of course what they eventually got. He wanted Protestant Ulster to remain as intrinsic a part of the United Kingdom as Yorkshire. Many a politician has failed through his lack of knowledge of history: geography is usually regarded as a somewhat simpler part of a school's curriculum. Yet it was on this very simple issue that the United Kingdom nearly foundered, or at least was close to floundering into civil war in 1914: were the Scots-Irish Protestants of northeastern Ireland Irishmen by reason of birth or Britons by reason of choice, religion and remote conquest? Nobody could then, as nobody can now, pretend that they were or are 'Englishmen'. Though the rich, the aristocrats of land and industry, might send their sons to the best English schools and universities there to acquire the accents and many of the attitudes of their English contemporaries—and not infrequently to become professional soldiers or sailors, often of great distinction, in the British forces —the majority remained as remote from English modes of thought as did the majority of Cork men or men from Limerick. Furthermore English social prestige, at that time, was so great that a surprisingly high proportion of all Europe's aristocracy was given, at least in part, an English training, if only by English nannies and governesses, from Moscow to Madrid. This, of course, remained skin-deep even if it ended in three years at Oxford or Cambridge, and—paradox again—it was two European emperors, both grandchildren of Queen Victoria, the Czar Nicholas II and the Kaiser Wilhelm II, both perfectly multilingual and trained, in so far as this was possible, to behave like English noblemen, who in the end solved, or at least postponed, the Irish crisis by starting a world war.

Yet it cannot be overstressed that what was happening between 1910 and 1914 was not, in effect, an 'Irish crisis' at all but a British crisis of the gravest political and constitutional magnitude. That much of the action took place on Irish soil, and that many of the actors of all political and religious persuasions were Irishmen or Britons with greater or lesser Irish connections should not be allowed to obscure this fact. Two great British issues were involved, the two which, interrupted and then only in part by the World Wars, have dominated British politics throughout this century. These can be briefly summarized as follows. The one was the extension of that political democracy which had been established in the last century into what might be called economic democracy, egalitarianism, the Welfare State: whatever the nomenclature the process is obvious and has been almost continuous, the main domestic plank in the Liberal and later the Labour Parties' programmes and only occasionally halted, though never really reversed, when the Conservatives have held office. The other great political tide, first but then only faintly discernible in the Irish Home Rule issue, has been the retreat from Empire, also foreshadowed in other terms in the previous century by the granting of Dominion status to Canada, Australia and New Zealand. There is no reason why these two vast, and in retrospect at least apparently irreversible, political trends should have become, also at least in retrospect, inextricably intertwined. There is, after all, no logical reason why an internally egalitarian society, such as say Sparta or in theory the First French Republic, China or even the Soviet Union, should not adopt ferociously imperialistic policies abroad: nor why a highly stratified society, such as eighteenth century Holland or contemporary France, should not withdraw from Empire almost completely. Yet in England, or rather Great Britain, these two great tendencies in some measure, though only in some, coalesced in the policies of the leaders of the Liberal and Labour parties. There is, of course, a very apparent emotional logic here too. If in domestic terms the dominant ideology has decided that all men are equal, it requires considerable dialectical skill simultaneously to convince oneself that Englishmen are automatically entitled to rule over Indians or Muscovites over Turcomen.

However that may be, the early twentieth-century liberal syndrome in England was essentially an amalgamation of the Welfare State concept and of anti-colonialism. It was immediately recognized as such by its enemies who have seldom distinguished between the two wings of the ideology, except when under the harsh spur of economic loss, and who fought a losing battle against its encroachment on what they regarded as their rightful privileges, both domestic and foreign, which began in the years just before the First World War and which, far more faintly, is still a joined battle. Then the cockpit was all Ireland. Today it is, in great measure, the Six Counties of Northern Ireland. But it was and is essentially a British, not an Irish, issue, for in other circumstances the cockpit might have been in Scotland or Wales. This has led to an immense mass of confusion, bewilderment and plain humbug both in Irish and British minds.

It is not my intention here to describe in detail the events of those distant, doom-laden years, but a brief chronology may be helpful.

September 28th, 1912, that is to say some six months after the passage of the Home Rule bill through the House of Commons and its temporary rejection by the House of Lords, was designated 'Ulster Day'. On that Sunday the Ulster Covenant—reproduced in the photograph facing p. 257—was signed, by perhaps as many as a quarter of a million Ulster Protestants, some signing in their own blood. One of the first signatories was Edward Carson. The document was modelled upon the Scots Covenant of the early seventeenth century, was drafted by a certain Thomas Sinclair, and was vetted, cut and approved by various Protestant divines, including a Presbyterian by the name of the Rev. Alexander McDowell who insisted that this declaration of resistance to Irish Home Rule should not be permanently binding on those who signed the Covenant but should be limited to the present Home Rule crisis. The purpose of the Covenant, in its original form, was to prevent by pressure, by massive lobbying, the implementation of a bill that had already been passed by one of the Houses of Parliament and that could now only be delayed by the other. It was thus a denial of the democratic process as expressed through parliamentary representation. Had it stopped there, this attempt to impede legislation by non-constitutional methods, under the banner of British patriotism, would have been bad enough. But it did not stop there. A Lord Clare would almost certainly, and immediately, have arrested both Carson and Craig and pronounced the whole performance illegal. Such, however, was not the style of Asquith, Birrell, let alone Redmond. Winston Churchill had already visited Belfast and, as a member of the government, had attempted to speak in the very Ulster Hall in which his father had 'played the Orange card' a generation ago. The hall had been banned to him, by threats of riot: he had spoken, rather weakly, in a tent: and by now he had moved to the comparatively calmer offices of the Admiralty. The British government did not respond to the implications of the Ulster Covenant. The Orange leaders therefore increased their pressure.

In September of 1911, at the height of the excitement that surrounded the Lords Reform and Home Rule crises, a group of men from the County Tyrone turned up at Craigavon. A formation would be a more accurate description, for these were members of an Orange Lodge who had learned the rudiments of infantry drill. No doubt many, perhaps most of them, were ex-soldiers, veterans of the Boer War. In any case this display of martial initiative by the Tyrone men struck a receptive chord in Ulster hearts. Almost immediately other Orange Lodges began to mobilize those irregular forces which coalesced, in 1912, to become the Ulster Volunteer Force. The secretary of the Grand Lodge of Ulster was a lawyer by the name of Colonel R. H. Wallace. He conferred with J. H. Campbell, K.C. (later Lord Glenavy) and discovered that there was a loophole in the laws of the realm which could be used to legalize this private army. Any two Justices of the Peace might authorize military activity by amateur soldiers within the area of their jurisdiction provided that such men were dedicated to the preservation of the United Kingdom's non-existent constitution, provided in fact that they marched about under patriotic slogans. Such J.P.s, it need hardly be said, were two a penny in Ulster. The drilling, and soon enough the arming, of this large force—it is estimated at its maximum to have amounted to about one hundred thousand men—proceeded apace. It was commanded by a retired British officer, a certain General Richardson, and it was armed with weapons bought abroad, principally in Germany and by Edward Carson. For two years the British government did nothing, or almost nothing, to prevent the creation, on Irish soil, of an alternative army, and the officers of the real British army came more and more to believe that this was an ancillary force and to sympathize with its avowed intention, 'to fight against Home Rule'. The Ulster Volunteer Force was, very quickly, an army in being, with the necessary supporting services such as signals, engineers and a medical service, even with a corps of women to carry out clerical and other such work. It lacked only artillery and a naval arm, nor was it fully equipped with the heavy weapons, such as mortars and machine guns, of the age. But it was, by 1914, most certainly an army, a small army but a formidable one. Furthermore it appeared to be an army without any visible enemy other than the Roman Catholic majority of the Irish people, for it could, or thought it could, rely on the sympathy of the regular British Army in its determination to prevent the actions of the British government as passed through the United Kingdom parliament.

Thus not only did the Orange Order have a leadership (a 'Provisional Government' for Ulster was set up in September 1913), but it very rapidly acquired a military arm for the support of that leadership and for the implementation of its aims. The Peep o' Day Boys had now become, at least in their own eyes, totally respectable. With political leaders, armed forces, and popular support among the Protestant majority, the future state of 'Ulster' was in existence, at least in embryo, as early as 1913. And in London the possibility of partition, the creation of those two Irish nations which Asquith had so recently deplored, was becoming a third, alternative policy to Home Rule for all Ireland, as desired by the majority of the Irish people, and to a continuation of the Union, as desired by Carson, Lord Middleton (the Unionist leader in the South) and the Irish Unionist minority. The stage in fact was being set for a British civil war to be fought on Irish soil. Postponed by the First World War, when at last it materialized, a few years later, much had changed. It fell into two phases, first a United Kingdom civil war fought between the Irish Republicans (1916-1921) and rapidly followed, after the Treaty that established the Irish Free State, by an Irish civil war (1922-1923). This lingers on, but the lineaments of the protracted struggle were already in existence once the Ulster Covenant was signed.

There is a popular misconception to the effect that militant Orangeism in the form of the Ulster Volunteers came into being as a counterforce to militant Irish nationalism. Precisely the opposite is true. The Ulster volunteers were created to fight against Home Rule, that is to say against the enactment of a law which could only be passed through the Parliament, and implemented by the Government, of the country to which they proclaimed such total and unswerving loyalty, and of which they were citizens. It was only when the Ulster Volunteer Force was in existence, and already partly armed, and when the will of the forces of the Crown to fight against it, if need be, were in grave doubt, that certain Irish nationalists, not at first Redmond's political party nor exclusively members of the I.R.B. or of Sinn Fein, decided that Catholic Ireland had better look to its own defences against the very real danger of a Protestant insurrection in the Northeast and perhaps elsewhere.

True there came into existence almost simultaneously with the U.V.F. the Citizen Army which James Connolly, the Labour leader, had created essentially as a workers' defence force as a result of police violence during the great strike and lock-out in Dublin of 1912. True, too, Connolly was an ardent patriot whose aspiration was to see a free and socialist Ireland, for he could not imagine the second without the first. But his small Citizen Army, consisting of a few hundred men almost all of whom were Dublin workers, was primarily and in intention an instrument in the class war.

It was not until early November, 1913, that Professor Eoin MacNeill, an Irish scholar attached to Cork University and, with Douglas Hyde, one of the founders of the Gaelic League, expressed in the League's Irish language paper the desirability to create a nationalist force comparable to the one already in existence in Ulster. On November 25th, 1913, a meeting was held at the Rotunda Rink in Dublin and volunteers enrolled. One of the first of the 4,000 Irish Volunteers to sign on at that meeting was a thirty-one-year-old teacher of mathematics at a teachers' college and a member of the Gaelic League, by the name of Eamon de Valera.

Eoin MacNeill, precisely because he was not connected with any movement, either open like Sinn Fein or secret like the I.R.B., remained in command of the Volunteers. It was not the intention of the I.R.B., whose members held many of the more important posts on his staff, to arouse British suspicions. Meanwhile quite soon Redmond, realizing that a new force was coming into existence in Ireland, began to show great interest in the Irish Volunteers, and not without a measure of success. Indeed in the summer of 1914 MacNeill split the movement, those who followed Redmond being henceforth known as the National Volunteers. However neither the National Volunteers, let alone the Irish Volunteers as a whole, were ever the armed force of Redmond's political party as the Ulster Volunteer Force was the mailed fist of the Orange Order and, through this, of the Ulster Unionists. Indeed by comparison with the Northerners they were hardly armed at all. A small consignment of arms was smuggled into Howth, near Dublin, on board Erskine Childers' yacht the *Asgard* in the summer of 1914, for by then the British government, growing alarmed at this proliferation of private armies, was blockading the Irish coast against such importations, north or south. This was interpreted by the Irish as meaning that while it was all very well for the Ulstermen to arm themselves, once the Irish Nationalists started to do the same it was time to clamp down on the import of arms. This judgment is probably unfair. To this writer it would seem that the arming of Ulstermen under the much waved flag of patriotism was an unprecedented act which bewildered the United Kingdom government, whereas the attempts by Irish nationalists to obtain arms from abroad was only too familiar to any student of Irish history. In any event, once the dangers of the developing situation were realized Churchill, at the Admiralty, acted with great vigour, and a large naval force was deployed off the Irish coast.

Nor was that the end of it. It was rumoured that deprived of their seaborne supply of arms the Ulster Volunteer Force was planning to raid British Army armouries in the north. To prevent this the British Army in Ireland was ordered, from London, to move units from the south into Ulster, for it was feared that the British forces already stationed in Ulster had been infected with Orange ideas, as had their predecessors at the end of the eighteenth century. The result, in the summer of 1914, was the so-called Mutiny at the Curragh.

For it was not only the British Army in Ulster that was pro-Orange, but the British officer corps, particularly those officers stationed in Ireland or of Irish Ascendancy background, as a whole. These included, first and foremost, the commander of the Cavalry Brigade stationed at the Curragh Camp outside Dublin, Brigadier General Gough, himself an Irishman. He had not only the backing, in London, of the Chief of Operations, General Henry Wilson, but also of the Chief of the Imperial General Staff, General Sir John French, both also Irishmen and fanatical Unionists. The cavalry officers could also count on the sympathy and often the support of the officers of other regiments. They were determined not to find themselves in a situation where they might have to open fire on fellow Protestants, even if the Ulstermen were to seize and loot British Army arsenals. General Gough and most of his officers threatened to resign their commissions if ordered north. In slightly more muted terms Generals Wilson, French and others threatened much the same. And this in the summer of 1914, with Europe on the brink of war.

Some infantry was sent north, but the Secretary of State for War, Jack Seeley, rapidly gave in to the rebel officers, none of whom was dismissed while those who had tendered their resignations were reinstated. True, Seeley was soon enough removed from the War Office, but by then the damage—the psychological damage that is, for the armouries were not in fact raided —had been done both in Ulster and in the rest of Ireland. The Orangemen assumed, quite correctly, that they were under the protection of the central authority to continue their 'fight against Home Rule', while the Nationalists and more especially the members of the I.R.B. were reinforced in their conviction that a free and unpartitioned Ireland, even within the limitations implied by Home Rule, would not come as a gift from London but would almost certainly have to be fought for. And the situation was soon enough drastically changed by the outbreak of the First World War.

Both Redmond and the Asquith administration now each made a cardinal error. Redmond pronounced himself a British patriot. There was no need, he said, for the British Army to continue garrisoning Ireland: 'his' Volunteers, working together with the Ulster Volunteer Force could, he assured London, keep Ireland quiet. Many Irishmen, even many moderate Nationalists, followed his line and volunteered for the British forces. Was this not a war to save 'plucky little Belgium', another Catholic country overrun by a powerful neighbour? Did it not follow that the war was about national self-determination? In which case Ireland could surely only benefit from an Allied victory. Even when the British government announced in September of 1914 that Home Rule, though on the statute book, would not be implemented until after the war, many Irishmen accepted this with good grace as merely an inevitable postponement of a binding promise formally made.

The I.R.B. thought otherwise. They immediately began planning an armed revolt at the earliest possible opportunity, preferably with German support in the form of arms and perhaps of troops as well. Sir Roger Casement was sent to New York and thence to Berlin to organize such support. The result, as all the world knows, was the Rising on Easter Monday, 1916.

In Ulster the Volunteers hastened, in large numbers, to enlist.

They were often enrolled as units and the famous 36th (Ulster) Division was essentially the Ulster Volunteer Force in British Army uniforms. That division first went into action at the Battle of the Somme, only a few weeks after the Easter Rising. It fought with almost incredible bravery, which in the context of the First World War meant advancing steadily across open ground raked by German machine gun fire. It soon left the divisions on either flank far behind and, at the cost of atrocious casualties, attained its objectives. But by its very gallantry the division's remnants found themselves holding a most dangerous and indeed untenable salient, fired on from three sides. They were ordered to withdraw, once again under murderous conditions. There was hardly a Protestant family in Ulster that did not lose a husband, son, sweetheart or at least a friend on the Somme. And the Ulster Protestants contrasted this tragedy of theirs most bitterly with what they regarded, and continue to regard, as the treachery of the Dublin 'rebels' a few weeks before, not always understanding that that too was a tragedy in which other brave men had died for another cause in which they too believed. The decimation of the Ulster Division is, to this day, celebrated annually in Belfast on the anniversary of the Battle of the Somme. That slaughter added yet further bitterness to the attitude of the Orangemen towards other Irishmen, even though some of those who died on the Somme were in fact Roman Catholics.

With the reorganization of the British government in 1916 as a Coalition rather than a Liberal government, and with the departure a few months later of Asquith and his replacement as Prime Minister by Lloyd George, the complexion of that government was drastically altered. Carson was now in the cabinet, as was his 'galloper' F. E. Smith, later Lord Birkenhead, another keen Unionist who had been much involved in Irish affairs. The prospects of Home Rule for all Ireland receded, and from now on the British government dealt with Sir James Craig as a potential Prime Minister rather than as the leader of an Irish faction. (For the details of this change of emphasis in London and of Craig's increased status in the Anglo-Irish crisis, the reader is referred to the opening chapters of Lord Longford's *Peace by Ordeal*, revised edition 1967, the New English Library, as well as to the biography of Lord Craigavon mentioned earlier.)

Furthermore the climate of opinion among the Irish majority

was changing rapidly. The Easter Rising had evoked little sympathy among the populace as a whole, and virtually no support outside of extreme Nationalist circles apart from Connolly's Citizen Army. Perhaps some 2,000 men were directly involved (but then there were only some 10,000 Bolsheviks in Russia in 1917). However the brutality with which the Rising was suppressed, the immediate execution after secret courts martial of all the leaders save de Valera, and then the trial and execution of Casement with F. E. Smith prosecuting for the Crown, shook Ireland out of the state of near lethargy which had prevailed, politically, since the fall of Parnell. British brutality, which by our standards would be wellnigh negligible, was intensely shocking in that gentler age, even though a World War was raging. The result was that throughout 1917 Sinn Fein gained in strength, at the expense of Redmond's Constitutionalist party. By 1918 it was the dominant power in the land. In October of 1917 de Valera, now released from prison and elected to Parliament as a Sinn Fein member in a by-election, was elected to the council of the Sinn Fein executive. A few weeks later Arthur Griffith agreed that de Valera succeed him as President of Sinn Fein.

This meant a complete change in the nature and intentions of Sinn Fein precisely at the time it was achieving predominance and was almost totally eclipsing Redmond's party. Griffith was a constitutionalist who had advocated a dual monarchy on the old Austro-Hungarian lines. Before 1914 he would have been satisfied with a somewhat more drastic measure of the Home Rule Act as passed by the Asquith government: in 1921 he signed the Treaty which created the Irish Free State, whereby the King of England remained King of Ireland. De Valera would have none of this. His sharp, clear mathematician's mind had taken him, of course, far beyond the simplicities of Euclidean formulae, but the concept of Q.E.D. remained. *Quod erat demonstrandum* was to him, and has remained to him, perfectly clear. Ireland, all Ireland, must be a totally independent Republic: the primary language must be the Irish language, the second language English: the state Church was to be Roman Catholicism, with tolerance of the other faiths: the economy, both industrial and agricultural, must be self-sufficient, thus preventing the danger of what is nowadays called neo-colonialism on the part of the British. How precisely this was to be achieved, whether through free enterprise on the old American model or by the socialism advocated by James Connolly, whom he admired greatly, or by a mixed economy, which was in fact what occurred, was left as a matter for the Irish people to decide once they should have achieved complete political freedom for all Ireland. Sinn Fein thus became the political development of those ideals for which the Volunteers had fought and died in 1916. De Valera was entirely conscious of this and expressed his views both in public and in private, with only a minimum of emphatic change, from that day to this. In his early days the mathematician was an empiricist and above all a soldier: only later did his career as a politician teach him that there are certain, limited virtues in pragmatism. And his empirics were, of course, anathema to Sir James Craig and his Orange followers. Thus was the gulf still further widened and deepened between Dublin and Belfast and also between Dublin and London, while the English, with their traditional political dualism and their consequent failure to realize that their enemy's enemy is not necessarily their friend, found themselves ever more involved in the support of the Scots-Irish minority in Ireland. Partition was on. With the Anglo-Irish War of 1919-1921 it became, from the point of view both of London and of Belfast, a certainty even though it was and has remained a geographical, historical and economic monstrosity. Even in Dublin pragmatists such as Michael Collins, Arthur Griffith and many of their political successors have, with greater or lesser distaste, accepted its inevitability: de Valera and the extreme Republicans, never.

Leaving aside, for the moment, the Ulster Protestants and the Unionists in the rest of Ireland, what emerged from the events of 1916-1922 was an Ireland united in its determination to achieve freedom from British rule, but basically divided as to the purposes to which that freedom should be devoted. Inevitably it was the activists of 1916 and of the Anglo-Irish war, the political leaders and ever more so the soldiers, who dominated the state that was fighting to be born and that came into existence with the Treaty negotiated in 1921. They were, as always and everywhere, a small minority of the population though they had the support, on occasion the active support, of the more passive majority.

The activists themselves were, from the very beginning, divided as to their social intentions. As stated earlier, Connolly's

socialist Citizen
segment of the
leaders who were
them were not nece
it would be no exa
preserve the existing
and economic power fi
of their leaders and thei
appearance on the Euro
atheist Bolshevism, which
ted as extreme socialism, o
determination to preserve soc
the Free State came into exis
had created, including a vastly
in being, though of course now
the beginning the old Irish Repub
British, contained ideologically di
ism has been inherited by the new ar
and south of the border, which early
a 'green', that is to say purely patriotic, I.R.A., known as the
Provisionals, and a 'red' I.R.A., that is to say a socialist or even
communist body of armed militants. The second claims legitimacy, though such a claim is odd from one arm of a schism
of which both are illegal in all parts of Ireland. The two I.R.A.s
have fought one another, with fatal casualties, in Belfast and
probably in the Republic as well. It would seem that the Red
I.R.A., being now under the control of international Communism as directed from Moscow, has been ordered to hold its hand
for the time being, while the Green I.R.A., in vague collusion
with certain Irish politicians now removed from office, is left to
do the dirty work, including murder, in the North. The Green,
or Provisional, I.R.A. is probably the larger, but less disciplined,
force active in Northern Ireland and the smaller in the Republic.

So long as the war against the English went on, the old I.R.A.
preserved its homogeneity of purpose. The moment the unsatisfactory Treaty was signed, and was rejected by de Valera and
almost half the Sinn Fein deputies in the Dail, or Irish parliament, the split became apparent and within a matter of months
this led to Civil War, Republicans versus Free Staters. Most of
the socialists were, as it happened, on the Republican side
though that was not what the Civil War was about, even though

nder Communist control, a
ic on the Soviet, Hungarian and

concerned with two matters: the reten-
chy, with the King of England still King of
the partition of Ireland, brought about by the
the Government of Ireland Act, rushed through the
Parliament in 1920, so that six counties of Ulster were
given Home Rule while remaining an intrinsic part of the
United Kingdom. This presented the Irish nationalists with a
fait accompli, theoretically subject to revision, when an end was
made to the Anglo-Irish war a year later.

While de Valera seems, at this time, to have been principally
concerned with Ireland's constitutional status and its continued
membership of the British Empire, some of the soldiers, led by
General Rory O'Connor, were more interested in partition,
which they were determined to destroy, and immediately, by
force. It was their intention to 'liberate' the six counties, which
contained approximately half a million Catholics and twice that
number of Protestants, thus ensuring a perpetual Unionist-
Orange domination in the area, soon to be reinforced by skilful
gerrymandering of the electoral boundaries, both for election to
Westminster and to Stormont as well as of the municipal districts. This was accompanied by particularly savage attacks,
especially in Belfast and above all in the shipyards there, on the
Catholic minority, which can be not unfairly described as a
pogrom. It was against this state of affairs that elements of the
I.R.A. rebelled.

It has been frequently said, by his enemies, that de Valera
'started' the Civil War. This is untrue, though his rejection as
President of Sinn Fein and the accepted political leader of the
Irish nationalist movement of the Treaty that Michael Collins
and Arthur Griffith had signed in London undoubtedly raised
the temperature immensely. It was the soldiers who started it.
In order to liberate the North they first had to secure a base in
the South, and occupied certain buildings in Dublin and elsewhere, the most spectacular being the Four Courts on the bank
of the Liffey. De Valera, having resigned his Presidency to
Arthur Griffith, merely enlisted as a private soldier in the Republican force, though he does not appear to have done any actual
soldiering and remained, of course, a most important political

figure even when disguised as a private. However the soldiers in charge of this new revolutionary and liberating force seem to have been quite uninterested in him or, indeed, in politicians as such, and simply brushed them aside. In this they bear a certain resemblance to their German contemporaries, also ex-soldiers, who were joining the *Freikorps* to fight for German lands in Silesia, Carinthia and elsewhere. Had O'Connor's men triumphed it is not inconceivable that they might, like the *Freikorps* soldiers, have provided the nucleus for some Irish version of a non-democratic state. That, however, did not happen.

The British government could not allow irregular Irish Forces, or indeed any Irish forces, to invade their newly created puppet state. Strong pressure was brought on the Free State government to neutralize the Republicans and arms were supplied to the government now headed by Griffith and Collins for this purpose. (Both were soon dead, Griffith of a heart attack, Collins ambushed and shot.) The only alternative was a renewal of the Anglo-Irish war, unthinkable not only for logistical reasons but impossible with the Irish patriots divided as they now were. A war, bitter and brutal as only a civil war can be, was the result. Comrade fought former comrade, prisoners were murdered and prominent hostages executed, often without trial. On the whole 'the passive majority' sided with the government forces, for the people were sick of bloodshed and arson. This, combined with British support in the way of heavy and light weapons, ensured the victory of the Free State forces within about a year. The surviving Republicans, including Mr. de Valera, were arrested by the Irish government. The peace of the graveyard descended upon a burned, plundered, impoverished Ireland. And in the North the Orangemen could and did congratulate themselves that they had not been compelled to become citizens of a country whose inhabitants behaved with such suicidal insanity. The scars remained and remain: to this day the Civil War is the principal barrier between the two major political parties of the Irish Republic, *Fine Gael* being descended from the party which won that war and ruled the Free State for a decade, *Fianna Fail*, de Valera's creation, drawing its inheritance from the Republicans. Both are in essence right-wing parties which in most other countries would long ago have merged. But Ireland is a haemophilic country where scars not only do not heal but are passed on, through the mother it is said, from generation to generation.

When the Boundary Commission was assembled, with a view to the revision of the Border, in 1925, it failed to reach agreement and in a welter of mutual incrimination dissolved with nothing accomplished. Half a million Roman Catholics, almost all of whom would sooner have been ruled from Dublin than from Stormont, remained subject to a Protestant majority which treated them as second-class citizens.

CHAPTER EIGHTEEN

In public as in private life fantasies realized can produce psychological problems with which it is more difficult to come to terms even than with the fantasies themselves. When, in war, almost the total energies of a nation are devoted to victory, its achievement will sometimes leave the victors in a state of bewilderment greater even that that of the vanquished whose dream has been destroyed and who are confronted with very real and immediate practical problems quite unconnected with earlier desires.

In Northern Ireland the the 'siege mentality' described in earlier chapters had long ago assumed the nature of fantasy. Bigoted politicians, backed by demagogic clergymen, had for generations told the people that the Roman Catholics were their bitter enemies who would destroy them, drive them from their homes and their jobs, and subject them to a merciless religious tyranny. In their schoolbooks (now fortunately revised) they learned much about the Inquisition and Bloody Mary and the savageries of 1641. They also learned about the glories of the British Empire, but precious little about the history of Ireland. Clive of India was a better known figure to Ulster Protestant schoolboys than was Grattan of Ireland. A whole conspiratorial interpretation of world affairs had struck deep roots in ignorant minds. The entire Roman Catholic body of believers, headed by the Pope himself, was planning, day and night, the destruction of the Protestants in general and of the Ulster ones in particular. Sly and cunning Jesuits, much given to casuistry and debauchery, were his principal agents, the Catholic population of Ireland their willing dupes and accomplices. Impossible to argue with such nonsense, as impossible as to try to convince a Nazi that there was no 'Jewish problem' or to show a young Chinese Communist that Mao Tse Tung is capable of error. The fantasy, like most fantasies, was impervious to reason. And now, with a stroke of Lloyd George's pen, the fantasy became the reality: the Border existed and the Six Counties of Ulster were politically severed from the rest of Ireland, including the other three counties of that province.

In Belfast it was of no avail to point out that the Protestant minority in the Free State was in no way persecuted nor their very substantial, quite disproportionately extensive, holdings in land and other sources confiscated: that Cosgrave's Free State government had fought the nationalist extremists, defeated them, and locked up most of the important survivors of the Civil War who might have caused trouble in the north: that the Dublin government was as bourgeois-capitalist in outlook as was the government at Stormont. As a result of the Border, the Orangemen were, if anything, more convinced than before that they were living in a state of siege, their enemy 'those people' on its far side, their ultimate defence against the diabolical Popish plot against them the might of Britain and, therefore, their cause the cause of Empire. On any one of their many tribal days of remembrance, there are more Union Jacks, more red-white-and-blue bunting to be seen in Belfast and the other towns than in the whole of the rest of the United Kingdom except, perhaps, in moments of supreme national crisis or rejoicing.

The fantasy had become the reality, and owing to exhaustion within the Free State that followed the Civil War the Orangemen were granted a full decade in which to prepare their defences against the permanent siege that they now foresaw as their destiny, forever.

The Roman Catholic enemy had two main columns. One, later to be dubbed by General Franco in another context, was the internal Catholic Fifth Column, incorporated into the besieged state for economic reasons, since without this accretion of second-class citizenry the little state would hardly have been viable. The four other columns were the hordes beyond the Border, led by the fanatics of the I.R.A. and backed by the vast powers of the Papacy. ("How many divisions has the Pope?" Stalin is said to have asked Churchill in 1945. To have asked such a question of an ordinary, semi-educated Orangeman would have produced a very different reaction.) It was against this two-pronged force that the embattled Orangemen prepared their defences.

The terms of the Government of Ireland Act gave the Stormont administration very considerable powers in the drawing of electoral boundaries. In those areas with a Protestant majority it was not necessary to use those powers to protect the majority. Almost everyone there voted Unionist, vast majorities were piled up, and indeed the Unionist candidate was not infrequently elected to an uncontested seat at Westminster or Stormont. It was in the areas where there was something like a Catholic-Protestant parity or even a Catholic majority that gerrymandering was practised with great vigour and considerable skill, particularly in the counties Fermanagh and Tyrone, the city of Derry and parts of Belfast. The technique is simple. Fermanagh is predominantly Catholic. It returns three members to Stormont, two of whom are almost invariably Unionists, the third a Nationalist or the member of some other opposition party. The electoral boundaries are drawn in such a way that the Catholics are always in the minority in two of the constituencies, in overwhelming majority in the third. The way the boundary of that third constituency twists and turns and loops the loop in order to encompass the maximum number of Roman Catholics is a splendid example of skilled demo-cartography at its best.

In the towns, and in particular those with a Catholic majority or parity such as Derry, Strabane, Dungannon, Newry and others, there is a refinement to the technique in the allocation of municipal housing by the Unionist urban authorities. The Roman Catholic priests insist that Catholic children be educated in Catholic schools and, of course, that they and their parents attend Church on Sunday and holy days. Since the Catholics are inclined to distrust their Protestant fellow-citizens, it was very easy for the municipal authorities to create what have been described as Catholic ghettoes, such as the Bogside in Derry, thus concentrating the electoral strength of their anti-Unionist enemies in districts where most of their votes would be wasted while claiming that, by so doing, they were merely giving in to the wishes of the people and the priests. To this must be added plural voting by property owners with more than one property, that is to say the richer and therefore almost always Unionist section of the electorate, a system abolished in the rest of the United Kingdom over twenty years ago and due to be abolished in the Six Counties now as part of the reforms that are slowly being enforced by Westminster upon Stormont. One example of these stratagems' success has been the municipal government of Derry, a city with a Catholic majority consistently administered by the Unionist minority.

Hand-in-hand with this political subjugation there goes economic discrimination. This is not inspired by the government as such, but by the Orange Order which controlled and controls that government. Forty years ago, a man applying for a job would be asked his religion, and if the foreman or the boss were a Protestant and the applicant a Catholic was likely to find himself unacceptable. Such crudity is no longer fashionable. It is simpler to ask him for his school credentials. After half a dozen such experiences the young man would, with luck, emigrate, thus compensating for the higher birthrate among Catholics than among Protestants. Of course there are Roman Catholic employers, and it is maintained by the Orangemen that they employ the same technique, but they certainly do not wield as much economic power as their Protestant equivalents at *petit bourgeois* levels. It must be stated here that the very biggest industries, most of which are now foreign-owned, do not adopt such discrimination as policy, though of course they do not desire sectarian troubles on the factory floor or in the shipyards: however the owners or managing directors of great international combines do not personally hire young men to work in the paint shop or the foundry.

In the public employment sector the Northern Irish government states that there is no religious discrimination whatsoever. So far as government policy goes this is undoubtedly true. The Royal Ulster Constabulary, for instance, was intended to contain a number of Roman Catholic policemen proportionate to the size of that minority in the Six Counties. In fact very few ever enlisted. Psychologically this is hardly surprising. The old Royal Irish Constabulary, a barracks police and therefore a para-military force, had been predominantly Catholic. As stated in an earlier chapter those policemen had almost always been stationed far from their homes: Ireland as a whole, in those days of more difficult travel, was big enough for this. Most of the men were, inevitably, Catholics. They were the first line of defence for British rule in Ireland and, as such, became the first target for Michael Collins and the I.R.A. in the Anglo-Irish war. Their barracks were destroyed, they themselves, torn between loyalty to their force and loyalty to their country, resigned in very large numbers until the British had to recruit another, irregular police force in England, the so-called Black and Tans, to replace them. Save in Ulster the R.I.C. vanished from the scene, though some of the men joined the Gardai, the new police of the Free State.

The Royal Ulster Constabulary was simply the Ulster branch of the R.I.C., but with a difference. In this new mini-state with its monolithic myths and fantasies, men could never be moved quite out of the control of that extra-legal political and religious force, the Orange Order. Mostly Protestants, they were drawn from a class in which Orange orthodoxy was in any case very rigid. Furthermore they had seen what had happened to their comrades of the old R.I.C. They had little love for the 'Shinners', the rebels, whom they often identified with the Catholic minority as a whole. Their job, their job with guns in their hands, was to protect the new state against what they regarded as dangerous, subversive elements. It is hardly surprising that very few Roman Catholics enlisted in this force, which soon had little in common with the old R.I.C. and had never borne much resemblance to the police forces of England, Scotland or Wales. An attempt, at the time of writing, is being made to change this as part of the reforms ordered from Westminster, to create an unarmed police force in Ulster on the English model rather than a force that resembles far more closely the State Troopers of Alabama or Mississippi. The R.U.C. are brave and usually well-disciplined men. They have handed in their guns, but whether they can change their attitude is another matter. To expect Ulster Roman Catholics to join such a force in large numbers, but always as a minority, would be equivalent to Palestinian Arabs enlisting in the Israeli police (some of course do as some Catholics in the Six Counties did and do) or Israelis becoming Egyptian policemen, an inconceivable phenomenon save on the part of secret agents.

Such then was the basic defence established within the 1920s within the besieged fortress against its 'internal enemies'. Against its external foes the R.U.C. was also the first line of defence.

They were backed by the Special Constabulary, a force of some 50,000 men created by the British in 1920 and handed over to the Northern Ireland government when this came into existence in the following year. This Special Constabulary was the equivalent of the Black and Tans in the rest of Ireland, but with one highly significant difference. The Black and Tans were usually men from Britain, imported to replace the R.I.C. as this force was destroyed by the I.R.A. or simply faded away. The Ulster Specials were local men, Protestants almost to a man, with all their prejudices and sectarian hatreds built in and ineradicable. (But see Appendix D.)

There were three branches of this Special Constabulary. The A-Specials were ex-soldiers and therefore accustomed to some measure of discipline. Having usually fought in the First World War, and seen something of the world, they had inevitably shed a certain amount of bigotry and acquired a measure of tolerance. They were, however, quite rapidly phased out and soon ceased to exist, as was the case with the original C-Specials who were older men enrolled only for the crisis of Partition. Soon enough the Special Constabulary consisted solely of what had been the B-Specials, but the original designation had by then become common usage and remained so until the dissolution of the Specials and after.

The B-Specials were recruited from the Ulster Volunteer Force as well as from the extremist Protestant riff-raff. A part-time force, they kept their guns at home, as they had done when in the U.V.F., indeed they were often the same guns. They remained therefore the armed branch of the Orange Order, which now controlled the new mini-state, and were the nearest thing to Nazi Storm Troopers that the British Isles have ever produced, behaving much as the S.A. did once Hitler had come to power. They took part, armed or unarmed, in Orange parades, but what is more important they immediately launched an intensive persecution of the Catholic minority comparable to the irregular persecution of the Jews by the S.A. in 1933 and 1934. The result was a state approaching civil war that lasted from 1920 to 1923, with casualties, mostly Roman Catholics, estimated at some 300. There were cases of B-Specials clubbing men to death and similar atrocities.

The B-Specials were not dissolved until 1970, on the orders of the British government, when they were still some 10,000 strong. According to the Northern Irish government's statements their primary purpose was to guard the Border against the I.R.A. raiders from the south, and since they were home-based this meant that a high proportion came from the Protestant element in the mixed Border counties where sectarian feeling is particularly violent. However they also continued to support the R.U.C. in riot control duties, as late as 1968 in Derry and 1969 in Belfast, duties for which they were entirely unsuited, and which they sometimes used as a pretext for bashing the Catholics. They became, for the Catholic minority in the north and for Irish nationalists in all Ireland, the most hateful symbol of Orange oppression in the Province.

As part of the current reforms the B-Specials were disbanded, to be replaced by another para-military force, this time with its arms kept in armouries. Some, but very far from all, of the B-Specials obeyed these instructions and handed in their guns. A surprisingly large number of new gun licences was issued in the year following their disarming. Exact figures are unobtainable, but it has been put as high as one thousand. Some, but again by no means all, enlisted in the new Ulster Defence Regiment, as did a mere handful of Catholics. In this respect in fact little has been changed since the siege ceased to be a fantasy and became a reality nearly half a century ago, for it takes more than two generations to change the minds of men, perhaps particularly of Irishmen, and above all of the Scots-Irish. For them, the Pope is still plotting their disaster.

Behind these indigenous defenders of Orange Unionism there stood, usually out of sight, the forces of the Crown. As military and technological demands altered, Ireland became, quite quickly, of far less strategic value to the British Chiefs of Staff. In 1938 Neville Chamberlain, advised of course by his Chiefs of Staff, was prepared to hand back to the Free State government those ports, the so-called Treaty Ports, in the south whose retention had seemed essential to the British when the 1921 Treaty was signed. However with the range of aircraft and the capacity of U-boats and surface warships what it then was, the possession of ports at least in Northern Ireland remained indispensable if there were to be a second world war. Indeed Derry, and to a lesser extent Belfast, proved extremely valuable to the British and Americans between 1939 and 1945. The British government were therefore prepared to give support to this little state in its desire to preserve its identity, even though in the imperialist context, as Empire declined, it was rapidly becoming a political and economic anachronism. From a purely party-political basis, moreover, the presence of a dozen Unionist M.P.s, who could be relied to vote the Conservative line, was acceptable to successive Conservative, or Conservative-Coalition, governments, even though the quality of Unionist politics in Ulster was becoming increasingly out of step and at times embarrassing to the men at the Conservative Central Office in London. Still, they were prepared, *in petto*, to use the Ulster Unionists for their own ends much as the Asquithian Liberals had used the much greater force of Redmond's Irish Party for theirs. Nor was the attitude of the later English politicians very different or noticeably less cynical. The stakes were again very high, though once again the real game was being played far from Ireland.

During and immediately after the Irish Civil War the Free State government had arrested some 15,000 men, mostly members of the I.R.A. or of Sinn Fein, its political wing that only lasted for about a further year for it had once again become an extreme nationalist organization that refused to recognize the Dail and the Free State government. The prisoners were quite rapidly released, the three most prominent, de Valera, Austin Stack and Liam Deasy being set free in July 1924. By the end of that year it may be said that the Cosgrave government had, so far as it could, written *Finis* to that tragic incident of Irish history, nor were there any reprisals against Republicans as such, though they met with a measure of unpopularity among those against whom they had fought, and did not always find it easy to get jobs: the middle and managerial class was fairly solidly opposed to them.

The I.R.A. however, now a secret and illegal society dedicated to the use of force and without the backing of the I.R.B. or indeed any other responsible political organization, was not prepared to give up the struggle. For the next twelve years the I.R.A. was primarily engaged in fighting the government of the Free State, both while the government was led by its Civil War enemies and, after 1932, when that staunchest of Republicans, Eamon de Valera, was Prime Minister and was devoting his entire, very considerable energies to reversing those parts of the Treaty to which he had objected since 1921, namely partition, membership of the British Empire, the retention of the Treaty ports by Britain, land annuities paid to Britain and British domination of the Irish economy. The I.R.A. during this period of increasing Anglo-Irish tension, culminating in the so-called Tariff War, was almost totally inactive in this field, and was using its very limited strength and resources (once again largely derived from Irish-American extremists) almost exclusively against the Irish government, robbing banks, murdering police-men and men whom it regarded as traitors within its own shift-ing ranks, intimidating and occasionally killing witnesses and even jurymen who had given evidence or convicted I.R.A. men, until at last the government had no choice but to hand over such cases to military courts. The I.R.A. of this period was no active threat either to the British or to Stormont. The violent anti-Catholic riots which blew up again in Belfast from 1933 to 1935 were in no way inspired by I.R.A. activity, though they were certainly not unconnected with de Valera's demands and with the Tariff War.

In fact when de Valera created his new party, *Fianna Fail*, in 1925 he rapidly siphoned from among the old Republicans all the responsible support that he needed to win a general election a mere seven years later. With the exception of two brief periods of Coalition government, that party has held office ever since. Becoming increasingly staid and bourgeois with middle age, it has nevertheless never abandoned its republican principles. The last English injustice to Ireland still to be righted is, in many Irish eyes, partition. It is not accidental or surprising, therefore, that several *Fianna Fail* ministers were, by allegation at least, implicated in an attempt early in 1970 to smuggle arms to the Catholics in the North: nor that a Dublin jury failed to con-vict: nor even that they were nevertheless dismissed or resigned from the government.

The history of the various campaigns carried out by the I.R.A. against Britain, Northern Ireland and the Irish authorities in the past thirty-five years has been admirably told by Tim Pat Coogan (*The I.R.A.*, Pall Mall, 1970). These campaigns have so far been invariably ineffective, and have served only to provide the Orange Order with a convenient bogeyman and to bolster anti-Irish sentiments in Britain. This is in part due to the rapid turnover within the small and, until recently, shrinking I.R.A. itself. Young men joined it for essentially romantic reasons, for the aura of secrecy, unthinking patriotism, even for the danger and the opportunities of violence. Like the young Communists of the 'thirties in England, like the student protesters of today, it became almost fashionable to pass through the I.R.A. But as they grew up, and as campaign after campaign fizzled out in failure and squalor, and occasionally in death, they departed again. It is one thing to wave flags, build barricades, make fiery speeches: it is quite another to lie in a hospital bed, and even more so to attend a friend's funeral. Both in peace and in war the attempts, first by the Nazis and now by various brands of Communists or anarchists, to use the I.R.A. as a political force have all so far led to total failure. It is far too incoherent a force. Even when it took to murdering, or attempting to murder, members of the Royal Ulster Constabulary or of the B-Special on the border in the late 1950s and early 1960s, such *crimes gratuits* merely served further to unite the Ulster Protestants behind their Orange Order. In Ireland proper it is merely a nasty and occasionally a dangerous nuisance. The Irish political scene south of the Border appears to be far less volatile now than at any time for the past sixty years. The relative importance of the I.R.A. could change, but at the time of writing its emergence as a political force of any importance whatsoever in the foreseeable future would seem improbable.

It is not my intention here to examine either the events of the last few years, which are too near us in time, the motives of those involved too obscure for rational analysis, let alone to prophecy any more than is strictly necessary.

In the mid-1960s it seemed that time had at last come for a measure of *rapprochement,* in economic matters, between the two Irish governments. The two Prime Ministers Captain (now Lord) O'Neill and Sean Lemass met, first secretly then publicly. In the Republic of Ireland this was generally greeted with approval and even relief, in the North with mounting apprehension and distrust. At the same time a new but very familiar figure appeared upon the Ulster stage, a fanatical, ranting, anti-Papist, super-patriot, nonconformist clergyman named Ian Paisley. The Catholic minority in the North misunderstood the climate of opinion and demonstrated in favour of those civil rights that had always been denied to them. The Orangemen reacted with traditional violence. O'Neill was dismissed and rioting of such brutality took place that the British were forced to intervene, sending over a very large army to preserve the peace and ordering reforms intended to bring the Six Counties of Ulster into line with the rest of the United Kingdom, reforms principally concerned with the police, the franchise and housing. These reforms are now being implemented, at snail's pace and, so far as housing and the reorganization of the police are concerned, largely at the expense of the United Kingdom taxpayer. One wonders how long any British government will continue to pay for the pleasure of nominal control over the politics of Northern Ireland. The reason why no reliable figures are available is given in Appendices B and C.

From a military and naval point of view, Northern Ireland was certainly a most valuable, perhaps even an indispensable, base during the Second World War. It has still some value, but with modern weapons systems can hardly be described as indispensable any more. Because it was used as a base in that war by the British and Americans, and because the Irish Free State was only benevolently neutral, Unionist spokesmen like to contrast the perfevid patriotism of Belfast with the treacherous poltroonery of Dublin, thus evoking memories of the 36th (Ulster) Division. In fact very many Irishmen, from Kerry to Antrim, volunteered for the British forces between 1939 and 1945. (There was no conscription in Northern Ireland during that war.)

Can the *status quo* be preserved in Ireland? The answer would seem to be that it probably can, provided the British government is prepared to foot the bill and provide the soldiers. So the question is once again shifted from Belfast to London. But can the soldiers be kept there? For nearly two hundred years now, London or Dublin has sent British troops to Northern Ireland in order to reinforce the local forces of law and order and help these subdue sectarian violence. Never did this drastic measure produce more than a brief, temporary respite. Only General Lake's brutal treatment of the United Irishmen in Ulster was a permanent 'success', and he was dealing with an essentially non-sectarian, foreign-inspired, ideological conspiracy, using methods that would surely be almost inconceivable to any United Kingdom government, or to British public opinion, today. The British soldiers of the '70s have acted, almost always, with quite remarkable restraint and under a rigid discipline in a task which all soldiers hate, since soldiers are not trained to act as policemen and cannot be expected to understand the weird religio-political emotions that have once again boiled over in Ulster. Greeted originally as the liberators of the Roman Catholic minority from the tyranny of the R.U.C. and the Specials, they soon found themselves regarded as the enemy, their presence resented by Catholics and Protestants alike, and themselves the target for gunmen of both factions. Their self-control in the face of almost intolerable provocation has been more than admirable, but it is perhaps asking too much of those young, armed men that they should carry out an unarmed, English policeman's duties. Furthermore one wonders whether the British government can afford to keep what is almost the whole of the British armed forces capable of infantry duties tied up as auxiliary policemen, achieving no solution. History does not stand still, and those brave, disciplined soldiers are likely to be needed elsewhere, perhaps even to fulfil the functions for which they were trained.

Does the Catholic minority really wish to be incorporated in the Republic? This is an almost unanswerable question. It is frequently said that with their high birth rate and incidence of unemployment they would suffer serious financial penalties if the British Welfare State benefits were sacrificed for the considerably lower degree of support that they would receive from a poorer all-Ireland Republic. On the other hand to live as second-class citizens is unattractive, to put it mildly. To be paid for having children is hardly a compensation for the danger that a child may be killed by a stray bullet in a sectarian riot. These are imponderables, for there exist no scales upon which they can be measured.

Do the citizens of the Irish Republic really desire the incorporation of the Six Counties within their state? The answer is that the politicians, all the politicians, at least in public, must and do insist that this is a Pole Star of their policy. In private they, and other Irishmen, are less determined. First, because the Irish nation cannot afford those great doles and handouts. Secondly because fifty years of Partition, like twenty-five years of partition in Germany, have produced characteristics on either side of the Border that further divide the populace. Thirdly, because the Irish businessmen are often, and openly, afraid of competition from the Scots-Irish whom they tend to regard as more efficient and more hardworking than themselves, in some cases correctly, in others erroneously so. On the other hand the economic unity of the country would almost certainly be advantageous to the whole island. If there is an economic 'border' to be drawn, the present political one is quite meaningless. In a 32-county Republic the partly industrialized eastern areas, both in Ulster and Leinster, would support and be supported by the largely agricultural west. It is likely that a well-balanced economy might result.

If Ireland and Britain both enter the European Economic Community, will this automatically solve the Border question? The answer is certainly in the negative. Belgium has been a unified country for well over a century and a member of the E.E.C. since is creation, yet Walloons and Flemings are still at enmity with one another, with occasional riots. The signing of treaties does not dispel the animosity of centuries, or not at least until more centuries have passed.

Will the reforms instigated by the last Labour Government and being pursued by the present Conservative Government in Britain solve the problem and unite the inhabitants of Northern Ireland? If British rule is to continue in the province, it is devoutly to be hoped that they may, or at least that they will decrease the tension. On the other hand one is justified to be as cynical about constitutional measures as about international treaties. The men who administer any constitution can very easily find means of denying its avowed spirit. The constitution that Joseph Stalin devised for the Soviet Union is probably the best, fairest and most democratic in the world, and is still in force. How many millions have been illegally murdered or sent to rot and die in the Soviet Union's labour camps since 1936? If they are so inclined—and there is no reason to believe that they are not—the Orange Unionist leaders, who will certainly continue to dominate Stormont, are quite capable of bending the most liberal reforms forced upon them by London in order to preserve the paramouncy of their own tribe in Northern Ireland.

There is an Irish legend, for which there is a measure of substantiation, concerning 'sleepy grass'. A man, it is said, can walk through a gate into a field which he knows well where such 'grass' has sprung up. It will cloud his senses, and he will be unable ever to find his way out again. The scientistic explanation of this phenomenon is that, in certain climatic conditions, a herb may grow on Irish soil which expels in the damp air some form of opiate or other narcotic, and that the inhalation of its poison may produce a hallucinatory, bewildering effect. Are the Six Counties of Ulster pastured with sleepy grass? Do its fumes reach into the very slums of the cities? Where, oh where, is the gate that offers escape from this apparently interminable, lost, dreary misery?

Appendix A

POPULATION

Any statistical analysis of the population of Ireland, and especially of the religious demography, for the period under discussion in this book is extremely hard to come by, and this for several reasons. The figures that follow should therefore be treated with very considerable caution, even though they be the best known to this writer.

The problem is threefold.

In the first place no census figures exist before 1801. That is to say the precise magnitude of the population explosion of the eighteenth century, concerning the existence of which there is no dispute, can hardly be estimated. No more can the scope of emigration, both from Ulster and from Ireland as a whole, be rated much higher than guesswork, as the contrasting figures of the historians show. Finally we have no reliable statistics concerning the religious faiths of the Irish, nor of the casualties endured by Roman Catholics and Protestants in turn during the wars and massacres that were an intermittent feature of Irish life from the reigns of Queen Elizabeth to that of Queen Anne, not to mention the chain of events associated with the '98 and the Act of Union. It is, however, safe to assume that both sides will have grossly exaggerated the miseries and murders inflicted upon them by the other. The various tables given below, should therefore be treated with caution not unmingled with scepticism.

Secondly, throughout the nineteenth century we do indeed have the statistics provided by the decadal census, beginning in 1801. Unfortunately, however, these figures—at least until 1861 and perhaps later—are themselves far from reliable. Large parts of Ireland, and especially the heavily populated West, were unmapped, often without roads, and the census officials ordered to deal with a foreign-speaking, sometimes semi-nomadic peasantry were confronted with a wellnigh impossible task. They did their best, but a margin of error, both before and after the Famine, of anything between 10% and 20% (in some districts) cannot be ruled out. Furthermore, until 1861 no attempt was made by the authorities responsible for the census to establish the religious faith of the people counted. Again, it is safe to assume that both the Roman Catholics and the Protestants would, for numerous reasons, have exaggerated their own numerical strength.

From 1861, and particularly from 1901, the figures are far more reliable but even during that period, even indeed today, not entirely so. To give but two examples: a Roman Catholic in a bitterly sectarian Protestant area might well prefer to disguise his religion from government officials, and vice versa. These, however, would be now a very small minority. Perhaps more important, and increasingly so among Roman Catholics and Protestants of all denominations alike, would be the number of people who would declare themselves members of a church which they seldom attended or attended for social rather than religious reasons. Even today it is an eccentric Irishman, and probably a member of the miniscule 'intelligentsia', who will stoutly announce that he is an atheist or even an agnostic. He will fear his friends' and neighbours' and indeed enemies' disapproval if he is not seen at Mass or at Chapel. Yet the real religiosity of the Irish has undoubtedly declined, though perhaps more slowly, as it has in almost all Western Europe. A curious, negative proof of this, at least among the Roman Catholic majority, has been the steady erosion of anti-clericalism. If you do not really mind very much what the clergy say, you will hardly get very angry when they say it. This is true, though perhaps to a lesser extent, among the Protestants of the North; certainly the extremists there have had to rely increasingly on the uneducated, on latter-day Peep o' Day Boys, keen on a punch-up rather than theology. All this of course may change again, but at the moment of writing it would seem that real sectarian bitterness is becoming a nurtured, hot-house plant.

When we come to the figures, then, we are confronted with a measure of confusion. For the late seventeenth, eighteenth and early nineteenth century Mr. K. H. Connell in his *The Population of Ireland 1750-1845* (Oxford University Press, 1950) gives in his 'Table 4' the following estimates, as revised by himself:

Revised Estimates of the Population of Ireland

	Modified estimate of number of houses	Persons per house	Population estimate	Traditional estimates
1687	—	5-6*	2,167,000	1,300,000
1712	524,773	5·3	2,791,000	2,099,094
1718	542,262	5·3	2,894,000	2,169,048
1725	579,343	5·25	3,042,000	(1,669,644-(2,317,374
1726	577,275	5·25	3,031,000	2,309,106
1732	580,353	5·2	3,018,000	2,000,000
1754	593,158	5·38	3,191,000	2,372,634
1767	636,069	5·47	3,480,000	2,544,276
1772	644,638	5·56	3,584,000	——
1777	672,639	5·56	3,740,000	2,690,556
1781	716,403	5·65	4,048,000	(2,500,000-(2,750,000
1785	711,355	5·65	4,019,000	2,845,932
1788	776,855	5·65	4,389,000	(3,900,000-(above 4,040,000
1790	812,513	5·65	4,591,000	3,750,344
1791	841,322	5·65	4,753,000	3,850,000

Census figures

	Modified estimate of number of houses	Persons per house	Population estimate	Traditional estimates
1821	1,142,000	5·95	6,802,000	——
1831	1,250,000	6·2	7,767,000	——
1841	1,329,000	5·9	8,175,000	——

*Five in single-hearth houses; six in larger houses.

To this writer, as indeed to Mr. Connell himself in his accompanying text, some of these figures would appear highly suspect. It is of course possible that the Irish population might have increased at so fantastic a rate between 1791 and 1821 (*ab initio* close on 50%) but there seems little social, medical, religious or economic reason, apart from the fall in emigration, why it should have done so in the course of a single generation. On the other hand the population per household, as given for the preceding period, would seem to this writer to be probably both too low and, by the very nature of Irish society as it then was, a poor yardstick. We read repeatedly of 'cabins' crowded with adults and children during this period, of massive itinerant labour on the roads or seasonally in the small cities. In fact to judge the Irish population in the three centuries preceding the Famine in terms of 'living space' would seem as misleading as to estimate the population of Russia, since the Revolution of 1917 if not earlier, by the same logic. Slums, urban and rural, are shared, for better but usually for worse; they are not susceptible to division into cubic feet of ownership or cubic metres of air space.

For this, and a later, period the population of Northern Ireland has remained, at least for the last century and a half, remarkably static. The figures are derived from census returns and from Whitaker. 1,443,000 in 1801 it rose to 1,649,000 in 1841, but declined during the Famine and Emigration years to a low of 1,237,000 in 1901 since when it has in general increased and in 1966 stood at 1,485,000. There has not in effect been anything like the vast fluctuations of population that affected Ireland as a whole. This is, in some measure, explicable in that Roman Catholic immigration counterbalanced emigration. In recent years, starting from the first reliable statistics of the 1911 census, there is only a very small, indeed virtually negligible, religious-demographic change.

1911	
R.C.	690,816
Protestants	366,773
Presbyterians	421,410
Methodists	48,816
+ others	

	1926	1937	1951	1961
R.C.	420,428	428,290	471,460	498,031
Presbyterians	393,374	390,931	410,251	413,006
Ch. of Ireland	338,724	345,474	353,245	344,584
Methodists	49,554	55,135	66,639	71,912
Others	54,481	59,915	69,362	97,929

Figures taken from Census and Whitaker.

The only marked decline since 1911 would be in the Roman Catholic population, due in large part to the fact that Ulster's three counties of a predominantly Roman Catholic faith were detached from the rest of the province at the time of the Treaty, partly to the fact that many young Roman Catholics have, for obvious reasons, chosen to emigrate from that area.

As for Belfast itself, I quote from D. J. Cowan's *History of Belfast*

Year	No.	
1659	589	(according to Sir William Petty—but it is questionable whether this is trusworthy).
1685	2,000	(a rough estimate).
1757	8,549	
1782	13,105	
1791	18,320	
1813	27,832	
1821	37,117	
1831	53,287	
1841	70,447	
1851	87,062	
1861	121,602	
1871	174,412	
1881	208,122	
1891	255,950	
1901	349,180	
1911	386,947	
1920	430,000	(estimated in round figures).

To these authoritative figures certain, and often more modern, statistics may well be added. In 1911 the people of Belfast included some 93,000 Roman Catholics, 118,000 members of the Church of Ireland, and approximately 140,000 members of the Presbyterian and other non-conformist faiths. More recent figures show, once again, remarkably little change for the city as a whole.

	1926	1937	1951	1966
R.C.	95,682	104,372	115,029	114,529
Presbyterians	137,384	137,939	134,831	120,158
Ch. of Ireland	133,100	140,310	131,885	112,316
Methodists	25,701	29,966	34,504	33,019
Others	23,284	25,499	27,422	36,072

There has been no important change of the religious demography in either Northern Ireland or in the Republic of Ireland
during the past five years. It would therefore seem that one
theoretical explanation of the recent eruption of violence in the
Six Counties—namely that the Protestants are being 'outbred'
by the Catholics—is a nonsense. Since every form of contracep-
tion, including apparently the oral device known as 'the Pill',
cheaply at present and perhaps soon enough for nothing, this
terror of genocide-in-reverse, nurtured over the centuries in the
minds of Protestant extremists would seem totally without justification. The hysteria will, alas, continue, but the hysterics might
remember that neither Commodore Paul Jones, nor General
Humbert, and let alone Wolfe Tone visited Ireland in order to
breed Catholic babies.

Appendices B and C

These appendices do not exist, and this is not merely due to the inertia which tends to afflict a writer as he nears the end of a book as long as this one. The reason for their absence would seem to me of sufficient interest to the reader to warrant an explanation.

The first of these appendices was to have been a statistical survey of unemployment in Northern Ireland, expressed as an annual average gross figure since 1921 and also as a percentage of the employable (or registered for employment) population, this percentage to be contrasted with similar percentages for the Free State/Republic of Ireland and for the United Kingdom as a whole. We have heard a great deal concerning the high incidence of unemployment in the Six Counties of Ulster, particularly in the western, predominantly agricultural counties. It has even been alleged, very frequently, that the Roman Catholic minority—being proportionately more numerous among the unskilled and therefore, in our age, more prone to unemployment, quite apart from their tendency to larger families—would not in reality relish incorporation into the Republic since they would thereby forfeit the higher degree of 'benefits' that they now enjoy in the North and have enjoyed since the creation of the British Welfare State a quarter of a century ago. This seemed to me, therefore, a social and economic phenomenon that should be documented.

Unfortunately I discovered that it is quite impossible to present the necessary facts in any neat, statistical form, and for the following reasons:

(a) The unemployment benefit, old age pension, health service and family allowance returns do not distinguish between the religions of the recipients. This I had assumed to be the case, but was prepared to make an avowedly tentative estimate.

(b) The definition of 'unemployment' and hence entitlement to benefit has been altered more than once over the past fifty years, thus making comparative statistics between various years scarcely valid.

(c) The definition of 'unemployment' in Northern Ireland is not identical with the same definition in the rest of the United Kingdom and is markedly different from that prevailing in the Free State/Republic. Thus spatially comparative figures would be not only inaccurate but positively misleading.

(d) Although direct state assistance (Welfare) is undoubtedly considerably higher in Northern Ireland than in the Republic, the social structure and social attitudes in some measure, but only in some measure, serve to counteract this discrepancy. To give but two examples, the amount of money that reaches the people of the Republic from emigrants to America and Britain would appear proportionately to exceed—though this is pure speculation—similar remittances to the poorer people of the North. There is also the activity of the churches.

(e) The Irish of the Republic are generously entitled to avail themselves of the National Health Service and other Welfare State benefits by the comparatively simple means of transporting themselves across the Irish Sea. Many—though how many it would be impossible to say—avail themselves of this privilege. Since Irish medicine is extremely expensive, save only for the very poor, many an Irish baby is born in a British hospital and many a major operation, if there is time enough, is carried out by English surgeons.

(f) In Western, agricultural Northern Ireland, as indeed in agricultural Ireland generally, there is a great deal of 'concealed' employment. A man will register as unemployed, and draw his benefit as such, but will in fact have a part-time or even a full-time job with a neighbouring farmer or friend. For this he will receive a wage below the minimum stipulated by law. On the other hand his low wage, combined with his unemployment benefit, will ensure him a larger net income than that which he would receive were he regularly employed. This of course also suits his employer who thereby acquires cheap labour and, since he does not declare that labour, he is exempt from paying insurance and so on. Both sides, in fact, profit from such flouting of the system devised by the bureaucrats. This typically sly peasant's manoeuvre is common both in parts of Northern Ireland and in the Republic. It contributes, though to what extent it would be impossible to say, to the vastly inflated unemployment figures in both parts of Ireland.

It will thus have become apparent why it is impossible to produce meaningful, comparative statistics for unemployment and other Welfare State benefits in Northern Ireland. In this writer's opinion real unemployment there is probably as bad as in the worst areas of the United Kingdom as a whole, and rather worse than in the Republic of Ireland as a whole, though perhaps on a par with that prevailing in Connaught and western Munster. As for benefits—though this is pure guesswork—it would seem that the very poor are slightly, though not much, better off in the North than in the rest of the island, when all factors have been taken into account. The emigration figures, themselves not only suspect but really unobtainable, would seem to bear this out.

To assume that for such slender financial benefits the Roman Catholic minority would prefer to remain in a society which can neither protect its children from murder nor its homes from arson would seem, to this writer, an insult to human nature worthy only of the liberal ideologues who presided over the famine and of our near-contemporaries who presided over Nazi Germany and who still rule Russia, China and Cuba.

*　　*　　*

The second unwritten appendix was intended to deal with the actual financial support supplied, over the years, by the United Kingdom as a whole to Northern Ireland. Here, again, the problem proved intractable, and for a number of reasons:

(a) Direct grants in aid have been estimated at between £100 and £200 million per annum. It is impossible to state how much of this returns to the U.K. Treasury in the form of income and other taxes.

(b) Vast treasure has been devoted, both by public and private enterprise, to subsidizing industrial development, particularly in the Belfast area, shipyards and industry, and in the new Craigavon industrial zone, as well as elsewhere. It is impossible, at least for this writer, to estimate at this date how much of this money—for which no satisfactory statistics are or can be available—is normal, capitalist or state-capitalist investment and how much is, to put it crudely, charity. Were I a British tax-payer, I should hope that all of these thousands of millions came into the first category.

(c) The sum of £270 millions has been mentioned for the proposed re-housing project. Presumably the houses will belong to the public authorities, and if properly built will presumably not decrease in value.

(d) What does it cost to maintain such a very large proportion of the British army in Northern Ireland, attempting bravely and at times failing 'to keep the peace'? What would it, on the other hand, cost to keep these soldiers elsewhere? The loss here would seem to be military and moral in the first instance, economic only in the second. Once again one is involved with problems that are not subject to statistical analysis.

There you are. It is frequently said that the United Kingdom government, any U.K. Government, cannot 'afford' to support Stormont for much longer. But who decides what the cost, in fact, is? Certainly not this writer, and hence this substitute for two uncompiled statistical appendices.

Appendix D

THE SPECIAL
CONSTABULARIES

On re-reading the typescript of this book I reached the conclusion that it displays a very considerable bias against the
Protestant extremists in the North of Ireland, which I would
not retract, but that I have been scarcely fair to the now dissolved
Special Constabulary, popularly known as the 'B-Specials'. I
therefore requested of Mr. Wallace Clark, author of *Guns in
Ulster* (Constabulary Gazette, Belfast, 1967) that he write the
following appendix explaining the position of the various para-
military organizations in recent years. Mr. Clark comes from
and lives in Maghera, County Londonderry, a district where
sectarian strife has been both violent and rooted in the traditions
with which this book is primarily concerned. His family has been
involved in Ulster politics for many years, one member thereof
having been a Unionist M.P. at Westminster until defeated by
the Rev. Ian Paisley in 1970. Though himself a former 'B-Special',
he was never an active member of the Orange Order. He is
therefore in a position to describe with the maximum objec-
tivity, the role of the Special Constabulary in the society to
which he has devoted his patriotic integrity. I have in no way
edited what follows, nor has he—for technical reasons—been
able to read the full text of the book to which he has kindly
contributed this appendix.

The Memorandum which authorized the enrolment of Special
Constables, who were to be the immediate precursors of the 'B'
men, was published in October 1920. This was a couple of months
before Lloyd George's Government of Ireland Act forced Home
Rule on Northern Ireland. There was nothing new in the principle of raising Special Constables to assist the Royal Irish
Constabulary; such a force had been authorized as early as 1832*

---

* Special Constables (Ireland) Act, 1832.

and activated a number of times during the intervening ninety years. In view of the criticisms of every aspect of the Special Constabulary, including the very legality of its existence, which led to its disbanding in 1970, it is worth remembering that the original decision to set it up was taken by what is now referred to as the Westminster Government, before the Northern Ireland parliament existed.

The need in 1921 for some effective form of security force was indeed urgent. Ireland was in a state of lawlessness unparalleled in any European country in this century. In most parts outside the six northeastern counties the Police had been forced by fire and bullet to leave the smaller towns. Intimidation of both plaintiffs and witnesses by the I.R.A. had brought the normal processes of justice to a standstill. The authority of the civil power was in such disrepute that the situation was getting beyond the point where the British army, or any army if it came to that, could deal with it. This was proved eight months later when Britain gave up the struggle, abandoned her adherents in three quarters of Ireland and signed the Truce. Had the loyalists in the South been banded together earlier, or had there been more of them to form part-time local forces to assist the military at this last minute, the Battle of Ireland which was so nearly won by Britain would have finished in her favour.

In the South, however, very few men indeed dared at this late hour to join the Special Constabulary in the face of the I.R.A. threat to shoot anyone who volunteered. In the North the same threat applied, and there was every reason to believe that it would be extensively carried out, but loyalists were numerous there and the courage of Ulstermen has never been questioned. Recruiting, however, even in Ulster, seemed maddeningly slow at first to the local leaders who had been appointed to form the force. 'I need men,' my grandfather, who was well known for his colourful speech, is recalled as having said in January 1922, 'and the younger and wilder they are the better.' If he took on any wild ones in the frustrations of the early days he very soon got rid of them, and the men he did raise quickly put a stop to intimidation in South Derry and set about the long task of beating the terrorists. At that time the future of Northern Ireland as a community must have seemed doubtful in the extreme to those who comprised it; even more so a few months later when the Treaty in December 1921 brought an end to the fighting in the south. This had the effect of releasing the full weight of the I.R.A. hardened by months of warfare, to attack the newly fledged community. Fortunately the Royal Irish Special Constabulary had by this time become strong and well organized.

It was led by such men as Sir Basil Brooke, afterwards as Lord Brookborough Prime Minister of Northern Ireland. He had played a major part in persuading the British Government of the necessity for an armed Special Constabulary. His fellow officers comprised the leading men in each of the six counties. The Force they commanded, sixty thousand strong, was in four divisions: Mobilized on a full-time basis were the 'A' Specials, usually organized in units of platoon strength stationed throughout the province. A high proportion of their platoon commanders were drawn from the great body of unemployed ex-officers in England. In the heat of the emergency there was only the most cursory check on backgrounds and many of those appointed were chancers who knew little of the situation in Ireland and cared less and whose misdeeds brought undeserved disrepute on the Ulstermen in the force.

Next in order came the 'B' Specials, part-timers, available for patrols on one or two nights a week and for such drills as could be worked in. They were unpaid except for an allowance of £10 a year to cover wear and tear of clothes. At first there was no uniform other than caps and armlets but as the months wore on many of the men bought their own uniform from the disbanding R.I.C. The 'B' Specials were led by their own officers with the rank of commandants but under the Police authority of the area. The third category, known as 'C' Specials, comprised older men who only turned out in case of major emergency or on occasions when the 'A's and 'B's were called away.

Last and by no means least was the 'C 1' Division, twenty thousand strong, situated mainly around Belfast and organized as an army division, trained like soldiers. This was designed to meet the situation of Britain withdrawing the regular army and leaving Ulster defenceless.

The outlook of the leaders of the Special Constabulary in those stormy days can be gauged from letters written by my grandfather at the time. On the 30th March, 1922, Harry Clark wrote to his neighbouring District Commandants:

'I have been discussing the whole situation with men in this district and we all agree that unless we are better supported by the authorities it will be impossible for the 'B' Force to protect the lives and properties of the loyalists in South Derry.

I need not remind you of what has happened during the past two weeks, murders and outrages of every description, which if unpunished are certain to be repeated.

I know that at present we are getting blamed for not having prevented these outrages and I feel that the few hundred 'B' men even if mobilized all the time could not possibly guard all the points of danger throughout the county, the enemy having the advantage of being able to concentrate on any given position. We are all strongly of the opinion that it is absolutely essential for the authorities to arrange for a big comb-out of the enemy strongholds with full power at least to intern all the leaders.

I feel that we must consider our own position; it is very likely that if things become quiet for a month or two the 'A' Special platoon in Maghera will be withdrawn, then the Sinn Feiners will have a free field to come down and massacre us all. We will all be marked men and our positions certainly serious and dangerous.

So far no offensive movement has been made against the three or four hundred men who marched into Maghera and cleared out the Police Barracks, murdered Kirkpatrick, blew up the Moyola bridge, captured Sergeant McKenzie and burnt down George McDonald's mills. Flushed with these great victories they will now feel strong enough for further outrages and I feel that the position is dangerous and urgent. My idea is that we should all have a meeting and send in an ultimatum to the Prime Minister threatening resignation unless active measures are taken at once. At present we are only making ourselves marked men and no object can be achieved as long as we are confined to our strictly defensive measures.'

The criticisms of the government for alleged failures to deal with terrorism which appeared almost daily in Northern Ireland papers during 1969 and 1970 struck a very similar note to this letter of fifty years earlier. In the first part of 1922 the weapon of internment had not been introduced, and it was almost impossible to catch and hold the terrorists.

A week later Harry Clark received from the I.R.A. a threatening letter promising death if he continued his activities in the Specials. He sent this to his County Commandant with the following note:

'My dear Colonel,

I attended Craig's meetings in Belfast yesterday; they are going to raise a hundred thousand pounds for propaganda at once.

I am afraid from all I can hear that the peace terms* are not worth the paper they are written on. I received a letter, as enclosed copy, on Friday night last which is also in my opinion not worth the paper it is written on and does not cost me a thought. Unfortunately however Mrs. Clark saw it and of course is more or less anxious. Sir Hiram Wilkinson got two, one a duplicate of mine and the other said that if he or anyone assisted to repair the Tobermore bridge they would be shot as the destruction of this bridge was an act of war by the I.R.A. I don't know how this strikes you but it has at least given a record in writing that the I.R.A. are at war with us. Why in hell should we be at peace with them? Personally as you know it has only been due to my very special efforts that peace has been kept in this district, that our men have not retaliated for the brutal murders of Kirkpatrick and McFadden. So far as I know there has not been a single act of retaliation in my area but if there is another murder, although I have no connection with it, I understand a body has been formed which will immediately destroy hundreds of Roman Catholics. About this there is no possible doubt.

We require seven more mobilized 'B' men immediately which I hope you will allow me to take on; in fact I think you already told me I might engage as many men as I thought necessary. Craig said yesterday that Winston Churchill had promised him any amount of money he required and it would be cheaper to take a few men to guard our property than to lose a quarter of a million if it is burnt out.'

The next few weeks April/May 1922, saw the crisis of the

---

* The Craig-Collins pact of 30th March, 1922, it in fact only lasted a very short time.

Battle of Ulster. Murder and arson took place every night. On May 25th Harry Clark pinned up the following notice for his men:

'I am glad to say that with few exceptions all the 'B' men in my unit, No. 3 area, have been congratulated on three occasions by the G.O.C. on the splendid discipline they have maintained, often in the face of great provocation. This discipline is very helpful to the Prime Minister as the other side are always trying to take a chance of blackening the Specials. In England they are only too ready to listen to such reports and to cry us down. You must know how very important it is to keep the English people with us; they could withdraw the army any day and leave us to the tender mercies of a hundred thousand Sinners from the south and west, so I urge all of you to continue the good behaviour that has been in this area and do not give any unnecessary provocation.

I will not tolerate any drinking or unlawful behaviour of any description.'

When 'Master Harry', as he was locally known, wrote these words, the fighting was very near its end, although this must have been far from obvious to him at the time. A few days later large scale internment was introduced, and this was followed on the 28th June, 1922, by the start of the Civil War in the south which took the pressure off Ulster. The I.R.A. and the Free Staters became so busy perpetrating on each other atrocities which equalled and in many cases excelled anything that had happened during the fighting with the British, that they had no time to worry about Partition. Ulster returned to peace and to start the rebuilding of her shattered bridges, and worse shattered public confidence much earlier than anyone could have foreseen.

The 'A' and 'C' Specials were disbanded during the next year or two. The term 'B' accordingly became obsolete, for the remaining force became simply the Ulster Special Constabulary, but the name which has stuck is the 'B' men. A stranger might have been surprised to hear one night when a callout was required a girl came running into my uncle's study shouting, 'Mr. Tommy, ye're till scatter the 'B's', but no-one in Ulster would have had any doubt as to what she meant.

My father, 'young' Harry Clark, had taken over local command from my grandfather in 1937 and very shortly afterwards his men were in action during the 'Maghera riots' when an attempt was made by the I.R.A. to burn the Barracks. The 'B' men mobilized within minutes of hearing the shooting and put the enemy to flight so quickly that they abandoned dozens of bicycles which were later sold for the benefit of the wounded policemen. Serious trouble in County Derry and elsewhere was forestalled or minimized by the presence of the Ulster Special Constabulary.

On the outbreak of the war many of them joined the armed forces but the Specials who stayed at home were kept busy throughout the period of the hostilities in patrolling the roads to prevent incursions by the I.R.A., while many of them took on a second part-time activity by joining the Ulster Home Guard. Without the Specials Ulster would have been over-run by the I.R.A. during the war, if not before it. Without Ulster's ports Britain would have lost the Battle of the Atlantic and with it the war. These are facts which scarcely anyone in Britain remembers today, but the British, have never cared about anything but football.

When I returned home from the war aged 22 it seemed as natural to join the Ulster Special Constabulary to defend my home from terrorist activity as it had been a few years earlier to join the Home Guard and, as soon as I was old enough, the Royal Navy to defend my country from the Germans. To a young man the political implications of joining a force such as the Ulster Special Constabulary never mattered very much. On analysis all that the act implied was that I wanted to maintain the ties which my family in Ulster have had for at least 300 years and which the inhabitants of northeastern Ireland as a whole have had for 2,000 years with Scotland and England. These ties require a little explanation. Up until a hundred years ago and the advent of the railway, travel by water was easier than travel by land—the sea united rather than divided. Dalriada and Ulidia lying close to the narrowest part of the Irish Sea, have for nine tenths of their history been effectively far closer to Scotland and England than to Dublin. It is hardly surprising if their allegiance continues to lie towards their age old allies and associates, in the same direction as the ties of kin and commerce. So it has been for the major part of recorded history. Ulster has usually been divided from the rest of Ireland and in many periods united to Northern England and Scotland.

To return to my personal attitude, if the south had chosen to secede from Britain, that was alright by me—I have never had any animosity towards anyone there and many links of personal friendship, but I had no intention of being coerced into seceding too by a bunch of shop boys armed with rusty pistols which was the I.R.A. image at the time.

Post war service in the U.S.C. offered occasional danger, much monotony and minimal pay. It was not 'hard liners' who joined, but those with a higher than average sense of public service. So joining the U.S.C. offered a chance to meet and work with some of the finest men one is ever likely to come across—men you could lead to hell and back but never drive an inch. The company would be robust.

When I set about joining I found that recruiting for the Specials was done locally, by application to the sub-district commandant who commanded a unit of platoon strength formed of men living near each other. The S.D.C.s knew all there was to know about a lad's background, family and character and were shrewd rejectors of anyone likely to prove unreliable— a system of selection far more thorough than the best organized impersonal screening. All applicants were subsequently vetted by the Royal Ulster Constabulary and anyone with the smallest police record was automatically rejected. There was never any requirement to be a member of the Orange Order first; there were no secret meetings or dark undertakings; the U.S.C. with the disadvantages of a part-time force was much too simple and loosely-knit for that sort of thing; the men in it were in general straightforward and kindly coming from many different trades and professions who had the one common bond that they were not prepared to see their country over-run by terrorists with political motives. Much of the bogeyman image of the 'B's so prevalent in the south arose from the fact that the I.R.A. operated mainly by night and most frequently in the winter. This led automatically to the fact that the 'B's carried out their duties almost exclusively in the dark. They were little seen by outsiders, a 'silent service' with no public relations and without any feeling of the need for one. This indeed led to their own undoing and eventually disbandment, for the news service field was left entirely open to their enemies and there were many, to spread whatever evil stories they could imagine against them.

In so far as the 'B' men thought about this matter in the 1950s they would have said that one could hardly expect anti-partitionists to like them, and they knew that their own very effectiveness was the strongest reason for the antipathy.

There were plenty of Ulster Protestants who did not approve of the Specials either.* If the I.R.A. stayed quiet for a year or so there were protests from those critical of the expenditure, small though it was, and from others who thought that that sort of thing would never be needed again. There are always these elements in a nation at peace overkeen to dismantle the defences. A point which critics were quick to seize on was the fact that there were few if any Roman Catholics in the U.S.C. This is regrettable to me and to many 'B' men but to anyone who knows at first hand the situation in Ulster and a little of her history it is scarcely surprising. In the early 1920s when the very act of joining the force put one's life at immediate risk there was no room for any compromise, and a man would only go out on dangerous operations with people he could trust completely, not think he might be able to trust. Irish troops, Protestant or Catholic, had come through the war with a reputation for great bravery but also for a tendency to shoot in action any officers or N.C.O.s they did not like. At home many an R.I.C. man was shot and many a barrack was captured through treachery by Roman Catholic members of that force. I could quote at least three instances of this within ten miles of where I live.† The place where a man hung his hat on a Sunday had little or nothing to do with this attitude. It so happens in Ulster that the Nationalist or Republican party is almost exclusively comprised of Roman Catholics and that most Roman Catholics have leanings in that direction, even if some choose to keep these feelings carefully concealed. The same comments apply in just the same way to Protestants and the Unionist Party. So in the early days of the Special Constabulary when one literally took one's life in one's hands night after night the Protestant 'B' Special chose Protestants for his comrades. This situation prevailed for long enough for it to become something approaching an unofficial rule of the force that Roman Catholics would only be admitted in very special circumstances. Once established, such

---

* The great majority of the 'hard liners' of the 1960s were men who had never raised a finger to help the Specials, let alone join them in the past.
† Bellaghy, Maghera and Draperstown Barracks.

an attitude is difficult, indeed almost impossible in Ireland, to break. But to repeat it had little or nothing to do with religious beliefs.

In 1950 the strength of the Ulster Special Constabulary was about 12,000 and it seemed part of the life of Ulster. The necessity for it was kept refreshed by intermittent attacks by guerillas from a neighbouring state whose politicians frequently protested an anxiety to co-operate and an abhorrence of violence. Most 'B' men if they ever thought about it, which would not have been very often, would have admitted a respect for the point of view of those in the south who had won their freedom after fierce fighting with considerable bravery and loss of life. Indeed there was among the loyalists of Ulster an increasing feeling of liberalism on these matters. Unfortunately there was never any *quid pro quo* in this respect and one seldom heard privately that the Ulsterman also had a reasonable point of view, that uttered, and never publicly, in the Irish Republic any admission he would have been disloyal to his background and traditions if he had not wished to remain part of the United Kingdom and be prepared to fight if necessary to do so. Such respect would have made possible the beginning of an understanding leading to goodwill and co-operation to the benefit of everyone living in Ireland.

The U.S.C. had a comparatively peaceful time for ten years after the war and remained in 'drill category' as opposed to 'patrol category' (that is training, not active service) for most of the period. Standards of drill, shooting and equipment rose steadily in this period. It was a far call from the day in 1922 when a local man brought back the rifle he hardly understood to show his mother, and was told to take it away. 'She's no charged, Ma', he protested. 'Charged or no charged, son, she's dangerous. Houl' till the door!' was the reply, a story which is still relished locally.

In the early 1950s I.R.A. activity in Ulster was confined to burning an occasional Customs' Post and a couple of raids for arms on military barracks, one successful, the other thwarted by a quick thinking sentry. The Northern Ireland government followed the age-old principle that if you want peace, you prepare for war, and steadily improved the training and equipment of the Specials. In 1955 after six years as constable and sergeant I succeeded my father as District Commandant of the local force. At 1 a.m. on the 12th December, 1956, I was woken by the familiar voice of my Sergeant Instructor shouting outside my bedroom window. 'Balloon's gone up, Sir, balloon's gone up,' he yelled and added that Magherafelt Barracks had been burnt down, something about a wounded man in the car and that there was trouble all over the country. My first job was to circulate orders to stand to round the outlying sub-districts.

'Tell Mr. Wallace the Innisrush boys are on the job' was one of the messages that came through to my mother just after I had gone out, a comforting one to her and others who had to sit there and wait and to whom it seemed that all hell was let loose in the countryside. The 'B's were busy setting up road check points some near home, others in remote areas on get away routes. Rumours, mostly of enemy success, circulated freely but in the morning proper reports came in and it seemed that the night which was to have been a dramatic start to the great new campaign had gone badly for the I.R.A. Five of their men were in police lock-ups, three caught at Torr Head, two at Armagh Military Depot; no Police Barracks had been attacked, a garbled report had confused it with the courthouse which was only slightly damaged by fire. No success of any consequence had been achieved in ten separate operations. Yet the terrorists had achieved a degree of surprise which it would be impossible to gain for many years. Even the most unimaginative during the nights that followed must have sensed the tension over the whole countryside as thousands of pairs of eyes stared into the darkness on the lookout for the enemy. Every loyal man or woman in Ulster seemed to contribute his or her share to the total sum of watchfulness.

During the next couple of winters there were many such callouts punctuated by long hours of road check points and guarding of installations such as transformers and bridges. My father came out of retirement to rejoin the force as a Special Constable, typical of the spirit of many older men who gave their services in any way which offered in direct or indirect support of the Special Constabulary. The main deterrent exercised by the 'B' men was their ability to saturate the country with road check points. Motorists sometimes commented adversely on this form of security, quoting individual cases where a car had only been searched in cursory fashion. One of the main objects was to give a sense of security to the loyalist population and this was certainly achieved by the mere presence of 'B'

Specials' patrols, the other was to ensure that the I.R.A. could not drive around the countryside with their faces blackened and tommy guns across their knees on the way to a raid. It would never have been possible to search all cars stopped in a thorough fashion for the disruption caused to traffic by such an operation would have been quite unacceptable.

In the later stages of this campaign the I.R.A. confined their activities to blowing up bridges between the north and the south thus separating Ulster physically as well as politically from the rest of Ireland. This was in complete contradiction to their avowed object, but one had long since ceased to expect logic from the I.R.A. The Police Barracks nearest to my home in Swatragh was attacked no less than three times but on each occasion the raiders failed to stay more than ten minutes, the average time it took the Specials to bring support. They could be under arms in seconds since each man kept his weapon at home—a practice which has been much criticized. The record however speaks for itself; in 20 years after the war the U.S.C. 'lost' only six weapons, one of them automatic; the British Army in Ireland lost about 600 including 50 Bren guns to raids on depots in the same period. The weapons dispersed were not only much more effective but a hundred times as secure.

Gradually it became obvious that the I.R.A.'s efforts were fizzling out once again. The British Army, it is worth noting, played a minimum part in the defeat of this campaign which was won by the Royal Ulster Constabulary with the huge support of the Specials. Trouble was nipped in the bud in Belfast and Derry and so confined almost entirely to country areas. There were no incidents of any account in the cities.

In 1962 the I.R.A.'s own publicity bureau announced the end of the campaign. It had caused the deaths of six policemen, wounded thirty-two others, and brought about damage to a total of a million pounds. It would be surprising in the face of this sort of attack if there were not a few people, including some in the Specials, whose feelings ran high against the Irish Republic. At least Ulstermen could pride themselves on the fact that they have throughout the existence of the province kept their extremists under much better control than has the government in the south. Up until about 1967 there were no reprisal raids across the border.

After 1962 the Government maintained the Ulster Special

Constabulary at its normal strength, knowing that it was only a matter of time until trouble of some sort or another broke out again. In terms of cost of deterrent the Specials represented remarkably good value. The force never cost more than about £800,000 per annum to run and in composition was the military commander's dream in being all teeth and no tail. The full-time administrative staff never comprised more than one per cent of the total strength and every other member was available for the security work of the force.

In 1966 when the 50th anniversary celebrations of the Dublin Rebellion in the Republic were echoed with demonstrations and provocative displays of the tricolour in the north, the background presence of the Specials prevented trouble of any sort breaking out although many had predicted bloodshed.

In 1967 I wrote a short history of the force mainly centred round local events. At the time the Ulster Special Constabulary seemed so much an essential and normal part of Northern Ireland life that its record did not require any particular defence, and one could paint the picture, 'warts and all'. But Ulster was asleep in one vital respect. In concentrating on warding off the attacks of the I.R.A., she had failed to see the growing communist element in her midst parading under the reasonable banner of Civil Rights and growing strong in its shadow.

'In England there is nowadays a large class whose one only object in life appears to be to take sides with any and every enemy of their country, be he Boer, Boche, Bolshevik or Sinn Feiner. This party never ceases to aid and abet these enemies by every means in their power short of endangering their own skins, at the same time never letting an opportunity pass of accusing our soldiers and police (in Ireland) of every abominable crime which man has been known to commit.'

This comment was written in 1922 at the height of the trouble in Ireland.* The attitude described, which perhaps stems from the rather attractive English tendency to support the under-dog, has become even more prevalent in the England of post-war days. In this numerous class the enemies of Ulster, and of the Ulster Special Constabulary in particular, found their readiest audience.

After 1967 events moved at a pace in Ulster which to the

* 'Tales of the R.I.C.', Blackwoods.

ordinary Special Constable appeared quite bewildering. He was puzzled, and inevitably some individuals became irate. History records that in 1970 after almost exactly 50 years of existence the Ulster Special Constabulary was disbanded. Prior to that its reputation had been destroyed in the eyes of the world, by an extensive and cleverly directed campaign of defamation. Vilification based on unrefuted lies followed by enforced disbandment is as shattering a combination of disasters as can happen to any corporate body. The fact that the U.S.C. disbanded in exemplary fashion, and that every weapon and piece of equipment was handed in correctly and on time when the order came, was just what would have been expected by anybody who knew them, and should prove to any outsider who might care to see that the force had high standards of conduct and discipline.

There were undoubtedly a few extremists or bad characters in the Special Constabulary who in the last year or two of its existence brought blame on the force. There are bad men in any group of 12,000. Perhaps the Specials' own leaders were at fault in not eradicating these men either before or after the alleged bad behaviour. It is still too close after the event to look at these things dispassionately and in perspective. Historians of the future, if there is any fairness in the world, will give the Ulster Special Constabulary the credit for having been one of the most dedicated and effective part-time forces ever raised within the British Commonwealth.

INDEX

Aberdeen, Lord, 292

absenteeism, 53, 58-9, 61, 171; failure of legislation against, 74

Act of Union, 64, 89, 102, 134, 144, 145, 146, 147, 148, 149, 158, 163, 167, 168, 181, 256, 266, 336

Adair, Captain, 230

Agar-Robartes, 306, 307

Age of Enlightenment and Reason, 51, 63, 65, 77

agriculture, 47, 59, 73; agrarian crime, 47, 59, 60, 64, 163-4, 237; depression, 256; 'rationalization', 235, 237, 238, 240

American Civil War, 49, 238; Revolution, 49, 70, 86; War of Independence, 82

anarchy, 47-8, 171

Anglesey, Lord, 194

Apprentice Boys, 41, 162, 282

Arendt, Hannah, 107

Aughrim, Battle of, 42n.

Anglo-Irish Truce of 1921, 312, 317, 318, 329; Treaty of 1922, 242, 341

Arms Act, 297

Asquith (Jenkins), 277, 292

Asquith, H. H., 278, 287, 292, 295, 300, 306, 307, 310, 312, 315, 316, 317

Atkinson, Stewart, 118, 120, 121, 126

Balfour, Arthur, 268

Bank of Ireland, 58

Barrington, Sir Jonah, 142

Bates, John, 205

Beckett, J. C., 146, 234

Belfast: cholera epidemic, 197, 199; housing, 196; industry, 195-6, 199, 279; proletariat, 197; riot of 1857, 201-23, 258, 259; typhus epidemic, 197

Bereford, John Claudius, 146

Biggar, Joe, 260-1, 265-6

Bindon, Sub-Inspector Harris, 204, 206, 207, 210, 212, 216, 217, 218, 219, 220, 221, 222, 228, 230

Birrell, Augustine, 287, 288, 292, 310

Blacker family, 115, 120, 121, 122, 123; Stewart, 120

Blair, Constable, 209, 210

Blaney, Lord, 143

Boundary Commission, 322

Boyd, Andrew, 195, 223, 227, 258, 262, 298

Boyne, Battle of the, 41, 42n., 129, 202; anniversary celebrations, 77, 127, 129, 192, 197

Brehon Laws, 21

bribery, 61

Brickfield, Battle of the, 261

Brooke, Sir Basil, 348

Browne, Samuel, 214, 220

Bruce, Rev. William, 67

Brunswick Clubs, 161, 163

B-Specials, *see* Special Constabulary

Burden of Our Times, The (Arendt), 107

Burke, Edmund, 87, 89, 91, 96, 98

Burke, Richard, 91, 98

Burke, T. H., 252

Burton, William, 206

Butt, Isaac, 157, 257

Callaghan, James, 68

Campbell, J. H., 311

Campbell-Bannerman, 278, 287, 288, 292, 293

Campden, Lord, 126, 132

Camperdown, Battle of, 114

Carhampton, Lord, 109, 123

Carlyle, Thomas, 165

Carnot, 106

carpet-baggers, 17, 18, 19

Carson, Edward, 282, 302, 303, 304, 306, 307, 310, 311, 312, 316

Carson (Montgomery Hyde), 304
Casement, Sir Roger, 242, 294, 315, 317
Castle, Dublin, 87, 88, 90, 91, 100, 102, 104, 117, 124, 126, 129, 134, 135, 136, 142, 158, 166, 188, 287, 299; secret police, 111
Catholic Association, 155, 159, 161; dissolution, 156, 157, 160
Catholic Board, 150
Catholic Committee, 87, 88, 89, 90-1; split, 98
Catholic Convention, 101, 102; petition of rights, 100
Catholic Gun Club, 225
Catholic Emancipation, 134, 147, 150, 151, 152, 157; Act of 1829, 153, 154
Catholic Relief Act (1778), 51; (1793), 102
Cavendish, Lord Frederick, 252
Chamberlain, Joseph, 265, 269, 272, 274
Chamberlain, Neville, 329
Charlemont, Lord, 62, 75, 76, 77, 78, 79, 80, 120, 124
Charles I, 24, 30
Charles II, 41, 45; restoration, 37
Chichester, Sir Arthur, 27, 28, 29, 30
Chichester-Clarke, Major, 297
Church of Ireland, *passim*; disestablishment, 181, 256, 260, 289
Church Temporalities Act, 181
Churchill, Lord Randolph, 266, 267, 271, 272, 273, 274, 275, 282, 283, 295
Churchill, Sir Winston, 261, 265, 267, 287, 300, 307, 310, 314, 324
Citizen Army, 290, 313, 317, 319
Civil Rights movement, 40, 68
Civil War, 312, 319, 320, 321, 324, 330
Clan na Gael, 252, 294
Clare, Lord *see* FitzGibbon, John
Clarendon Code, 38, 280
Clarendon, Lord, 199
Clark, Wallace, 346ff.
Clarke, Captain, 120
Clarke, John, 228
Clarke, Tom, 278, 293
Coercion Acts, 252, 260
coinage, shortage of, 58
Collins, Michael, 287, 288, 291, 293, 318, 320, 321, 326; *Life with Michael Collins* (O'Connor), 294
Commission of Enquiry (Belfast riots), 220, 223, 225

Connaught, Composition of, 22
Connolly, James, 290, 313, 317, 318
Constitution of 1782, 70
Cooke, Rev. Dr. Henry, 178, 179, 180, 182, 185, 186, 187, 194, 226
Cope family, 115, 118, 119, 120, 121
Corn Laws, 59; repeal, 234
Cornwallis, Lord, 146
Cosgrave's Free State Government, 324, 330
Craddock, Colonel, 125
Craig, Sir James, 282, 283, 302, 304, 305, 306, 307, 310, 316, 318
Craigavon Ulsterman (Irvine), 304, 316
Crawford, Fred, 296
Cromwell, Oliver, 31, 32, 34, 35, 36, 39, 40, 41, 46, 52, 55, 56, 76, 139, 190
Cullen, Archbishop, 241
Cumberland, Duke of, 151, 194, 195
Curragh, Mutiny at the, 314

Dalrymple, General, 124
Darnley, Lord, 165
Deasy, Liam, 330
Defenders, the, 68, 79, 80, 84, 92, 109, 115, 116, 117, 118, 119, 122, 123, 262
Derby, Lord, 284, 285
Derry siege, 41, 192
Desmond wars, 21, 29
de Valera, Eamonn, 293, 313, 317, 318, 319, 320, 321, 330, 331
Devlin, Bernadette, 92, 238-9
Diamond, Battle of the, 84, 111, 115-127, 129, 130, 131, 136, 142
Disraeli, Benjamin, 257, 266, 267, 268
Dissenters, the, 74, 75, 77, 91, 92, 93, 94, 97, 98, 107, 110, 115, 116, 119, 121, 122, 129, 133, 157, 161, 182, 198
Dolly's Brae, Battle of, 207-8
Donegall, Lord, 60
Down Protestant, The, 224
Downshire, Marquis of, 183
Drew, Rev. Dr. Thomas, 200, 201, 202, 203, 204, 206, 207, 224, 226, 227
Drummond, Thomas, 188; creates national police force, 189
Duffy, Charles Gavan, 241

Easter Rising, 278, 288, 291, 293, 315, 316, 317
Education Acts, 281
Elizabeth I, 14, 20, 22, 23, 24

Elizabethan Wars, 13, 189

emigration, 49, 57, 59, 61, 63, 92, 171, 177, 199, 200, 232, 235, 287, 326, 336, 338, 339, 343; of craftsmen, 146

Emmet, Robert, 94, 106, 128, 145

Emmet, Thomas, 145

Encumbered Estates Act, 236, 237, 301

Encumbered Estates Court, 236, 256

Enniskillen, Earl of, 160, 192

evictions, 48, 60, 170, 172, 199, 234, 237

Famine, the, 149, 163, 165, 166, 167, 169, 173, 197, 199, 200, 232, 233, 235, 238, 240, 244, 336, 339

Fenians, Fenianism, 112, 128, 231, 240, 241, 242, 243, 244, 245, 246, 248, 250, 252, 278, 289, 291, 293; Clan na Gael, 252, 294; Rebellion, 258, 260; terrorist campaign, 249, 271

Fianna Fail, 321, 331

Fine Gael, 321

Fitt, Gerry, 297

FitzGerald, Lord Edward, 105, 106

FitzGerald, Vesey, 156

FitzGibbon, John (Lord Clare), 77, 82, 83, 89, 90, 91, 101, 102, 106, 111, 123, 126, 132, 146, 147, 188

FitzGibbon, Lady Louisa, 89

Fitzgibbon, Lord Justice, 271

Fitzmaurice, George, 221

Fitzwilliam, Lord, 87, 111, 126

Flood, 52, 62, 76, 101

Fontenoy, Battle of, 64

Foundation of Maynooth, 89

Fox, Charles James, 96, 100

French invasion of Ireland, 112-13

French Revolution, 38, 70, 86, 87, 88, 96

Gaelic Athletic Association, 294

Gaelic League, 294, 313

'gallow-glasses', 13

Geddes, Samuel, 212

George I, 58, 70

Giffard, John, 138

Gladstone, Herbert, 270

Gladstone, W. E., 252, 256, 257, 260, 265, 266, 267, 269, 271, 272, 273, 274, 276, 277, 283, 286, 292, 300

Goldsmith, Oliver, 52, 190

Goold, George J., 221

Gordon Riots of 1780, 51, 153

Gosford, Lord, 124

Government of Ireland Act, 320, 324, 346

Grattan, 52, 54, 62, 63, 68, 69, 71, 72, 76, 82, 87, 90, 97, 125, 126, 133, 144, 147, 150, 151, 155, 279, 291, 323; *Memoirs*, 87

Gray, Sam, 162

Great Hunger, The (Woodham Smith), 168

Green, Chief-Constable Thomas, 218, 228

Grey, Sir Edward, 287, 292

Grey, Earl, 151

Griffith, Arthur, 300, 317, 318, 320, 321

Grouchy, General, 113, 126

Guns in Ulster (Clark), 346

Hackett, John, 202, 204

Hamilton, James, 20

Hanna, Rev. Dr. Hugh, 226-7, 228, 229, 230, 261, 283; letter to the Protestants of Belfast, 231

Hardwicke, Lord, 146

Hartington, Lord, 269, 274

Healy, T. M., 293

'Hell or Connaught' activities, 35, 36, 49, 108, 122, 126, 139

Henderson, Head Constable, 206, 210, 211, 220, 222, 223

Henry VIII, 14, 20

Hill, Adam, 205

Hill, Sir George, 143

Hillsborough, demonstration of 1834, 180ff., 193, 226

History of Belfast (Cowan), 340

History of Ireland in the Eighteenth Century (Lecky), 90

History of the Irish Rebellion in 1798 (Maxwell), 145

Hobart, Major, 90

Hoche, General, 106, 113

Holland, Francis, 206

Holy War in Belfast (Boyd), 195

Home Rule, 133, 231, 261, 264, 267, 268, 269, 270, 272, 273, 277, 279, 289, 290, 291, 292, 293, 295, 300, 301, 306, 307, 308, 310, 312, 315, 316, 317, 346; Government of Ireland Act, 320, 324, 346; first attempt at, 54; first Bill, 257, 265, 274, 276; riots of 1886, 258, 273, 295; riots of 1893, 297

Hood, Major, 212, 216, 218, 219, 230

Humbert, General, 341
Hungry Forties, 238
Hyde, Douglas, 294, 313

industry, industrialization, 189, 257;
  beer, 73; cotton, 72; linen, 39, 48,
  57, 72 (decline), 63; ship-building,
  147; woollen, 73
Inquiry into the Conduct of the Constabulary, 221
Insurrection Bill, 125, 127
intermarriage, 39, 93
Invincibles, The, 252
I.R.A., see Irish Republican Army
I.R.A., The (Coogan), 331
Irish Constabulary, 173-4, 206, 226,
  228, 259, 326, 327; creation of, 159,
  188; become 'Royal' Irish Constabulary, 231, 260
Irish language, decay of, 44
Irish Nationalists, 258, 259, 274, 276,
  277, 287, 293, 314, 315
Irish Republican Army (I.R.A.), 60,
  68, 112, 320, 324, 326, 328, 330,
  331, 332, 347, 348, 350, 351, 352,
  353, 354, 356, 357, 358; Provisionals,
  224, 319
Irish Republican Brotherhood, 242,
  243, 244, 246, 247, 252, 253, 258, 289,
  294, 295, 300, 312, 313, 330
Irish Unionists 253
Irish Volunteers, 313, 318, 319
Irvine, St. John, 304

Jacobins, Jacobinism, 70, 74, 79-80, 82,
  83, 91, 94, 104-6, 108, 110, 113, 120,
  121, 126, 128, 131-3, 143
James I, 24, 41, 43, 76
James II, 41, 43, 45
Jephson, Richard, 120
Johnstone, William, 202
Jones, John Paul, 66, 341
Jones, Jonathan, 209, 211, 216, 220
Jowett, Benjamin, 198
Joyce, James, 253

Kane, R. R., 299
Kenmare, Lord, 88, 89, 90, 98
Keogh, John, 90, 91, 98, 100
Kilkenny, Confederation of, 34
Kilkenny, Statute of, 21, 237
Knox, Bishop, 226, 227

Lake, General, 110, 136, 137, 139, 141,
  143, 333

Lands Acts, 236, 252, 257, 260, 270,
  279, 292
Land League, 264, 273
Land War, 236, 237, 252, 260, 264,
  270, 287
Lansdowne, Lord, 302
Lawless, John, 161, 162
Lecky, William, 56n., 67, 90
Lemass, Sean, 332
'liberals', 131, 132
Liberal Clubs, 163
Life with Michael Collins (O'Connor),
  194
Limerick, Treaty of, 43, 44, 45
Lindsay, Chief-Constable Thomas,
  212, 213, 214, 218, 228
Lisburn True Blues, 67
Lloyd George, David, 269, 287, 300,
  301, 307, 316, 323, 346
Londonderry, Marquis of, 184
Long, Walter, 307
Loyal Order of the Orange and Blew,
  The, 151
Loyola, Ignatius, 15
Lyons, Thomas Briscoe, 130

MacMahon, Hugh, 20
MacNeill, Professor Eoin, 313
Maghera riots, 191, 352
magistrates, stipendary, 188, 191
Making of Modern Ireland, The
  (Beckett), 146
Mansergh, Professor, 255
Marshall, Rev. George, 120
'mass-houses', 46
Maxwell, 145
Maynooth Jansenists, 235
McCarthy, Justin, 276
McClure, Rev. William, 186
McCormack, Richard, 91
McCracken, Henry John, 139
McDowell, Rev. Alexander, 310
McGee, William, 212, 213
Melbourne, Lord, 193, 194, 195
middle class, emergence of, 51
Middleton, Lord, 312
militia, 117, 127; authority to search
  houses, 125; creation of, 116; Mili-
  tary Lodges formed, 123; Mona-
  ghan Militia, 136-7
Monaghan Fencibles, 257
Montgomery, Rev. Henry, 178, 179
Montgomery, Hugh, 20
Montgomery Hyde, H., 304
Moore, Thomas, 52, 233, 279

Most Favoured Nation Clause, 71
Munro, Henry, 139
mutinies of 1797, 132

Nappach Fleet, 79
National Convention, 101
National Volunteers, 313
Newcastle Declaration, 276
Niall of the Nine Hostages, 14
nonconformists, *passim*
North, Lord, 64
Northern Star, The, 124, 128, 136, 137
Northern Whig, 197
Northland, Lord, 120, 123
Northumberland, Duke of, 192
Not an Inch (Shearman), 296-7

Oakboys, 60, 78, 264
Oates, Titus, 45
O'Brien, William Smith, 198, 199, 242, 243
O'Connell, Daniel, 145, 148, 150, 151, 155, 156, 157, 158, 159, 160, 161, 162, 163, 179, 180, 193, 194, 198, 206, 214, 225, 241, 244, 248, 249, 258, 259, 291
O'Connor, General Rory, 320, 321
O'Doherty, Cahir, 22-3, 26
O'Donnell, Rory, 18
O'Faolain, Sean, 149
O'Mahony, John, 242, 243
O'Neill, Hugh, 13, 14, 17, 18, 24, 26; Earl of Tyrone, 17
O'Neill, Owen Roe, 28, 31, 36; rebellion of 1641, 34; rebellion of 1642, 24, 32, 33
O'Neill, Terence, 88, 92, 297, 332
Orange Boys, 116, 121
Orangeism in Ireland and Britain (Senior), 121, 138
Orangeism in Ireland and Throughout the Empire, 182, 224
Orangeism, Orangemen, 41, 42, 77, 94, 124, 126, 145, 148, 151, 153, 154, 155, 158, 160, 162, 179, 191, 192, 193, 194, 202, 207, 253, 254, 260, 284, 295, 307, 308, 315, 321, 324, 334
Orange Lodges, 42, 68, 84, 85, 94, 102, 112, 123, 136, 137, 141, 142, 145, 153, 160, 192, 203, 221, 225, 258, 273, 296, 311; dissolved, 195
Orange Order, 61, 84, 109, 110, 111,
118, 120, 121, 122, 127, 129, 130, 136, 138-9, 140, 141, 150, 151, 152, 154, 155, 161, 162, 175, 180, 188, 193, 194, 195, 204, 205, 225, 226, 262, 274, 277, 283, 285, 298, 304, 312, 326, 327, 328, 331, 332, 353; opposed by Irish Government, 123
Orange Society, *see* Orange Order

Paine, Thomas, 75, 87
Paisley, Ian, 92, 103, 178, 283, 332, 346; Paisleyites, 51, 61, 68
Pakenham, Thomas, 105
Palmerston, Lord, 263
Parliament (Irish), 61, 62, 63, 64, 65. *See also* The Castle *and* Stormont Administration
Parnell, Charles Stewart, 157, 244, 250, 251, 263, 264, 265, 266, 270, 271, 276, 278, 283, 289, 291, 317; death, 253; and Kitty O'Shea, 253, 277
Partition, 42n., 319, 320, 334
Party Processions Act, 191-2, 201, 203, 207, 208; repealed, 260
Patriot Party, 61, 62, 71, 74
Peace by Ordeal (Longford), 316
Pearse, Padraic, 128, 289, 293, 319
Peel, Robert, 150, 193
Peep o' Day Boys, 61, 68, 78, 79, 80, 84, 92, 107, 115, 116, 117, 119, 121, 123, 129, 139, 148, 155, 262, 283, 312
Penal Laws, 45, 51, 62, 63, 65, 66, 88, 89, 97, 99, 100, 124, 280; abolition 109; effects of, 45, 47, 48; repeal, 70, 78, 147
People's Democracy, 68
Peterloo Massacre, 153
Pitt the Younger, William, 71, 72, 76, 89, 96, 100, 102, 108, 132, 147
Plantation, 13, 15, 24, 34, 36, 40, 121, 129; motives behind, 19, 21
police force; created, 190; lack of, 111; Town Police of Belfast abolished, 205
population, 336-41
Population of Ireland, The (Connell), 337-8
Portrait of the Artist as a Young Man (Joyce), 253-4
potatoes, diet of, 47, 165, 169, 172; crop failure, 166, 173, 174
Power, John O'Connor, 269
press gangs, 60, 109
Preston, General, 34

Price of My Soul, The (Devlin), 239
primogeniture, principal of, 13, 17
Protestants, *passim*; Ascendancy, 56,
    63, 67, 69, 71, 73, 74, 77, 82, 83,
    87, 88, 92, 98, 120, 124, 126, 236;
    see also Orangeism, Orange Lodges,
    Orange Order, etc.
Purplemen, 141

Raleigh, Sir Walter, 22, 25
Rebellion of 1782, 55, 63, 74
Rebellion of 1798, 34, 55, 107, 113,
    140
Redmond, John, 276, 287, 288, 289,
    291, 295, 300, 306, 307, 310, 312,
    313, 315, 317, 330
reforms of 1793, 104, 107, 115, 133
Reform Bill of 1832, 99, 153, 157, 179
Reform Bill of 1867, 128, 268
revolutionary cycle (18th-century),
    reasons for, 56-7, 68
Ribbonmen, 47, 158, 163, 188, 190,
    191, 192, 264
Ribbon Society, 202
Richardson, General, 311
Rights of Man, The (Paine), 74
Riot Act, 217, 219, 220
riots of 1898, 288-9
Roden, Earl of, 207, 208
Roman Catholics, *passim*; deprived of
    higher education, 46; deprived of
    parliamentary franchise, 46; for-
    bidden to carry arms, 67, 77, 78;
    and Irish nationalism, 37; mas-
    sacres by Cromwell, 35ff.
Roseberry, Lord, 286, 293
Royal Irish Constabulary, *see* Irish
    Constabulary
Royal Ulster Constabulary, 68, 224,
    260, 304, 326, 327, 332, 333, 353,
    357
Russell, Lord John, 199
Russell, Thomas, 145

Salisbury, Lord, 268, 270, 272, 273,
    286
Sarsfield, Patrick, 43, 261
Saunderson, Colonel, 307
Saurin, William, 159, 160
Schomberg, 42n.
schools, denominational, 281-2
'scorched earth' policy, 27
Scott, Sir Walter, 165
secret societies, 115, 116, 121, 141, 159;
    illegality of, 119, 125, 194, 195

Seeley, Jack, 315
Senior, Hereward, 121, 138
Senior, Nassau, 198
servitors, 23, 24, 25
Shaw, Bernard, 279
Sheridan, 52
Short View of the State of Ireland, A
    (Swift), 57
Sinclair, Thomas, 310
'siege mentality', 40, 42n., 279, 323
Sinn Fein, 60, 68, 300, 312, 313, 317,
    318, 319, 320, 330, 349, 351
Sirr, Major, 142
Sloan, James, 119, 121, 122, 123
Smith, Adam, 172
Smith, F. E., 316, 317
smuggling, 46
Special Constabulary (B-Specials, etc.),
    68, 110, 328, 329, 346-59
Sperber, Manes, 140
Stack, Austin, 330
Steelboys, 60, 78, 164
Stendhal, 165
Stephens, James, 242, 243, 246, 247
Stewart, A. T. Q., 307
Stormont Administration, 324, 325,
    335
Strafford, 41
Swift, Dean, 48, 57
'swordsmen', 27, 28, 43, 46
Synge, 279

Tandy, Napper, 106, 114
Tariff War, 330, 331
Thackeray, 165
Thirty Years' War, 15, 34, 35, 94
Thompson, Robert, 216, 218
Thoughts on the Volunteers, 67
Thurot, Admiral, 65, 66
Tithe Composition Act, 181
Tithe War, 181, 193, 194
Tone, Wolfe, 38, 74, 75, 82, 83, 87,
    88, 90, 91, 95, 96, 97, 98, 99, 100,
    101, 102, 103, 104, 106, 111, 113,
    114, 135, 139, 149, 291, 341; *Auto-
    biography* 90, 94-5
Toynbee, Arnold, 133
Tracy, Samuel, 204, 212, 213, 214, 216,
    217, 219, 220, 221, 222, 223
trade and commerce, 71; in Protestant
    hands, 50
Trevelyan, 199
tribalism, 108, 232
*Twenty Reasons for Being an Orange-
    man* (Drew), 202

Ulster Covenant, 310, 312
Ulster Crisis, The (Stewart), 307
'Ulster Custom', 48, 59, 92
Ulster Defence Regiment, 226, 329
Ulsterman, The, 210, 225, 227
Ulstermen, 42, 50, 63, 78, 94, 107; emergence of, 39
Ulster Unionists, 313, 318
Ulster Volunteer Force, 42n., 68, 311, 312, 313, 314, 315, 316, 328
'undertakers', 22, 23, 24, 25, 26, 27
unemployment, 342-4
Unionist Party, 84, 152, 225, 253, 255, 272, 274, 277, 281, 296, 303, 325. *See also* Act of Union
United Irishmen, 74, 82, 83, 84, 92, 94, 97, 98, 102, 104, 106, 111, 113, 120, 125, 126, 127, 134, 135, 137, 139, 143, 150, 163, 175, 198, 205, 241, 242, 333; Presbyterian, 135, 141

Verner, James, 118, 120, 126; family, 192
Verner, Colonel William, 193
Versailles, Peace of, 71
Victoria, Queen, 73, 173, 195, 260, 268, 271, 308; visits Dublin, 167
Volunteer movements, 64, 66, 72, 75, 77, 78, 80, 82, 84, 115, 124, 129, 148; Convention, 77; spread of, 67

Wallace, Colonel R. H., 311

Waring, Rev. Holt, 182, 185
Wellesley, Lord, 159, 160, 188, 191
Wellington, Duke of, 152, 159
Westminster Confession of Faith, 178
Westmoreland, Lord, 90
Whig Club, 87, 88, 95, 97
Whiteboys, 47, 59, 60, 66, 80, 84, 106, 107, 121, 158, 159, 264; Whiteboy Act, 122
Wild Geese, the, 28, 32, 34, 43, 46, 109, 149, 170
Wilde, Oscar, 279, 304
William of Orange, 41, 42n., 44, 52, 67, 203-4
Williamites, Williamite War, 42, 43, 56, 64
Wilson, 116, 118
Winters, Dan, 115, 116, 117, 118, 119, 122, 126
Wolfe, 125
Woodham Smith, Cecil, 168, 172, 173, 174, 233, 234
World Crisis, The (Churchill), 267
Wyndham Act of 1903, 264

Year of Liberty, The (Pakenham), 105
Yeats, W. B., 128, 279, 294
Yeomanry Association, 146
York, Duke of, 150, 151, 152, 153, 155